MW01177956

GETTING OUT OF HERE
ALIVE

THE BALLAD OF
MURRAY
McLAUCHLAN

VIKING

VIKING
Published by the Penguin Group
Penguin Books Canada Ltd, 10 Alcorn Avenue, Toronto, Ontario, Canada M4V 3B2
Penguin Books Ltd, 27 Wrights Lane, London W8 5TZ, England
Penguin Putnam Inc., 375 Hudson Street, New York, New York 10014, U.S.A.
Penguin Books Australia Ltd, Ringwood, Victoria, Australia
Penguin Books (NZ) Ltd, cnr Rosedale and Airborne Roads, Albany,
Auckland 1310, New Zealand

Penguin Books Ltd, Registered Offices: Harmondsworth, Middlesex, England

First published 1998
1   3   5   7   9   10   8   6   4   2

Printed and bound in Canada on acid free paper ∞

CANADIAN CATALOGUING IN PUBLICATION DATA

McLauchlan, Murray
Getting out of here alive: the ballad of Murray McLauchlan

ISBN 0-670-87659-3

1. McLauchlan, Murray. 2. Singers – Canada – Biography. I. Title.

ML420.M163A3 1998   782.42164'092   C98-931056-6

Visit Penguin Canada's website at www.penguin.ca

This book is dedicated
To Denise, who suffers bravely through
my attempts at telling the truth
and
To my children
Sarah Sackville-McLauchlan (formerly Amy)
and
Duncan McLauchlan
some unvarnished truth in case I'm no
longer around to tell you in person

Special thanks to: James Ian McLauchlan, Rosemary McLauchlan Hunter, Sandra McLauchlan, Calvin McLauchlan, Bill McLauchlan, Bernie Finkelstein and the helpful staff at True North Records, all of whom helped me fill in the gaps.

Thanks as well to: Meg Taylor, Kathryn Dean, Cynthia Good, and Jacqueline Kaiser, for putting the process in motion, and to John Allemang, who started the ball rolling.

CONTENTS

Foreword ix

"By the Bonny Banks of Clyde" 3
Being a Little Kid 10
The *Samaria* 15
On Being a Bigger Kid 20
Weaning in the Fifties 22
The World Expands 26
Sins of the Father 35
Look! Up in the Sky! 37
Meeting Robert Bateman 40
The Hysterical Boatman 44
Childhood's End 50

Art School Years 65
The Boy Snaps Awake 73
The Move to Manhood 84
Leaving Home 95
Riding the Rails 99
Yes, I'm Moving 109
Sometimes the Bear Eats You 118
Spinning Wheels Grab the Road 122

I

II

III
Trying to Get Going 129
Why, Because You Have to? 138
Yorkville 146
The Commune 154
Ghost Story 163
New York City 172

IV
The Ship Isn't in, but You Can See the Land 183
Goin' Back to New York City 191
Farmer's Song and Beyond 204
Massey Hall Debut 216
Goodbye to You Too, Pa 222
Bars, Boats and Limousines 226

V
A Very Good Year 239
Crash and Burn 248
The Comeback Kid 256
Life Gets Really Complicated 268
You Thought *That* Was Complicated 278
The Beautiful Girl Child 286
A Smoking Hole Where I Used to Be 292

VI
Love's Bubble Springs a Leak 303
Floating Over Canada 308
Floating, Part II 324
What Else Can You Show Me? 333

VII
Goodbye, Mama 347
Picking Up the Pieces 352
Swinging on a Star to Swinging on a Star 362
And Then Came Duncan 371

Epilogue 381

Discography 387
Index 389

Foreword by Peter Gzowski

🔊 "SCOTS WHA HAE WI' WALLACE BLED," I'd written—well, Robbie Burns had written and I'd cribbed for the occasion—"Scots wham Bruce has aften led," and then, taking off from the original, that being as much as I could dig out of my childhood memory anyway, I went on,

> Murrray McLauchlan is nae dead—
> Just growing older.

The occasion was Murray's fiftieth birthday party. It was early summer, and he was finishing this lovely book, though no one at the party knew how lovely it was, except maybe Denise, who said (not at the party) that she'd cried at some of the passages he'd read to her, and, to some extent, me, since I'd read by then most of what the editors at Penguin had been able to wring out of him (I don't think I cried, though I certainly laughed out loud a few times). We were gathered in the garden of Murray and Denise's house, overlooking one of Toronto's verdant ravines—a motley group, whose very motleyness, I suppose, reflected Murray's remarkable history: musicians; a poet or two; the novelist Alison Gordon (Murray's partner in his triumphant appearance on CBC Television's *Great Canadian Quiz*); no painters so far as I knew, though the landscape artist Doris McCarthy, unable to attend, had sent along a painting as a birthday gift, but some aviation people; some radio people; me; my life partner Gillian Howard, who likes Murray and Denise as much as I do; Murray's brother Calvin; Denise's Mom; a few cousins and aunts; the music entrepreneur Bernie Finkelstein; and quite a few people whose identity (introductions not being a major part of etiquette at gatherings of this sort) I had no idea of, all drawn together on a glorious summer afternoon to pay tribute to a man we liked, admired or—in many cases—loved. I went on:

> Like flats, Labatt's or orange bills,
> He, at fifty's o'er nae hills,
> He still needs nae Viagra pills
> (Or so he's told her).

Flats, for the uninitiated, are—or were—flat fifties: tin boxes of cigarettes you could buy for about a quarter when Murray and I were learning to smoke, something he's been much better than I at learning *not* to do. (He has, in fact, turned into something of an antismoking zealot.) Labatt's, of course, is a reference to Labatt's 50 (it's still around, isn't it?) and orange bills . . . well, pink has only one syllable. But the poem was for Murray, and he'd get it.

This was actually Denise's suggestion. I'd been wracking my brains for something to bring along to the party, which in my case, as usual, meant huddling with my incomparable assistant Shelley Ambrose and wracking *her* brains, and Shelley had called Denise, who was producing the party as a surprise for Murray (it worked, too), and Denise, without wracking anything, said what he'd like most of all from me was something I might write for him.

Hmmm. On the one hand, exquisitely appropriate. High on the list of things Murray has done for *me* over the years are two pieces of writing. One, indeed, was a poem. Not a parody, either, but a clever and original work, which he composed for one of the golf tournaments that are now held in my name all over the country to raise money for literacy, and of which, typically, he's been a generous supporter. One of the traditions of those tournaments is to have a poet laureate, who spends the day with us and finishes our closing ceremonies with a poem written on the spot. Dennis Lee started it all a dozen years ago, and we'd had all kinds of other distinguished writers since, from Margaret Atwood to (bless her memory) Bronwen Wallace—a Who's Who of Canadian poesy. But I was sure Murray could handle it. I remembered the first time I met him, when, still in his early twenties, he came shuffling into the old CBC building on Jarvis Street to be on the program then called *This Country in the Morning*, and, as well as singing, presented a poem or two. Besides, just read some of the songs he's written since. Maybe not "wiping his face like a shoe," whatever that means, but much else that sticks in the head. Anyway, he was a smash hit, though I think the pressure kind of spoiled his golf that day, and the only line I can remember from his epic was about golf really being "flog" spelled backwards.

The other occasion when he wrote something for me was more ostentatious. In 1995, I was asked to accept a Governor General's Award for the Performing Arts (the capitals are His Excellency's). This both astonished and delighted me—astonished, since I considered myself neither performer nor artist (the award was for work I'd done on radio) and delighted because it sounded like a splendid occasion. Among its splendours was a gala evening at the National Arts Centre in Ottawa, where a concert would be held in the recipients' honour, and it was up to the award winners to choose both who would perform for us—the other anglophone honorees that year were Anne Murray and Maureen Forrester—and who would read and write our citations. I thought immediately of Murray—for both roles—and Gill, when I consulted her, agreed enthusiastically. But the more I thought of it, the more I thought, singing is *work* for him—and he's already done so much of it on my behalf, at literacy concerts everywhere from St. John's, where he sat at the piano and did one of the elegant 1940s ballads he seems to write so well since Denise has come into his life, to Yellowknife, where I can still see him doing, of all pieces, "Farmer's Song" ("wiping his face. . ." and all)—and virtually every kid in the place, most of whom had never even seen a farm, singing along with all the familiar words. Besides, I wanted the world to see the Murray I knew: thoughtful, articulate, honest (not unlike this book, come to think of it). So I arranged for Ashley McIsaac and Laura Smith to perform, and asked Murray if he'd honour me by doing the citation. As he had with the golf poem, he either felt or feigned intimidation when I asked him. But he wrote an eloquent and touching piece, and when I heard him read it at the ceremony, I may well have reacted as Denise did to parts of this book.

Later on, on a visit to our home in the country, he brought along the manuscript, which he'd signed and had framed. I'm not sure I'd like the Governor General to know this, but I treasure that memento as least as much as—maybe more than—the sumptuous gold medal that now sits in its velvet-covered case on our mantelpiece.

On the other hand, I am to poetry what Newfoundlanders are to swimming—smart enough to stay out of the water. Ah, well, if Murray could do it . . .

Now's the day and now's the moment,
Raise your glass in Murray's gloamin'
Join the wishes of the poem 'n'
List' the piper.

Och, the frost's nae on *his* punkin,
His stride is bold, his cheeks not shrunken.
He's young at heart like Bonnie Duncan,
Just somewhat riper.

Though I'm kind of proud of turning Murray and Denise's meandering and enchanted garden into a "gloamin'," and though, as it turned out, advising people to "list' the piper" was a prescient thing to do, since there were a couple of pipers waiting in the wings at the party, I will confess that much of those two verses was constructed with an eye—or ear, I guess—on Duncan, Murray and Denise's son.[*]

I have quite a few friends who are on their second marriages. I'm on my second myself, if you count living contentedly with the same woman for fifteen years a marriage. (If there's a better ode to that part of life than Murray's "Second Time Around," by the way, I'm not aware of it.) And more than a few of them have young children. I imagine all those second-time fathers are determined, as I would be if Gill and I had decided to have a family of our own, to do for their second families what they were too busy or too stupid to do for their first. This doesn't mean they—we—were bad fathers the first time; from what I know of Murray, both before and after reading what he has to say here, quite the opposite was the case, for he dotes on his daughter, and is as proud of her nightingale's singing voice as of anything he has achieved himself. But none of the second-chance fathers I know come anywhere near Murray in passion and determination. He loves Duncan in a way that puts the rest of us to shame—spoils him even, but why not?—and his young son, as well as Denise, has inspired new music from him—including, notably, "The Old Tin Star," as sweet and poignant a Christmas song as anyone anywhere is turning out these days.

Murray will be sixty-five when Duncan is the captain of his university football team, in his seventies when Duncan stars in his first movie and even older

---

[*] I know I'm overexplaining, but think of all the work I'm saving Ph.D. students of the future. Wouldn't it have been nice if Burns himself had been so considerate?

when he wins the Nobel Prize for literature. But he's fifty now, and, yes, that's him on the front of the toboggan, laughing even louder than his diminutive, beautiful passenger.

> He's poet, pilot, painter, bard—
> Too much for one wee business card.
> For thee and me he stands on guard,
> Yet still at ease.

In a longer poem, or if Burns had set the metre differently, I could probably have gone on with my list. Chiropractor? Well, probably not, but I remember once when Murray and Denise showed up at our cottage for some golf and my tricky back had hobbled me, Murray ordered me onto the floor and drill-mastered me through a series of exercises from which, miraculously, I rose like Lazarus. (Around our house, this routine is still called "doing your Murrays.") Or chef, maybe, though I've witnessed only his prowess on the barbecue. Or Scrabble player. Golfer even, for he hits the ball an astonishingly long way, even though, like his life, it may not always go in the direction he's planned. Certainly debater could have been in there; one of the most memorable dinner gatherings Gill and I ever assembled featured Murray and Denise and Bob and Arlene Rae, when Bob was premier of Ontario, with Murray and the premier in full conversational—and enjoyable—flight for most of the evening. Bob won, I think, but he was up against a formidable opponent—who'd have been even more formidable if he'd been arguing with someone he actually disagreed with.

But poet, pilot, painter, bard will do. The poet we've already established. The pilot, as you'll learn in these pages, is a man possessed. My guess is that when people who don't know Murray hear that he flies, they think, Oh, sure, he goes up and tools around sometimes as a lark. Well, maybe. But he's a folk singer who's licensed to fly anything up to twin-engined jets (see his adventures with our Armed Forces) and who finds a Saint-Exupérian ecstasy in being above the clouds, and, when he's aloft, he is as meticulous and professional as he is on stage. He loves everything about planes, and if I have any warnings about becoming friends with him, they would be: (1) Don't sit with him when he's a passenger on a small aircraft, as I did one sunny day when we were going from Halifax to Cape Breton—Murray kept up a running commentary, not all of it complimentary, on every wind current and flying manoeuvre—and (2) Don't let him start to show you the videos he's made of the latest air show he's been to—they go on longer than the search for Amelia Earhart.

But if he offers to take you up, go with him. You'll see flying as you never have before. One day, he picked me up in a float plane in Orillia, near where I live, and we soared up and over Muskoka, banked left to Georgian Bay to overfly Calvin's cottage and came back along the Severn River, drinking in the lakes and the rivers and the forests, reliving memories of summers past, gazing down at the Lilliputian rich people of Muskoka and the ant-like cars along the byways, laughing and chortling to ourselves, and for a couple of hours I knew what it was like to be an eagle—or at least an eagle's lucky friend.

He's almost as good a painter. Maybe, in fact, better. As I read through his early years in Toronto, I thought from time to time, Hey, Murray, stick *with* this. Listen to Doris McCarthy—painters as great as she is don't take an interest in just anyone. But maybe if he'd just painted, we wouldn't have those songs. In any case, he's painting again now: big, bold, colourful canvases that capture the spirit of the land—or, in the case of one that holds pride of place in his living room, of flying.

And bard? He practically defines the word, Celtic origins and all: a national minstrel, a spinner of tales, a recorder of people and places. Surely one of the most remarkable things about him is that the kid from Toronto has come to understand not only the landscape of the wilderness but what it means to us. For all the genius of "Down by the Henry Moore" or "Honky Red" or his other sketches of urban life—or even the unforgettable "Farmer's Song"—my own favourite among all these songs, for what it's worth, is the haunting "Beyond the Timberline," which describes, accurately, where the real Canada begins. And for all the impact of all his music, I wonder if the truest thing he ever created wasn't the film he put together a few years ago, flying his plane across the country he loves, dropping in to share songs with friends, drawing together his flying skills, his musical gifts and his painter's eye in a statement about the land, which is, I think, what I was thinking about when I wrote about Murray standing on guard. He really cares about this place, and knows and loves it well.

And know what?

The son of a bitch can write, too.

So lay the proud usurpers low,
As Burns would have it did he know,
And wish him fifty more to go
With fair Denise.

And then, in the summer air, the pipers began to play.

Peter Gzowski
Lake Simcoe
August 1998

GETTING OUT OF HERE
A L I V E

I

"By the Bonny Banks of Clyde"

A LITTLE BLACK VAN TRAVELS ALONG the south side of the Clyde River. It is August of 1996. Forty-four years have passed since I left this place. I've been to every nook and cranny in Canada. I've been to the United States, Australia, Japan, Germany, South America—many places, but never back to the town in Scotland where I was born.

A young CBC television producer named Leslie Haller is also travelling in the van. She's a person who exudes a kind of wholesome niceness that's rare even in well-bred Canadian girls. We're on our way to Eleven Drums Avenue, Ferguslie Park, Paisley, Renfrewshire, Scotland, and we've been warned against doing so by several people, including my cousin Ritchie. Last night, after my concert in George's Square, downtown Glasgow, he remarked, "My God, you're no going there! It's aw drugs an' guns an' mayhem!"

We have a Scottish cameraman with us, and he's brought along his nephew as the sound recordist. The cameraman is about sixty, with a denim-tweedy look, a pork-pie hat and a salt-and-pepper beard. He typifies the kind of staunch socialism you find around the world wherever there are good Scottish union men. There's a pong of trade unionism about him. The operating principle of this mindset is: Thou shalt not a finger lift or a shovel move if it ain't in the contract. If it ain't in the contract, it ain't your job! (This was confirmed when I learned that his camera hadn't been rolling when the really interesting stuff was going on.)

Neither of our Scottish crew seems unduly concerned about going to Paisley. Mind you, they don't seem overly enthusiastic either. I've been regaled with stories of bloodletting in the streets and bars by all and sundry since arriving in Glasgow. I've been warned repeatedly about going anywhere or doing practically anything.

If this propaganda is to be believed, then I guess all the bandy-legged little Scottish guys must somehow transform themselves at some magic hour into the homicidal, ear-slitting Glaswegian toughs of legend. Sometimes I think idly that the Scots pay more than casual attention to the fine art of yanking your chain.

I keep looking out the window for hints of the familiar—a hill, a landmark of some kind—and drawing a blank. I was not quite five years old when I left, and the memories of a child are so different—smells and strange jumbled images.

Glasgow Road, Gauze Street, High Street. I know the names, but only because they've been part of my family's litany for so many years, in so many stories. Well Street, Underhill, Greenhill Road. Wait, I recognize the water tower or whatever it is! It's a great big grey-brown rusty tank with an external frame, and I know it, not just from grainy photographic mythology. No, this really hits me. I'm unexpectedly excited. I know I'm on my native soil now! It's ma 'hood, man!

Yes, Greenhill Road, then—it's just here. Yes, left there—there it is, that's it! Left on Drums Avenue. Look to the left there. Yes, pull over!

I have the strangest feeling as I slowly get out of the van and stand across the street from the house in which I drew my first breath. This nondescript little grey council house leaps out of a hundred old photographs, and as I look, the scene in front of me seems to keep changing from colour to black and white. I can almost see my Uncle Jimmy standing beside his ancient Ford Prefect by the front gate. I feel like my shape is changing. A tiny person deep down inside me is rattling a tin cup on the bars.

Eleven Drums Avenue is a two-storey grey-beige stucco semi-detached Scottish council house. It takes characteristics like plain and nondescript to a high art. A low hedge forms a border with the sidewalk, and on the right is a small iron double gate, which opens onto what was once meant to be a driveway. The former driveway in turn leads to what was once meant to be a garage, but is now just a rundown shed. The house is small, smaller than my memory of it, but of course, I remember it from the perspective of a child. It appears to have been cared for.

I reach into the van for my camera, snap off a quick picture from the other side of the street and slowly begin walking across the road towards the house.

Halfway across, my eye is drawn to movement at the upstairs window, the window of the room in which I was born. The curtain is pulled aside, and I can see a shock of white hair and the face of an old woman peering at me. As I continue across the road, looking at the house, the window slides open.

"What you want?"

She has a great Paisley accent. There's no evidence of hostility, but there is some pugnaciousness in her tone. Which is understandable. I could be anyone— a rent collector, taxman, cop. There is no traffic in this neighbourhood, and someone who is stopped and looking at your house would naturally be treated with suspicion.

I immediately launch into my dog-and-pony show.

"Hello, my name's Murray McLauchlan. I've come all the way from Canada to see this house again. I was born in it, right in the room where you're standing. I'm famous in Canada. I make records and win awards and stuff, and these people who are with me are from a television program called *Adrienne Clarkson Presents,* and we've come here, you know, to Ferguslie Park, to put the house in the film, like *Roots.* Do you think it would be okay if we went around the back? What's your name, missus?"

"Anna Docherty," she replies. "Hang on, I'll be right doon."

While I'd been talking with Mrs. Docherty, I became aware of a commotion behind me. Voices insinuated themselves from my back brain to my forebrain, voices that had a certain unmistakable cadence. "Ooooooh, yeh! Gwan! Whooo *him*? Heh, heh, heh—all be onna telly, eh?"

It was the signature sound of the other side of Ferguslie Park, the one that looked like West Beirut.

I turned and looked across the street to where the sound was coming from and immediately experienced that prickly feeling you get on the back of your hands when you know a terrible shit storm may be about to happen. Several of the local lads had more or less surrounded the van and were busying themselves interrogating the occupants. The largest had no shirt, several tattoos, a shaved head, combat pants, Docs and a can of what appeared to be Newcastle Brown Ale clutched in his hand. This could go any way, but it seemed most likely that it was going to go badly. I had visions of everyone lying in the street with broken ribs and no teeth while the denizens of Ferguslie Park scampered off in all directions laden with camera equipment.

Some part of me remembered that I'm a six-footer and that I weigh a hundred and eighty-five pounds—not big by Canadian standards but reasonably imposing in Scotland. When you're in the water with a shark, it pays to remember that you're sometimes just as intimidating to the shark as it is to you. I was wearing black jeans, Docs, a black tee-shirt, sunglasses and had short hair and a scruffy growth of stubble on my face.

I found the nerve to start walking across the street instead of running away and leaving the camera crew to die. Instinctively, I knew the best defence was a good offence, so I walked up to the roughest looking of the bunch, stuck out my hand and began the dog-and-pony show again.

"Hello, my name is . . . all the way from . . . born here . . . TV show . . . absolutely, no question about it, you'll all be in it—everybody in Canada will see you . . . no, nobody here knows who I am but back there I've got gold records and they gave me, like, you know, the OBE."

Across the road, Mrs. Docherty was looking on with interest. I had a firm grip on the shirtless tattoo and was pouring it on while pumping his hand.

"Yeah, we went off to Canada in 1953."

What I'd hoped would happen did. As other people began to drift over, attracted by the developing commotion, the first lot automatically elected themselves to be the gatekeepers of the situation.

"Aw, yeah! He's alla way frae Canada. Yeah, makin' a show ferra telly . . . yeah, Canada!"

So, what had seemed to be a potentially fatal incident rapidly turned into a sort of local festival in Ferguslie Park. By this point, a white police van was circling the block every three minutes. I wasn't concerned anymore, but they obviously were, judging by the way they were rubbernecking as they drove by. I don't know if they'd decided to make sure we weren't killed or if, in the manner of the Belfast constabulary, they just turned up whenever a crowd gathered, hoping to contain a riot or something.

With the beer can brigade now looking after our interests on the street, Leslie, our crew and I walked back across the road, through the gate of the house and then, with the kind permission of Mrs. D, around into the backyard. I remembered so much: a tree, a shed, that big tank you could see from the yard. There was the spot below the kitchen window where I used to be put outside in my pram and where my mother claimed she'd heard me singing back to the birds.

"You want to come in for a wee bit?" asked Mrs. D.

I'd been hoping the invitation would eventually come. We all went back 'round to the front.

"Bugger off! You're no coming in here! I know where you live!" said Mrs. D. to one of the beer-holding youths.

He'd opened the front gate to join the activities in the house. She pushed him out and shut the gate forcefully. There was no anger in her actions. She'd obviously known the lad since he was in nappies, and I think she was sorry about where he'd fetched up—a layabout, unemployed, drunk at noon on a Sunday.

We all went in the front door—cameraman, sound man, producer and me—into a cramped little hallway with a room to the left, different but still the same. There, the fireplace—no longer coal but gas. That's where I learned how to put my lips together and whistle!

"Hello, Mr. Docherty. Nice of you to let us look around the house!"

Mrs. D.'s husband was parked in a chair in front of the telly, watching, or rather staring at, some children's show. He looked as if he'd grown roots the day he retired and hadn't moved since.

"Uh," replied Mr. D., without looking up.

"Do you mind if I go upstairs?" I asked Mrs. D.

"Suit yersell."

As I moved up the narrow, almost vertical staircase from the tiny hall space between the sitting room and the kitchen, my shoulders actually brushed the wall as I ascended. I had to duck. I walked through the door on the right and into the dim claustrophobic bedroom. The crew set up, and as they did, Mrs. D. began a lengthy monologue.

"Nobody wants tae work anymore! There no the fortitude tae get oot and make somethin' o' yersell!"

Her words began to trail off to the side of my conscious mind amidst a background noise that sounded like the buzzing of cicadas in summer.

Well, here I am, right on the exact spot where I was dragged reluctantly into life.

Who are we? Who are all those people in all those passionate couplings down through the dim recesses of time that sprinkled their stardust into the soup that is us? There is no me. I am a compromise of individuals. For a microsecond, I have a fantasy about all the thousands of men and women who designed my DNA doing the Gay Gordons in a giant ballroom.

Mrs. Docherty came back into focus, and I realized I'd been nodding my head and saying "uh-huh" a lot without having been there at all. I moved to go back downstairs. The room was too small.

"What did ye say yer mam's name was?" said Mrs. D.

"Margaret McLauchlan."

"Oh, aye. No, I canny think o' her."

"How long have you been in the house?"

"Twenty-five years."

"Well, then, there you go. We left forty-four years ago."

"Oh, aye."

Mrs. Docherty was almost as wide as she was tall. She wore a plain print floral housedress, and her feet, swollen slightly, bulged over the edges of her slippers. She was tiny, surely not more than five feet tall. She led the way into the kitchen, assuming I would want to see it, and began to remark on what had been moved around, which window had been replaced, the door being blocked off so the stove could go there. The kitchen was small and slightly shabby with its worn and scuffed linoleum.

I guess the size of the house was having an impact on me. Almost absent-mindedly, I said, "I can't believe my mother raised six children in this house! Where the hell did she put them all?" Mrs. Docherty fixed me with a look that the Scots reserve for the pitiably stupid. In a tone that suggested the reasoning behind such a question was incomprehensible to her, she simply said, "I'd nine!"

When we left the house and emerged onto the sunlit sidewalk of Drums Avenue, there were still a number of people gathered to see what all the fuss was about, including some young boys who'd ridden over on their mountain bikes. I took them to be about six years old, judging by their size. It turned out they were eleven. So much for the quality of life for kids in the area.

"What you doin' here?"

It was the lad with the shock of red hair and the freckles to match. I squatted down on my heels and told him what we were up to.

"What's your name?" I asked him.

"Rambo."

"How'd you get a name like that?"

At this, the other boys laughed as if it was a big "in" joke.

"My faither gi'ed it tae me," he said, looking down at the ground.

The lack of detail in this simple statement spoke volumes, and I thought I'd just leave the matter alone.

"What's it like living here now, Rambo?"

"S'awful! S'aw drugs an' murder. Somebody shot dead just doon road the last week."

"What do you think about all that, you know—drugs and stuff?"

"I hate it!"

This was the sweetest-looking little kid with the most penetrating merry blue eyes, proud and straight in his little football shirt. It made me shudder to think how he was probably going to wind up as I glanced over at our pal with the bottomless can of Newcastle.

"Well, when you get bigger, I guess you'll be one of the guys who'll help put a stop to all that, eh? What do you want to do when you get bigger?"

I realized with dismay that I sounded like a parody of the worst kind of patronizing politician on a neighbourhood baby-kissing tour. Rambo fixed me with that peculiar Scottish look—yes, the one reserved for the pitiably stupid—and answered my question simply and directly:

"I wanna get out!"

With all my heart, I wanted to put him in the van and take him away from Ferguslie Park to any place where he'd have a chance.

I walked across the street to the van and sat down on the fender next to the shirtless skinhead. We just quietly looked around for a little while, then he looked at me levelly. "It's good tae see somebody got out of this place and actually made somethin' of hisself!"

"Come on, man! You've got all your fingers and toes. If you want to badly enough, you're not so far gone you still can't make something out of yourself. There's a lot of world outside here!"

As soon as the words came out of my mouth, I already hated the way they were sounding.

There it was again. There was the look that pigeon-holed me as a foreigner after all, guilty of stupidity beneath contempt.

"Ye want tae try an' get on a job wi' a accent frae here? Good luck tae ye! Yer born here, ye fuckin' die here!"

There he was, the proof of the wisdom of my mother, sitting on the front of a black van, another casualty of the class system so entrenched in Britain, the class system that was my mother's mortal enemy, for it threatened her children.

Being a Little Kid

🍂 "HOW OLD WERE YOU WHEN you came to Canada?" seems to be the question that follows: "Born in Scotland? You don't have an accent!" Well, yes I do, but I've had to learn to speak something that you lot could understand!

"Oh, you came over when you were only five! Well, I guess you don't remember much."

On the contrary, even Scottish children, in spite of what you may have heard, are capable of forming connections in the neural pathways at a relatively early age.

A number of things have happened recently in the life of my young son. He is five at the time this is being written. His name is Duncan. He was only four when the first event in the sequence occurred.

One day, I was driving him home from school in my eighteen-year-old BMW 320-i. By this time the poor old thing could barely be described as four wheels operating in unison, but I was determined to keep it running as long as I could. We stopped at a red light, and as we sat there, the engine suddenly stopped. I knew what it was right away because the fuel pump had been making horrible noises for a week or so, and I figured that one day soon, its demise would signal the end of this car. It would cost more to put in a replacement than the whole car was worth. Besides, the body structure had been compromised by rust and rot. I knew as soon as I heard the silence that this was it.

"What's wrong, Dad?" asked Duncan.

"The car is dead, Duncan," I replied.

I was using an adult way of speaking without literally meaning what I said. The car had always been in Duncan's life, though. To him it was an animate thing with a personality, like a pet. It was a loss for him, and he had to come to terms with it.

I had the car towed back to our driveway, and the next day a truck came from the auto wrecker's yard to take it away. When Duncan came home from pre-school, it was gone. I explained to him that it had gone to a place where they could use it to make other cars go, and this seemed to satisfy him.

For the next few days, Duncan would announce to anyone he met: "Dad's car has died!"

Then, in August of '96, my sister Rosemary died. Duncan was quick to realize that something big and not happy had occurred, and he began to ask questions.

"Is Auntie Rosemary dead?"

"Yes, Duncan, she is."

"Why is she dead?"

"Well, she got very sick, so sick that she couldn't get better and the doctor couldn't help."

"What did she get sick of?"

"She got a sickness called cancer. You see, Duncan, sometimes people are sort of like cars. They need all the important bits they have or they just don't work anymore. Well, cancer makes some of the bits in people so broken they just can't be fixed. That's what happened to Auntie Rosemary, and she just couldn't stay in the world anymore. We loved her very much, and we'll miss her very much, but we'll still have all the wonderful things about her to remember, so we won't be so sad."

"Is she in heaven?"

I had never mentioned heaven or anything of a particularly religious nature. I felt that moment's hesitation so familiar to parents who don't want to commit to a particular point of view but sense it's not the time to engage a frightened four-year-old in a theological dialogue.

"Yes," I answered.

Then Duncan's maternal grandfather died very suddenly and unexpectedly in the prime of his life. An aneurysm on a major heart vessel let go. Here, gone— just like that. It was a terrible shock to Duncan's mother, and we were all in a state for a while.

A month or so after the funeral, Duncan walked up to me and announced, "Grandpa and Auntie Rosemary are coming back in a thousand years in the silver car!"

Duncan had taken the information he had and formed his own beautiful little resurrection myth, and as far as I was concerned, it was just as good as any of the others around.

"I'm really glad!" I said.

What's the point? Sure, I remember all kinds of things from when I was a kid growing up in Scotland or about coming to Canada, but they're all jumbled up in time, oversized and mythic, the gaps filled in with a child's imagination.

Here are some of the things my mother told me:

On the night of my birth, June 30, 1948, my life was saved by a good Scottish midwife. I was strangling in the birth canal with the umbilical cord wrapped around my neck, and she was able to intervene.

I was born for good luck according to the Celts, for I was born with a caul, a cap on my head formed by the placenta. Though I've occasionally had reason to doubt this belief, by and large I think it's probably true.

One day, so my mother said, she had to shoo off a cat that had got into my pram and was in the process of suffocating me by curling up for a sleep on my nice warm head. I believe this to be true, for I've never had a great fondness for cats.

I don't remember any of these things.

My first real memory is more consistent with a Scottish upbringing. I remember I'd been given a thrupenny bit (a coin worth three pence) for an ice lolly (equivalent to a popsicle). I'd got out the front gate with it and was toddling off down Drums Avenue with my money held proudly up in the air as I headed for the ice wagon. An older boy came up, whacked me on the head and took it.

I remember the great hairy red cows being walked down our street on the way to the abattoir where they would be slaughtered.

My worst enemy was a collie named Laddie. He looked just like "Black Bob," the heroic dog owned by the shepherd Andrew Glenn in the Paisley *Sunday Post* comic strip. Laddie was anything but heroic and seemed to have a particular fixation on my posterior.

The thing was that, like all Scottish male children, I was virtually never in long pants except for formal occasions and spent all of my waking hours either in short pants or wearing a kilt. Now the kilt, as any proper student of Scottish lore would know, was never designed to be worn with undergarments. It was designed as rough country wear that would shake off water, drape down and keep the wearer warm even after wading through a stream. Adding a pair of cold wet underpants to the ensemble would have been somewhat self-defeating. Even at the tender age of three, I was possessed of a strong sense of tradition and was thus unencumbered by any of the trappings of modernity.

Well, to Laddie, my bum was a beacon. He would make a beeline straight for me from a block away and run me down. Now, remember, this is a dog that is genetically disposed towards herding sheep, so be sure there was no escape. Perhaps to him I was just a wee tartan sheep, for he made it his mission in life to herd me home by sticking his icy cold nose up the back of my kilt and bumping me while he barked.

That was how they'd find me, howling at the front gate with a border collie buried up my backside.

There are other memories, strange and disjointed.

I remember sitting in front of the coal fire one evening and suddenly finding that through the proper contortions of the lips and a strong exhalation of air, I could produce an ear-shattering whistle.

I remember walking up and down the stairs of the tenement blocks across the street and mouthing rhythmic nonsense syllables as I stomped my feet, then listening for the echoes up and down the stairwell.

There were evenings when one of my uncles on my father's side who was a piper would let me blow into his chanter in front of the fire while he played the melodies of Scottish pipe tunes with his fingers.

When I was considered old enough, I was sent away to nursery school in the daytime and placed in the care of large and forbidding-looking nuns. I don't know what particular brand they were, but they certainly seemed austere and aloof to a small child like me. The reason I was packed off during the daytime was that everyone in the house who could pass for an adult was working, and the rest were in school. There was no one home to mind a toddler. I didn't understand this at the time, and I remember feeling frightened, abandoned and very unhappy.

I'm not trying to paint a dark picture of early childhood in Scotland. A different mindset governed issues of child rearing in those days, one that did not lend itself to the gentle nurturing of budding self-esteem. Life was often hard, and the thinking was that the sooner a child understood that reality, the better it was for him or her. Chances were that if a frightened child started crying in a dentist's office when they saw the drill, they'd be told: "Stop your crying or I'll really give you something to cry about!" It was generally accepted that cuffing children on the back of the head, or frightening them half to death, were just two techniques for inducing children to behave themselves.

One day, I got into big trouble at nursery school. I sneaked into the girls' washroom when one of the wee girls was on the throne and pulled the chain on her while she was still seated. I thought this was the funniest thing there ever was and I was still howling with laughter when the nuns arrived.

A brief description of the Scottish commode must be offered for the full dimension of this prank to be impressed upon your imagination. First off, this is no insipid little trickle of a North American toilet. This is atomic disposal. This is the Victoria Falls of water closets. The seating area itself is conventional, save for the hidden refrigeration unit that chills the seat to a bracing minus ten degrees Celsius. But it is the waterworks themselves that strike the user mute with awe.

Approximately one-half mile up the wall is a porcelain tank containing roughly five thousand gallons of water. Suspended from this vessel is an equal length of stout chain of a type considered satisfactory for anchoring ocean liners. One grasps, and with a mighty heave, pulls upon a wooden handle attached to this chain to activate the mechanism. The results might be likened to opening the floodgates on the Aswan Dam, for a raging flow is let loose, accompanied by a terrifying sucking roar.

When my unfortunate victim perceived herself perched over a vortex that was not only soaking her already chilled backside, but also threatening to carry her away to oblivion, she set up a scream that would have wakened the dead as far away as Edinburgh.

My mother was sent to fetch me and accompany me home in my disgrace, but not before I'd received what in Scotland is referred to as a "cuff on the lug." I have a distinct memory of my mother trying desperately not to laugh.

My sister Rosemary looked after me at home. She was like a second mother to my brothers Bill and Calvin and my sister Sandra. I know she resented my mother for the loss of social opportunities in her younger years and I know also that they fought about it once or twice. It's the curse of the older sister in a working-class family to be robbed of her teenage years by duty, but I never remember feeling any sense of resentment or any harshness from Rosemary when I was little—quite the opposite, in fact. She was full of fun and stories.

The memories that are missing from those years are of my father and my oldest brother, Ian. They had gone—sailed to Canada to try and get set up so the rest of us could come over. I guess they must have left when I was still three.

Life has rhythms and paces, and when you go along with people—your family, your husband or wife—you're moving at the same pace and living your life intertwined. It's as though you're all part of the same thing. You're all reading from the same book.

When you're forced to be apart by war or emigration, you lose track of something fundamental. You lose your place in the book of their life and they in yours.

It's as though you're running on parallel roads at different speeds and you see that the other person is no longer beside you to wave at for reassurance.

I always wondered why it was that I could never seem to find my father even when he was sitting there in front of me. Maybe the answer lies in 1953. One day that year, things began to change. There was unfamiliar activity. Things were being put in boxes and crates or gotten rid of. There was excitement. There was talk about going to Canada.

Now, as far as I was aware, there was only one other place in the world other than Ferguslie Park, and that was California. California, as I well knew, was where my Uncle Tommy lived, and he was the uncle, my mother's brother, who sent us packages with oranges in them.

It seems hard to imagine, but even that long after the war, there were chronic shortages of food and clothing and there was still rationing on some items like butter, sugar and meat. Fresh fruit was almost nonexistent or so expensive that it might as well have been unavailable. Uncle Tommy would send us parcels from the United States with the most wonderful things in them: tinned hams, sweets and all kinds of goodies, including oranges—big fat California navel oranges.

The first time I bit into one of those golden fruits, after being instructed not to eat the peel, I was gobsmacked. I thought I'd blow up it was so good. I loved oranges as much as rice pudding with raisins, and that was saying something!

Well, I knew oranges were tied for the best thing in the world and I knew they came from California, so if we were going to go to California, that was perfectly all right with me!

The Samaria

WE WERE ON A TRAIN. THE train was going to someplace called London. I remember being upset because London didn't sound at all like California. I was assured, however, that we weren't going to wind up in London. I was told we would overnight in a hotel, and then in the morning, we would go to someplace called Southampton, and there we would get on a great big boat, which would carry us to Canada. I was reassured to be told that we were actually going to California after all.

The train ride was a great adventure for us kids. It was a corridor train— which meant it had a walkway down one side of the coach and compartments on the other. The train was beautifully appointed, and we felt like royalty because we had our own compartment and ate terrific things in the dining car, on tables with beautiful white linen and flowers. We had our noses pressed to the glass all the way to London.

My mother, Margaret McLauchlan, was determined that we would all rise to a higher station in life than working class, and sometimes this desire would manifest itself in odd ways. We all regarded her with the utmost surprise when, on arriving at the train station in London, she secured an Austin Princess taxi and commanded the driver in the thickest upper-class-twit English accent: "'Lambra Hotel, plyuz!"

She was taunted about this for about the next decade.

It was April of 1953, one month and a bit away from my fifth birthday. I was old enough to be intrigued rather than frightened by the sudden change in life—the bustle of the stations, the crush of people, and finally, the awe-inspiring sight of the dock and the ocean liner berthed there. In my child-mind's eye, I remember the ship being so big that the other end disappeared over the edge of the world.

In reality, the *Samaria* was a single-stack Cunard liner from the prewar era, which was due to be scrapped in the not-too-distant future. She was a substantial vessel at 19,200 tons, at least until you looked at the *Queen Mary*, which was berthed next door. The *Queen* weighed in at 81,000 tons, so I guess the *Samaria* wasn't large as the liners of the day went. Being an older vessel, she didn't have gyrostabilization, a wonderful innovation that helped damp out the pitching and rolling of a ship in heavy seas.

With a deep bass whistle that tickled a little boy's tummy, the *Samaria* slipped away from the dock, and after a brief pit-stop at Calais to take on more hopeful New Worlders, she set off across the North Atlantic.

The position of our stateroom (I always think that term has a far more regal sound than reality justifies) left no doubt about the ongoing health of the ship's engines. And if we'd been any farther down towards the keel, they'd have had to provide a tin pot for bailing. I liked all the strange rumbles, creakings and groanings. Perhaps because of the din of so many of us growing up in such a small house in Scotland, the lack of quiet was reassuring.

My older brothers Bill and Calvin were sharing an inside stateroom with no porthole, somewhere on the keel. Their life immediately took a turn for the better, however, because a rather oily steward had taken a shine to my sister Rosemary. He felt that the way to a young girl's heart was through her brothers, so the boys found they had lots of opportunities for movies and treats of various kinds.

Early on, Calvin ran into the visible evidence of our station in life. While exploring the ship, he came across the barrier that blocks the stairs to keep folk like us from contact with the upper classes and the well-to-do, who inhabited the upper decks. He was offended to realize there were people who thought he was not good enough to associate with them. I don't think he ever forgot that feeling.

One of my favourite things was the sound of the lyre-shaped chimes that the man in the white jacket would ring with his little mallet as he walked the companionways announcing the various sittings for meals. Compared to our usual experience, meals on board were a special event. I had never eaten out in a restaurant in my life, and dining on board ship was like doing that at every meal. There were lovely clean white tablecloths, and the dishes were shiny and matching. Best of all, the usual bets were off as far as childhood treats were concerned. It was open season on all manner of delicious and wonderful things that, being ration-bound all our lives, we had never eaten before.

Then we sailed into the teeth of a springtime North Atlantic gale. By the next service, you could have shot a cannon through the dining room and not hit a soul. It became very rough, and virtually everyone on board other than the crew became deathly seasick. Remember those gyrostabilizers we didn't have? Fortunately, I was gifted with some good nautical genes somewhere in my ancestry because I seemed to be unaffected by the ship's motion.

By increments and then more progressively, the *Samaria* became an unpleasant place to be below decks. One of the stewards, a good-hearted man, took pity on me, and it was arranged that he would escort me to the deck for some fresh air. The memory of this excursion is forever etched in my mind with the most astonishing clarity. I had never really seen the ocean before, except when I was bashing jellyfish with my sand pail on the beach down at Prestwick, and those excursions were reserved for better weather conditions.

When the steward, holding me firmly in his arms, stepped through the hatch onto the pitching deck, I was confronted with the sight of the Atlantic in full fury. We had emerged onto a deck that was protected from the wind and flying spray. My guardian had chosen well, for the noise of the storm was quite deafening. I was exhilarated!

There were huge grey-green waves, long and rolling, and as the ship pitched up and down, one would occasionally loom up as high as the deck. The wind battered the tops and grabbed their whitecaps, carrying them forward so that, often, you could not see down into the troughs of the waves but only a flat rage of blowing spray.

Suddenly, a nearby hatch slammed open in the wind, and a poor man lurched out. He must have been deathly ill to brave such weather without protection, for he was dressed only in his shirt and trousers. I watched in fascination as he retched. The contents of his stomach were picked up by the wind and flew horizontally without losing an inch of altitude, striking the wall some twenty feet away.

Gradually, as the storm subsided over the next couple of days, life returned more or less to normal. People began to stir. The ship smelled more of broth than the sourness of seasickness, and the colour of people's faces returned to normal.

I befriended a little German kid, and we took to playing on the flat top of a storage hatch with our toy cars. I had a Standard Vanguard of which I was very possessive, and he had some foreign contraption called a DKW. The cultural differences between German and Scottish became immediately apparent, for try as I might, I could not get him to make a proper engine noise. He kept uttering "RRRRAAAANNNNNGG, RRRRRAAANGGGGG!" instead of "BBBRRRRRMMMMM, BBBBRRRRRRMMMMM!" and would not be persuaded to do otherwise.

Gradually, we became shipboard friends, and the language barrier didn't seem to matter much. I suppose it wouldn't have, as language is less of an issue to young children just learning the linguistic ropes. After a while, life on the ship became the only life, and I adjusted to it as normal, even though the voyage lasted only a little more than a week.

Then, land! Someone pointed to a hazy strip on the horizon and said, "Quebec."

It was May 7, 1953, and the whole process was beginning again: noise, bustle, confusion, finding and wrestling with belongings, endless queues for immigration, interrogations, stamps, papers and more papers. Finally, exhausted, we boarded the boat train in Quebec City bound for Toronto.

It seems hard to comprehend now, but in those days, air transport, particularly transoceanic air transport, was a fledgling enterprise accessible only to the few who were wealthy enough to take advantage of the new services. The airliners were the big piston-engined classics like the Douglas DC–6 or the Lockheed

Constellation. People put on their best clothes to fly. The democratization of travel had not yet begun, and most people, particularly immigrants (read, the lower classes), travelled by ship. Quebec City was the gateway to Canada because that was as far up the river as the big boats could get. The St. Lawrence Seaway had not yet been completed.

The train ride to Toronto seemed to take forever. We stopped at every fire hydrant on the way. Not only that, but the train was both filthy and shabby, in sharp contrast to the beautiful British train we'd been on only a week and a half before. There were no compartments, and the dining facilities consisted of a man in a paper hat walking up and down the aisle with a pushcart full of stale ham-and-cheese sandwiches. We children were all cranky and exhausted because there was no way to rest on the train. The tracks were rough and uneven, and the thing lurched all over the place. God only knows how my mother and Rosemary coped with the situation. As far as my brother Calvin was concerned, if this was Canada, we could turn around and go right back to Scotland.

At last we arrived in Toronto, where we were met at Union Station by my father and Ian. They were both strangers to me, and even my brothers had some adjusting to do, for my father had changed a bit in the time he'd been in Canada. He'd put on a few pounds and gone a bit thinner and greyer on top. Bill and Calvin had to face the greatest adjustments because they'd been used to being the top men around the house and now suddenly here was this dad guy, who seemed to think he was running the show.

We were bundled into assorted taxicabs bound for a boardinghouse on Soudan Avenue, where we would be staying until we could move into a proper house. It was during this ride that I made my debut as a radio performer in Canada. I was induced to sing "A Gordon for Me" into the microphone of the cab's two-way radio for the enjoyment of anyone out there who might be listening.

A Gordon for me, a Gordon for me
If you're no' a Gordon, you're nae use tae me
The Black Watch is braw, the Seaforths an' a'
But the cocky wee Gordon's the pride o' them a'

This was one of the songs we all sang as kids, which glorified the highland military regiments. In very short order, though, the dispatcher thundered back over the speaker, "What the hell is going on in there?"

And so we arrived in the New World, everything twice as big and twice as much. Me, with my unintelligible Ferguslie Park accent and my tartan kilt.

On Being a Bigger Kid

🍂 WE MOVED INTO A HOUSE AT 5 Stayner Avenue, a big house by our standards. It was out on the north side of Toronto in what was called North York but in reality was pretty much open fields. There were still original farmhouses in the area although the bulk of the local housing consisted of little boxy postwar bungalows. To the east was a marsh that separated our house at the end of Stayner from the heights of Briar Hill. There was an old farmhouse on the north slope that I was told contained a witch and so was to be avoided at all costs, but the hill itself was loaded with wild strawberries, which I picked and stuffed myself with while keeping a watchful eye out for witch goings-on.

It hadn't taken me long to make friends with some of the local kids. They picked up as many Scottishisms from me as I did Canadianisms from them, so a sort of hybrid language was created among us.

They were all highly amused by my kilt. "Murray wears a dress! Murray wears a dress!"

The kilt was soon retired.

In those days, there wasn't much development in the area, so there were a million hidey-holes to play in and places to run wild. There was the marsh to hunt in for tadpoles and birds' eggs. You could make bulrush forts deep in the waving expanse of the cattails. There were a number of good places to swipe chestnuts for playing "conkers." This was a game we'd played in Scotland. A nail was used to drill a hole in a chestnut, which had been hardened using various secret strategies. Then a shoelace was inserted and threaded through the hole. Finally, a thick knot was tied in one end of the lace and the chestnut pulled down snug against it. The players would then take turns smashing their chestnut into their opponents' until one or the other of the competitors' carefully chosen weapons was demolished.

We were getting pretty well settled into our new world by the fall of 1954, and then along came Hurricane Hazel! It was the 15th of October.

It's rare for a big tropical storm to veer inland. Usually they hit the Gulf coast of the United States and blow themselves out, having been separated from the forces that gave them birth, or they follow the Gulf Stream up the east coast and eventually whirl out into the colder waters of the North Atlantic to die. Hazel arrived very much alive and packing a hell of a wallop.

The whole storm came and went over a couple of days, but the full fury of it lasted for perhaps eight or nine hours. I was scared out of my wits. I thought the world was coming to an end. The house shook like an animal, beaten by the wind and lashed by sheets of unbelievably heavy rain. When the storm finally subsided, my little marsh, which had been several hundred yards from our house, had become a lake with wavelets lapping just a few feet from our side door.

The waters subsided over time, but for several years, the level in the marsh remained much higher than normal.

That winter was a paradise for all the neighbourhood kids. There was unlimited ice for skating, impromptu shinny games and sliding on your boots or belly after a mighty running start.

It was around this time that I got the idea I could skate. I don't know why, but it has always been an assumption of mine that I was born knowing how to do everything.

"I can skate!" I announced emphatically to my sister Sandy. "You just go like this," I said as I scliffed across the basement linoleum in my stocking feet. I was doing my best imitation of the big kids I'd seen playing hockey.

Somewhere, I guess from one of the neighbours, a pair of cast-off skates was found for me, and off I went to the frozen expanse of the marsh to make good on my bragging.

I didn't know there were so many ways to fall. I fell on my backside, on my stomach, painfully on my side. My feet slid out from under me in front, and I cartwheeled backwards, cracking my head on the ice and seeing stars.

I sometimes wonder, when I see children nowadays who are all padded up like little gladiators before they venture past the hot-chocolate machine from the warm changing room, how it was that my friends and I ever managed to survive the experience of learning how to do most of the things we eventually mastered.

Well, I did master the art of scrabbling along in a more or less straight line, desperate arms flailing for balance, balance made more difficult by frozen toes and ill-fitting skates. I did not immediately master the twin survival skills of stopping and turning, however. The down side of this was the discovery of an entirely new way to fall. There I'd be, pumping away hell for leather and there, directly in front of me, would appear an area where the stubble of bulrush stalks protruded just above the surface of the ice. My feet stopped immediately, but the rest of me didn't and I went flying. I didn't know it was possible to hit the ice so hard. I just lay there, gasping like a beached fish.

Eventually, I got proficient enough that I became a candidate for the attentions of my big brother Bill. He was naturally athletic and already knew how to skate but had also quickly mastered the stickhandling and shooting skills that were fundamental to the game of hockey. Gradually, his knowledge filtered down to me.

I don't know exactly how Bill taught me to play sports. It just seemed to happen naturally as a result of goofing around. He taught me so many things over the years: hockey, throwing a football, swinging a golf club, working on cars and swearing. I idolized him when I was a kid.

It's one of life's great curiosities that events which cause havoc and great hardship for adults can simultaneously create opportunities for play and adventure in the lives of children. In the rich explosion of life that often follows some cataclysmic event, wonderful things happen.

The spring after the hurricane, there was an explosion in the frog population. There were spring peepers, leopard frogs, bullfrogs—all there to be caught, examined and prodded into jumping. Everywhere you looked in the water, there were things swirling, swimming and snapping at other things: mosquito larvae, dragonfly nymphs, diving beetles, and of course, you had a front-row seat for viewing the miraculous development of tadpoles.

Most amazing of all, though, was the sound. As we sat on the front porch on a warm summer's night, a thunder of song filled the air as every frog, great and small, gave voice. That singing, filling the air as I sat quietly listening, is an indelible part of my childhood memory. We had never heard such a sound in Scotland. It was a reminder that this was someplace new and unexplored.

Weaning in the Fifties

AT ONE POINT, THERE WERE TEN permanent residents in our modest two-storey house on Stayner Avenue. In addition, guests would arrive for Sunday dinner to add to the general confusion. There were all of the kids—some now grown up, such as my brother Ian, who worked as a travelling salesman for a coffee company. He came and went a great deal. My sister Rosemary was now working downtown at Dominion Securities and was the very height of sophistication.

My brother Bill, having had the benefits of an aggressive Scottish education system, was doing much better than expected at Bathurst Heights Collegiate. My brother Calvin had suffered from rheumatic fever soon after we'd settled in the house, and the doctors had warned, as was the custom in those days, against any exercise or stress because of possible heart damage. During his long slow recovery, he'd sit and watch other boys at play while he comforted himself by eating chocolate bars. As he gained weight, Calvin, always an intellect, always wearing glasses, was stung by the cruelty visited on him by his peers. He bided his time and learned about his inner nature.

My sister Sandy, with whom I've always felt an almost supernatural empathy, was growing up fast in saddle shoes and crinolines.

Grandma Fisken, my mother's mother, had come to live with us. She was a woman from a completely different age, to whom an electric kettle was a suspiciously newfangled and unnecessary invention. She took on the duties of shepherding me, although it was hard for her to keep up: she was well into her eighties.

Alistair Hunter, who ended up marrying Rosemary, was around so much I can't really remember whether he lived with us or not. It certainly seemed as if he did. He was terribly fond of our mother because she was such a great conversationalist. That's why he used to come around to visit when we were living in Scotland. He'd come across the ocean too and resumed his old habits. Alistair sat up late at night, after finishing his correspondence course lessons in accountancy, and handmade me my first-ever and best-ever six-gun holster— hand-tooled leather with a fast-draw swivel. Those are the kinds of things a kid doesn't forget.

Then there was me. I was so far down the pecking order that I felt pretty much left on my own to seek whatever adventure or mischief presented itself. This was with the clear understanding that I would do nothing that might attract the attention or the wrath of my father.

My mother and father were both working at this point. My father had found employment before we arrived in Canada, at Inglis, an appliance-manufacturing firm at Laird Drive and Eglinton Avenue. He was a machinist, and this, of course, was a vulnerable trade, dependent on the ups and downs of the economy. That fact would continue to have a profound effect on our family life.

My mother was in the first of a succession of positions that she would occupy. She was working for the Toronto *Telegram*, taking advertising over the phone for their want ads. She'd adopted the *nom de profession* Miss Burns because this was the tail end of the era in which, if women wanted to have a job, they could be neither married nor pregnant.

Neither of my parents drove an automobile. In fact, they never did throughout their lives, always relying on friends or, later on, sons if a trip had to be made. If it was the Saturday grocery shopping that needed doing, my mother would walk to the store, then call a taxi to get her home with twelve bags of groceries. Twelve bags of groceries which, at sixty-five dollars, made up our biggest weekly expense.

I don't remember having any sense that money was in short supply, but I guess it was. As I got older, I began to notice that I never got anything new in the way of clothing or anything else for that matter. Everything came well broken in by a succession of brothers or neighbours' children.

The lack of a car never seemed to be of any great consequence either. It was considered a luxury to own a car if you were of British background. Sensible people took the bus or the train when they went anywhere, and there were far more important things to be done with your money. It was the same with that other North American big-ticket item, television. We didn't get one for a number of years. We did, however, have a rotary phone with Russell 1–4197 written on the circle in the middle of the dial, and we kids evolved a very clever system for entertainment involving its use.

The family in the house at a slight angle across the street did have a television set, and if the curtains were open and you sat just so, you could see the screen from the day bed in the glassed-in sunporch of our house. My sister Sandy, upon finding out there was something on that we desperately wanted to watch, called over on the phone to the house across the street, and we'd all sit on the day bed listening to the sound on the phone as we watched the picture through the window. This was a conspiracy that was possible only with the full cooperation of the neighbours' kids. The plan worked very well until someone older would begin to wonder why so-and-so hadn't called and then trace the phone cord out to the porch. I think my mother, much as she tried to hide the fact, got a kick out of our ingenuity.

It was also true that TV couldn't compete for my imagination with the lure of radio. Network radio was still alive and well at this point, and I listened to *The Lone Ranger, Jack Benny* and *Amos 'n Andy Show*. The great thing about radio was that you could still do other stuff while you were completely absorbed in the story or skit. You could draw or make a model while at the same time radio was exercising your imagination in the same way that books do. What a pale ghost of its former self radio is today!

Another great thing about radio were the winter hockey broadcasts with Foster Hewitt. I can still recall the smell of the rug and hear the gentle thrumming of the electric-pump motor on the oil-fired furnace as I lay there listening to the broadcast of the Toronto Maple Leafs games. For me, there is only one hockey club in the world and that is the Leafs.

My father, however, was a fan of the Detroit Red Wings, a habit he'd picked up in Detroit when he first came to North America in the twenties. As far as he was concerned, Gordie Howe was and would always be the greatest hockey player who ever lived. It was best not to debate this with him.

I, on the other hand, lived, breathed and ate the Toronto Maple Leafs. George Armstrong, Bobby Pulford, Dick Duff, Red Kelly, Johnny Bower—these were not mortal men. I had no idea what Maple Leaf Gardens actually looked like and I had no illusions about ever being able to go there, but the screaming crowds on the radio and the excitement of Hewitt's voice had me convinced it must look like heaven in that movie where David Niven starred as the young RAF pilot who was taken prematurely from life by an angel. In my mind's eye, I saw banks of golden clouds with white-robed spectators seated in them stretching all the way to infinity from the sun-drenched surface of the ice. The goal judge was Vincent Massey in a white lamb's-wool wig.

One winter day, our ragamuffin little public school hockey team was treated to a skills-demonstration, courtesy of the Leafs organization. We were like drops of water on a hot skillet as we waited for our heroes to arrive. When they finally did, we were struck dumb with awe. It was Bob Pulford, Dick Duff and Billy Harris who appeared in their perfectly creased grey flannels with those beautiful iridescent blue team jackets that sported the pure white stripes and the proud white maple-leaf crest.

It was impossible for any normal person to skate that fast. They put on skating and passing demonstrations with complex three-way combinations, jinking around our plain little rink like unleashed lightning bolts. They had the most beautiful CCM Tackaberry skates that sliced into the ice with a slash and a grind and threw showers of snow high into the air when they cut hard to a stop. Oh, those skates—skates that little boys in hand-me-downs could only dream of.

There was a shooting demonstration, and Bobby Pulford let go with a shot at the net from between the centre and blue lines. It hit the net dead to rights, went straight through it and punched a hole in the boards.

Well, God could have taken us all to heaven right then and there because there was nothing left in this whole wide world for us to see after that!

The World Expands

{🐾} WHEN I LOOK AT THE WAY children grow up now, in the last years of the twentieth century here in North America, it makes me stop in amazement and contrast their lives with the freedom of my childhood in the fifties. Nowadays, children are accompanied everywhere by a responsible adult, and virtually every moment of their lives is regulated and organized into some supervised activity or another. I understand, of course, that the world has changed. Still, I look at the spontaneity that has disappeared from their lives and I'm sad for them.

By contrast, when I wasn't actually in school, I was left to do whatever came to hand in the form of play or to pursue whatever form of adventure presented itself. Some of these activities were quite dangerous, such as jumping off the twelve-foot-high roof of a local construction shack over where the new housing tracts were being built. We were pretending to be wartime paratroopers jumping into France, carefully collapsing and rolling when we landed so as not to break our legs on impact. It was all in the spirit of testing our boyish courage. Other activities were really foolish, like exploring the dark labyrinths of newly laid sewer pipes.

There were almost constant pick-up sports, and the game we would be playing would depend on the season. In the winter, there was shinny at the Danesbury Public School rink. Run home after school, get the skates and stick, run home for dinner, go back, play till the guy came to turn the lights out and flood the rink for the overnight freeze, walk slowly home with frozen toes, boots crunching in the snow, down to the basement to sit on the linoleum and go "Ow, ow, ow" as fingers and toes and ears came back to life.

In the summer and fall, there were pick-up games of baseball and full-contact no-holds-barred unregulated tackle football with no pads. It was always great to compare cuts, scrapes and big blue-black bruises while bravely pretending that they didn't hurt.

My friends had names like Neil Korman (from our side of Marlee); Steve Goodman (from the other side), who had great electric trains; Peter Dvorsky, who left the neighbourhood one day after his parents were tragically killed in a car accident; Brian Stepak, who was a really good natural athlete; and Joey Schwartz, my best friend.

The only Gentile kids I was hanging around with were the Nelhams from next door. Their dad, Austin, worked down at the Royal York Hotel and always had great stories about the goings-on during the Grey Cup weekend. The older son, Bobby, was a really good hockey player, already in the junior leagues by that time and dreaming of a career in the NHL. I looked up to Bobby. The younger brother, Tommy, was a bit too young for me to play with. The sister, Donna, was the right age, but she was a girl and I wasn't that keen on playing with girls yet.

One day I came home and my mother met me at the door. She looked tired and sad. She told me to go next door and stay at the neighbours' for the rest of the afternoon and she would come and fetch me later. I was not to come into the house. There were a number of strange cars in front, and one of them was an odd-looking station wagon with no windows. It was dark-coloured and very clean. I figured out pretty fast that something was wrong, and it scared me that no one would tell me what was the matter.

It turned out that my Grandma Fisken had died. I was immediately overcome with remorse and fear because I was sure her death was my fault. I'd been sick, and she'd been looking after me. I'd made a game out of getting her to come upstairs as many times as I could until she'd lose patience with me. First some juice, then a cracker, then flat ginger ale. When I told my mother what I'd done, she sat me down and assured me it hadn't been my fault that Grandma had died. It was old age and being so worn out from life that had finally convinced God to call her home to heaven.

I felt better after my mother's assurances, at least as far as my feelings of guilt were concerned, but I now had a new realization to come to terms with: the dawning of awareness that people went away and they didn't come back. I suddenly got curious about this God guy, who snatched people up without even asking anybody.

One morning, I awoke with a red, spotty rash and feeling rather poorly. It was determined that I had the measles, so I was quarantined in the house and confined to my bedroom. My brother Calvin brought me home the entire collection of John Wyndham books. Some of them were made into quite dreadful movies, but the original books were great. *The Day of the Triffids, The Midwich Cuckoos, The Kraken Wakes,* et cetera, were the best kind of terrifying science fiction for an impressionable kid.

By this time, I could read very well, so I just dived right in and practically ate those books for dinner. My favourite was *The Day of the Triffids.* In this story, the spores from an alien plant species drift to Earth one day and take root. It is quickly discovered that they are rich in a high-quality and valuable oil, so they are cultivated in vast plantations. Two things are both interesting and problematic about these plants. The first is that they have a long and dangerous whip-like stinger at the top, which lashes out at whatever threatens the plant. The second curiosity is that they can uproot themselves and move around at will. These plants represent no danger to the world as long as they are well confined. Did I mention that they are incredibly fecund?

One night, the world is treated to an unpredicted and unprecedented display of celestial energy pulses so spectacular that virtually everyone who isn't working in a vault, bunker, mine or confined to a hospital goes outside to watch.

The next morning, the world wakes up blind, except for the fortunate few who weren't watching the night before. You can imagine the chaos. Of course, now that there's no one to exercise control over the Triffids, they quickly break out and become dangerous. This was great stuff! I just wolfed those books down, and they scared the shit right out of me!

Not long after I recovered from the measles, my sister Sandy and I were outdoors in the early evening by the front porch. We began to notice a greenish glow in the northern sky, and as we watched, it got brighter. Then it became columns of light. Colours began to appear. Shapes began to swirl and dance around the sky and it seemed the whole event was emanating from a point directly over our heads.

I suppose there must have been a burst of activity in the sun around that time, with the attending solar flares. What we were looking at was a spectacular and unusually bright display of the Aurora borealis. But I had never seen the Northern Lights before, and having recently read the John Wyndham books, became convinced I was going to be struck blind. I dashed inside the house and hid in the darkest place I could find!

In the summer and fall of 1955, certain things began to capture my attention that I hadn't noticed before.

There was a sort of summer background noise, kind of always there, like the mountains surrounding Vancouver that no one notices after a while. It was a low rumbling humming bumblebee sort of noise. It sometimes pulsed, sometimes took on a jagged saw-toothed sharpness. It always seemed to be there, except, of course, at night.

One day, the noise was close by and extra loud. I looked up to find the source, and there in the sky was a yellow aeroplane. It had a greenhouse canopy. It had blue-bordered white circles with bright red maple leafs in them and big black letters and numbers on the side as well as beneath the wing. I could see there was a man flying it. I found suddenly that I really wanted to do that too!

There were also other noises: strange noises, muffled hissing roars with overtones of high-pitched shrieks. These were the sleek fighters and interceptors with their jet engines.

My brother Bill knew everything there was to know about aeroplanes, and I quickly learned from him that my bumblebees were Harvards—basic trainers used by the RCAF, and the noise they made came from the tips of the propellers exceeding the speed of sound as the craft climbed to altitude. There are still many of these wonderful old planes flying years after they trained a generation of pilots to fight in the Second World War.

The two other silver streaks were the Canadair F–86 Sabrejet, and the Avro CF–100, which was being built out in Malton at the A.V. Roe factory. These aeroplanes made a really big impression on me, especially the Sabre, which I thought was the most beautiful thing I had ever seen. I still think it ranks up there with the Spitfire as one of the most beautiful designs ever.

The Downsview RCAF base, where they now have the de Havilland factory churning out Dash 8s, was at that time the home of an active fighter squadron. There were both combat and training activities going on, so the field was very busy. The lure of following the aeroplanes to the fence was too much to resist, and as time went by, it became a regular activity to make the journey up to

Wilson Avenue, which bordered the south side of the base, and sit by the fence watching the jets on their final approach for the runway. These were the beginnings for me of what would become a lifelong passion for aviation.

The natural world also captured my attention around this time. I found myself spending many happy hours examining things and wondering about them.

We had a family friend who would often visit. He was the sort of fellow who'd come for a night and stay for a week. I think he was rather a lonely man, and my mom and dad were always very open hearted about taking in lonely strays who had no real family.

This fellow was a good-hearted and likeable soul named Frank Berry. Unfortunately, when Mr. Berry came to visit, all the good manners and behaviour my mother had tried to instill in us would be tested to the limit. He had, as bachelors will, developed some of the worst habits, and the worst of these was a cavalier disregard for the most basic principles of personal grooming.

When he came over, he would relax on the couch and kick his shoes off. He had several kinds of body odour, all competing for attention, but the worst of it, by far, came from his feet. We kids had to make as discreet an exit as we could from the room because it was impossible for us to prevent our reaction to the assault on our noses from being written on our faces.

One happy day, Frank Berry met a young lady by the name of Mary Stuart. She was a lovely soul, kindly by nature, and I was immediately fond of her. Unfortunately, she was not very healthy. She had pleurisy and was prone to extended fits of wheezing and phlegmy coughing, the kind that makes you stop breathing when you're listening to it. She was a really good influence on Frank, though, and he rapidly shaped up.

Mary noticed I was spending a lot of time looking at animals and birds and reading books about them. She had quite a keen interest in birds herself. One day, she read in the papers that a remarkable event was taking place in the area, and then she did a wonderful thing for me.

Every so often, there is a mini-explosion in the small rodent population—deer mice, voles, and other such creatures. Even more rarely, as if on a given signal, there appear the next day, seemingly out of nowhere, a great number of huge white Arctic owls. Of all the great predatory birds, these must be the most magnificent. They fly like ghosts in and out of the winter mists without making so much as a whisper when they pass.

When Mary learned that the owls had come to southern Ontario, she arranged an expedition by car out to the countryside. We drove until we found a farmer's field that was ringed with the great birds. There must have been a hundred or more perched regally on the upright posts and along the lengths of the split-rail fence. We got out of the car and stood watching quietly. There was no sound except for the wind rustling in the sedge grass and rattling the desiccated leaves in the surrounding poplars.

Every so often, without any apparent reason, one of the owls would rise up silently from its perch, flap out over the field and pluck from the snow some hapless rodent. There never seemed to be any competition for these morsels or any order for which bird was to make the kill. It was such a graceful and leisurely hunt, as though they were casually gossiping and eating a box of chocolates. How did the owls know from such a great distance away that the mice were there under the unmarked snow? This will always be a great mystery to me.

Mary pointed to a pile of brown oblong things next to the bottom of a post. She explained that they were owl pellets. She said that when owls swallow mice whole, which is their habit, they digest everything soft, then excrete the bones wrapped in the fur. Needing no further prompting, I immediately collected a large number of the pellets and spent many happy hours at home in secret trying to reconstruct the skeletons of mice from the jumble of bones and skulls in the fur.

Little things can become turning points in the lives of children. To come to an early appreciation of the myriad wonders and miracles that lie all around us is so pivotal. I will always think kindly of Frank and Mary for helping kindle that particular fire in me.

Another thing was making itself evident. I began to discover, through rendering sketches of the aeroplanes or animals I found so interesting, that I was keen on drawing as well. I always seemed to be scribbling away at one thing or another.

And there was music, specifically the discovery that you could make your own.

My future brother-in-law, Alistair, gave me my very first little Marine Band harmonica, and I read the instructions in the box very carefully as I figured out how to play "Red River Valley" from the numbered-hole, sucking-and-blowing system. Blow, blow, blow. Blow, blow, blow. Suck, blow, suck, blow. It was magic!

My father, who had a passion for music, had recently purchased a Hammond Chord Organ. He was a very talented and capable baritone who had loved and sung church music all his life (Handel's *Messiah* was always a favourite). He'd been a member of a Gilbert and Sullivan society back in Scotland and was offered the chance at one point to turn professional.

The organ was a pretty simple affair, with a shortened piano keyboard that you played with your right hand, and accordion-style buttons for chording with your left hand. There were two bass pedals, which were harmonically linked to whatever chord button you happened to be pressing at the time, so you could keep up a back-and-forth rhythm with your left foot while you played on the rest of the machine with your hands.

In the evenings or on Sunday afternoons, my father would relax for a while by playing hymns or some of the old sentimental songs. "My Love Is Like a Red Red Rose" was always one of his favourites. Sometimes he'd play "Peg O' My Heart," which was "their song," as it contained my mother's pet name in the title. My sister and I would roll our eyes and disappear in the face of so much mush.

In the afternoons, though, when no one was home, I would fool around with the thing, trying to figure out songs, until one day I could play "La Paloma," complete with Latin-rhythm bass parts. I thought I was pretty hot shit then!

Life had changed a great deal in many respects by 1957, but one of the most significant changes was getting a television set. I remember vividly when the thing was first plugged in: the very first sound I heard was Andy Devine yelling, "Hey, Wild Bill, wait for me!" Andy played Jingles on the *Wild Bill Hickok Show,* with Guy Madison as Wild Bill.

I guess we were entering the golden age of black-and-white TV because it sure was paradise for kids. There was something for everyone, from the dusters like *Hopalong Cassidy* and *The Lone Ranger* to *The Mickey Mouse Club*, which fed my romantic attachment to Annette Funicello. For my sister Sandra there was *American Bandstand*, although I used to watch that too because I thought Pat Mollitieri was a great dancer.

Sometimes adult and child interests would overlap on the same program. I remember watching open-mouthed with amazement as Sandra went completely ape-shit the night Elvis Presley first appeared on *The Ed Sullivan Show*. My father's face looked like a thundercloud.

My mom and dad took Sandy and me away for a week's vacation that summer in a rented cottage up on Gull Lake near the town of Gravenhurst. That was a major adventure because I'd never been away from home before for any length of time. It was a small cottage and it wasn't on the water, but there were pines around it and the walk to the lake wasn't too far.

We would walk down to go to the swimming beach at Gull Lake Park, where the floating bandshell was, and set up camp with all the paraphernalia of towels, bags and books. For a special treat, we might get a cardboard poke full of fresh crinkle-cut French fries (we still called them chips), sprinkled with salt and vinegar. That was the best thing in the world. I still love the smell of chips wafting on the breeze of a warm summer's day.

At night, they put on music concerts at the bandshell, and it felt very grown up to be out so late walking down there after dark. I'd never heard a real live band play before.

One night, they had a Mexican trumpet player by the name of Raphael Mendez playing as a guest soloist with the RCAF military band. The band were very impressive in their splendid uniforms. They played a program of big band swing music, as well as the more conventional military fare. This was the first time I'd ever heard the arrangements of Glenn Miller, Tommy Dorsey or Les Brown, and the music just blew me away.

The show stopper, though, was when Rafael Mendez, after several dazzling numbers, got up, and with only the mouthpiece from his trumpet, played "Flight of the Bumblebee" on a length of pipe. Well, I thought I'd died and gone to heaven. That was just the most spectacular thing I'd ever seen.

One afternoon, I was paddling around in the water at the park. There was a line of cork floats that marked the boundary of the swimming area and served to keep the boats away, but there was no demarcation to show shallow from deep.

I was fond of pretending I could really swim. I thought I was fooling everybody when I'd walk along the bottom, turning my face from side to side in the water and moving my arms in a simulation of the Australian crawl. Every so often, I'd overbalance and tip forward, thrashing about till I got my feet back under me. This worked fine until the moment I thrashed my feet back under me and found out nothing was there.

I went under and got a big snootful of water. I thrashed my way back to the surface but I couldn't yell for help because I was spluttering and choking too much. I was absolutely gone with panic and started clawing frantically at the water, with my eyes clenched shut. It's fortunate for me that while I was clawing,

_____

33

I was pointed not out towards the deep but back instead towards the safety of the shore. I guess my simulations of the Australian crawl paid off, because I was actually capable of propelling myself clumsily through the water and at last gained a foothold on solid ground.

I stood there in the waist-deep water, shaking, snotting and peeing all at the same time. My heart was racing at two hundred beats per minute. Gradually, I calmed down a bit, and as I did, I realized with surprise that not only had I saved myself from drowning, but I had successfully swum for the first time in my life. Pretty soon, I was thrashing back and forth with a new confidence and yelling, "Hey, Mom, look at me!"

As far as life at Danesbury Public School was concerned, things were going along pretty well. I liked school and I was a good student, though I found out early on that I could do pretty well without having to put out much effort.

We'd been having the life scared out of us periodically by the civil defence authorities. There was an air raid siren on the roof of the school, which they insisted on testing at regular intervals. We were supposed to treat these tests as though they were real and were instructed about what to do when the nuclear bomb went off. There was a silly little song they played called "Duck and Cover," I think. It was supposed to remind us to get down on the floor under our desks and put our hands over our heads. Right, as if *that* was going to help! We knew what the bomb was, and we knew we'd be as well off to go outside and play in the bright light as do what they said in the stupid song!

Nuclear war seemed a real possibility. The threat of annihilation was everyday background noise, and the bogeyman of choice had become the Russians. There was a big event that year which shook things up even more, given the atmosphere at the time.

We all stood outside one night and watched the sky.

"There! There it goes!" someone yelled.

We all watched the bright little dot moving rapidly across the background of the stars. The Russians were overhead. It was *Sputnik*!

Sins of the Father

৬ THERE WAS A RECESSION. ONE of those events that they write about in the *Globe and Mail* in dry, academic terms, terms that mask the emotional impact such things can have on everyday people.

Factories had to scale back production in response to shrinking sales. There were cutbacks. News commentators spoke about acceptable levels of unemployment. There were layoffs.

Inglis, like most manufacturing companies, had to respond to the times, and my father, missing the seniority list, was one machinist too many. He and a lot of other poor souls suddenly found themselves idle through no fault of their own.

My father had a hard life. He'd emigrated to the U.S., a young man full of optimism with a good trade, then met and married my mother, who lived across the river from Detroit, where he was working at the auto plants. He'd begun a family in Windsor, Ontario—just in time for the crash of 1929. The Depression brought a cycle of downward-spiralling desperate times that finally forced them to return to Scotland, a move my mother was bitterly disappointed by, just in time for the Second World War.

The back-breaking work and sleepless nights of the war years gave way to the rationing and dead-end economics of the Scottish postwar, and my father had to find the courage to pick up and emigrate for the second time, virtually starting over at the age of fifty.

Now, here he was, out of work again in what was supposed to have been the promised plenty of the postwar world! Here, once again, was the gnawing anxiety, come to visit in the years that should have been his time to relax and enjoy life a little. For a man as Scottish and proud as my father to be home idle while his wife was working and his older children were contributing to the family finances was a terrible come-down. Being laid off was even worse because it precluded looking for other work. You might be recalled at any time if production orders picked up. It was like spending life in an airport waiting for a flight that would never come.

He gamely picked up the slack where he could by being helpful around the house and getting caught up on all the little things that needed doing. At the end of my school day, I would come home and find my father in the kitchen with an apron on, peeling potatoes or scraping carrots for the evening meal. No one really talked about anything, but there was a lot of tension in the house.

I knew the bare facts about what was going on, but I didn't know the details of my mom and dad's early life. I didn't understand how things could affect people emotionally. I was only nine or ten years old, I suppose. Anyway, it wasn't the habit of my parents to share the darker details of family life with the kids, particularly the younger ones.

I was coming in the back door one day after being outside playing at some boisterous game or other, so I was revved up and full of energy. The back door was protected by a lean-to porch and consisted of an outer multipaned glass door and the wooden inner door.

I threw the outer door open, thinking to burst through the inner door before the other one swung back in on its spring, but the inner door was slow in opening and the multipane came in sharply and hit me. My shoulder went through one of the glass panes with a crack, and there was a further crash-tinkle as the rest of it fell onto the stoop. The inner door gave way into the kitchen at exactly that moment, and standing there was my father.

Without a word, he hit me on the side of the head. He hit me hard enough that I saw lights, and my ears rang. He hit me again, and as I howled and tried to escape, he kept on hitting me all the way up the stairs and into my room. Head, back, shoulders, backside, nothing was spared. Then it stopped.

I was terrified, shocked, hurt and betrayed, but most of all, I was white-hot with rage. When we were little kids, we'd all had the odd cuff on the backside to assist us on the path of righteousness when we were throwing a tantrum or engaged in wilful wrongdoing, but nothing like this had ever happened before. The effect of the full force of an adult temper on a kid is terrifying at the best of times, but I thought my father had gone insane and was going to kill me.

I'd always been afraid of my father, but for some time after this happened, I hated him. Eventually, I got over it, but the lingering effect remains in the way I'm hard-wired. I have a hair-trigger attack reaction to being even playfully slapped or cuffed around the head.

Not long after this incident with my father, I was struck by a male teacher at my school. I had been ejected from the classroom for some minor form of disruptive behaviour and was waiting out in the hallway to be escorted to the principal's office. This particular teacher had been walking by and stopped to interrogate me as to why I was standing there. I guess he didn't care for the tone of voice I used when I answered him because he hauled off and slapped me one across the face.

I can still recall the exact feeling I had, even after all these years. If I'd had the size and strength to leap on him and tear his eyeballs out with my fingernails, I would have screamed with joy as I did it. From idling speed to enraged with no warm-up, just like that!

This incident affected my basic circuitry as well. I have had a lifelong hatred for any form of arbitrary authority. My natural reaction to someone saying, in effect, "You will go there! You will do this!" is: "You will go fuck yourself!"

I learned much later in life, during one of the many revealing conversations I had with my mother about my father, how he'd cried his eyes out with remorse the very few times he'd ever lost his temper and taken it out on one of the children.

I know now the pressures that were on him in his life and I know also that he was a deeply sensitive man who had difficulty communicating his feelings without the aid of a few drams. I understand all that and more, and I've long since forgiven him and made peace.

Look! Up in the Sky!

ONE FINE SPRING DAY, I WAS outside running around in the schoolyard at Danesbury. It was 1958 and I was ten years old by now. My dad was back at work, so the tension had been relieved, although the last of his occupational problems was still to come. My mom had changed jobs and was now working for the Robert Simpson Company in their new building up on Lawrence Avenue. She was in the Customer Service and Complaints Department. She could walk to work now, which was great. The down side was that now she was compelled to listen to people bitching all day, or even worse, she had to try to catch them at defrauding the company by returning merchandise that had already been substantially used.

The neighbourhood was changing rapidly. It was transforming into suburbia more and more with each passing day. Tract housing was spreading to the north and eradicating the wild places in which we used to play. Most painful of all was the sight of what used to be the marsh at the foot of Briar Hill.

Dumptrucks and bulldozers had begun to arrive, and soon they were dumping and levelling masses of dirt and rubble. It was horrible to watch. All those things that wriggled and croaked and were there for us to investigate, the red-winged blackbirds that would sit up on top of a bulrush and call my name, Murrreeeeee—all of it was torn to bits and buried in a few short weeks.

They were nuking everything that anybody might care about, to prepare the ground for the Spadina Expressway, and they were doing it quickly before anybody wised up to just what was being lost. The expressway was eventually halted before it destroyed Chinatown and Kensington Market, but it was too late for my childhood playground. Now it was just a big ugly flat muddy scar, and the nights were strangely, sadly quiet.

So, as I was saying, there I was at school, trying to contrive new ways to torment the girls as ten-year-old boys are wont to do, when a new noise in the sky caught my attention, one I hadn't heard before. It was deeper, with a great rumble and a shrill overtone. I looked up, and there in the sky was the most awesome and beautiful aeroplane I had ever seen. It was large, and its brilliant white skin shone in the sun. Its black-tipped nose flowed smoothly into a large triangle of wing that spread all the way to the tips of the twin exhausts. It had that circle with the beautiful red maple leaf on it, and I could see the numbers two-zero-one written large on the side of the fuselage. It flew majestically by at what couldn't have been more than a couple of thousand feet above the ground, plainly visible in all its glorious detail. It was the *Arrow*!

There is a book called *Empire of the Sun* that was made into a brilliant movie by Steven Spielberg, I believe. In the story, a young boy, who is held prisoner in a Japanese internment camp, stands by the fence overlooking the nearby airfield and watches the kamikaze pilots conducting their short ceremony before climbing into their craft for the final flight. He is moved by the purity of their sacrifice, and he begins to go there every day to stand gravely and silently with his hand up to his forehead in salute. He reveres the aeroplanes almost as objects of worship.

One day, the airfield is attacked and strafed by an American squadron of P–51 Mustangs, and the boy is so moved by the sight of these avenging angels that he runs to the top of the highest structure, in harm's way, jumping up and down and screaming out his chant, "P–51, Cadillac of the skies!" over and over until he collapses in tears from exhaustion and hysteria.

When I saw that scene in the movie, I was immensely moved. I was rocketed back to that day in the schoolyard when I first saw the *Arrow* fly. I was over-whelmed with emotion, although I just stood there mute. I wanted to run after it and follow it wherever it went!

Years later, when I met the man who had flown the *Arrow* on that day, it was one of the biggest thrills of my life. The diminutive Jan Zurakowski is still pos-sessed of the steely eye of the test pilot and of an immense dignity, even though his career was finished forever with the gutting of A.V. Roe. He remains one of my greatest heroes.

Two of the sadder things I have seen in my life have been, first, the destruc-tion of my original neighbourhood, where not one shred of anything familiar remains except my old house, school and one or two other buildings, and, sec-ond, the nose section of one of the *Arrow* prototypes, butchered by the cutting torch, sitting forlorn as a broken promise in the National Aviation Museum.

Spring slowly gave way to summer, and with the season came some real and unprecedented independence. Even though family finances were tight, a way had been found to send my sister Sandra and me to summer camp for a couple of weeks. It was a camp run by the University Settlement House and was called Boulderwood. The camp, which was on the familiar waters of Gull Lake, was set up so that disadvantaged or less well-to-do kids could attend by taking advan-tage of subsidies or various income-related discounts. Sandy and I didn't seem to be stigmatized by this evidence that we were seated below the salt at the table of life, as it were. We were both just happy to get away.

I loved the swimming, canoeing and games activities, but all that came at a price. Boulderwood was also a music camp, devoted entirely to types of music that were excruciatingly unhip for a guy who could play "La Paloma" on the chord organ! I would find myself seated in the middle of twenty shrieking recorder flutes, all competing for the right key as they butchered "Sur le Pont d'Avignon." That was torture, but things got worse!

Once it was determined that I could sing quite well, I was given a feature role as the Go-Between in a hideous little operetta called *The Marriage of Oh Chou San*. It was being produced for the camp by the music director, a lunatic who spent a great deal of his time shouting.

Sometimes, on those nights when my idling brain is searching for choice humiliations to keep me from needed sleep, the lyrics from this early stage expe-rience will suddenly begin to replay themselves. It started out:

Oh, it's perfectly plain to see
That the rat is more powerful than all the rest.
It is indeed.

The most amazing thing is that I can still remember this entire lyric.

I think that during the actual performance, I got one or two of the stage directions right. The rest of the time, I was floundering around red-faced, with people hissing directions at me from every side.

I guess it's universal with children that they are never quite as grown up as they wish to appear, even though they may put on a brave front. There is always the dread that once your parents have left you somewhere, they will never come back.

On visitors' day, I was determined to act very grown up, but when I caught sight of my parents, I ran so fast for them that I don't think my feet ever touched the ground. I hit my mother at a run, still in the air, and clung to her like a monkey with my eyes closed. It's no secret. I loved my mummy!

Meeting Robert Bateman

MY BEST FRIEND, AS I MENTIONED before, was a guy named Joey Schwartz, who lived up on the other side of Stayner, between Marlee and Dufferin Street. We pretty much did everything together. We shared a common enthusiasm for various kinds of sports and projectile weaponry, especially archery. Sometimes we'd test our friendship in the usual boyish ways.

In the summer we'd ride our bicycles up to the newly completed pool at Bathurst Heights to swim. We'd have all kinds of contests of endurance and strength, swimming lengths underwater or diving from the board backwards.

One day, we were having a game of arm punching. You know, you hit me and I pretend I don't feel it, I hit you, you do likewise. The punches get a little harder with every turn until someone winces or quits. Well, neither of us would quit, and the blows got harder and harder, and we both started getting madder and madder. Finally, we were trying to beat the hell out of each other for real and had to be hauled apart by the lifeguard. I think we were mad at each other for a couple of days and then we forgot why we'd been mad in the first place, so things got back to normal.

We had a common interest in the subject of animals and a consuming interest in the romantic wildness of what we called "The Great North Woods." This, as far as we were concerned, was anything farther north than Gravenhurst, Ontario, which was as far north as I had ever been. Anytime either of us got far enough north to see rocks made out of granite and towering white pine trees, we were thrilled to death!

I had been immersing myself in fanciful books such as *Longhorn, Leader of the Deer*, which was a rather anthropomorphized version of the life of a white-tailed buck. I had been consuming, from cover to cover, any copy of *Outdoor Life* or *Field & Stream* that I could get my hands on. I was laboriously making copies in pencil of the heroic cover art from these periodicals, spending hours toiling over pictures of leaping pike and bold mountain sheep.

Joey had been going down to the Royal Ontario Museum on Saturday mornings to attend meetings of an organization called the Toronto Junior Field Naturalists' Club. This was the junior chapter of the Federation of Ontario Naturalists, a conservation group engaged in many worthwhile projects—from saving marshlands for habitat to the establishment of what would eventually become the Bruce Trail.

Joey's father allowed him to make the long bus and streetcar trip down to Bloor Street and University Avenue on his own. I'm pretty sure Joey enjoyed the independence but figured it would be good to have the company of a friend, so he asked me if I wanted to go. My parents were giving me a small allowance by this point for doing chores around the house. Because I was the first one home from school, I was already learning basic cooking skills, and it fell on me to peel potatoes and whatever else needed doing in advance of dinner.

It wasn't hard to get permission to make the trip with Joey, providing I could pay my fare out of my allowance and cover any other expense that might be incurred. So when the next meeting was scheduled, I went along.

The club was divided up into categories of interest, and you joined one or the other subgroup depending on where your preferences lay. You would do your projects and research, and the various groups would then be heard from at general meetings. In that way, information about all kinds of animals could be exchanged. The groups were set up to study mammals, fish, insects, birds and plants. I chose the study of mammals because of my passion for Longhorn.

From day one, I enjoyed myself hugely, and because of that, I also learned a great deal. I was very lucky in my choice of groups. I walked into that first meeting in one of the lecture rooms with Joey and sat down. After a short while, a very pleasant looking young man with a mop of sandy hair walked in and said simply, "Hi, my name is Bob!"

Bob was, of course, Robert Bateman, who would one day gain international fame as a wildlife painter. At this point, however, he was still a teacher and wouldn't even begin painting seriously as a career until he was forty-seven. His professional shift was the world's gain and teaching's loss because Bob was a natural-born teacher.

I remember him lecturing us on the life and habits of a tiny little humble animal like *Sorex fumeus* (smokey shrew, to you civilians). For a bunch of kids who were interested in the large and powerful predators, this would normally have set attention spans drifting to thoughts of hockey or lunch—but not in Bob's class! He would appeal to our sense of the macabre by bringing in stuffed field specimens. He had a pantomimist's gift for imitation and through his facial contortions and body postures, he'd bring the little animal to life in caricature as it blundered blindly along the forest floor, bumping into things and taking bites, its little brain going, "Edible or not edible?"

It's amazing how much kids learn if you can make them laugh!

Bob could also draw, and that really got my attention. He would be discussing the anatomical differences between a cheetah and a leopard—long bones, lung capacity, presence or absence of retractable claws, etc.— and at the same time, using simple chalk on a blackboard, he would create, with a few circles and lines, amazing dynamic representations of the animals he was talking about.

Bob was also incredibly generous with his life and his time. As I mentioned, he was still working full time as a teacher, over in Burlington, I think, yet he went out of his way to organize amazing field trips for us.

On one occasion, we had a campout up on the Niagara Escarpment. This is a long ridge, part of which rises down by Niagara Falls and continues with few breaks all the way up to Tobermory on the tip of the Bruce Peninsula. The Escarpment is riddled with caves, and these, being the convenient shelter they are, provide a home for countless bats and other varieties of animals. Down in the deeper recesses and at the bottoms of shafts, there are the bones of other hapless creatures who either fell in or were dragged there after being killed. Some poor creatures had no doubt become lost and died of starvation.

We spent the entire weekend cave-spelunking. I can't remember if I actually told my parents what we were up to. I probably didn't because by this point, I was in the habit of not telling them about a lot of things I was up to! I think the attitude towards risk was still wonderfully casual in those days, which was why we could go on such an expedition.

The caves were a labyrinth. There were little caverns and chambers, tall narrow cracks, chimneys and long tight passageways that had to be negotiated by crawling on your belly and dragging yourself forward like a worm—only forward because going back was impossible. There were others behind, and the passageway was only a couple of feet high and a couple of feet wide. It was claustrophobic, frightening and thrilling to us, but I'm confident that it wasn't as dangerous as we thought. I'm sure that Bob would never have put us at any major risk. The best thing was that at the end of the day, we'd have terrific specimens of bat bones and strange skulls of this and that.

We had a campfire that night, and Bob's brother had a guitar, which he strummed with his thumb as we all sang goofy versions of "The Green Grass Grew All Around." It was wonderful going to sleep on the ground out in the woods, listening to the night noises, ducking into the sleeping bag when a mosquito would try to fly into my ear, wondering what might be crawling in there with me. The next morning, I was startled awake by a frog, or maybe a toad, which had decided to have a seat on my forehead.

One of my proudest achievements while I was going to the club was to have one of my drawings featured on the cover of the monthly magazine. Unfortunately, I can't remember what the name of it was anymore. The drawing, naturally, was a heroic representation of a white-tailed buck. I was becoming convinced that what I wanted to do with my life was to be an illustrator, just like the people who drew the covers for *Field & Stream*.

I know that Robert Bateman fed my enthusiasm for drawing by his example and helped inspire my great curiosity about and love of the natural world. All of the really good teachers lead by example, and he was a terrific model to all of us. I am delighted that his love for his subject matter and his comprehensive knowledge have resulted in such a great success as a painter!

The Hysterical Boatman

❧ BY THE END OF JUNE 1959, I HAD turned eleven and had started to pack on the pounds in preparation for the big height increase to come. I was built like a little rhino. I had a brush cut that required frequent applications of something called "butch wax" to keep it standing up properly. I was beginning to regard girls with more interest than enmity and was trying hard to hide the fact. Other things around the house had also changed.

My brother Bill had become the proud owner of a magnificent 1954 Chevrolet Belaire sedan, on which he lavished his attentions. It was quite a change to have a car in the driveway all the time. I had taken long journeys by car—but they had mostly been with my brother Ian on his sales rounds through southern Ontario. During one of many summer trips, rocking along the roads with a sedan full of Mojabo coffee for delivery to the small towns, Ian had met the love of his life and the girl he was going to marry. Charlene Bates worked as a waitress in her dad's restaurant in Harriston. I remember getting to spend a lot of time pumping change into the jukebox and listening to Rompin' Ronnie Hawkins sing "Mary-Lou" while Ian was busy courting. Not too long after that, they married, and Ian moved out to begin his life as a family man. Rosemary, my sister, had married Alistair Hunter, and they were out on their own as well, so the house was a lot less crowded.

That Chevy marked the beginning of a lifelong love affair between my brother Bill and the automobile, which goes on to this day. I used to like going out to the driveway and just sitting in his car. Of course, the green Chevy quickly got co-opted for family duties—from grocery pick-up to picnics—and I seem to remember that Bill sometimes got a little sulky when the car he'd spent so much time caring for would be forced to cruise some dusty country backroad, picking up dirt as we searched for an obscure beach at Musselman's or Heart Lake. I loved going to Cedar Beach for picnics and eating jelly aspic and white-bread sandwiches on a blanket. Hell, I still like aspic, though I've since graduated to whole wheat.

There's a tendency for resentments to grow in Scottish families because it's hard to have anything recognized as being yours. I guess Bill was feeling a little bit of this. It sometimes seems that the sole purpose of your possessions is for the collective use of the family. If you have a job and you live at home, you turn your money over for household expenses and get only walking-around money back. Clothes are often used by more than one person.

My brother Ian used to come back from a road trip ready for a bath and a night out, only to find that all his clean shirts were on someone else's back for a date or a job. Sometimes he'd be looking for his sports jacket and find out that Bill or Calvin was wearing it. Come to think of it, I was wearing Calvin's suit when I eventually had my first date.

One of the things you learn quickly not to do in Scottish families is complain. First of all, it attracts attention that you do not want. It's like when a chicken clucks too much in the coop and it starts all the other chickens pecking at it. Second, you learn that no one wants to know. In my family, democracy was viewed as an indulgence of the Hellenic Greeks, not something we practised in our daily lives. If you took your complaints to the family council at the dinner table, chances are they would be met with the standard: "Stop complaining before you really get something to complain about!"

Above all and most important, you did not want your little hiding place in the pecking order to attract the attention of the head rooster!

Speaking of the head rooster, my father had begun to experience dizzy spells of an unknown origin, which made it unsafe for him to be working over high-speed whirring machinery. His days at the factory were numbered, and he began to cast about for other employment.

That summer, we got to go up north again. This time it was to a cottage that belonged to friends of my parents, two delightful people named Bob and Ellen Crowley. The cottage was on the shore of Wood Lake, along the Vankoughnet Road, near Bracebridge, Ontario. The Crowleys had a son named David who was a year or two older than I, so I had a playmate and coconspirator. He knew how to do a bunch of things that I didn't, and I learned from close observation and his frequent condescending tutorials.

Bob and Ellen were just about the most convivial people that you'd ever want to meet. Ellen had that kind of big-hearted laugh and sad-eyed warmth that spoke of troubles overcome and hardship understood. Bob never seemed to have a harsh word, was easy with a laugh and had a great elfin twinkle in his eye. He was both trusting of me and generous to me. I liked both of them very much.

Bob Crowley had built his own boat, a simple craft of perhaps twelve or fourteen feet made of varnished plywood. It had a five-and-a-half-horsepower Johnson outboard motor on the back, with the standard black rubber fuel lines connected to the bright red gas tank. He carefully instructed me in the operation of the motor, and when he was satisfied that I could run it, he let me take the boat out by myself.

When supplies were needed, it meant going all the way across the lake to pick up something at Milne's marina. I loved to get that little boat up on plane and bounce across the wave tops! It was the first wind-in-your-face screaming-for-joy freedom I'd ever had. I prayed there'd be something they'd forgotten to mention so I'd have to go twice.

"No, it's okay. I'll go over to Milne's," I'd say. And if it was pouring down with rain? "A little rain never hurt anybody!"

I wanted to drive Mr. Crowley's boat, even if the weather was keeping the ducks on the water.

Alec Milne was a great burly Scot who ran the only marina and grocery store on Wood Lake. He'd been there since the beginning and would likely have been in his late sixties at the time we were visiting. He was as strong as any two other men I'd ever seen. I watched, awe-struck, as one day he picked up a heavy motor—a big thirty-five-horsepower Evinrude—with one hand, then calmly stepped down into a boat and swung it onto the transom as though it was some little old West Bend fishing motor.

Alec was also the local paramedic and was always on call in case of emergency. I don't think he had any formal training, just bags of experience.

One day, I was practising my spin casting from the dock, trying to get the lure out there a good distance. I was throwing one of those big red and white Mepps lures with the nasty triple hook on the back. I figured that if I let out a little extra line on the back swing so the rod would bend and then threw as hard as I could, I'd pitch the thing out there as far as those guys at the Sportsmen's Show. I really let the thing rip and was rewarded by the sound of a dull thud and a very sharp pain in the muscle at the top of my left shoulder blade.

Bob Crowley took me over to Milne's, and Alec calmly pushed the two hooks that were stuck in my back right through, then cut the barbs off so he could remove them. This was made possible only with liberal applications of Novocaine spray before the surgery. A couple of stitches closed up the minor tearing around the entry points where I'd pulled the flesh open before I realized quite what I'd done. I was as good as new, though I was a damn sight less casual about my spin casting after that.

David Crowley and I used to go fishing in the small boat. We'd putt around here and there, dropping hooks baited with worms or minnows. Sometimes, we'd catch bluegills or little perch that boldly struck up from the weeds at things far too large for them to be concerned with. I still had the leaping bass from *Field & Stream* in my mind as the picture of what a fish should look like, and I was pretty convinced by this time that there was nothing resembling that in Wood Lake. Then—Kapow!

My fishing rod bent over at a crazy angle, and I felt an almighty tug such as I'd never imagined. I was so goddamned excited, I nearly blew up and pissed my pants all at the same time. David was yelling, "Keep the rod up!"

What a comic sight I must have been, scrambling around as the poor fish, fighting for its life, cut under the boat in a vain attempt to wrap the line around the bottom of the motor. I almost fell in, trying to get the rod under the back to clear the fish.

Finally, the struggle was over. The fish was in the boat. It was what a real fisherman would call a marginal keeper. To me, that bass was the size of a submarine! I was never so proud as when we brought our fish, for David got one too, back to the cottage. They were like our trophies of war. We actually ate the things!

There was another boat up at the cottage that David was really fond of driving. It was a contraption called a Sea-Flea. It was, in fact, a small three-point hydroplane, a miniature version of those big monsters like Miss Supertest that race on the Detroit River—aircraft-engined 160-mile-an-hour fright machines that regularly kill their drivers.

This little boat worked the same way. It would get up to speed, and as it did so, it would rise, until only the tips of the three small keels and the propeller remained in the water. The driver sat midships with his hand on the twist-grip throttle of the twelve-horsepower motor mounted on the transom. There was no steering wheel. The boat was directed by moving the motor from side to side by hand.

Small would be an understatement. This little hydroplane was only eleven or twelve feet long, weighed nothing, and even with that small motor could reach speeds of over thirty miles per hour. I watched David roaring around the lake in it, and I was pea-green with envy. I was also convinced by this time that, given my boundless experience as captain of the plywood yacht, there wasn't a boat in the world that I couldn't drive.

My long face was finally noticed, and David decided to let me have a try. I eagerly hoisted myself into the small cockpit. It was really more like sitting on a raft with little four-inch uprights forming a coaming around you. The motor was started, and as I left the dock, I heard David yelling, "Be careful when you slow down that you give it a little power or . . . ." The rest of what he said trailed off as I got too far away to hear him over the motor. I opened up the throttle, and the bow climbed up into the air at a crazy angle, forcing me to move my weight forward to get it down. It settled down and forward as the hull came up on plane and then, just like that, I was going like greased snot!

This was great! I had never gone this fast in anything in my life! I felt like I was driving a rocket. There was no cowling on the engine, so the noise level was incredible, adding to the excitement. The thing was bucking along the waves like a wild animal and skidding sideways as it cornered. There was a really impressive rooster tail, sparkling diamonds and white foam mixing in the brightness of the summer sun. Round and round I roared in a big racetrack oval, passing the dock and whooping with joy once a lap. I never wanted to stop!

At last I realized I was getting tired and hungry. Besides, I figured it wasn't fair to hog the boat all day. I guess anyone who has a nodding acquaintance with hydroplanes can figure out what happened when I decided to bring the boat back in. As I was describing the final turn back to the dock, I chopped the throttle to slow down. At the same time, the bow rose up steeply and the back end settled way down in the water. Something made me look behind me, and when I did, my blood ran cold. The wake, filling in behind the boat, had converged into a mountain of water, higher than my shoulder. This tidal wave was now sweeping towards the transom. It was obviously going to wash right over the boat and sink it!

I panicked and quickly opened up the throttle again. Off went the Sea-Flea for another lap. I came back around and tried to let off the throttle more slowly and gently this time, but it only delayed slightly the onrush of the tidal wave. I opened the throttle and went 'round again, thoroughly rattled and afraid by now.

I don't know whether this is a male characteristic or just mine, but I've always been more terrified of looking like an asshole than of actually being killed. This time was no exception. I was less terrified of drowning than I was of sinking David's pride and joy off the end of the dock in full view of the lovely and talented Lorna Westcott, who had recently captured my attention and who, I was sure, was watching this drama unfold.

I tried everything I could think of to get that boat stopped, but the same thing kept happening. Finally, I was in a full-blown tearful panic, orbiting the lake and shouting each time I passed the dock, "How the hell do you stop this thing?" I guess the folks on the dock couldn't hear what I was saying because they just kept waving and smiling. I guess they figured I was having a great time, what with all the whooping and yelling I was doing.

Finally, there was no choice. I got as close as I could and cut the power. The wake washed right over the back, and I sat there bawling as the boat foundered. I was rescued immediately, and no major damage was done to anything except my pride.

I was mortified! If the earth could have opened up and swallowed me, I would have been grateful. To make not only an asshole out of myself in the full glare of the public eye, but to be reduced to snot-nosed crying as well was more than I could bear.

Naturally, my boating skills became the butt of family humour for years. All it took was for someone to yell, "How do you stop this thing?" in mock eye-rolling fear to turn my face red and my mood black.

By the way, for all you hydroplane wannabes out there, the part of the message I missed was, "When you shut the power, you'll get a big filled-in wake chasing you. Don't worry! Let it come. Just before it rolls over the boat, give her a quick shot of power and the wake will fill in around the stern with no problem!"

A new awareness about my mother and father began to emerge during that time at Wood Lake. The cottage had one of those designs where the internal walls that divide the rooms go up only as far as the rafters, so you could quite plainly hear the goings-on in the other chambers without intending to.

After my sister and David and I had been packed off to bed, the adults would spend their time talking, sipping rye and ginger and playing cribbage. I noticed the different way my mom and dad conversed with their friends. There was an easy intimacy of close friendship that enfolded me like a warm blanket and made me feel safe. It was a great way to find out how my mother and father felt about things they never would have talked about had they known I was awake and listening.

After they went to bed, we would have to bite the covers to keep from giggling as my father, slightly tipsy, joked with my mother about the intimacies of married life. There was the shirring of the covers and the pleasant sound of muffled laughter.

It was a side of them I'd never seen before, and even though I didn't under-stand exactly what was going on, I was reassured by the feelings of love and warmth that their laughter and easy intimacy suggested.

Childhood's End

IN THE FALL OF 1959, I BEGAN MY last year of public school at Danesbury. I'd gotten pretty used to doing well in school and was usually at the top of my class—or second if there was a particularly bright girl. I had been really enjoying science classes because of the interests in the world at large that I had been cul-tivating. Of course, we weren't doing hard science yet—rote memorization of sci-entific principles, that sort of thing. It was still pretty interesting stuff: pond food chains, life cycles of various creatures, elementary geology, you know the drill.

To the great credit of my mother and father, they had created an atmosphere around our house in which it was understood and accepted that naturally you would do well in school. If you got eighty percent on a test, there would be a parental inquiry as to why you had not achieved full marks. I toed the line until my last year of high school, by which time I was well advanced into sullen rebellion.

My other favourite subject was English, specifically literature, although that was not part of the curriculum that was hived off from English in general.

I still thought of music and drawing as being quite separate from school. They were things I did for me. There were music classes at Danesbury, but they gen-erally consisted of singing the most appalling little ditties, in groups.

> I took my little sailboat to sail around the world
> And in and round the meadows
> The river wound and curled.

On and on the song meandered through rose-infested gardens until reaching the earth-shattering conclusion that there's no place like home.

Sometimes it would be the inevitable collection of shrieking recorders shrilling some tortured version of an unrecognizable song and setting the dogs to howling.

I was drawing incessantly on every available piece of flat material that came to hand. My artistic efforts had taken on a new urgency. I found that being an artist was a great cover story for looking at art books—books that just happened to contain certain representations of women in an unclothed state.

My teacher in the sixth grade was a tall man with an iron-grey brush cut and an extremely gruff manner. He was notorious for spicing up history lessons with gory war stories, full of detailed descriptions of amputations and the thrusting of bloody stumps into fires to cauterize them. I recognized him for what he was. I had by this time done battle with a few bullies. This was the first one I had met who was all grown up.

During that year, I remember many instances where he browbeat, belittled, humiliated and generally made life hell for the weakest, the underachievers, or anyone who was unfortunate or just plain dumb enough to come under the full glare of his attention.

I breezed through my science exam that year with lots of time to spare. When I finished, I knew that I'd either aced it or got as close as I was going to get. I looked it over and found nothing I could change, so I began to draw on the back of one of the foolscap answer sheets. I drew a highly detailed and, I thought, rather good representation of an American alligator.

The next day, when the results were announced, Mr. Brushcut looked directly at me and said, "If you had enough time to scrawl all over your exam paper, you had enough time to write a perfect exam! Failed!"

I was dumbstruck. I had never failed at anything in my life, and I knew for sure that I must have scored in the upper nineties on the exam. My sense of justice was so compromised that, for the second time in my life with teachers, if I could have killed the bastard on the spot, I would have whistled while I did it. Mr. Brushcut, I don't know where you are now, but I sure hope you grew into a better man than you were in those days.

Memories, distorted perspectives and scale. I sometimes take a detour through my old neighbourhood and stop for a while at Danesbury School. It seems to be an urge I have to recapture some piece of me that I know I'll never find. It's a plain little building, red brick, box-like. The vast field where I used to run my races, the big sliding hill that led down to the unpainted boards of the hockey rink—they loom so large in memory, so small in reality. I have to drive away. I feel too much like a ghost!

In the fall of 1960, I started at Lawrence Heights Junior High, a middle school that acted as a transition to the harder work of high school. Here we had different teachers for each subject, and we moved around from room to room for the lesson periods. However, the most noticeable thing at first was that it was a heck of a lot farther to walk to school in the morning. That meant getting up earlier. This I didn't like, as I was already demonstrating a distinct preference for nocturnal life.

The school was located at the southern edge of the land that would later become the Yorkdale Shopping Centre. Construction was already underway on Canada's first big indoor mall, and it would open to the public around the same time that I left Lawrence Heights for bigger things.

So my trudge to school, which had been only three blocks, now exceeded my mother's trudge to work by a small margin. (She was still up at Simpson's, listening to the customers bitch.) It was a walk during which the full-bore bite of the January north wind was guaranteed to get your body fully awake.

I actually enjoyed the new school. There was a whole new group of kids to get to know, and the curriculum was much more demanding. I needed the scholarly challenge because, quite frankly, my biggest problem in school had become boredom. I could walk through it with half a brain and still have plenty of time left over for daydreaming.

It was at Lawrence that I received my first formal musical training. There were music classes with real, serious instruments that you would find in a real, serious symphony, and you could take them home to practise! You were given the opportunity to select the instrument you wanted to play, but if you were slow to react, one would be assigned to you by default. That was why you saw in the orchestra a group of young ladies playing double bass or tuba. They had been reticent to commit themselves.

Our teacher was a German man by the name of Karl Waldhauser. I had never encountered anyone quite like him before. In fact, other than the kid on the boat, I had never encountered a real German before. Mr. Waldhauser was a *real German*.

My mother had told us stories about keeping a big butcher knife in the kitchen drawer in wartime for sticking in the heart of the first German paratrooper who might have the misfortune to land in our yard. My mother, like all Britons, took the threat of a German invasion seriously. She did not yet know of the close relationship between Herr Hitler and his astrologer. It was now a full fifteen years after the war, but a portion of my brain was still devoted to thinking of the Germans as the Enemy.

Mr. Waldhauser had what appeared to be a duelling scar on his cheek, such as one acquires during one's tempestuous years at Heidelberg University. He had, we learned, flown Stuka divebombers for the Luftwaffe. God only knows what the poor man had been through and survived, only to wind up in some obscure backwater junior high in suburban Toronto trying to impart some of his great passion for music into the thick skulls of a group of completely indifferent preteens!

He had a love for the Russian Romantic composers, and I can only imagine how excruciating it must have been for him listening to us sawing and tooting our way through a piece by Shostakovich or Tchaikovsky. He yelled a lot and used an extraordinary amount of body language to help us through whatever we were playing. I chose the violin and actually did learn to read music during my two years at Lawrence, but usually I would just go through the piece a couple of times to memorize it, then pretend I was reading to satisfy the good Mr. Waldhauser.

What could be worse than equally out-of-tune violin and clarinet sections duelling with each other? I guess the answer for Mr. Waldhauser was probably the war.

The teacher who had the most influence on me from those days, oddly enough, had nothing to do with either music or drawing. He was a history teacher, an Englishman named Guy Petlock. I had never cared much for the subject before, and rightly so. It had all been rote memorization of names and dates, and it seemed to bear no relationship to anything that mattered to me. What did I care about the Wars of the Roses or the Magna Carta?

Mr. Petlock would see me fighting the wind while I walked by the sickly yellow-brick apartment buildings on Marlee Avenue. On cold winter mornings, he would pull his old Vauxhall sedan over to the curb and beckon me inside. I went eagerly not only because I could get out of the cold, but also because it was an opportunity to observe his driving technique, which was truly awesome.

This Vauxhall was an old English car with a four-speed shifter up on the column and no syncromesh in first gear, which meant you had to double clutch down or stop the car completely to get it into first. Well, Guy Petlock had the automotive mastery of a Jackie Stewart. His feet danced on the clutch and brake pedals. He would heel and toe the accelerator and brake as he down-shifted for a corner, just like a race driver. Under his skilled hand, that old Vauxhall became a Maserati.

He, like Robert Bateman, was also a natural teacher. No facet of history we studied was ever without anecdotes and research on the central players in the drama. Mr. Petlock could take a subject like the papal annulments sought by Henry VIII and the eventual formation of the Church of England and have you come out not only having learned about the events, but also having reached an understanding of who Henry was! His character took on flesh and form, and we saw his foibles as both tragic and comic. Mr. Petlock made human beings out of the players of history, painting the aristocrats as they were, warts and all. When we came to see them as human, they became interesting to us and we were hooked on history!

Most important of all, Mr. Petlock got it into my head that history doesn't end. I came to understand the process by which one event flows into another and subtly influences outcome. I came to see the complex web of events that brought us to where we are now, at the junction of an infinite number of possibilities.

Now, when I travel, I can't go anywhere without visiting the places where things of significance occurred and seeing or touching the artifacts of the times. Some of the things I have seen, great and small, have had a profound influence on me. I have walked on Drumossie Moor where the Battle of Culloden was fought, stood on the *Arizona* Memorial at Pearl Harbour, visited the gravesite of John Kennedy in Arlington, Virginia, and when I've been in Washington, DC, I've never failed to visit the *Spirit of St. Louis* at the Smithsonian Institution.

The smallest things can sometimes have the greatest impact. I found this to be true one day as I wandered through the Smithsonian. There in a glass display case was a piece of complex-looking machinery. I walked up to see what it was and realized I was looking at the Norden bombsight from the *Enola Gay*. I imagined the eye of the man in contact with the sighting lens who was about to drop the bomb on Hiroshima. Here was an object that was frozen in time on the precipice of an unspeakable horror. The sight of it was chilling! Beside the bombsight was a letter of evaluation written by the bombardier. It was a matter-of-fact report, indicating that he had found it to be satisfactory. The letter was made more horrible because of its very banality. Thousands of lives snuffed out in a flash, just another day's work!

The past can talk to you. Its ghosts call out from the places of events. They inhabit the objects of heroism and tragedy. If you haven't learned to hear them, what defence is there against the times when lies are passed off as fact? Guy Petlock gave me a great gift, a love and respect for history. I hope I can pay him back by passing it on!

In 1961, I turned thirteen.

There had been a guy in the sixth grade, when I was still eleven, a repeater named Don, who was slightly older than the rest of us. He was the source of a tremendous amount of bullshit, but on occasion, his words carried the blinding light of universal truth. One day, during a boyish game of making outrageous statements that were greeted with cries of "You don't know shit!," Don made an astounding pronouncement: "If you rub your dick while you're pissing, your piss will turn white!"

We all thought this was ridiculous, but when we got home, every one of us all rushed off to the bathroom to try it anyway. Of course, the boyish stream became undirected and soaked areas that should not have been hit, and time had to be spent on a hasty cleanup. It had quickly become apparent, however, that the real interest lay in the rubbing, not in the colour transition of the liquid. We all quietly dedicated our maximum efforts to exploring further the potential of this rubbing.

One day when I was twelve, I was devoting myself wholeheartedly to experiments in this technique, when something happened that changed my life forever!

Don was right!

So here I was, thirteen years old and trying to catch any glimpse of forbidden flesh with a newfound restlessness that I couldn't trace to any particular source. I developed a bit of a crush on a rather thin but very sweet girl in my class. She had horn-rimmed glasses that swept up at the edges, with little decorations and sparkles where the arms met the frames.

On a class trip to Midland to see the Martyrs' Shrine, where Jean de Brébeuf and Gabriel Lalemant had met their end, we sat together on the bus holding hands. On an impulse, in a supreme act of courage, I put my arm around her and kissed her full on the lips. At that exact moment, two female heads appeared over the seatback in front of us. From that moment on, I was frequently referred to as "Hot Lips."

There were more changes at home. As I mentioned, my oldest brother and sister had left home when they got married, so there was actually some lebensraum in the place.

My brother Bill, being the oldest male in residence, got his own room at last. My sister Sandra, being a young lady of sixteen, naturally required her own chamber. My mother and father had this quaint old-fashioned idea about sleeping together, so the one room that was left over was split between my brother Calvin and me.

My father had finally left Inglis. The dizziness he was suffering had, in the opinion of his employers, become too dangerous for him to work as a machinist anymore. The spells may have been noise induced. I can't really remember what the cause was supposed to have been. I think the cycles of work and layoff had become too much, and my father was probably not entirely unhappy about trying something else.

He took a real estate course with a view to getting his agent's licence and even went so far as to begin driving lessons because he thought it would be necessary to operate a car were he to work in that field. Sometimes I think of my father, now long dead, and my heart goes out to him. He had such a hard life, full of disappointments and hard work. He carried so much responsibility and had so much pride. To keep continually hitting the wall must have eaten away at the heart in him. Now, here he was once more, almost sixty and trying to start over again!

Fate intervened in the person of my sister Rosemary, who was working downtown with Dominion Securities. She helped secure a position for Dad as a bank messenger with the company, and so a new era began for him. He would walk all day, carrying stock certificates and negotiable securities from one financial institution to another. Then, after his day was done, he would take the subway to the Eglinton station at the end of the line; take the Eglinton bus; transfer at Bathurst to the Glencairn bus, nodding in his seat from fatigue; get off at Marlee Avenue and walk home. I remember the sight of him as he made his way up the street. He had that working-man's walk, down on the heel with the toes pointed out forty degrees, stooped, walking like his shoes weighed a thousand pounds.

Rooming with my brother Calvin was great! For one thing, he was out most of the time. For another, he had the habit of throwing all the change from his pants pockets onto the dresser at night and leaving it there. As subtly as I could manage, I pilfered this gold mine for whatever sundries I needed. I'm pretty sure Calvin figured out where his money was going.

He was also quite the sophisticate as far as I was concerned. He was reading books like *Marketing and Media* and going off at night to meetings of the Young Men's Ad and Sales Club, preparing himself for a career in advertising.

He was also bringing home some wonderful LPs (monaural long-playing vinyl records, for those of you who weren't around when dinosaurs walked the earth). It was because of Calvin that I first heard Ray Charles, Sonny Terry and Brownie McGhee, and Johnny Cash's first album on Sun records. It was the very beginning of what would become the huge commercial boom in pseudo-folk music, and Calvin was sort-of-dating a young lady who was a coffeehouse sophisticate. I think her name was Moya.

She came around the house a couple of times and I remember being impressed because she played the guitar. I tried to conceal the fact that I was pretty impressed with the rest of her as well. Anyway, the hip records of the time started to find their way into my life, and I spent time listening to everything from Lightnin' Hopkins to the Limelighters. For comedy, there was Bob Newhart and Stan Freeberg, who were doing a new kind of hip comedy that drew from the analyst's office and the agency world, rather than the Borscht Belt.

Calvin liked to fall asleep after he came home by listening to the radio. He had a little beige clock-radio at the head of his bed, and I would lie half awake while Stan Getz and Charlie Byrd played bossa nova. Some nights it was a folk music show hosted by a guy named Randy Ferris. It would always open up with Joe and Eddy singing "There's a Meeting Here Tonight," then go on to play current folk records of the Joan Baez ilk, or classic recordings from the Library of Congress featuring Woody Guthrie. There were Allan Lomax recordings of "Leadbelly" and old Canadian sides of Wade Hemsworth singing "The Blackfly Song."

This was a rich and varied diet for a kid. I had always liked music, but now, for the first time in my life, it really started to get under my skin.

One day, Calvin brought home a beat-up guitar.

"Don't touch it!" he said.

That is how I began learning how to play the guitar.

By this point, my collection of artistic representations of naked women was becoming somewhat less than artistic! Many of them were not exactly what you'd call "art shots." They were tending more towards the *Playboy* model. They were numerous enough that, even though I tried to conceal them, my mother, with that instinct common to all mothers, ferreted them out. Quickly realizing that nobody draws that much, she made preparations to read the riot act to me.

My brother Calvin, in one of the most noble acts of his life, intercepted her. He convinced her it was just a harmless phase I was going through and that I'd grow out of it eventually. I guess he was armed with all the newest psychobabble of the time because whatever kind of purple smoke he blew up her rear end caused her to back off.

I was rapidly coming to a crisis in my education as I neared the end of junior high. According to the North York Board of Education, I was supposed to attend high school at Bathurst Heights up on Lawrence Avenue. My father's view was that if it was good enough for my older brothers and sister, then it was good enough for me.

I had already made my career decision, though. I was going to be a magazine illustrator. I'd convinced myself that this would be the most glamorous and rewarding profession a person could aspire to. There was one problem, though. No meaningful art programs existed at any of the North York schools. I knew I had ability. I thought I could succeed. I damn well wanted to go to art school!

There began a family debate that went on for some weeks. My mother was quickly won over to my point of view because she could easily see how much this meant to me. She knew I was as serious as it was possible for a thirteen-year-old to be.

My father took the position that I should not attend art school—the idea was foolish and impractical. He didn't see art as a solid profession and was of the opinion that I would only come to financial grief with nothing to fall back on.

It might be that my father saw through me. The career justification story, I came to realize myself, was really just to mask the fact that I wanted to go to a place where I could draw and paint all the time. I didn't want to spend my time in a trigonometry class at Bathurst!

Eventually, my father was won over, as was so often the case when my mother championed my causes. An audition was arranged at Central Technical School. Located downtown at Bloor Street and Bathurst, Central was a school with an excellent reputation for a first-rate art department. It also combined high school subjects with a full art curriculum, so it filled the bill on both counts.

On the big day, I went down with my mother and was directed into the office of Charles Goldhammer, who was in charge of the art department at that time. I was clutching my portfolio of heroic wildlife art, figure studies and copies of various paintings I had laboriously made, hoping to impress.

It seemed to take forever, and I sat there sweating as he pored over my work. At last, Mr. Goldhammer announced that I had "promise" and I would be accepted as a student if the paperwork could be worked out between the North York and Toronto boards. This was trickier than it sounded, as the North York Board would not pay for a student to attend a school outside its district unless it could be amply demonstrated that absolutely nothing whatsoever in North York would serve the purpose.

It took some time to establish that the art courses they offered wouldn't do. Finally, however—and God bless my mother and father for really fighting like demons on my behalf—the paperwork was done, and I was thrilled at the prospect of beginning formal training at Central in the next year.

My brother Bill was becoming interested in racing at about this time and would take me along occasionally, in an Austin Healey Sprite he had acquired, to hill climbs up at Hockley Valley or to club races down at Harewood Acres. He eventually had the Sprite modified with a bored-out engine, a roll bar and a more robust clutch, to take up the mammoth amount of power the engine was now generating.

Going to the racing events was great fun for me. I got to see some amazing machinery in action: Cad-Allards, Ace Bristols, even homemade cars like the Macon Special, which terrorized the ice races at Lake Couchiching.

Bill was a debenture holder who had invested early at Mosport Park. We went out there when it was finally completed and the races had begun. I loved barrelling along Highway 401 with the exhaust roaring away, sitting in front of the roll bar with the wind buffeting my head.

I saw some great race drivers there: Stirling Moss, Joakim Bonnier, Olivier Gendebien—all big names in Formula One, as well as winners in sports car competition at Le Mans.

Eventually, when I was older, fourteen I guess, Bill took me down to the United States to see the U.S. Grand Prix, which was being held at Watkins Glen in upstate New York. I was about as excited as a kid could get without blowing up. This was the longest trip I'd ever made away from home, as well as the first time I'd ever been to the U.S. This was going to be a major racing event with the world championship hanging in the balance, and all of my heroes would be there.

The drive down was just spectacular. The scenery around the Finger Lakes, heart of the lands once ruled by the Iroquois, was breathtaking. The switchback roads running up through the low mountains and winding back down through the peaceful rural valleys were just huge amounts of fun, and Bill had a ball, chucking the car around. As the day wound down, we arrived at the cottage of two friends of his from Rochester named Brian and Sally Metcalfe, where he'd arranged for us to stay. The place was on the shore of Seneca Lake, not far from the town and the racing circuit. We settled in for the night, but I had a hard time falling asleep in anticipation of the next day's events.

Morning dawned bright and beautiful. We drove to the circuit, parked and then hiked over to a well-chosen vantage point from which to watch the race. We set up our comfort gear and settled in to wait for the start.

At last the flag dropped, and the race was underway. What a spectacle! It was the first Formula One race I'd ever seen or heard, and I do mean heard! The noise of the massed, high-revving cars was just awesome! We were well situated to see my heroes, and there they were: Jim Clark "The Flying Scot;" Graham Hill, father of today's Damon; Richie Ginther; John Surtees; Jo Siffert—the entire cast of the movie *Grand Prix* that had starred James Garner. It was a great spectacle!

The race was eventually won by Graham Hill, who clinched the world championship in his BRM. My hero, Jim Clark, failed to finish when the engine in his Lotus blew up.

One of the highlights of the day had been the appearance of the new Lola Ford GT cars, which were demonstrated by Dan Gurney and Ritchie Ginther. These cars represented Ford's hopes for eventually winning at Le Mans, and after seeing them, I was sure convinced. The cars were breathtakingly beautiful, with mind-boggling performance. It was all Ginther could do to stop his car fishtailing out of control when he put his foot down coming out of a corner. What a noise that "small block" V8 made as it was wound out!

Altogether, it was a thoroughly satisfying day, and I was a bit sun-whipped but as happy as a clam when we packed up our stuff and headed back for the little sports car with the surprised look on its face. The engine started, and Bill moved the car out to join a steadily thickening stream of race fans heading out of the park. In no time, we found ourselves in a long line of cars jammed bumper to bumper on the two-lane road leading away from the track area. The stop-and-go irritated Bill as he rode the clutch, inching forward only to wait forever to move another couple of inches. We could see some sort of disturbance way down the road—flashing warning lights, people standing around on the road. Suddenly, a cop appeared and pointed at Bill in the Sprite, indicating that he wanted him to pull out of the line. It turned out he was commandeering the car to take him down to the scene of the disturbance, which was about half a mile down the road. I jumped out to make room for the cop, the car having only two seats and all. Off they roared down the road, leaving me trudging down the far side, away from the line of vehicles that was slowly inching forward.

Eventually, Bill got down to where the accident was, and the cop got out to assess the situation. Ever ready to seize an opportunity, Bill began to gesture wildly for me to hurry and get the hell down to where he was so we could jump the line of cars and get out to the highway. I began to run down the road at a steady lope to join him.

By this time, it was beginning to get quite dark. The sun had set and the twilight was deepening, so I picked up the pace a bit. As I ran, an emergency vehicle pulled out from the scene of the commotion and began to charge towards me. There was no room on the road. It was pretty well filled up with the width of two cars and completely filled by one car and an ambulance. I had nowhere to go.

As the vehicle neared, I jumped the ditch on my side of the road, intent on continuing my running on the other side by the farm field. I was still running fast when I jumped it. I didn't see the barbed-wire fence that bordered the other side. I bounced off it and landed on my back in the ditch, as stunned as a cow hit by a hammer.

I lay there for a couple of minutes, then struggled to my feet. I was fascinated when I looked at my left arm because even in the dim light, I could see that there were several stripes on my forearm that had not been there before. I held my arm up and looked at it dumbly, seeing each layer of my anatomy neatly revealed: skin, fat, underlying muscle tissue. I noticed idly that there was no blood. I thought that was odd. I guess I've got a good shock reaction because I wasn't bleeding much at all, just oozing here and there. I realized my shirt and pants were hanging in tatters and that I had numerous minor and major lacerations.

I got out of the ditch and began hobbling-running towards Bill. I think he just about shit when he saw me. When the cop noticed the condition I was in, we were immediately given the high fast road to the hospital, such as it was, in Montour Falls.

After numerous applications of Novocaine spray and a bad moment where the nurse scratched her head in confusion—she wasn't sure if she'd given me my tetanus shot from the right bottle—they gave me a bunch of stitches to put my edges back together and then a great big shot of Demerol—WWWooowww! As far as I was concerned, I could run into a dozen barbed-wire fences if they'd keep giving me this stuff! I was a thoroughly happy little race fan until the next day, when reality came calling with sharp pointy teeth.

By the way, the guy who originally caused the whole kerfuffle was a drunk riding on the trunk of a car and cheering his fool head off. He'd fallen when the car lurched and cracked his chin on the pavement. He was at the clinic at the same time as I was. He got four stitches and a mild hangover.

I had a lot of great times with Bill. Everything I know about what my wife Denise calls "Boy Stuff"—from turning a wrench to whacking a golf ball—I learned from him.

When I think about it, I was fortunate in having two such different brothers as Calvin and Bill because they each exposed me to very different worlds.

II

Art School Years

❧ IN THE FALL OF 1962, I BEGAN my four years at Central Technical School. I took the Glencairn bus down to where the streetcars looped at Bathurst and St. Clair, then the well-loved and familiar Bathurst streetcar down to Bloor Street. That same old streetcar, red and yellow, that had for years taken me down to the CNE, the Royal Winter Fair and, best of all, the Sportsman's Show, with its casting competitions and retriever dog trials. Now it was taking me to uncharted territory.

I guess I thought I was hot shit, going off to art school, worldly and sophisticated in my chinos and Hush Puppies, hair in a fall-down brushcut like the Kingston Trio wore.

The first thing I noticed upon entering class A1A was that there were types of people I'd never seen before, except in the pages of *National Geographic*. The faces that greeted me were Chinese, Japanese, Russian, Portuguese, Italian and Finnish, as well as various brands of British. But even they were different from what I was used to. They were from Cabbagetown or the new projects over at Moss Park near Queen and Parliament. I was the only native-born Scot. Multiculturalism wasn't just a noble abstract at Central. In those days, it was an inescapable fact of life.

It's hard to imagine now, but when we first came to Canada and for some years afterward, well into the fifties, Jews could not purchase a cottage at Wasaga Beach up on Georgian Bay. It wasn't an official policy, far from it. It was an unofficial one, which was worse! It was simply that no one would sell to Jews. The same social exclusion was visited on the Italians, who were initially ghettoized in the area around Dufferin and Eglinton. They were dismissed among members of the White Anglo-Saxon Protestant community as "guys who hung around on the street corner, scratching their balls and insulting your sister!" The only Italian I saw when I was a kid was a man named Vince, who used to come through our neighbourhood in an old bus, selling vegetables.

There was no intolerance in my family or any overt racial prejudice that I can ever remember hearing, other than the casual bigotry of my mother doing imitations of a particularly troublesome Jewish lady she'd encountered at work. She would perform with full Yiddish accent. She referred to Forest Hill, a wealthy neighbourhood to the south of us, as "The Gilded Ghetto." I don't think there was any maliciousness in my mother. It was only her way of using humour to ease the tensions that occur when cultures collide.

I have a memory of witnessing an incident that took place on our front porch at 5 Stayner. A man came up one day and asked my father to sign a petition that was being circulated around the area. It was backed by a group of people who were trying to stop the sale of a recently constructed house at the end of our street to a family that wasn't white. I think the family wanting to purchase was from the Middle East. My father told the man, in no uncertain terms, that he should be on his way.

We had two very close family friends, introduced originally to us by my sister Rosemary, whose names were George and Marjorie Day. They were a mixed-race couple, which was very uncommon in the fifties. He was a Burmese gentleman who had fought in the Pacific theatre with the Gurkha regiments and had wound up being parachuted into New Guinea to recruit head hunters. It was his job to convince them to kill the Japanese instead of him or each other. She was a very refined and sweet English lady, somewhat shy and reticent. They were obviously very much in love.

George and Marjorie were often at our family occasions—New Year's and the like. George's adventure stories from his days in the jungle were fascinating stuff to me. I can never remember anyone remarking that there was anything unusual about their relationship.

The point of these observations is that because of my upbringing, coupled with the natural curiosity of youth, I had no trouble adapting to the new realities of life at Central. As the years there passed, however, the influences I encountered would stretch the tether that held me to my parents' home until it finally broke.

In my first year, I quickly realized that, in spite of my high opinion of my own abilities, I knew practically nothing about drawing or painting. I didn't even know how to find out what I didn't know. I also discovered that going to art school was expensive! The cost of art supplies, even at the school discount shop, was ruinous. Ways and means had to be found to top up the income.

The most important thing I realized all too quickly was that I was what some would call "a dweeb." There was a look that art students had in the more senior classes, a sort of studied scruffiness. They had mastered the art of putting together a bohemian image that I, taking the bus to school with my process cheese on white, cotton poplin raincoat, Hush Puppies, and art supplies in a fishing tackle box, did not possess.

There were two divisions in the art department at Central. There was *us*, the lowly ones who were still enduring elements of a conventional high school education. We still had classes in English and math, etcetera, but no languages (something I could have used). By grade ten, all that would change, and we would be reduced to studying only English and Economics.

Then there was *them*. They were known by the identifier Special Arts. They were slightly older, were not required to attend high school classes and had either finished their grade twelve or become old enough to give up legally (you could quit school at age sixteen or go into some special technical course). Special Arts, then, was a catch basin for the eccentrics and the stylish misfits. I paid very close attention to everything they did.

The first year I was there, the new building, which would house the Art Department separately, had not yet been finished. Our art classes were in the same old stone building as the two thousand or so students of other disciplines, like drafting, aircraft mechanics, bricklaying and welding.

It reflected a type of thinking held over from the prewar era that artistic ability was considered simply another technical skill that could be mastered, like auto mechanics or wall papering, as long as you were willing to put your nose to the grindstone and study!

In many ways, the art courses at Central were geared that way. As well as drawing and painting, there were classes in research, package design, art history and printing techniques. The purpose of the exercise, it rapidly became apparent, was to take people such as myself and train them for a useful trade in greeting card design, conceptualizing Kleenex boxes or sharpening pencils for some senior director at an advertising agency. Ironically, just to drive this point home, I won the Hallmark cards scholarship while I was at Central. Though I was grateful for the financial assistance—two hundred and fifty dollars, I think it was—I had a vision of myself, a character in a Dickens novel chained to an art table, shivering as the last lumps of coal smouldered in the grate, giving my last breath to Mr. Hallmark. I decided not to pursue this path.

The work was tough sledding because I was learning how to create representational images from square one. Circle, square, perspective, special relationships, colour, tone, blending, all the building blocks of a basic technical repertoire had to be mastered before I could move on any further.

Our life-drawing classes (renderings of human figures) were still being held in the highest point of the old school building, a room up in the central tower that dominated the place architecturally. As winter moved into spring that year and the weather warmed, the windows would be opened. I would try to position myself as close to the casement as I could get. I loved to be distracted from the overweight male in a loincloth for a short while and enjoy the commanding view of the southern Ontario landscape.

If I ever want to consider how much Toronto and the area around it has changed in thirty-six years, all I have to do is remember how, when I looked out of that tower window on a clear day, I could see all the way to Rattlesnake Point out on the Niagara Escarpment. That must have been over thirty kilometres. There were a lot fewer cars clouding up the atmosphere then, and the tallest things on the Toronto skyline were still the Bank of Commerce building and the Royal York Hotel.

I buckled down and worked hard that first year and got pretty good marks. I had a few new friends who would move through the system with me as the years went by, guys I would wind up hanging around with a lot after school.

I had found the odd way of adding a little money to the kitty for art supplies. A few of the drivers around the sports car club scene were interested in having portraits done of their cars, so I painted them for twenty-five dollars.

When I turned fifteen that summer of 1963, a lot of things had begun changing really fast, not the least of which was me! I'd grown at an alarming rate and was pushing up towards six feet. I was in the full grip of adolescent awkwardness and was often moody.

I had been reading voraciously, but now the books were Steinbeck's *Grapes of Wrath*, Algren's *A Walk on the Wild Side*, Hemingway's *A Farewell to Arms*, as well as Ken Kesey and odd things like Jean Genet's *Our Lady of the Flowers*. In addition, I was reading any kind of smut I could get my hands on. I was often busy under the covers at night and had reason to be glad that Calvin went to sleep playing the radio.

A certain worldview was forming. I was becoming cynical about accepted dogma of any kind, and I'd begun to romanticize about a life free from the treadmill of striving for status and possessions. I had begun to see any attempt at authority exercised by anyone as a threat to my freedom. In short, I was becoming what every other tiresome male adolescent had become since the dawn of time—a sensitive pain in the ass.

I had begun to play the guitar at every available opportunity. I'd record songs from the radio on a little portable Philips tape recorder that belonged to Calvin (thanks again, Cal), then laboriously picked them apart and tried to learn the chords. Some of the things I was figuring out wouldn't exactly qualify as the hippest in the world. Not too many kids now would be caught learning the Burl Ives version of "Little Brown Jug."

I had somehow saved, begged and borrowed enough money to buy my first guitar, a six-string Kay, which sounded like it was made of plywood, probably because it *was* made of plywood. I laboured away, strumming, repeating, strumming, trying to sing. Occasionally, my efforts would irritate my father so much that a shout of, "Keep the noise down up there!" would come booming up the stairs. I should have known better than to try to compete with *Bonanza* (a horse opera about a noble family chieftain named Ben Cartwright and his sons, with which my father identified like crazy). There is no greater incentive than the irritation of a parent to keep a teenaged boy dedicated to whatever he is doing that produces the effect. I kept at the guitar with single-minded dedication.

I had been paying close attention to the style of certain members of the Special Arts section, and as I entered my second year at art school, my look began to change. Gone were the chinos and Hush Puppies, they were replaced with jeans, cowboy boots and blanket ponchos. My tackle box had made way for an army-surplus knapsack for carrying supplies, and I'd acquired one of those all-important vinyl snap-tight art cases to carry my portfolio of works-in-progress. I was chucking the process-cheese-and-white-bread-sandwich bag lunches and making my way up to the Java Shoppe Restaurant on Bloor Street for a nutritious lunch of chips and gravy with Coke while I hung out with my friends.

I began to suffer from descending hairline. This was an early sign of the battles to come with my father. He would give me some money and order me to go and get a haircut. I would sneak off somewhere with a pair of scissors and give it a few snips myself, then divert the money to some other purpose.

Queen's Own Rifles military cadets was compulsory for all male grade ten students at Central Tech, and I, of course, was determined to make as much trouble about it as I could. I was very antiwar by this point. I guess I was being influenced by the books I was reading and the leftist folk music I was listening to. In fact, with the growing awareness of what was going on in Vietnam, I was pretty opposed to anything that even smacked of the military.

My favourite story was that one about Christmas Eve in the trenches of the First World War when the troops started carolling each other across no-man's land till they finally walked out and wished each other Merry Christmas, poured each other drinks and shook hands. For one magic night, the soldiers saw not the enemy, but just other men, with families and friends, men like themselves. Peace broke out because the dehumanizing hatred and fear that characterizes war was banished by the humanity and love of Christmas. It took a few well-placed bullets directed by the officers at their own men to get them back to the business of slaughter the next day.

To speak in my own defence, I wasn't just an empty vessel for dogma. I still believed there had been moral justification for fighting the Second World War to defeat fascism, but I was coming to the conviction that settling political disputes with military force was an outmoded way of doing things and, furthermore, unless there was a clear moral issue at stake, it was inexcusable. I don't disagree with that now!

We all reported to the old gymnasium for the first day of cadets. There was a sawed-off little guy from automechanics in a natty little uniform who announced himself as Sergeant So-and-So. He proceeded to start barking orders at us. We had rehearsed our strategy well.

We went about everything we were ordered to do with the speed of molasses.

We misinterpreted instructions many times—every time. By the time we were finished with him, Sergeant So-and-So was apoplectic with rage. We kept up our campaign of glacial compliance until the word came down from on high that cadets was no longer compulsory. Then we quit!

That year was the first time I was ever formally kicked out of school. We had an English teacher, a middle-aged woman, who had a characteristic I found particularly irritating: she expected everything to be explainable, understandable and polite. I had always enjoyed English Lit because I read voraciously, but in her class I began to run into trouble.

The problem began when we were given an assignment to do an oral report on a book of our choice. I chose J.D. Salinger's *Catcher in the Rye*. This was supposed to be a cut-and-dried exercise: get up, speak about the book, sit down. Well, somewhere in the presentation, I alluded to the fact that I thought the outlook of Holden Caulfield, a right cynical little shit by anyone's definition, was consistent with the way many people of his age actually think.

This induced the teacher to enter the fray. She got up on her hind end and began to heatedly argue that not only was the book of questionable value, but she would not accept that young people ever thought or conducted themselves as Holden Caulfield did. She instructed me to apologize to her and to the class.

I replied by suggesting that she had reached such a state of dryness that it was unlikely she would have any idea whatsoever of what was in the minds of young people. I suggested that she was breaching the rules of engagement by editorializing. I suggested a few other things that eventually got her so angry that she left the room in tears.

I was asked to leave school that day and sent home with a letter to my parents, explaining the situation from the point of view of the school. It was their instruction that I would not be allowed to return unless I was willing to make a formal apology to the teacher in writing. There was no point in arguing my case to my father, so I did what I was told. It was no skin off my nose anyway. English class would be history by the end of the year, and I figured, What the hell, I already know how to read!

We had moved into the brand-spanking-new, architecturally modern art building by second year, and the work had picked up a gear and become more challenging. We were still dealing with the basics, but now we were more often called on to put our accumulating knowledge together in the form of creative works.

Sometimes an assignment could be both tedious and challenging. We might be required to spend weeks of spare time at the Royal Ontario Museum doing an exact copy in watercolour of a Chinese wall fresco or a lifelike painting of a suit of sixteenth-century Spanish armour. These types of projects were hard work, but almost without realizing it, I was learning how to look at something in all its complexity and see what was really there. I was learning to stay with something until it was finished, even though I might prefer to do something more spontaneous.

At the same time, in Virginia Luz's history of art class, we were exposed to slides of the trips she'd made together with watercolourist Doris McCarthy to the caves at Lascaux and Altamira, or to Egypt and the temple of Queen Hatshepsut on the banks of the Nile.

She was trying to make us aware of the rich and diverse creativity of the human race through the millennia and of the close relationship between artistic creation and spirituality. I endured the lessons with some impatience because I really just wanted to draw and paint and didn't see the use of it all. The point was being made subtly, and I was missing it on a conscious level. Yes, I loved history, but I loved a more dynamic form of it. What I didn't realize was that, whether I liked it or not, my horizons were being broadened in ways that would pay many dividends throughout my life.

Other areas of my education were proceeding along quickly too! I was hanging out after school at Brunswick Billiards, better known as "The Hole," an underground pool room at College Street and Brunswick Avenue. I was learning about "shape" and "side-stuff" and the lexicon of Snooker while spending my after-school hours with the Portuguese Ed Costa, the Russian Nick Hapanovitch, and the Italian contingent of Joe Lograsso and Carlo Provenzano. We were developing our own little version of the "Rat Pack."

Ed would eventually teach me the life-enhancing skill of checking into a hotel with empty luggage, doing a lot of room service, then leaving the luggage and walking out the front door. That's why, even if you pay cash for a room, they won't so much as turn the phones on these days unless you've got a credit card.

Nick Hapanovitch was a strange hard-luck kind of guy with his funny scuttling walk, always asking questions about everything, always coming to conclusions that didn't work, then coming to other conclusions. He was funny, though, always made me laugh. Eventually, we would ride the rails across Canada together.

There was Allan Snikkar, a Finn who lived down near the University Settlement off St. George Street. He was crazy as a bed bug. It seemed he was the kind of guy that other guys were always thumping on. There was a part of him that maybe didn't like what he saw in the mirror too much, and taking abuse seemed to get him some attention. He made lots of dark jokes about his mother.

Allan was one of the few people I used to go on sketching and painting trips with. He had a lot of talent and did really good work. One of our favourite painting destinations was the lagoon at Hanlan's Point over on the Toronto Islands. The derelict sidewheeler ferry *Trillium* was resting in the pond there, rotting away in what looked to be its terminal days. (It was eventually restored and now navigates the waters of Toronto harbour again.) It was great to go over to the Islands and just paint for the sheer love of it.

There was a guy named Neil Sharpe who lived in the new high-rise project over at Moss Park with his mother. He sort of looked like Buddy Holly and, like me, was interested in playing the guitar. We put together a duo and did a performance in the auditorium at Central during a school talent show. We sang "Good Old Mountain Dew." It terrifies me that, somewhere, there is a recording of that performance because the whole evening was taped for posterity.

Neil and I were going to start a band together. I even approached my dad about the idea of helping us out financially, getting suits and stuff. We had it all worked out. We could make a bit of money playing school dances and parties and we'd pay him back. I needn't tell you what my dad's reaction was.

Because I was hanging out with the downtown kids, without noticing it, I was turning into a little downtown rounder and leaving it later and later before getting on that streetcar to go back home. It didn't matter all that much because nobody would have been home when I got there, except maybe my sister Sandy. She was just about through the thirteenth grade at Bathurst Heights and had less distance to travel, but she too had her social life and wasn't always home early.

The Boy Snaps Awake

THERE WERE SOME INTERESTING young ladies in my circle of acquaintance at Central Technical School. There was a girl named Susan that I was sort of going around with. She was one of "the two Susans." I thought of them in quotation marks because they were like the Bobbsey Twins. They went everywhere and did everything together, and I'm sure they told each other everything they did on the rare occasions they were apart. I spent an extraordinary amount of time and energy trying to devise ways to get Susan out of her panty-girdle—one of those waist-to-mid-thigh contraptions with the feminine floral print, more effective than any invention ever created at preserving the hymen. But all my scheming was to no avail!

There was Sally Simone, a tough-talking little lady with a lot of pairs of eyelashes. With her lacquered black hair, frosted lipstick and a cigarette dangling from the corner of her mouth when she wasn't in school, Sally was the unelected ringleader of "Da Goils."

There was Sandra Ko, a very beautiful girl on whom I developed quite a crush. I was terribly awkward around her on the few occasions I did get to talk to her alone. I usually had her in mind when I'd find myself idly singing the words to the Beatles "You Won't See Me."

I'd come a long way, though, since my first date, when I'd asked a girl I'd picked up at the Eglinton Park swimming pool to go out with me. I'd arrived at her house wearing my brother Calvin's suit and taken her by bus to see the movie *Hud*, starring Paul Newman and Patricia Neal. I was too young to get into the movie and she probably was too, but I bluffed us in anyway. I spent the movie paralyzed with indecision as to whether I should put my arm around her. I was shorter than she was, and by the time I took her home, I think she just hoped I'd go away. I never saw her again and I can't remember her name.

So at this point in life, things had occasionally gotten steamy, but there hadn't yet been an occasion for doing "the unspeakable that's better left unsaid," to quote Loudon Wainright III.

One night, before going to sleep, I was idly listening to the Randy Ferris folk music show on the radio, when something happened that was, quite simply, a turning point in my life.

I had grown into a slightly rebellious teenaged boy, hungry for freedom, yearning for experience, with budding left-wing sentiments. I was moving easily into the attractions of the downtown streets and had a strong desire to do creative things, for my life to count for something. I was, however, still unfocused. By this time, I knew very well I'd never be happy working in an art studio for some agency, so I was beginning to wonder what my next move would be. I had improved a lot on the guitar, had a small repertoire of songs, and such people as had heard it didn't seem to mind my singing. I was a voracious reader and was even trying to write poetry. I loved the power of words.

"And now, here's a new recording from a young New York singer who's making quite a reputation for himself!" said Ferris. "Bob Dylan!"

The song that followed was "Don't Think Twice, It's All Right" from the *Freewheelin' Bob Dylan* album, and as soon as I heard that rolling Travis-picked guitar, coupled with the railroad harmonica and bittersweet words, I snapped awake and was never the same again. I had about me an inarticulate longing, and there it was on the radio. That was the sound of my longing! It sounded like down the road.

Years before, when I was small and there wasn't a lot of noise about at night, I would sometimes lie awake and hear the whistle of a freight train as it left Toronto. That sound always filled me with restlessness, and it would often take me some time to get back to sleep. Well, here was this weird music that reached way down inside me, grabbed hold of that feeling and yanked it right out of my throat. I knew then and there what I was going to do. I was going to do that!

I got my hands on both of Dylan's albums, but *Freewheelin'* was the jewel. It had everything in it: songs that were funny; songs about injustice, love, loss; songs that spoke out against war, but not in a way that just preached at you. They picked you up and carried you along with their art. You came to them of your own free will!

Over time, as I discovered the other new writers coming out of the New York singer-songwriter scene, I came to realize that what was going on was something radically new. It wasn't just poetry and it wasn't just music. It sure wasn't the popular shit you were hearing on the regular radio stations. This new thing, the idea of combining folk or pop music and relevant poetic lyrics, seeing them become something more than the sum total of their parts, was exactly the sharp-edged form of expression I'd been looking for. I wouldn't develop the legs to walk that road for some time, but I could see right away where it was going and I wanted to be on it.

In the meantime, I applied myself to learning every Dylan song I could, from records or from one of the emerging magazines that published lyrics and music for contemporary and traditional folk songs. My appearance got a little scruffier, my hair a little longer still, and my romantic notions of the open road began to occupy more and more of my daydreaming time.

That summer, I got a job that took me away for the entire season. It would be my first really lengthy absence from home, and I was looking forward to freedom from supervision.

Through Allan Moffat, the son of my parents' friends from Peterborough, the opportunity came up to work as a counsellor at a YMCA camp called Wanakita. It came up at the last minute because somebody else dropped out and couldn't do the gig. I don't remember there being much of a checking-out process for the job. Heaven knows if there had been, the YMCA would never have allowed the likes of me around anybody's children. I suppose I was well enough qualified, though, having been a camper at Boulderwood and having a good knowledge of campcraft from digesting Ernest Thompson Seton's *Two Little Savages*. I also had a good background in natural science from the years with Robert Bateman, as well as a Red Cross swimming certificate I'd picked up along the way.

I arrived at Wanakita on the shores of Lake Koshlong up in Haliburton a few days after my sixteenth birthday. There was a short get-acquainted-and-find-out-where-everything-is period, and then we were assigned to the cabins we would be occupying with our charges. The camp wasn't very fancy: simple green-shuttered cabins with bunk beds; a big mess hall with screened-in sides, where all the campers ate; a separate small cabin for the camp nurse (the only female there); and the camp director's house. There was a sandy beach with an assortment of canoes nearby and a swimming raft floating out in the water.

Nowadays, when kids go camping, things are quite different. There's horse-back riding, wind surfing, water skiing—a wide variety of upscale amusements. Wanakita wasn't like that. The camp program was classically old-fashioned. There was swimming, canoeing, hiking, campcraft (learning to construct shelters in the bush and make various implements for fun and survival), sing-songs around the campfire at night and the crowning event of a camper's two-week stay: the canoe trip.

You would get to make the canoe trip only if you could demonstrate your ability to handle the canoe properly and if you had learned all the skills in campcraft and swimming. This journey into manhood was the big reward for diligent effort, and when it was done, each kid would get a bright bandanna called a "Tripper's Scarf" to be worn around the neck as a badge of honour. It was pretty much up to the counsellor to shepherd the boys through all the learning on his own, using whatever advice he could get from the camp director or any other source he could find.

Wanakita handled quite a high number of what were then called "problem children." That meant pretty much everything: behavioural, medical, all of it. These were kids with varying degrees of withdrawal, hostility, learning disabilities, mild autism or severe allergies, or just bright kids who didn't fit somebody's mould. I waited with some interest for the first bunch to arrive.

My first group was a harbinger of things to come. There were seven boys, and among them were a bed wetter, a firebug, one slightly withdrawn kid who'd spend long periods lying on his stomach in his bunk, rhythmically raising his head and then letting his face fall on the mattress. There was one kid who was a bit slow but made up for it by being almost fifteen, as tall as I was and outweighing me by ten or fifteen pounds.

The first game they wanted to play was "Kill the Counsellor." The name pretty much sums up the rules of play. All of them would jump you at once, without warning, and try to wrestle and pummel you to the ground. The only defence was to fight for your life because if dominance in this little pack was lost, you were as good as dead! Boys would fly through the air, either screaming in fear or laughing wildly, depending on whether they were coming at you or being thrown off you. For me, this was a great fitness course.

Another characteristic of my little lads was that they were generally a bit mopey about being at Wanakita. I guess some of them thought their parents were just trying to get rid of them for a while by sending them to camp. Sadly, I think there may have been some truth to that in some cases.

At first, they would rebel against authority, namely me. Some of them would come to camp with reams of comic books, and that was okay with me because I like comic books, especially Marvel comics. The thing was, though, they'd refuse to do anything in the way of activities offered by the camp. They were determined to mope in their bunks all day and read comics. So I let them! I never said anything about it. I just sat in a chair and read comic books with them!

After a couple of days, it would dawn on them that perhaps they were missing some of what the camping experience had to offer because their counsellor was pulling a fast one on them. Of course the bastard was willing to let them read comic books all the time because then he didn't have to do anything! He could goldbrick his way through the whole summer while still getting paid! Pretty soon, a tiny voice from the wilderness would pipe up, "Is this all we're gonna do?"

Then we were off to the races. I had learned how to win by not fighting!

I can still remember the faces on some of those boys. I can still remember meeting their parents on visiting day and realizing with a shock why some of them were so troubled. Sometimes it almost broke my heart to send them back home.

There is a kid whose face sticks out a bit more than the others. His name was Ernst, and he was a real keener. He was also a lightning rod for major and minor misfortunes, as is often the case with people who try too hard to do everything right. Ernst had worked like a Trojan and gotten his canoeing and campcraft down to the point where, along with the rest of the cabin, he was ready for the big canoe trip.

Now these trips were nothing too major, just three or four days' paddling the Gull River and Kennisis Lake. We'd sleep rough, without tents or Coleman stoves or any of the stuff that people take now. In those days, you could still pull a canoe out of the water and make a lean-to for a camp by cutting saplings. You could collect wood and put your groundsheet and bedroll in front of a nice campfire, then sleep under the canopy of the stars. Try that now in southern Ontario and you'll get busted by some "Smokey the Bear" type for creating a fire hazard.

We'd cook out on a grill over an open fire, boiling water in a pot for hot drinks and cooking bacon and eggs in a black iron skillet in the mornings.

It was a huge adventure for the kids, many of whom had never been out of the city. It was a rite of passage and a symbol of accomplishment.

I guess it was our second night out. We'd pulled over on the shore of the lake and made camp. The boys had all settled down in their various constructions, as comfortable as they could be, given the fact that they were using spruce boughs for padding and there wasn't any mosquito protection when the sun went down except the smoke from the campfire.

We'd had our cookout dinner of hot dogs and beans with Gumpert's freeze-dried mystery, and we were all dog-tired from a full day of paddling. I hunkered down in my bedroll and drifted off to sleep, idly watching the sky for shooting stars. Sometimes I think that watching the night sky, without any lights from cities or towns to dull the splendour, should be a condition of continued citizenship in Canada. It never fails to change you in some subtle way.

"Murray, Murray! Ernst is burning the canoe!"

I lurched out of my bedroll in the darkness, waking as I rose, realizing that even though it was still night, it wasn't dark. There was a huge commotion, boys running around in circles, and there, in the middle of the fuss, was an overturned fibreglass canoe with the bow burning like a torch!

Now Ernst, bless his little heart, had decided that after I went to sleep, he was going to pull off a demonstration of campcraft such as the world had never seen, knowing that when I awoke and saw what he had accomplished, I would forever hold him in awe. He had decided to construct a canoe shelter, so he quietly positioned the canoe as best he could and propped it up on one gunwale with a stout stick. He then rigged up a couple of support posts and stretched a tarp from behind the canoe over the supports, to form a sort of awning. He padded the interior space with spruce boughs and then meticulously laid out his ground sheet and bedding. Then, for the coup de grâce, he dug a trench in front of the structure and built a smoking wet-wood fire in it, adding more damp wood once it was finished and going. The idea was to create a curtain of smoke in front of his lean-to that would drive the mosquitoes away, a sort of protective barrier at the entrance.

All told, Ernst had done a beautiful thing. The only trouble was, he hadn't cleared the trench of pine needle mulch down to the rock, so after he fell asleep, the fire started to smoulder, and as it smouldered, it began to travel. It described a serpentine path around the general area, branching out every so often, then dead-ending, only to start off again from somewhere else on its leisurely course. It must have meandered around for some time without ever coming up and breaking out in flame. When it finally did, though, it was right under the bow of the canoe and it lit up real good.

I dragged the canoe to the water and dunked it to put the fire out. Then I took care of the still-burning ground fire and got everything calmed down again. It was still the middle of the night, so we all tried to get back to sleep.

The next morning, I got up and inspected the damage. The sweeping curve on the bow of the canoe was pretty much burned off all the way to the flotation bulkhead, but I thought it was still safe enough to use. In spite of damage to the air chamber in one end, it would float okay on the other one, even if it was filled with water.

Ernst was about as hang-dog as I've ever seen anyone, his moment of glory shattered, his self-confidence in tatters. We had a kangaroo court to figure out what his penance should be, and we came to a decision that was satisfactory for everyone. We would take the freight out of the other canoes, so they could take three paddlers, and load it all in the burned canoe. Ernst would paddle that one solo. It was quickly evident to the boys in the three-man canoes that being lighter with more power made life a good deal easier, so they weren't at all unhappy about the way things were working out.

That's how it went for the whole day. We'd make progress easily, winding up half a mile ahead of poor Ernst, who was struggling bravely to move his heavily laden, deformed slug through the water. It was okay, though, because Ernst felt he was working off his shame, and while the other guys were embellishing the stories they'd tell on their return, they were starting to feel sorry for him.

When Ernst was finally awarded his "Tripper's Scarf," he was beaming with happiness and a sense of accomplishment. Having done the manly thing and taken his punishment with resolution, he had earned his redemption and was no longer a pariah in our little troop. There was a visible change in the kid as it sunk in that he'd actually finished something he'd started.

That transformation happened with a lot of the campers. They'd come to Wanakita reticent and unsure of themselves, but while they were there, they'd blossom and emerge from their shells. They'd take pride in the things they learned and were able to accomplish, and I think they were subtly changed forever. I've always remembered my time at Wanakita with great fondness because, without knowing what I was doing, I think maybe I actually helped some kids.

Of course, there was another life that summer as well. There were extracurricular activities of all kinds between group arrivals, and on days off.

I discovered, with the help of another counsellor named Glenn, the Lake Koshlong bootlegger. We'd either hijack a canoe or hoof down to the bootlegger's place and get ourselves a mickey of some exotic hooch (cheap scotch seemed to be a favourite) and a pack of cigarettes. I had started smoking regularly, in keeping with the manly way of doing things. It took me about twenty-five years from that summer to finally quit, and I grew to regret ever having picked up the habit, but those were innocent times.

Anyway, once we had our prizes, we'd paddle out to a rock in the lake that was high and dry. There we'd spend a leisurely time sipping whiskey, smoking cigarettes and shooting the breeze about nothing in particular.

As evening neared on the days off, we'd strike out on foot down the dirt road and head over for the lodges on Lake Kashagawigamog. There were a bunch of them over there, but my interest lay in one particular establishment. I had developed quite an interest in the daughter of one of the lodge owners, and I was heading over there at every opportunity to see her, even to the point of occasionally playing hooky on work nights.

I'd stay as late as I could and usually wound up walking the dark roads back to camp, trying to make it before dawn. I'll never forget some of those long walks. I felt like Ichabod Crane making his way through Sleepy Hollow. Some nights it was so dark you only knew by the feel of your feet whether you were on the road or not, and there were an awful lot of things crashing around in the bush that weren't on two legs.

There was a lively competition going on between myself and another counsellor named Gavin for the attentions of the lodge owner's daughter. Gavin was blond, good looking, muscular, good at everything athletic, and other than being my rival, was a reasonably nice guy to boot. I pulled out all the stops. I became every bit the sensitive and brooding folk singer. This was made easier by the fact that I'd brought my guitar and had already learned every Bob Dylan song ever written.

I guess it worked because Cassie (that was her name) got permission from her dad to run a coffeehouse once a week up in a recreation space at the lodge. I was the main attraction, singing "The Lonesome Death of Hattie Carroll" or "Don't Think Twice, It's Alright" while posing as the romantic vagabond.

Cassie was really sweet, and I found it easy to sit up and talk to her. She was pretty enough that I don't much remember what we talked about. I'm glad she had an understanding father. After I'd left home, I drove up on my motorcycle a few times to see her and visit the camp again. Then life took over and I didn't see her after that.

I came back from camp very fit and tanned, but more than that, the ties that had bound me to home had really stretched. I was much more mature and self-reliant. The first night, after we'd finished our dinner, my mom brought out her Du Mauriers, my dad brought out his pack of Player's filters, my sister brought out her smokes and Calvin brought out his. I yanked a pack of Export straight-cut out of my pocket and lit one up. There was a raised eyebrow from my mom to my dad, but he didn't say anything. This demonstrated another of the many unwritten rules in Scottish families: "It's your life. If you're old enough to buy your own, you're old enough to smoke!"

The new year at art school would be the beginning of my studies with two of the most influential teachers in my life and the time of life when things of great significance began to occur.

Bob Ross was my life-drawing teacher. He was legendary for gruffness and toughness. He did not suffer fools gladly, but if he was convinced that you really cared about learning something, he developed a twinkle in his eye. He was a tweedy rumpled old man by the time I met him. He was prone to spending a few minutes at the beginning of each class getting everyone off to work, then, donning his beret, he would be off around the corner to the Brunswick Tavern. He would return before the class was over and often be more outspoken than when he'd left.

Bob had been a student of Frederick Varley, which showed in his art. He taught me a lot about drawing, which still shows in my art, but more important than that, he taught me something critical about my attitude to everything I do, whether it be writing songs or drawing.

One day, I was standing in front of my easel. I was halfway through a charcoal sketch of one of the women who modelled for our classes when Mr. Ross arrived back from the Brunswick. I was standing there feeling pretty good about myself because the drawing was going well, or so I thought. I was beginning to develop some confidence in myself as an artist.

I didn't hear him coming up behind me. Suddenly, his voice barked out, "McLauchlan! There's two kinds of people in this world. One guy is standing in front of his easel drawing, and what's in his head is a picture of himself doing it! The other guy is just doing it! Which kind are you?"

After all these years, I still measure everything I do by that standard, and if the work passes that test, I feel good about both the work and the guy who does it. God bless Bob Ross, who provided me with a litmus test for wanking.

Doris McCarthy was my watercolour teacher. Doris wasn't gruff and tough, except in the critical sense. I was amazed by her boundless energy and her enthusiasm for art. It seemed to come from some inner place.

You know how people who are very religious become transformed when they contemplate things spiritual? Doris had that look when she gazed on a piece of art that transcended the mundane. She was thrilled when someone got it right without letting their ego get in the way. Brother, did she have a keen eye for ego!

Watercolour is a fast and dangerous medium. You have to make quick decisions, then commit yourself wholeheartedly to your course of action. Once you blow a painting, that's it! Unlike working in oils, you can't paint over your mistakes and try again. It's gone, ruined, finished!

I struggled in Doris's class because I'd choke. I'd be paralyzed with indecision when I stared at a piece of stretched paper. I was afraid the thing I did would be the wrong thing. Fear of painting and impotence have one thing in common. The more you become preoccupied with the potential for failure, the more likely you are to fail. When I got going at all, I'd usually overwork a painting that should have shone with light, into a state of opaque muckiness.

Doris would look at the work I did, and I would wait with dread. It was just that her face always told me how far I'd missed the mark. She was sometimes frank and painfully blunt in her criticism, and even though it was meant to be supportive and helpful, it stung nonetheless.

Gradually, however, with her help, I came to understand that I was having difficulty making my creative decisions quickly and firmly because I was considering the painting and not the subject of the painting. In other words, I was off in my head trying to render my opinion of a thing, rather than the thing itself. Relax, Doris taught me, trust your instincts and have faith in them. Any fool can paint a picture! The trick is to learn how to see!

Doris, I'm delighted to say, is back in my life as I write this book. I was invited to make a speech in her honour at the City Hall in Scarborough. They were naming a street after her. I went and I told that simple little story about learning how to see. I described how she and Bob Ross still continue to influence my thinking. I was very moved to see her face beaming back at me in full understanding of what she had meant to me. You don't get too many opportunities to pay back your teachers.

Doris has become immensely influential as a painter in watercolour and oils. She is probably best recognized for a series of stunning paintings of Arctic icebergs and her moody impressions of Georgian Bay. She is not a young woman, but you'd never know it by the way she conducts her life. With the same boundless enthusiasm and energy as always, she tears off across Canada on painting expeditions. I'm still nervous about letting her see my work.

There were a lot of good teachers at Central. They were all working artists and worthy of respect. However, these two affected me the most, and their philosophies of creativity would have important applications in my later years as a songwriter. I try to look at things honestly, to really see what's there, unclouded by my own opinion. I'm constantly worried that I'm just doing something out of the vanity of trying to be clever.

The Move to Manhood

❧ IT WAS THIRD YEAR, AND I WAS beginning to spend most of my time in the new art building. The only remaining academic subjects were English and Economics. I suppose the Economics classes were to prepare me for managing the mammoth income I'd earn as an artist.

I liked being in the new building. It was much better suited to our work. It had been purpose-built, with huge amounts of natural light shining into the studio rooms. It was constructed of an architecturally modern combination of rough concrete, terrazzo, glass and steel. It appealed to the snobbish little shit side of me that, for the most part, we no longer had to mix with the common people.

The social boundaries between me and the Special Arts bunch had all but disappeared. I was hanging out with a crowd that included Bob Snider (now making a name for himself as a writer/performer of very eccentric and beautiful songs). There were parties. There was staying up late drinking cheap sauterne and hanging out the window of some Annex flat rented by a couple of older students.

I had also started going over to Yorkville Village, which was still a pleasant, relaxed place on a sunny afternoon. It was coffeeshops and little clubs, a taste of Europe with its sidewalk cafés. The "Summer of Love" hadn't happened yet, and there weren't really any rock 'n' roll clubs. That was all still down on Yonge Sreet. At that time, folk music was the king thing on campus, and all the major clubs were featuring it.

Up at Avenue Road and Pears Avenue north of Yorkville was the Village Corner Club, where Ian and Sylvia had played when they were starting out. That place would soon become a very big part of my life. Down at the intersection of Yorkville and Avenue Road was the Purple Onion, where I coughed up what was, for me, a lot of money for an admission and a coffee to see a big-time singer like Bob Gibson. He played the twelve-string guitar and sang everything from Bertolt Brecht to double-entendre blues songs like "Keep Your Skillet Good and Greasy." I saw Sonny Terry and Brownie McGhee there for the first time, and it was the best ten dollars I ever spent. I didn't know anybody could play that well.

There were other clubs along Yorkville. There was John McHugh's Penny Farthing, where the Mynah Birds, one of Neil Young's early bands, would soon play. The Mousehole coffeehouse was going at that point, owned by an English lady named Patti, who would eventually marry Bernie Fiedler. He would, in turn, start the Riverboat coffeehouse, the most illustrious of them all.

Down in the area around Gerrard Street and Bay, there was still the remnant of the old Gerrard Street Village, a hipster community soon to be levelled to make room for a hospital parking lot. The Bohemian Embassy still clung to the periphery of this area. It was hidden up a narrow cobblestone alley called St. Nicholas Laneway.

Nick Hapanovitch and I would meet up there. He'd found the place first and really liked it. It wasn't just a folk club. It had comedy reviews written and performed by guys like Chris Beard and Barry Baldaro, who would later become famous in the U.S. comedy-writing trade. Don Cullen perfected the skit where he put on a clerical collar and read the text of a Campbell's soup can as a mock sermon. There were poetry readings and, of course, there was chess. There were even some types with sunglasses and berets—you know, throwback beatniks.

The Embassy was more like the classic coffeehouses of legend: a cheap, stimulating place to hang out for people who didn't have much money and didn't go in for bars. I definitely didn't go to bars because the drinking age was still twenty-one!

There was plenty of good music down there, but one of the groups I remember best was the Dirty Shames. They were a loose-knit ensemble of very different personalities, often compared to the Jim Kweskin Jug Band from the States. The Shames were different, though. Everybody got their chance to step out front and shine. It might be Jim McCarthy, playing his big Guild twelve-string and singing "Sailor's Tango," or Amos Garrett, the legendary guitar player who turned a Stratocaster into a steel guitar on Maria Muldaur's "Midnight at the Oasis." It might be Chick Roberts doing a gritty version of a Dave Van Ronk song, or the wonderful funny beautiful Carol Robinson cracking up the crowd. She would eventually become a regular on the *Ray Stevens Show* and gain fame as Miss Penelope in the Ontario lottery commercials.

I started sneaking out of the house at night after everyone had gone to sleep. If I hustled, I knew I could catch a late bus to the subway to get down there. One thing was certain, though. It would be a long dark walk home in the middle of the night, ducking for cover if I saw a police car, to avoid any hassles from the cops.

There was a good reason for going all the way downtown to hang out at the Embassy, other than socializing with Nick and a few of the other art school guys who'd decided to come too. Every chance I'd get, I would collar the poor guitar player. I'd already spent the whole time he'd played watching his hands like a hawk and taking note of things he did that I hadn't seen before. I'd try to get him to sit down for a moment and show me how a particular lick or picking style he'd done was accomplished. My targets were often Jimmy McCarthy and Amos Garrett because they seemed to play there more often than anyone else.

One night, I sat down with Jimmy. I guess he was in a magnanimous mood because he took the time to show me this weird thing he was doing on the guitar, which I later learned was developed by Merle Travis and was called "Travis Picking."

You'd set up a rhythm by picking alternate bass strings with your thumb, eighth notes in a four-beat bar. Then you'd pick out melody in a counter-rhythm on the top strings with your first three fingers while your fourth acted as a brace. Jimmy wore metal banjo picks on his fingers to play, as did Amos, so I got a set and started figuring out this technique.

One of the two coolest people at art school during my early years had been a guy named Michael Bain, from whom I got the idea of wearing cowboy boots and eccentric, ragged clothing. He also played guitar and would occasionally be up the alley across from school at lunchtime, picking and drinking wine. His coolness and general bohemian demeanour, I quickly noticed, earned him the attentions of Miss Heather Rigby, the other coolest person and the object of some of my most heated fantasies.

Heather could often be seen and heard clicking her way down the hall in these incredible thigh-high Napoleon boots. She had the boots pulled on over a pair of jeans that looked like they'd been spray-painted on her butt. When you viewed her in her full line of retreat, the effect was breathtaking.

Now I burned with idealistic zeal, and my creative juices were coming to the boil, but it hadn't been lost on me that if you "look like Michael and play the guitar, Heather will come!" There were other juices burning hot in me now, and between those and the fact that I was hanging around in coffeehouses, my allegiance to the visual arts was being replaced by a new loyalty. I was a rapidly developing folk poet and a walking set of raging hormones.

My brother Calvin had moved into a little walk-up flat downtown on Cottingham Street, with fleur-de-lis bricks holding up the shelves. He'd become a copywriter at Foster Advertising, and with his newfound stature came independence.

I know my brother was just as eager to escape the spectre of Scottish working-class life as I was. Any trace of an accent had been obliterated. He'd wanted to reinvent himself in his own image, and now he was on his way!

The down side was I wouldn't be able to catch a ride to school in his sporty Corvair. (He'd scaled up his automotive image since his first car, a white bucket fifty-nine Ford.) I'd been sleeping in later and later in the mornings, what with being out all night and sneaking back in the mornings before my mom and dad woke up. The ride had helped soften the blow a lot.

The up side was that now I had my own room for the first time in my life. I could close the door and not have to deal with anyone! This was great! I could spread out, draw all night, sleep with the light on or stand on my head and jerk off if I felt like it.

There was a little club on Yorkville that I wandered into one night. It was very small, just a few tables. It was officially named Rive Gauche, I think, but everybody called it the Left Bank. I had my guitar with me and I got up the nerve to try a few songs for the patrons. To my astonishment, the owner asked me if I'd like to sing there on Saturday and Sunday. I wasn't writing anything much yet, but I had a good repertoire of songs. It took me about a second to say yes.

So began my career as a folk singer. This was my first job, and I was as happy to be doing it as a person could be. It was (How do the pop psychologists say it now?) so "validating" to be taken seriously enough to get hired. Besides, the twenty-five dollars I was earning for the two days would help pay for art supplies. I didn't know you could also pass the hat in a place like this, where people weren't obliged to pay admission. It was a standard folkie way of eking out a little extra income. I was nervous as a cat, but I did pretty well in those first couple of days— well enough to get hired more regularly.

I met a girl.

She was German, really petite, cute and blonde. I'm not going to be a son of a bitch and say her name. She took my cherry, you see, and now she might be out there somewhere dreading that her friends or her children might be shocked or, worse, laugh at her for screwing some old folk singer. Or maybe there's a husband who likes to maintain a fiction and wouldn't take the news so well that he wasn't her only lover. Whatever! Maybe it's just that I think of her so tenderly after all these years that I couldn't hurt her, even without meaning to.

She was in Special Arts. She was one of the crowd that hung around with Bob Snider (who, incidentally, had developed the same madness for Leonard Cohen as I had for Dylan ever since he'd read *The Spice Box of Earth*). His girlfriend was an Englishwoman named Elizabeth Lumley-Smith, and they were a fun and attractive pair. He—like a great sad-eyed bird turning around and surprising you with a wonderfully whimsical sense of humour. She—well read, talented and somewhat proper, drawn to this humorous oddball like a moth to a flame.

In the middle of the scene up at the Java Shoppe restaurant, the German girl and I kind of fell into step for a while. I was utterly paranoid about getting into any kind of involvement. I had a head full of the romance of the open road and a repertoire of songs about not being tied down. But I don't think she had forever on her mind, and I certainly wasn't the first boy she'd gone around with at school. There were even some dark rumblings among the cattier girls that perhaps she was a little loose. She was a little bit older than I and wise in the ways of boys. She was the perfect girl for me.

One day, she and I left school quite a bit earlier than the school board would have liked. We just felt like playing hooky. I don't think there was really a plan. We didn't feel like going back after lunch, that's all.

We wandered around for a while with no particular place to go, then found ourselves on the Bathurst streetcar going north. We headed up to the loop, caught the Glencairn bus to Marlee, walked to Stayner, opened the front door to my father and mother's house, walked up the stairs, turned right into the front bedroom on the east side and lay down on my bed.

We began to kiss and fondle and explore. Things began to get heated up. I was beginning to feel a great discomfort in my fashionably tattered, very tight jeans. There wasn't enough room in there for what was going on. Then she uttered these words: "It's okay! It's the safe time of the month!"

She took off the top layer of her clothing and when she did, I thought I would die right then and there. She was dressed in the kind of garments that boys in sweating fevers see in their dreams after reading forbidden books. She had framed her pale body in fishnet and garters, and below an arch of lace was her treasure, pink and inviting with its dusting of blonde.

I had never been schooled in this most consuming of human endeavours. I was a blind-deaf-mute in a minefield, praying for guidance. She gave it to me! She taught me the dance steps slowly, carefully, one by one. She laughed good-naturedly at my clumsiness and eased me through my nervousness. Eventually I relaxed. I learned how to swim all over again. I gorged on her until, wrung out with gluttony, we both dozed off.

That was how my sister found us. When I awoke, she was standing in the doorway with a thoroughly disgusted look on her face. She turned on her heel and left the room. To her eternal credit and in the spirit of profound decency, she never ratted me out!

After that, I looked forward to those occasions when it was "all right, the safe time of the month" and tried to take advantage of them as much as possible.

My German girlfriend would soon prove to be thoughtful and generous in other ways.

One night, there was a party in one of those flophouses that a few of the art students were sharing. There was a lot of drinking and carrying on. A few people drank themselves pretty stiff and got clumsy. There was the odd beef, a bit of shouting, shoving, nothing serious. There were a few couples practising their biology lessons.

I was sitting on a couch strumming away on my guitar, the one I'd saved so hard to get. A guy came reeling by, lost his balance and fell over on me. There was no place for me to go, and my guitar was between us. He fell full on the face of my precious Kay and broke it into kindling. I was heartbroken, but worse than that, I was planning to go from this party directly to my Saturday gig at the Left Bank, and now I didn't have a guitar to play.

I went to the club anyway, hoping for the best. Fortunately, a guy was there that I knew, and he let me borrow his guitar so I could play my sets.

During one of the breaks between songs in my first set, I mentioned what had happened to my guitar that night. I was trying to make light of it, but I guess the way I felt showed pretty clearly on my face. After the set was over, a woman walked up to me. She'd been sitting in the crowd and listening. She asked very politely if she could talk to me. She was plain and slightly overweight, not richly or eccentrically dressed, just an average-looking person. She said her name was Elizabeth Taylor. For a second, I thought she was either having me on or she was one of the nutters who were starting to frequent Yorkville.

She said she thought I was really good and she was sorry my guitar had gotten broken. Then she took sixty dollars out of her purse and held it out for me. "I'd like you to take this to help you buy a new guitar."

"Look, thank you very much and everything, but I can't accept a handout. Anyway, I don't know when or even if I could pay you back."

"Please take it. I'd only spend it getting my brother out of jail anyway."

There was something about her. She seemed to have a deep sadness. Something in me understood that what she was doing was important to her, so I took the money. I wrote down her address and phone number and promised to pay her back as soon as I could.

I eventually did earn enough money to pay Elizabeth Taylor back. I went down to see her in her little second-storey bedsitter in an old house near Bathurst and King. Her furnishings were sparse and the decor institutional green, with a prominent crucifix up on the wall. I told her how grateful I was, and that was the truth. I would have died rather than not pay her back.

She gave me more than money, you see. She was kind to me and she didn't have to be. She trusted me with the simple faith that I would come through. Because she, a stranger, would trust me, I worked that much harder to be worthy of it. She is one of the reasons I believe in the essential goodness of most people.

Eventually, I tried to pay her back in another and more personal way by writing a song about her. It was called "As Lonely as You."

> I think of your room
> I think of you there
> I think of you dragging your body upstairs
> With your bed and your chair
> And your stale perfume
> I never knew anybody as lonely as you.

My German girlfriend, meanwhile, had been working like a demon. Unbeknownst to me, she had been fundraising among all our friends and acquaintances. She got them together, and they presented me with another eighty dollars. I was so moved I didn't know what to say or do. It's always been difficult for me to figure out how to act when people demonstrate that they actually care about me. I either turn mute or say something flippant. All I can say is thanks again.

One night at a party, I opened the wrong door and found she who had captured my innocence in a compromising position with another fellow.

I wasn't mad. She cried a bit—the requisite amount, I guess. She asked me to forgive her.

"For what?" I remember asking.

I figured it for her way of saying it was time to move on, and that was okay with me. So we drifted apart and that was that. I still think of her with great tenderness and gratitude. My best compliment is that I hope my son meets someone exactly like her some day.

That same year, Dylan came to Massey Hall for the first time. I probably would have sold my family for medical research to get a ticket. I scraped together the money for a seat in the front row of the first balcony.

The place was stuffed full of art school rebels and coffeehouse habitués. Sprinkled in among them were obvious Peter, Paul & Mary fans who knew Bob had written "Blowin' in the Wind." The air was blue with cigarette smoke from people intent on disregarding establishment conventions like fire regulations. There wasn't any noticeable reefer smoke. There wasn't that much of it around yet. It pays to remember that a few joints in those days got you a trafficking charge and a year of hard time in Kingston Penitentiary.

That night, just before the concert started, I was as keyed up as I've ever been. Walking through the front doors of Massey Hall had been like walking into church. This wasn't entertainment; we were here to testify! We were here to surf the wave that was sweeping North American apartheid and hypocrisy away.

From the moment Dylan walked onto the stage alone—just his guitar and harmonica, black turtleneck, buckskin jacket, suede motorcycle boots, a tangled mass of hair picking up the blue-white shaft of the spotlight—the air just crackled. You could have heard a cricket chirping in the back seats of the highest balcony. It wasn't only people's eyes and ears, it was also their need to believe that was focused on that stage.

He never said a word all night. He didn't have to! It was all in the songs. One devastating powerful song after another, each one ringing true.

Then he sang something I hadn't heard before, without introducing it by name. He started in straight away.

"Hey, Mr. Tambourine Man, play a song for me!"

I realized that thing was happening to me again.

This song was reaching down inside me, and I had no defence against it. It tore out the nameless longing I have, the one that can't be satisfied, and flew it in the air like a flag.

I left the hall that night, changed forever. There was a new target to shoot for. I had an intimation of what freedom was really all about. It wasn't about going where you wanted and doing what you felt like, it was about finding out things and facing them squarely, without flinching away. Freedom was a path you followed in your head, not with your feet. I didn't know exactly where I was going with all this, but it was okay as long as I kept growing while I went.

I'd been going to the Village Corner Club a lot more frequently and hanging around longer when I did. I'd gone up there to see Jesse Fuller, the old black one-man band who'd originally written "San Francisco Bay Blues," and I'd bought a membership card for the place. That was a common procedure with the coffee-houses. There was a different door price for members and nonmembers.

They had open-sing nights hosted by a young man named Nick Garber. He was a really good entertainer, though more in the conventional folk style. He did novelty and foreign-language songs, as well as good-time things like "The Pied Piper of Hamelin" while playing either a big twelve-string guitar or his banjo. He did numbers like Pete Seeger's version of verses from the Book of Ecclesiastes, "Turn, Turn, Turn," which would later become a huge hit for the Byrds.

Nick was part of a show-biz family. His brother Victor would eventually become a big Broadway star in New York. His sister Lisa became a rock singer, and his mother Hope became my manager for a short period.

The open-sings were great fun and enjoyable to see if you liked a wide sampling of different types of music. There was also the chance of parlaying a successful appearance into a gig at the club. That was well worth trying for. The club still had a certain gloss and reputation as a result of the number of major acts that had played there. It was a big step up from the Left Bank!

I threw my hat in the ring and took a shot at it by auditioning for Nick Garber. He was the gatekeeper, and he was kind enough to open the gate. I performed my mixed bag of folk traditional and contemporary New York singer-songwriter stuff. I was beginning to sound a lot like the regulation railroad boy, and I think I went over pretty well. I was invited to come again!

There was a regular group of people who frequented the place. It was really a social club for bohemians, in isolation from the rest of the developing Yorkville scene to the south. There was the owner, of course, Shelley Abrams, and her consort, a great big strapping bluegrass picker named Mike Cavendish. There was Myron Cooper, a painter who looked like he'd stepped off a wall from an Egyptian tomb. There was Derek, an eccentric Englishman who recorded everything that moved on a monstrous Farograph tape recorder—BBC green with Bakelite knobs. There was Sonny and Peter, a good-hearted blond singing duo who were also an item. There was Billy Fulghum, a soft-spoken guy from the right side of the tracks with an ongoing curiosity about the wrong side. He loved the blues and used to sing in the open nights himself with a rendition of "Jelly, Jelly, Jelly" that got the girls to squirming. Billy sought out trouble in the company of a folk singer named Doug Brown, a tall gangly dark-haired guy with a rapier wit and good suits. There was Noni Raitblatt, looking strangely out of place with her lacquered nails and her South Forest Hill sleek good looks. She not only later brought me food when I was starving, she also saved my life. And there was a solo girl who always wore dark sweaters and antelope suede skirts, with big round dark sunglasses like Holly Golightly in *Breakfast at Tiffany's*. She read poetry and looked fairly serious about everything most of the time. Her name was Patty Sockwell, she who would one day be the mother of my first child.

That old house on Pears Avenue developed into a retreat for me, and it played a pivotal role in shielding me from harsh reality long enough to get on my feet after leaving home. The regulars became an extended family and gave me a tremendous amount of support and encouragement.

Meanwhile, with the shifting of my focus towards becoming a rebellious and iconoclastic young folk poet, staying up late to party, sneaking out to coffeehouses and discovering sex, things were deteriorating both at home and at school.

I was limping towards the end of my last year, barely getting by in some courses. Had it not been for fear of my father, I would probably have behaved badly at home. As it was, I was sullen and uncommunicative. I tended to spend a lot of time in my room or just be away when I could manage it. I virtually never saw any of my old friends from the neighbourhood anymore.

In my fever to emulate Dylan, I had thrown the baby out with the bath water! I had developed a certain worldview. Everything—patriotism, religion, materialism, longing for security, "working for the man," sentimental ideas of sex and basic human relationships—was crap! In Bob's defence, I have to point out that none of this was his fault. I wouldn't want him crying himself to sleep at night over my going wrong as a youth. It was true that his songs were serving to focus ideas planted by the authors of the many books I'd been reading up to that point. Being a young man, though, I felt the only way to an ideal world was to start over from scratch. So I'd absorbed all the social criticism without appreciating the humanity in many of the things I read. There was a great intoxication in being angry about injustices that was far more satisfying than the hard slogging of actually trying to do something about them.

More and more I was becoming conscious of the clock ticking as I neared the end of my time in art school, measuring the days until the necessity of getting a job would be upon me.

My father held a perfectly reasonable point of view. Once you were old enough and had finished your education, you were expected to put yourself to work. It was your duty to help the family situation by paying for your room and board and helping with the mortgage payments on the house. Everyone else had done that, and I would too.

I felt trapped. I didn't want to get sucked into anything yet. I didn't know how to handle the fear that if I got stuck somewhere, I might not be able to be somewhere else that I really wanted to be, even though I didn't know what that place might be yet. Besides, Nick Hapanovitch and I had a half-baked plan about hitching out west to see the Rocky Mountains. I still had romantic ideas about being a free-roaming knight of the open road. It seemed I'd never really gone anywhere or done anything at all! I couldn't stand the idea of getting tied down before I'd even had a chance to sniff the air of freedom. I wanted to be an artist, for Christ's sake, not be chained to a drafting table in a greeting card company! Although it would later prove untrue, it looked to me at the time that all my schooling was pushing me towards that little work cubicle of my nightmares. Everything was coming to a head.

There was a particularly demanding final-year project. It was a history-of-art book we were required to make, and that book became a symbol of the growing schism between me and Central Tech. The gateway to success in this project was money. If you could find the money to have an expensive binding done and acquire costly four-colour reproductions of classic works for inserts and had an unlimited budget for Letraset, you would do really well.

People who didn't have money were reduced to razoring pictures from the public library and praying they wouldn't get caught. I did a lot of praying for that project, and I resented its bias towards the advantaged.

On the day I graduated from art school, I drank half a bottle of wine. Then I burned that book right there on the sidewalk in front of the brand-new concrete art building.

Leaving Home

I HAD BEEN SPENDING MY AFTER-SCHOOL time going from the Java Shoppe restaurant to the Village Corner. I was coming home late. I was spending most of my time hanging out there on weekends. I was playing more gigs there and elsewhere.

I was trying to write songs now, and I'd spend hours in my room when I was home working on them. They were clumsy self-involved songs about the gritty reality of the "real world." I was learning new songs by writers like Tom Paxton and Montreal's Bruce Murdoch. Gradually, I was metamorphosing into my fantasy of the road-hardened folk-singing version of Tom Joad.

I had a new girlfriend as well—much moodier and dark eyed. She had a beautiful face with a profile you could have taken from an Etruscan vase. She had her own little flat over on Madison Avenue in the Annex, and often Bob Snider, Elizabeth Lumley-Smith and a motley cast of art school reprobates would gather there. We'd drink wine and debate the merits of Leonard Cohen's attempts at music. We'd listen to Bob's off-beat poetry, or I might try to sing something I was working on. It felt good for us all just to be together with no expectations.

A lot of times, I just wouldn't come home at all, and the tension was growing at home as I became more distant and my father became convinced I was turning into some sort of a bum. My mother was still running interference. I think in her heart, she understood I genuinely did possess an artistic temperament and

I had no choice but to flail around until I got my legs under me and figured out where I was going. Time and time again, while she grew sick at heart worrying about what was to become of me, she would head off confrontations between me and my father.

Meanwhile, Nick Hapanovitch and I had formed a plan. I think it was pretty much my idea, and Nick was the only person crazy enough to be willing to do it.

I was hungry for experience, specifically the kind of experience described in the books I'd read—the rough honest life of the open road. How the heck was I supposed to sing or write about living hard and riding freights, about the humble heroics of the migrant worker, or most important, about turning your collar up to the wind and leaving your girlfriend if I'd never done anything tougher than walk down the street to a coffeehouse?

Nick and I made a deal. He'd always wanted to find out what it would feel like to have his head shaved bald, but he hadn't had any luck finding anyone to do it for him. Maybe he was experiencing some opposition at home. Anyway, he agreed to bum and ride freights with me (a good idea anyway because you'd need a companion to help you in case of danger or injury, we figured) plus he'd build me a guitar case of plywood that I could sling across my shoulder with a carry strap (he could do all kinds of useful things: make shoes, do carpentry, etc.). I, in turn, would, immediately before our departure, shave his head bald. Nick began to work on the case while I prepared to tell my father about our planned journey all the way to the Pacific Ocean.

I wanted to stall for time. It wasn't that I didn't want to find a way to help contribute to the family eventually. I just wanted to go and have this authentic adventure first! I didn't look on this as the time I meant to actually leave the nest. I was only seventeen! I just wanted to delay any major commitments for a little while, hoping against hope that maybe I could make something out of being a folk singer. That desire had now completely replaced my original plan for a career in visual arts.

The day after art school finished, I asked my father if I could talk to him. We went upstairs where we could have some privacy. I described to him what I wanted to do, and as the questions began, I knew I was already in trouble.

"What do you think you're going to do for money? You'll get none from me!"

"I don't know. We'll get odd jobs or I'll sing for my supper."

That got no reaction at all.

As far as my father was concerned, my attempts at music didn't hold any promise of anything but wasting my time when I should be making a living. He thought it was high time I assumed the responsibilities of life. He made it clear that under no circumstances was I going off wandering around like a bum when it was time to help support the family that had supported me!

I looked at him hard for the first time in a long time, not just his face but all of him. He was now into his sixties, thinning grey hair brushed straight back, neatly pressed grey flannels, oxblood loafers, the smell of cigarettes and Vitalis or maybe a little Aqua-Velva. I could see he'd aged a lot recently. He had extra weight on him now. Even for the not-so-well-to-do, Canada is the land of plenty. He looked careworn and beaten. It had taken a lot out of him starting over again so many times. I guess I wasn't helping.

I tried to argue, and his temper flared. Then out came the ultimatum. Oh, the things we say and having said them, realize there is no going back and everything is changed forever.

"You'll either live by the rules of this house or you'll get out!"

There was a bit of a silence as both of us realized just how far we'd pushed things.

"Well, I guess that's that, then!" I said. "I'm leaving."

"Well, don't expect to come crying when you land flat on your back!"

Then, for the first time in my life, I saw my father cry as all the frustration I'd caused him, all the anxiety and anger, all the disappointment he felt in knowing I'd gone wrong broke his reserve.

I didn't want to hurt him! I didn't want to hurt anybody! I might have been afraid of him, but I loved him and it hurt me to think our bridges were burned.

All I'd wanted was some gesture of support from him, some acknowledgement that my dream, as unrealistic as it might have seemed to him, was important enough not to be shot down in flames without my giving it a try. It's got to be the worst thing in the world, even if you think you might be stupid, to be treated as if you are.

I quietly went and got what few things I thought I'd need for right away: spare jeans, poncho, rucksack, knife, guitar, not much really. I went downstairs and let myself out the front door, knowing I'd never live with my mom and dad again. All this time, as bad as I'd felt, I hadn't cried. I never did.

I felt sad as I walked away down the street, but I also felt as though for the first time in a long time, I could take a deep breath as the tension lifted from my shoulders. I felt guilty for running out on my parents when I might have been able to help make their declining years more comfortable. I understood my father's position perfectly and not only that, I agreed with it! I didn't resent having to leave. I couldn't live by the rules of the house as they applied to matters of work and responsibility. If I couldn't contribute, I was a burden. Sooner or later it would have come to this anyway.

My father remained true to his word. He refused to come and see me play until the night I opened at Massey Hall myself, and he wouldn't come to my wedding.

Two years later, I finally managed to write a song about that day.

Child's Song
Goodbye, Mama, goodbye to you too, Pa
Little sister, you'll have to wait a while to come along
Goodbye to this house and all its memories
We all just got too old to say we're wrong
I've got to make one last trip to my bedroom
I guess I'll have to leave some stuff behind
It's funny how the same old crooked pictures
Just don't look the same to me tonight.

I learned later that there were some harsh words between my mother and father about the way he handled that day.

I didn't have any particular place to go, so I went down to the Village Corner. I got in touch with Hapanovitch, who had just about finished the guitar case, and made plans to meet him in a day or so when, after completing my part of the bargain, we'd leave town.

There were actually several people living in the building the club occupied. It was really just a big ramshackle house, of which the main floor had been opened up to create the concert space. Upstairs, there was an apartment and a couple of rooms, all of which were occupied. Nick Garber lived up there, as well as a cab driver named David. The apartment was occupied by a very eccentric folk singer, Tannis Neiman, and a wonderfully warm lady by the name of Jeanine Hollings-head. Jeanine later became Colleen Petersen's manager and confidante until

Colleen died. There was no problem with my crashing at the club. People came and went all the time, so I grabbed a mattress in the basement for the couple of days I needed to get organized.

Riding the Rails

 TWO DAYS LATER, I MET UP WITH NICK at the house of a friend, and we got all the necessary implements of destruction for the savaging of his head. I was determined to make him look as good as Yul Brynner because he'd done such a great job on my guitar case. It was made of thick plywood lined with fake sheepskin over foam and had a heavy webbing strap riveted onto the back for slinging it over one shoulder. Rather than being a series of sculpted curves that followed the contour of the guitar itself, the case was angular and brutal looking. It was a German expressionist guitar case—perfect.

I began with the scissors, hacking away at the extremities of hair and getting as close to the scalp as I could. Unfortunately, what was revealed the closer I got to the scalp was that Nick did not have the smooth skull of Yul Brynner but rather something more challenging. In the middle of the top of his head was a pink growth that I could see was going to present some problems. In addition, the shape of Nick's skull would have kept a phrenologist happy for weeks, with its sweeping planes and majestic bumps. I began gingerly shaving up from the base of the neck, up around the ears, up the side and then carefully, oh, so carefully, worked my way around that pink protuberance so as not to slash it open with a careless hand. Finally, the job was done, and Nick surveyed himself in the mirror. To my surprise, he pronounced himself happy with the results.

So with my guitar case done and his head shaved bald, our deal was complete, and nothing remained but to hit the road. I went back over to the Village Corner Club and said some goodbyes, packed my rucksack, prepared my bedroll and tried to get some sleep in preparation for our departure the next day.

In the morning, I got up and took stock of my finances. Counting my foreign currency, bonds and the contents of my safety deposit box, I had a grand total of thirty-five cents to my name. Fortunately, that was exactly enough to get a bus ride on the TTC up to the northern limits of town, so at least I knew I could get out of Toronto. After that, all bets were off.

I met Nick and we got on the bus. We rode that bus as far as it would take us, stuck out our thumbs and stood there. Then we walked with our thumbs out. We walked and walked. I think we walked halfway to Wasaga Beach because it took us all day just to get there.

What a sight we must have been to some respectable person driving along the road. There was Nick, looking like an escaped, demented convict from a Dickens novel, his head glowing above his shirt collar, shuffling along with his quick-step, crab-like walk—a Russian version of Ratso Rizzo from *Midnight Cowboy* without the limp. Then there was me: a six-foot beanpole, poncho like Clint Eastwood's in *A Fistful of Dollars*, tattered jeans, a mop of hair sticking out in all directions as though I'd just stuck my finger in a light socket, coffin-like guitar box on my back, loping along the side of the road in slope-heel cowboy boots. If people weren't outright terrified of us, they probably figured we were heading off to join the circus. It became a pattern across the country that the only people who'd give us a ride were as eccentric or outright crazy as we were. I'm serious about the walking. I think we got but one long ride and one short one all that first day and literally walked most of the way to Georgian Bay.

It was June, though, and the nights were warm, so being as we were embarked on an adventure and all, we weren't downhearted when we had to sleep rough and go hungry that first night. Heck, that was the whole idea!

Next morning, we stretched out the kinks, picked up our stuff and started walking again towards the northeast, following the road, heading up the east side of Georgian Bay with the idea of making it up to Sudbury and then turning left.

We walked and walked and walked. We walked pretty much all the way over to Penetanguishene before we sat down and began to examine our situation with a view to figuring out how we might make better progress. We both wanted to get out of Ontario before we died.

I guess it was about this time it dawned on us that we weren't too far from one of the major north-south railroad lines that connects Toronto and Sudbury. In fact, we'd heard a couple of trains go by fairly close, and we determined that if we were going to be truly authentic "bindlestiffs" and ride the rails, there was no time like the present to get started.

We found the tracks, and it was evident we'd found the right ones because they were bright and shiny with the wear of the heavy iron wheels. We walked along till we found a level crossing and then went down the tracks a hundred yards or so to wait. We figured the train would slow for the crossing, then before it sped up again, we'd be able to hop right in through the open door of a comfortable freight car and ride north in luxury and security.

We sat there in the June sunlight, listening to the insects humming in the brush and the shrill songs of the red-winged blackbirds, and every so often one or the other of us would put an ear to the rail to see if we could hear a train coming.

Well, all things come to those who wait, as the saying goes. We finally heard a distant thunder and the long whistle of a northbound freight, and at last we could see it looming up in the distance.

We hunkered down by the side of the tracks, trying to keep out of sight in case the engineer spotted us and figured us for boarders. We didn't want our first freight ride to end in getting beaten to ratshit by railroad cops.

It was a big black and red CN freight with three engine units on the front, and we could hear it slowing down as it neared the level crossing. The air horns blasted out their lonesome harmonies as the big engines drew up to our position, and the ground shook with the weight and the movement of them. I guess we should have waited a hundred yards down on the other side of the level crossing because as soon as the three big diesel-electrics got through, the engineer just poured the coal to them and they were already accelerating when they reached us. By the time any cars came by, the train was back up to ten or fifteen miles per hour and gaining speed rapidly.

I figured right away that the damn thing was going way too fast to get on, but Nick spotted an open boxcar door coming along and got up running, yelling for me to follow. I shouted, "No Way!" but I guess he didn't hear me because as he was running, the open boxcar door came by, and he threw his belongings in. He couldn't keep up with it, though, because the train was already travelling as fast as a really fit man could run, and it was gaining speed.

Desperate not to lose his belongings, Nick made a grab for the ladder on the back end of the boxcar as it came by. He got hold of it, but it pulled him right off his feet, and I knew immediately he was in really serious trouble. He'd caught hold of the ladder on the back end of a car, which meant he was only a couple of feet from the front wheels of the next car. As he was dragged along, desperately hanging on and trying to pull himself up, his legs were bouncing along the tracks until they were knocked over between the rails, dangling in front of the oncoming car. I was helpless as I watched him being carried away. I knew that if he lost his grip, he was a dead man, or at the very least, a legless one.

For what seemed an eternity, I watched him struggle to haul himself up inch by inch, until he'd managed to get himself high enough to swing his legs out of harm's way. When he thought he was clear, he let go, bouncing and rolling painfully to a stop on the gravel and cinders.

Some start to a great adventure! I was really sobered by how close we'd come to seeing one of us get killed, and this was only the second day. Once we got over the shakes, we took stock of our situation and realized it was only half as good as it had been ten minutes ago—Nick didn't have a single possession left.

We sat down, and I opened up my rucksack and undid my bedroll. Like true comrades and hobos, we split what we had left fifty-fifty. I gave him my spare shirt and a blanket from my bedding. We packed up and went back out to the highway and started walking north.

Fortunately, Nick hadn't lost what little money he'd brought when he'd pitched his belongings in the boxcar. It was still in the pocket of his pants, so we weren't completely destitute, though we weren't far away.

We walked and we walked and we walked up Highway 69. We walked till our bones ached. We weren't eager to try our luck at train hopping again, no matter how tired we were. We'd been pretty rattled by our first attempt. We got the odd ride in the back of some old pick-up truck or some local farmer's station wagon, but they were usually not going very far. We tried to keep an eye out for the Provincial Police. We figured that if they noticed us and gave us the once over, they might chuck us in the slammer as vagrants or something. I'd already been detained by the Buffalo police at one point on an armed robbery charge (I didn't do it!) when I'd gone down there with some pals from the camp counsellor days to get drunk and go to the Palace striptease theatre. I wasn't eager to repeat the experience of dealing with the business end of the police.

We worked our way north. If anybody was foolish enough to say, "Hey, what have you got in the case? A body?" there was an opportunity to do a couple of songs for small change. So we were able to stay solvent enough to keep ourselves in cold beans and rolling tobacco when we'd settle down for the night under a bridge or some other shelter.

We worked our way up till we could see the giant stacks of INCO belching the smell of money over Sudbury's lunar landscape, and then we turned west. That was an important moment for us psychologically, for as we began to follow the sun, we were moving into places we'd never been to before and geography we'd never seen.

Up north, the rides, when they came, tended to be longer, so we could cover more distance. Generally, people were going from town to town, not just farm to farm. They were also less worried about what we looked like up there, and it seemed to be easier to get picked up. Nick and I would take turns being the one to sit up front when we caught a lift with someone who wanted to talk to break the monotony of a long drive. Sometimes those were the roughest rides of all, sitting there trying not to let your head fall on your chest while some guy with a mickey of rye between his knees started his sentences with "The trouble with this fuckin' country" and then went on and on and on!

We worked our way west, past the paint-peeling air of Espanola with its fragrant paper mill, past the cutoff at Serpent River leading up to the big uranium mine at Elliott Lake, until we reached Blind River.

We came into town on foot as evening drew nigh. Our courage had returned and we'd decided that the next likely-looking opportunity for catching a free railway ride would be taken advantage of. We'd been told by another helpful knight of the road that there were some switching and siding facilities at Blind River and the trains would be crawling through town at very low speed there, making them easy to hop. As long as we were careful not to let the railroad cops see us, we'd be okay.

This time, we waited on the side of town where the trains were entering so we'd catch them slowing down instead of speeding up. As the dusk deepened we waited for our transport, talking in whispers to pass the time.

Finally, after a couple of hours of waiting, we heard the freight coming, its long warning air-horn blast carried in echoes out over the North Channel to lose itself in the distance. The ground began to rumble under us as the awesome bulk of the three-engined half-mile-long monster approached. I think we both experienced a moment of primal fear and wanted to shrink back from the violence of the machinery that bore down on us. The engines paraded majestically by as we hunkered down in the weeds, avoiding the eyes of the engineer. The train continued to slow until it was ambling along at easy walking speed. Along came an empty flatcar, nicely located between two boxcars, giving us the impression that there would be some protection from the wind. We walked along beside it for a second as we threw our belongings up on top, then jumped on easily. As darkness settled over us, we were on our way west to a destination we'd only know when we arrived. We were full of excitement—our first freight train!

The engines picked up speed as the train plunged back into the Ontario bush, heading for Iron Bridge. The ride was a long way from Pullman car comfort, and the noise was deafening.

The track beds are uneven up there with the frost heaving of winter and the weight of the huge freights, so as the train dashed along with the bucketa-bucketa-bucketa of the iron wheels riding over the track joints, we were propelled up-down-side-side. There wasn't much to hold onto on the flatcar, so we were tossed around like two sacks of potatoes unless we lay down flat with our arms out like angels.

As we lay there rocketing through the night in a mind-numbing cacophony of metallic noise, we were struck mute with wonder by the feast for our eyes overhead. It was a crystal-clear warm summer night, and above us, stationary, as the dark silhouettes of the white pines rushed by over the tracks, was the full glory of the Milky Way. As if in a tribute to the stars, every firefly in the bush was flashing its inviting little beacon, excited to a frenzy by the rushing train. Every time we came to a long curve in the tracks, there was a sustained shrieking from the protesting wheels, and showers of orange sparks would erupt from the sides of the train. The stars, the fireflies, the incredible noise—I felt really alive and absolutely in the moment, no past, no future! I was finally answering that long wolf howl in the night from the passing freights I'd heard when I was a little boy!

On through the night we roared on the back of our dragon, through Thessalon, blinking in the unaccustomed glare from the lights of gas stations and the acid sodium glare of yard utility floods, until finally, as morning began to visit the edge of the world, we pulled into the outskirts of Sault Ste. Marie. Exhausted and slap-happy, we dropped off the edge of the car before it got so far in towards the depot that we might be spotted. The hobo gods had smiled on us and made our first freight train ride one I'd remember vividly for the rest of my life.

We didn't really want to linger around the Sault. We were intent on pushing west, so after a few hours of furtive sleep somewhere out of sight, we walked and hitched our way through town. Mostly, though, we walked.

We didn't spend much time thinking about it in our excitement at being out on the road, but we hadn't been eating very much. We were tired and hungry and sunburned. Both of us had those scabs on our faces that you get from dried-out sunburn blisters. We hadn't washed ourselves or our clothes since we'd left Toronto. To each other we just looked dusty and rough and normal. To anyone else we must have looked like the kind of people you instinctively shrink away from in the street.

We were getting depleted and weakened but not realizing it. The brain plays tricks on you when your body starts to feed on itself. I felt light and strong, although when I thought about it, I did feel ravenously hungry.

It was in this condition that we hit the black hole of Superior, long stretches of the Trans-Canada where there are no towns and the only vehicles on the road are tourists or long-distance truckers. Rides were hard to come by. There weren't many places where the trains slowed down enough to get near, never mind get on. And we'd run out of money.

We had laboriously made it as far along as Wawa when we came to the decision that we'd better try to find some kind of temporary work so we could eat. We went up to the big open-pit mine there and applied for labouring jobs. We filled out forms and were told to come back the next day. We couldn't really stay in town because we had no money and we didn't want to get busted for vagrancy, so we made a little bush camp in a rocky area of woods over the road that led up to the mine. Hungry and unexpectedly cold in the chill night air, we huddled down to a fitful sleep.

The next day, when we went back, they said they were sorry but there wasn't anything for us right at that moment. If we wanted to wait, there might be work in a month or so. Well, we knew we'd starve to death in Wawa before that, so we hit the road again.

I finally did get a letter from the company the year I completed my first record. It came to my parents' house and said there was a job for me now if I could make my way there.

We went back to the Trans-Canada and long hours of walking in the hot July sun, thumbs stuck vainly out in hope of a ride. I was starting to get pretty light headed. If we came to an open meadow, I would go into it and crawl around on my hands and knees among the raspberry bushes, stuffing the berries into my mouth as fast as I could pick them. Day after day we walked and walked, with only an occasional short lift from a utility pick-up or some such work vehicle.

Then one day I found myself going through the garbage can at a roadside picnic area like a marauding bear. I think if there had been a bear in attendance, I might have fought it for the can's contents. I'd found a treasure, an unopened pouch of Shirriff instant mashed-potato flakes. I tore it open and began to stuff the dry flakes into my mouth greedily. In my hunger, I was acting like an animal, trying to eat anything that would sustain me. It was at that moment that a camper truck drove up.

I don't know what makes a person choose between turning away or being the Good Samaritan. Maybe some people are more afraid than others of strangers or of people who just look different. Maybe this man saw me in the final stages of picking through a garbage can to eat and just couldn't turn away from our need. Whatever the reason, rather than moving on at the sight of two rough-looking young men at the rest stop, he called out to us to come over. He filled up a picnic table with sandwich makings, biscuits, fruit and cold drinks. Then he invited us to eat our fill.

We ate like prisoners in a gulag—never raising our eyes from the food, not talking, just continuously stuffing food into our mouths, barely chewing it before swallowing it down. We ate until we could eat no more.

When we'd recovered some of our strength, we exchanged stories. We told him of our plan to head west to the mountains and work our way there and how we'd fetched up in the traveller's flypaper north of Superior. He was just a nice retired guy from out west who'd worked all his life and was now rambling around for a while, seeing the country.

I got the guitar out at his request and sang a couple of songs for him. I judged him to be a Johnny Cash type, and I wasn't wrong. "Wreck of the Old '97" was a stone hit!

We hung out for a couple more hours, and then it was time for him to hit the road, but not before he gave us a bunch of food to take with us. He even slipped us a couple of dollars against our protests, to help us on the way. We weren't panhandlers after all! We either worked for our money or I'd sing for food or change, so a donation without being able to give something back went against the grain. I didn't think my couple of songs was much of a payback for his generosity.

Our Good Samaritan got back into his camper truck and headed east while we, revived by his kindness, headed off in the opposite direction on foot.

Sometimes I would have a fantasy that the guy was my guardian angel because from that moment on, our luck changed. We never got stuck or really starved again, and we always seemed to find work when we needed it.

We got a fast succession of rides and found our way up to White River, which at that time held the record for the coldest temperature in Ontario. There was a sign saying that on the outskirts of town. This was a place where the trains had to slow right down, so the opportunity for a little free transport was once again in the cards. We walked down the tracks to the spot where they split up and led into the various sidings, where old boxcars and tankers sat idle. We hunkered down to wait as we had before, and consistent with our newfound luck, we didn't wait very long.

When our transport arrived, it was another regal multi-engined freight. This one was a prize, though. As it slowed down coming into town, we could see a series of flatbed cars carrying combines, farm tractors and other equipment—all shiny in their bold primary colours. They were those big monster prairie tractors with the enclosed cabs to protect the farmer against the worst extremes of flat-country weather. Maybe one of them might have an open door!

We jumped up on one of the flatcars as it glided by and hid down behind the giant wheels until the train was out of sight of the town. Once we thought it was safe and we wouldn't be spotted, we emerged and started trying the cab doors. We were both in luck! I climbed up into the comfort of the padded seat of a big double-wheeled John Deere and put my feet up to enjoy the ride. This was the closest to luxury I'd been for a while—a padded seat, quiet comfort and not having to make conversation to pay my way in someone's car! It was a pity there wasn't much in the way of scenery, given my vantage point. I slid off the seat and made a little nest out of my bedroll blanket, then fell into an exhausted sleep, lulled by the motion of the train.

I was awakened by a change in the motion. The train had slowed right down and was coming to a stop. It had gotten dark. Disoriented, I climbed out of my tractor cab and saw that Nick had done the same. We hopped down and scuttled off out of sight. There were men walking the train, but it was long enough that our end of it was still in the relative gloom of the outskirts of town.

Nick and I were both very leery of being caught by the railroad cops. They had a reputation for being badasses who'd beat the shit out of you if they found you. If you were a bum and riding the rails, who would care if you fetched up in a ditch anyway? We didn't have any firsthand experience of this, but we weren't eager to acquire any either.

We walked out to the main road and then into town. There was a small, brightly lit café right by the train station, so we decided to part with a little of our Good Samaritan money and spring for a cup of hot coffee to take the chill off our bones.

We walked in the front door of the place. It didn't have many tables, but several of them were occupied by a group of men, ordinary working men, rough and confident in their oily denim overalls. There was the sound of their laughter as they exchanged yarns and gossip. Through the blue haze of cigarette smoke, a couple of them noticed us coming in, and the conversation quieted down some as we were appraised. The waitress was not sure about us at all, but when she saw we had money for our coffee, she relaxed. Then came the magic words:

"What's in the box?" one of them asked.

"Guitar," I replied.

"Well, give us a song, eh?"

I took out the mighty Echo guitar I'd bought with Elizabeth Taylor's help and launched into a mini-concert. Those guys were amazed! I was pretty good by then and I gave them the full Johnny Cash treatment. I sang "Old '97," "Folsom Prison Blues," "Country Boy," "I Walk the Line,"—all the best hard-driving country blues I knew.

We never had to pay for the coffee. In fact, we never had to pay for the soup and sandwich or the pie. Best of all, my audience turned out to be not only the engine crew from the freight we'd been riding on, but the replacement crew that was going to take her on to Port Arthur and Fort William (Thunder Bay, to you modern types). They hadn't been born yesterday, and it was pretty obvious to them that we hadn't arrived in town at exactly the same time as their train by some coincidence. They knew what we were up to.

Once the food and the music were finished and it was time for the freight to be moving on, the men in the replacement crew came up to us and took us aside.

"Go on to the outside of town and wait down beside the level crossing there. You don't want to try getting on too near here or the cops'll get on to you," said the engineer.

"I'll keep the speed down until we start round the first bend after the crossing, and that'll give you a chance to hop up the ladder and get into the second unit."

We did as he said and hustled out of town quickly to the assigned spot, not wanting to miss this golden opportunity. We got down in the culvert beside the level crossing and in a couple of minutes heard the blast of the air horns and the odd whistling rumble those big diesel-electric engines make. Around the bend the big monster came, creeping slowly, its lights dazzling in the darkness. You know how small animals run around in confused circles when you catch them in your car headlights at night just before they dart off to the left or the right? That's a feeling I always had when a train was coming towards me.

The engineer was as good as his word. The first engine rolled by in a tumult of noise, and he waved us back. We swung easily onto the ladder of the second engine, walked back, opened the door to the cab and went in. I got up in the engineer's seat and slid the window open, putting my arm out just as you would if you were out for a summer cruise in the family car. I even found one of those engineer's hats—not the silly ones with the big puffy crown that you get at hobby stores, just a normal oily old engineer's working hat. I stuck it on my head, think-ing it would camouflage me if we were spotted and people would take us for crew. Then, as the full implications of what I was doing hit home—here I was living out a kid's fantasy, riding up in a locomotive as it thundered through the north woods, going west with an engineer's hat and my arm out the window, nonchalant as you please—I started laughing out loud. It didn't get any better than this!

Yes, I'm Moving

THERE WOULD BE MORE TRAINS as we moved west. There would be hair-raising rides with drunks, and occasionally there would be guys who wanted to beat us up and rob us of what little we had. We learned that running like hell was a lot smarter than fighting.

There was the wonder of emerging from the last of the trees and low hills of eastern Manitoba and seeing the Prairies for the first time. They had an amazing effect on me. I felt larger. I know that might sound strange, but I had begun to notice that when I was around a lot of people and buildings, I felt oddly dimin-ished, as though I was just one of many. Out here, though, I felt like I could reach out, pat God on the shoulder and ask how things were going. I wanted to fill my lungs up, run and yell out, just for the sake of being alive!

We slept in Sally Anns and prayer missions when we needed a safe bed and a shower. Mostly we fit right in. The hostels were full of the usual winos, unemployables, western-bound Maritimers and hard cases of various kinds, so we didn't look unusual.

It was the summer of 1965, and somewhere along the road I'd had my eighteenth birthday, though it had gone by without my noticing it. Most of the time, one day ran into another, and I didn't precisely know what the date was.

Nick was looking a little rougher than usual. We'd made camp under a bridge one night, setting up on the banks of a little creek somewhere in western Saskatchewan and building a campfire to keep the chill off. It was the best of both worlds because we could wash in the morning but we'd be sheltered if it rained. In the middle of the night, the temperature dropped off quite a bit, and Nick woke up with his teeth chattering. He built the fire up and huddled up as close as he could get before falling back to sleep. The trouble was, the wind picked up and went 'round. Nick woke up quickly the second time, but he was already smoking. He rolled around a bit, put himself out and then took stock of his condition. He was okay, but he'd burned a bunch of holes in the clothes and blanket I'd lent him when he'd lost his stuff way back at the first freight-train attempt. There wasn't anything left to split up, so he was a pretty sorry sight, burned dark from the sun and wind, dirty, his clothes all full of holes.

Nick had a good head for business, though, and he came up with various stratagems for adding to our survival money. He was a real stickler for wanting to make sure we always had a plentiful supply of rolling tobacco and papers. We'd have big fights when we had a limited amount of money and had to make the choice between food and coffin nails. I smoked a lot, but when I was hungry, it was food that was on my mind.

Nick was wise, though. He knew that cigarettes weren't just something to suck on yourself, they were cash in the bank during hard times. The poor guys in the missions rarely had enough money for a pack or even the makings for that matter, but most of them, being drunks, always wanted a smoke. They might not have a dollar, but they always had a nickel. We were both adept at rolling cigarettes that looked as good as tailor made, so we'd roll up a batch from our tobacco stash and sell them at two for a nickel. The mission was a safe place to carry on an enterprise like this because you wouldn't get rolled yourself for your tobacco and your cash.

There weren't any hippies out hitchhiking on the roads yet. That wouldn't start to happen until after the "Summer of Love," as it was called, and that was a little ways off yet. The hostility and suspicion that later seemed to greet the longhairs everywhere hadn't infected people in general yet, so most of the people we encountered accepted us as just two guys trying to find work, even if we were a little odd looking. In fact, a lot of people really tried to be helpful to us and occasionally took us in for the night. There wasn't anybody trying to roll us over and have their way or anything like that.

There was a fellow in Calgary who put us up for two days at his apartment in the Sundial Towers. Maybe we looked so young and dumb that people tried to stop us from getting ourselves killed, so they took us in. I don't know. This man let us have the run of his place even when he wasn't there, and he trusted us not to steal from him. We rested up, showered and got our clothes clean and were well fed to boot. As far as I could tell, he was just keen on folk music, and I represented the genuine article in his eyes. I sure sang him a lot of songs. If there was anything else on his agenda, it wasn't apparent to me.

We worked our way on out of Calgary, up the rise of brown hills to the west. As we rose up out of the big bowl that Calgary sits in, the day was clear enough for us to finally see the Rocky Mountains. I'd never seen any really big mountains before, and at first, I wasn't that impressed. They didn't look all that big! What I didn't realize was how far away they were.

After a while, it didn't seem to matter much that the farther west we went, the more the mountains seemed to stubbornly keep their distance—because the beauty of the Bow River Valley captured my full attention. With each passing mile, it just seemed to get more beautiful. I filed away the picture of it in my head against some day in the future when I'd be looking at places where I'd like to settle down.

Finally, we entered the gateway to the Rogers Pass. As the world closed in on us again, it had the odd effect of making us talk very quietly. We'd look to the left or the right and see giant wedges of rock jutting up. The perfect lines marking the formation of the Earth's crust had been tilted at crazy impossible angles by the enormous forces of compression. There was a sense of great stillness in these brooding sentinels. We'd grown used to the windblown freedom of the open country, and the Rockies, by contrast, seemed quite claustrophobic.

Then we met the neighbours. It seemed every time I turned around, there was a bighorn sheep staring back. Elk were everywhere. Seeing so much big game was both cheering and reassuring. They were great to look at, and their presence in such numbers assured me there wasn't anything around that would eat them or us. I had gotten used to the roadside magpies, black and white with their impossible tails, but now there was a new voice around at the campsites—from the pugnacious Steller's Jays.

We made slow progress in the mountains. We had come all this way to see them and we hadn't thought too far ahead about what we'd do when we got here. We were thinking about work opportunities that would allow us to hole up and make some cash. We really needed to stop travelling for a little while. People said there was work to be had everywhere in British Columbia, but we thought we'd go take a sniff around Banff before we got out of Alberta, just to see what it might have to offer. We found out pretty quickly that we weren't Banff kind of people.

It seemed to me at the time that the population of Banff consisted of four cocktail waitresses, twenty railroad workers, two or three thousand ex-Nazis who all owned accommodations for tourists and approximately fifteen thousand members of the RCMP. The horsemen were the only people who talked to us, and that was only to strongly suggest that we continue our walk right through to the other side of town and keep going. They've had problems in Banff over the years with outbreaks of elk attacks. Every so often, the big ruminants try to run somebody down right on the grounds of the Centre of Fine Arts. I think I know why.

Well, we didn't want to upset the tourists or anything, so we humbly set forth on the westbound trail, and like before, we walked and walked and walked. That was alright, though, because everywhere you turned, there was something interesting to look at. Sometimes we'd spot a nice-looking stream that seemed to originate from a waterfall way up high on the side of one of the rocks, and we'd go climb a couple of thousand feet up a mountain just to enjoy the view and get away from the highway for a while.

We'd been walking all day by the time we made it to Revelstoke. We were curious about whether or not life would be different now that we'd crossed the B.C. border.

We were trudging along the main road looking for a place to get out of sight and roost for the night when a beat-up car drove by. The guy who was driving yelled out of his window.

"Where ya playin' tonight?"

"Your place," I shouted back.

He stopped the car and yelled for us to get in. He was big and fat and more than a little drunk. At first, I was cautious, but he was in a good mood and he seemed harmless enough. We got in, and off we roared in this beat-up buggy with the bad muffler to what could only be described as a shack on the outskirts of town. It was comfortable enough, as well as warm, but it looked like it had been built as a chicken coop or something and then been added to as necessity demanded. It was a hodgepodge of materials from tarpaper to plywood to corrugated iron. It had little sleeping pits and alcoves that were partitioned off from the main section by greasy curtains, and in them were cots piled with questionable bedding and old soiled sleeping bags. It smelled a bit more like a den than a house. Nevertheless, we weren't proud, so we happily settled in to enjoy the man's hospitality. He broke out the whiskey and I broke out the guitar, and before long, I was in about the same condition as our host and we were all having a rollicking good time.

Somewhere during the course of the evening, the subject of what we were doing wandering through Revelstoke came up, and I told him, to his obvious amusement, of my dreams of experiencing the hobo life. He seemed to find it hard to believe that anyone would want to be a bum on the road if he didn't have to be. I did mention that we'd arrived here seeking some kind of work to build up our cash reserves. I stressed that we weren't panhandlers and that we didn't beg for anything. We always worked for, paid for or performed for whatever we got, although that usually wasn't very much.

This man turned out to be pretty well connected locally. He had a phone and he picked it up to make a couple of calls after he'd assured himself by asking us directly that we were willing to work hard. After he'd finished talking, he informed us that there was work at the sawmill operated by a friend of his down in Arrowhead, about twenty-five miles to the south. We could start tomorrow if we were willing to go down there. What the hell, I thought, might as well go! We stumbled off to our various pits to attempt a woozy sleep. Our voluminous host thundered the fact of his existence all through the night with an earth-shattering snore.

At dawn, as the birds shrieked and the insects stomped mercilessly through the woods, after a nourishing breakfast of grease and black coffee, we set off south in search of gainful employment.

Arrowhead wasn't all that far south of Revelstoke. It was just a hell of a job getting there! Most of the way, the road wasn't much better than a mud logging track, though that didn't seem to slow down the trucks moving along it. Carrying their twin-trailer-loads of fir logs, they charged ahead at breakneck speed.

More than once, we had to jump clear when they came around a corner. It made us think twice about trying to catch a ride. There was even a cable ferry to negotiate across a fast-flowing river. I'd never seen one before, and I was fascinated at the way the power of the current drove it across.

As the afternoon drew to a close, we made it to the sawmill. You could easily tell when you were coming near it because of the distinctive smell that comes from the big conical incinerator where they burn the sawdust, chips and other waste from the making of lumber.

We were directed to the office where the boss was and timidly knocked on the door. We made our introductions and were assured that he'd been expecting us to show up, though we were a bit scrawnier than he'd hoped we'd be. He announced his name as Marmaduke, and I could have sworn there was a second's pause while he waited to see if either of us snickered. We were careful not to do that because Marmaduke was big enough to pick both of us up, one in each hand, and toss us into the nearby lake without breaking into a sweat.

He hired us on the spot with a bone-crushing handshake and said we'd be starting work the next day. In the meantime, the foreman would show us where we'd sleep, and tomorrow he'd instruct us in our duties.

We were escorted back out, through the lumber stacks and up a small rise towards a group of three or four shacks. There was nothing to distinguish one from the other; in fact, other than being a good deal more run down, they were a lot like the cabins at good old Wanakita.

We went into the one that would be ours, and I quickly realized that the similarity to summer camp ended at the front door. This shack had been home to a lot of itinerant men since being built. I figured the last time it had been cleaned was the day the construction shavings were swept out the door.

It was called a "Batching Shack," meaning a bachelor's accommodation. There were two men already in residence, and they'd spread out pretty well, but we cleared a space around two spare cots and threw our worldly belongings on top of them. The two gents who would be our cabin mates were okay, just migrant workers like any of a number of others we'd met by this time in the cabs of trains or in the Sally Anns. We'd hardly be seeing each other anyway, as it turned out, because the shifts were so long.

The cabin had wall-to-wall litter and cold running water, which was pressured by an elevated cistern somewhere. Heat and part of the cooking surface were provided by a small wood stove, and the rest of the cooking was a mix of Sterno and a small hotplate. The lights were of the bare-lightbulb variety and powered by a gas generator that needed constant feeding. The generator was barely up to the task of powering the hotplate.

We shared our home with a great variety of creatures who knew a good thing when they saw it and had developed a preference for Ritz crackers and oatmeal instead of pine nuts. I heaved a sigh of relief when I ascertained there were none of those annoying little critters that like to secrete themselves on your person and feed on you.

Our new companions were bushed after their day in harness, and we were in a similar condition, with a whole day's travelling behind us, as well as the lingering effects of Revelstoke hospitality. The last thing I remember hearing was the throaty yowl of a wildcat somewhere out in the quiet night. This sure isn't Kansas, Toto, I thought to myself.

We were blasted out of sleep the next dawn by the bellow of the sawmill whistle. I felt a stirring response deep in my being, springing from the instinct for honest toil that has been the lifeblood of generations of good Scottish shipyard workers. Shrieking "Fuck off!" at the top of my lungs, I rolled over and tried to go back to sleep. I might as well have been in prison, though, for there was to be no lying abed after the whistle blew.

Nick and I choked down something to drink and eat and headed down to report for work. The foreman was waiting and took us over and showed us where we'd start.

Now, the way this particular sawmill worked was like this. There was what they called a piking pond, which was like it sounded. It was a collecting place for the giant logs that would soon be cut up in the mill. Men with long piking poles walked across the floating logs, guiding them, one by one, till they were lined up with the metal stanchions of a dolly car that was immersed in the water. The dolly car, with its enormous cargo, was pulled up the tracks of a marine railway by means of a strong chain, emerging from the water at a forty-five degree angle. It was terribly important for the logs to be centred and balanced when they were floated onto the dolly. They weighed several thousand pounds, and if one of them came loose, there was a pretty good chance of someone being killed! When the car got to the top of the track, it hit a stop and the log was launched forward onto a cradle. It was held firmly there while a man stripped the bark from it using an immensely powerful high-pressure hose. The pump that powered this hose was about the size of a D-9 Cat.

Once they were stripped clean, the logs were taken up by mechanical grips, then drawn inside the millhouse, where they were run through the Rube Goldberg mystery of the sawing machine itself. This monstrous machine was set up so that, in the hands of a skilled operator, it could get the maximum number of board feet of lumber in all sizes from each log. It was awesome to see and hear this huge machine whipping and turning giant lengths of heavy wood this way and that, back and forth, as though they were matchsticks.

Out of the end of the millhouse on a conveyer belt would come various sizes of rough-cut lumber: six-, eight-, and twelve-foot lengths of four-by-four, one-by-six, two-by-four. They weren't really those sizes yet because, as I said, they were unfinished, meaning they hadn't been planed smooth.

This conveyer belt ran past various piles of lumber that corresponded to the sizes emerging from the mill. The boards had to be sorted and stacked by labourers running back and forth, dragging them from the conveyer and stacking them in the appropriate pile. This is what Nick and I were assigned to do.

We started at eight o'clock in the morning, got a fifteen-minute water break at ten, then lunch at noon for one hour and you'd better hope you brought it, then back to it with one water break of fifteen minutes till the five o'clock whistle signalled the end.

The work was murderous. Neither of us had brought gloves, and none were provided. Halfway through the first day, our hands were raw with blisters and black with splinters from the rough wood. It was exhausting work running back and forth on the catwalk in the sun, lifting and pulling. The only mercy was the occasional lapse that occurred when a log was slow being loaded into the system.

Worst of all, there was a big fat guy who drove a forklift truck, and he'd sit there under the shade of his roof watching us bust our asses building a pile of lumber up six feet high until it was hard to get the planks up on top. He'd just sit there sipping on an icy cold Coke, enjoying our suffering. Then, when it seemed we couldn't get the pile any higher, he'd stir his lard, drive the forklift over and pick it up to carry it away and stack it somewhere else. Meanwhile, we'd start over again. While I'd run back and forth like a scuttling crab, sweating and hurting, at least the forklift fatso gave me something else to focus on. Shit, I started to hate that guy!

No matter what you do, sooner or later, somehow, you start to get used to it, and it becomes routine. Nick and I thought we'd probably die the first couple of days, but eventually our hands toughened up at about the same time our backs got accustomed to heaving and hauling. We were fairly wiry and tough from life on the road anyway, so it was really more a matter of adjusting to the work, as opposed to going straight from the couch to the conveyer. We collected our first pay at the end of the week, and that did a lot to cheer us up. Compared to what we'd been able to scrounge when we were travelling, two dollars and seventy-five cents an hour was a princely wage. When I got that in my hand in the form of one hundred and twenty dollars cash money, I was a happy guy, even if I was having trouble opening and closing my hands.

As we started the next week, I realized I'd barely touched the guitar since we'd started and when I had, I couldn't do much with it because my hands were so sore. I started to think about moving on.

I got a reprieve in the form of a job change. It didn't pay any more, but the work was a lot more fun. Practically anything would be better than what I'd been doing!

I got moved over to the position at the top of the marine railway and was given the high-pressure hose to blow the bark off the logs. This was a blast (no pun intended)!

It's a good thing somebody warned me because the first time they turned the thing on, I nearly went for the snake ride of the century. I wasn't expecting it to have that much of a kick. I learned how to brace my back against a post in such a manner that when the water came on, I was forced back into the post rather than up in the air. I quickly developed the required technique and precision in aiming, and I got an immense feeling of power watching eight- and twelve-foot sections of bark cartwheeling off in the spray. It was also cool!

For Nick, though, it was still hard slogging, and he was thinking really hard about calling it quits. We were halfway through the second week in the same place anyway and we weren't exactly planning on getting married and raising a family! We resolved that the next day would be our last, and we let the foreman know we'd be moving on.

Just before we quit to go and get our pay on that last day at Arrowhead, I was cleaning a log when I idly noticed that the water from the hose carried a fair distance when you aimed it up a little higher. I also noticed that the fat guy with the Coke in his hand was well within range. It was with a happy heart that I knocked his big lard-ass off the forklift!

Sometimes the Bear Eats You

ﾍ NICK AND I KNOCKED OFF WORK in high spirits that afternoon. We were light-hearted at the prospect of getting moving again. I guess there's more of the natural vagabond in me than I thought, because unless I'm actually at home, I still get itchy feet when I'm stuck someplace for more than a few days. It's been a lifelong compulsion for me to get in the car and just go. Maybe that's why I love aeroplanes so much. The joy is in the going; the anticlimax is always the getting there.

We went off to our shack to eat and rest up for the morning. We both had money burning a hole in our pockets for the first time since we'd left Toronto, and we were giddy with a sense of security. Arrowhead had one more little experience in store for me, though, before it let me get away.

I mentioned the constant feeding of the generator for our shack. What that meant in reality was that near the motor, one of those Briggs and Stratton howlers, there was a jerry-can that was used to top up the gas tank. You'd know the motor needed feeding when it started to run roughly and the lights flickered. We took turns with the feeding, and it worked out democratically for the most part. If you were the unlucky man who went out and found the jerry-can was empty, you had to make the long trudge down through the lumber stacks to the millhouse, where you could fill it up from the main tank. That walk seemed a lot longer at night. There was hardly ever a soul around because most of the full-time employees lived elsewhere.

On this last night, it was my turn to take care of the generator when it began to announce its needs, and naturally, when I went to fill it up, the can was empty. With a grumbling "Shit!" I picked up the can and started out for the mill. I had a flashlight with me so I was less concerned about the noises in the surrounding bush than when I was walking home in the dark from the lodges back to Wanakita. Besides, even though we were in a pretty wild area, the noise and smell of the mill tended to make the critters give the place a pretty wide berth. They were still smart enough to not care for people all that much. All the same, I was indulging in that kind of quiet tuneless whistling which, if you're really listening to your inner voice, tells you you'll be much happier when the journey is ended and you are safe indoors.

I was walking by the lumber stacks, looking up at the beauty of a rare crystal-clear sky, when I heard a distinctive sound close by. It was a low rumbly phlegmy kind of "Wooooof"! I stopped in my tracks and clearly heard the same noise again, this time accompanied by scraping and shuffling sounds.

I shone the light over to where the sound seemed to be coming from, and what I saw made the blood run right out of me so I nearly fainted. There were two little red eyes shining back at me, and they were attached to the biggest head I had ever seen in my life. There was room enough to land an aeroplane between the ears. Behind the head was a great hump of a shoulder and below it were two legs that looked the size of fir logs leading down to a pair of paws with equipment that made Freddy Kreuger's gloves look like pen-knives.

There was no place to go. It was useless to run. I thought I was a dead man, and as I stood there with the light shining on the first grizzly bear I'd ever seen except in the outdoor magazines, I felt a wet warmth as my bladder let go down my pant leg.

I wasn't really conscious of words, but I remember what my fevered brain was processing in those few seconds. First was the blinding realization, as I looked at my death, that the world is not a romantic game you read about in books. It's real and has bad breath and it's dangerous enough to kill you. The second thought was that the bear was a female. Don't ask me how I knew. I wasn't about to walk around behind it and look between its legs. Maybe some part of me was thinking that if it was a male, I'd probably already be dead and it wouldn't be just standing there quietly looking at me.

I don't know how long we stared at each other, perfectly still. Perhaps it was only a few seconds, but it seemed like an eternity to me. The grizzly half rose and turned around and lumbered away in a loping shambling run. I turned around and stumbled, rubber-legged, to the shack.

Nobody minded not having any lights that night.

I cleaned myself up and calmed down enough to think about why I wasn't spread out in a red heap somewhere out there in the sawdust. I figured the bear was just passing through, maybe hoping for a little opportunistic feeding on camp leftovers, but nervous about the stink of so much humanity. I also figured that when I stumbled into its path and shone the flashlight in its face, I was lucky that my scent didn't carry (maybe the breeze was helping me), and because it was dazzled and had poor eyesight anyway, it couldn't see what I was. Maybe the bear just saw me as an irritating mystery instead of a threat and chose to shuffle off rather than investigate further. I'll always be grateful to that bear for its decision!

Nick and I hit the road again the next morning and for me, the sky had never seemed so bright or the world so full of life. I was more conscious of smells and sounds and I felt amazingly light and strong. I wondered if I was feeling a sort of rapture at my deliverance.

Now that we were west, it didn't seem to matter that much whether the direction we took was that particular one or not. We had a huddle and decided to work our way over to the Okanagan region.

We headed down to Penticton, the little resort town that had grown up as a result of the fruit-growing business that was the staple of the area. To me, the countryside around the whole Okanagan Valley looked just like the old *Wild Bill Hickok* shows. It was warm and dry, with grasses and sagebrush instead of the big trees we'd recently been seeing. I had fantasies of getting on a horse and disappearing over the hills. The only trouble was that I'd been on a horse only once in my whole life—and that one had run away with me. I'd had to be rescued from the middle of a circle of curious cows where I'd been dumped on my backside by the little pinto pony as it fled off back to the barn. I was just a kid then.

Penticton was a lively and interesting place compared to what we'd been used to. It was the height of the summer season, and all the little motels and the grander accommodations were chock full of tourists. The town sits right between two lakes, Skaha and Okanagan, so it's not only got scenery, it's got watersports of all kinds, as well as guest ranches and lodges surrounding the area. On Lake Skaha, there were a lot of high-performance drag-racing boats. I guess there was a regatta coming up or a competition of some kind, because these stack-piped supercharged chromed deathtraps were roaring up and down the lake making an unbelievable racket. It was still okay in those days to burn a lot of gas and have a big engine that made tons of noise. There were a lot of cars on the main drag—muscle cars and chrome hot rods—that made as much noise as the boats. The place was full of open fruit stands and curio shops, but they were all local businesses, colourful and individualistic in their design. There was none of that horrible franchising—McDonald's, Arby's, Tim Horton's, Burger King, Wendy's, Taco Bell—that now makes the outskirts of one town indistinguishable from any other.

Best of all, there were the girls. When Mom and Dad came to the Okanagan, they brought their daughters, who promptly shed most of their clothing and headed for the beach. They were all over the place, these succulent little volcanoes of post-pubescent energy. It was heaven and we were inclined to stay around.

We'd been figuring on finding work in the orchards, but it was too early for the apricots or the peaches to be picked. They wouldn't start to ripen for a few weeks yet. We had to watch ourselves because even though we had money and weren't vagrants, we looked pretty rough and tumble, and as was the case in Banff, the cops weren't inclined to have people like us around frightening the tourists.

Unlike Banff, though, they had to have a certain tolerance for the migrant workers needed for the fruit-picking season, workers who were usually rough looking. So the cops had opted for a hands-off policy as long as the poor and the transients who were waiting to be hired kept themselves out of conflict with the mainstream.

We'd developed pretty good instincts about where to go by this point, and we quickly found the outdoor squat where those like us made their camp. Down on the banks of the canal that joins the two lakes, a group of young men had banded together for self-protection, and we pitched our bedrolls there at night. Self-protection was a necessary thing. Remember all those daughters? A lot of young men were attracted to the town by this candy, and they weren't above massing together in drunken groups and entertaining themselves by beating up on the marginalized. They were just another version of those assholes who drive down Church Street in Toronto and beat up on gays. You had to watch out for them.

Once I got talking to a few of our canal mates, I found out that while they were waiting for the fruit picking to begin, they had adopted a slightly more sinister means of making ends meet. They were preying on the teenaged girls.

No matter what you actually have in the way of clothes, everybody looks equal in a bathing suit. These guys, who were fit, tanned, and in a couple of cases, pretty handsome, would head for the beach and be indistinguishable from any of the other tourist boys in the town. They would spot the giggliest, the shyest, the most inexperienced girls who looked like they were over sixteen and put a major move on them. Pretty soon, the girls would find themselves in some quiet place minus something that their fathers cared about more than they did.

It didn't matter what the outcome was after that, the results were the same. If the girl fell in love with our canal-side shark, he'd use her desire to make him happy, to get money from her. If she was flipped out that she'd lost her cherry and didn't want her parents to find out, that was even better. He'd use her fear to extort money from her under threat of telling her parents.

This awakening to how lousy people can be dampened my enthusiasm for lingering too long in the canal district of Penticton. There didn't seem to be any prospect of immediate work there either, so after hanging out for a couple of days, Nick and I decided to make the big push through to Vancouver.

Spinning Wheels Grab the Road

☙ IT WAS THE LAST WEEK IN AUGUST 1965 when we finally made it into Vancouver. The mountains themselves were an anticlimax, given that we'd been seeing nothing but mountains for some time, but it was a relief when the countryside opened up to the expanse of the Fraser River Delta. For the first time since I was a little kid, I could smell the distinctive tang in the air that I remembered from the boat trip across the ocean. I couldn't wait to get my feet wet in the Pacific, so we made our way downtown, all the way down Burrard Street to the bridge, then down the slope and along Beach Avenue. I took off my boots, rolled up my pants and waded in. The water was freezing! I stuck my hand in and took a few drops up to my lips just to make sure it was indeed salty. I really didn't have to because, as I mentioned before, the sea always announces itself as authentic by way of your nose. There's a feral, musty quality to the smell, not salty really. If the coming and going of life has a smell, then this is it. The ocean smells like sex, but more subtle!

I took out a little bottle I'd been saving for this occasion. (I'd promised to take a little of the Pacific Ocean back for a friend.) Dipping it down into the water, I watched the bubbles rise to the surface as it filled. As I slowly screwed the cap back on, I stared out to the west, towards the distant mountains of Vancouver Island, and thought, "Now what?"

I had focused on this moment, but I hadn't given any thought as to what would happen once I'd reached my goal. Keep going? Try and get work on a freighter and go out across the Pacific?

For a few days, I'd been having the feeling that while I was aimlessly rambling, I wasn't moving towards the primary goal in my life, which was to find a way to be creative in music or art without starving to death in the process. I was not exactly homesick because home as I had known it was no longer an option. Even if I'd decided to eat humble pie and return to the fold, I was sure I wouldn't be accepted back by my father—and I wasn't about to do that anyway!

I guess I was scene-sick. I missed being involved with my music and my friends. I wanted that feedback I'd get from playing in front of people who understood what I was trying to do.

The most wonderful thing I'd found about being on the road was the freedom. I had never drunk so deeply from that well before—waking up in the morning, wetting a finger to stick up in the wind and thinking, "Guess I'll head this way for a while." Action and consequence were forever linked in my mind now. Work or go hungry. Be wily or get killed. Move out and meet people or retreat into loneliness.

The Oxford dictionary definition of anarchy is "an excess of freedom." I like that definition. I was beginning to figure out that the kind of total freedom I was indulging in had a price. It meant an existence without form or substance—moving around and surviving for the moment, without the commitment, passion and growth that give life its meaning. I realized it was time to go back to Toronto and dive into the music!

In the meantime, our immediate survival and comfort was the issue. We weren't about to spend any of our hard-earned money on a hotel, no matter how cheap it was, so we headed back over to the Vancouver Sally Ann for the night.

Vancouver was still more like its original self in 1965. It was a railway and resource town. There were log booms, lumber mills, potash piles and a big salmon-boat fleet, as well as the busy seaport of the Burrard Inlet. It was a muscular town, and the Salvation Army hostel reflected that, with a rich and dangerous mix of wharf rats, Gastown rummies, ship jumpers, migrants, mental cases and down-and-outs.

Nick and I bunked down on cots next to each other. It was just a large room with a great number of men snoring and moaning, muttering and stirring. I didn't feel too good about going to sleep, but the sheets were clean and so were we, from taking a shower in the communal baths. It felt awfully good to get under the hot water, even if we were watching each other's backs the whole time. I had even used up some of my precious cash to purchase a few toiletries. Heaven knows, maybe I was thinking of romance with one of Vancouver's abundant ladies of the evening because I'd even bought a bottle of Aqua-Velva. I'd splashed a little on after I shaved while idly humming the jingle, "There's something about an Aqua-Velva Man!" Guitar and bedroll safely stowed under the cot, I left the toiletries out loose for the morning and lay on my back, listening to the fitful stirrings of the social ladder's lowest rung. Finally, tired out, I must have drifted off to sleep.

I snapped awake in the morning, and the first thing I did was to stick my head over the side and look under the cot to check my stuff. Shit! Things had been moved. I frantically checked everything I had and did a quick inventory. The only thing missing was the bottle of Aqua-Velva. What the hell? I had rolling tobacco and other valuable items stashed. Why would somebody steal my aftershave and nothing else?

I found out soon enough. The empty bottle was in the shower room. I'd forgotten that aftershave has alcohol in it. Some poor shaking wino had been so desperate for a drink that he'd guzzled it down.

We wandered around in Vancouver for a couple more days. I even visited my brother-in-law Alistair's brother while we were there. I don't suppose he knew what to think about the way I looked. The last time he'd seen me I was a pretty clean-cut kid.

So that was it! We turned around and headed back east.

I was a different creature now—more like a horse that can smell the barn and starts picking up speed. I wanted to put in long hours and make a lot of miles. I wanted to push harder than Nick did, and it seemed we quarrelled more about little things, especially the old argument about what to buy first, food or tobacco. Because we were moving faster, there were fewer opportunities to replenish our meagre cash stocks, and we found ourselves tired and hungry again. A lot of the glamour of sleeping rough had worn off by this point, and I was cranky and irritable a lot of the time.

Finally, in eastern Saskatchewan, things came to a head. Nick wanted to make a diversion off the highway and cut south towards the U.S. border to a little town called Carnduff. He had some kind of connection with the place from when he was a kid and he wanted to go back and see it again. It was just some little rural obscurity down the country roads in the middle of nowhere and over fifty miles out of our way, to boot. Who knew what kind of transport we might be able to catch? I figured we'd probably get stuck down there for the rest of the rapidly disappearing summer. I didn't want to know about going to no Carnduff!

We had an argument about it right there on the side of the Trans-Canada. It heated up to the point where other stuff that we weren't really arguing about started to get said—personal stuff, "the trouble with you" stuff.

There was a bunch of bad language that lit up the atmosphere, and the next thing I knew, I was stomping off down the road on my own. I got lucky and caught a ride right away, and that was that. I just left Nick there on the side of the road to trudge down to Carnduff, Saskatchewan, if he fucking well felt like it and fall down a hole for all I cared.

I was already in Manitoba before I cooled down enough to start feeling like a total shit. I'd just dumped my travelling buddy, a guy who on more than one occasion had saved my ass and who'd made me laugh when I didn't feel like it— all because I didn't want to take the trouble to slow down and do something that was important to him. It was too late to do anything about it now. The likelihood of finding each other again was remote, and though I felt bad, I still wasn't about to go back.

Nick and I never did really connect again, although I ran into him once or twice. Our bond had been art school, our friends and our great adventure together. Once that was done, life pulled us off in different directions, and there was little reason for seeking each other out.

I kept moving day and night if I could, walking long distances. It was September, and the nights were getting chilly as I hit the tree country west of Lake of the Woods again. The eastern forests looked like old familiar friends. It was odd to still be so far away from home but feel at home anyway. I grabbed what freights I could. I caught rides in people's cars and didn't even make a pretence of trying to have conversations. I'd usually fall into an exhausted sleep within seconds, to the disappointment of the driver, who wanted someone to help keep him awake.

Once or twice, when there was no other option and there was a way to get in, I stowed away in the back of a stake truck or semi. I was getting light headed again because I kept pushing on and not working on the problem of getting food. I was eating very little, but when I noticed I was starting to see angels blowing golden ram's horns up in the sunset clouds and that sometimes, for no apparent reason, I would sit down by the side of the road and burst into tears, I started taking better care of myself.

I made the right turn at Sudbury and started heading south, past Parry Sound. I guess Bobby Orr would have been going to public school there at about that time. On down through cottage country, rapidly emptying now that the season was over. Past Penetanguishene, site of our near-disastrous first attempt at train hopping and into the rolling green hills of southern Ontario. In the short time

125

I'd been away, I'd forgotten how really beautiful this landscape was—lush, rich, with well-kept farms, fields of ripe corn standing tall in the sun. I was glad to see home again.

I got back to Toronto and headed straight for the Village Corner Club. I didn't go near 5 Stayner Avenue.

When I showed up at the club, it was like old home week. There were drinks and stories, and there was music, and I felt happy to be back in a place full of people I thought of as my second family. I cleared up the matter of where to lay my head fairly quickly—my old mattress in the basement was still vacant.

So I was back! I'd gone out and I'd ridden the rails. I'd toiled in the mills, busked, hustled, run away from danger and lived to tell the tale. I felt I was now possessed of the requisite authenticity to be a folk singer, and I had a great deal of confidence in my ability to survive.

I was six feet tall and weighed, give or take an ounce, only one hundred and twenty-nine pounds.

III

Trying to Get Going

🎝 THE ROMANTIC DECKS WERE CLEARED in a hurry. Shortly after my return, my dark-eyed girlfriend and I had packed ourselves into Billy Fulghum's brand-new white Mustang fastback for an impromptu trip down to New York City, just to take in the sights and visit a friend I'd met in Yorkville named Anne Hershoran. She was working for a music business manager named Herb Gart, and Billy was looking to get into that end of things. As a matter of fact, he was looking to get into that end of things with me.

We walked around Greenwich Village like tourists and generally rubber-necked. The only trouble arose when the girlfriend wanted to do things that no one else wanted to do—like shop, for instance. She also seemed to be unexpectedly fond of complaining, so by the time we got back to Toronto, everyone was happy to see the end of the trip, and she seemed happy about seeing the end of me.

I was still crashing at the Village Corner Club, footloose and fancy free. I'd begun to try writing songs in earnest and was performing some of my early efforts at the club on my own featured nights now. Time was slowly passing the old place by, though, and it was devolving into a hangout for the regulars, rather than the folk showplace it had once been. There were a couple of new faces around. Danny Magroder (the first of many aliases) was a black man up from the States who was an amazing singer. He could break your heart with his read of "Who Can I Turn To," and then he'd do a song that had the power of Richie

Havens singing "Handsome Johnny." He turned out to be a bit of a bad penny. There was another folk singer living upstairs. He was notable because he had glasses like Buddy Holly and he always had a little grass on him, even though the regulars and the owners of the club really had a hate-on for "dopers."

That girl I mentioned before, Patty Sockwell, was much in evidence. She was a regular face on most nights. She had her own apartment downtown but I think at the time she was being subsidized by her mother. She was still the most exotic-looking of the women around the place, with her combination beatnik–Holly Golightly fashion statement. She had added a cigarette holder for effect and could be seen sitting in the club, looking intensely at the performer, pulling on the end of this thing and letting the smoke spill out of her mouth in a big cloud. She never inhaled.

It was an incestuous little world, full of intrigues and gossip. The situation at the time was that Patty had the hots for Billy, whom she perceived to be a roman-tic smoky-voiced Southern bluesman. Billy was extremely flirtatious but very married, and his wife, Barbie, was not only sweet, but also gorgeous. So Patty was getting absolutely no closer to her ultimate goal. She was only eighteen and act-ing a lot more sophisticated than she really was.

Nick Garber, who hosted the open sings and lived like a churchmouse upstairs, had made not-so-subtle overtures to Patty and appeared to be making no progress at all. As happens with men, he was becoming a little sullen about his lack of success and was upping the pressure and the level of persistence. Clearly, something or someone had to give.

One night, after things had wound down and I was in the basement prepar-ing to drift off, Patty appeared. I think she'd finally gotten pissed off at not get-ting anywhere with Billy, but that's just a guess.

"Can I get in with you?" was all I needed to hear.

I moved into her downtown apartment after that. Nick seemed a little dis-gruntled, but he got over it. Billy was relieved—I think he just wanted the little girl to be happy!

The apartment had a pull-out sofa-bed sitting in the middle of a parquet floor and very little else in the way of furnishings. But that was okay. For the first little while, the sofa-bed was all we needed. We didn't even lock the door, so when Billy and Doug Brown came over to hang out, we didn't have to get up to unlock it. We'd receive our friends relaxing in bed, usually without pyjamas.

It was a pretty good time, though a short-lived one. Billy had quite a romantic attachment to the idea of riding the freights, so on many nights he, Doug Brown, Patty and I would end up going over to the west end of the freight yards. There was a great big neon Canada Packers sign down there that flashed alternately red and blue. We'd sit under its garish light watching the engines butt the freight cars into line with a machine-gun staccato while we talked about our dreams and drank screw-top wine. It was about then that Billy and I concluded an understanding that he'd try his hand at managing my career.

Trouble finally reared its head in the form of Patty's landlord. He was a person of some obscure European extraction. He'd paid careful attention to the way she dressed and the hours she kept. There were occasional complaints from the neighbours about the noise from my guitar and about strange people, mostly men, coming and going at all hours. He started banging on the door unannounced to make damage inspections of the floor or check the appliances.

I'd begun to make periodic forays outside of Toronto to work clubs. There was a circuit then, and club owners who heard about a performer doing well in one location would often give them a try in their own place. The folk festivals like Newport, Philadelphia or Mariposa recruited from the club system almost like a farm team in hockey. If you made a big enough splash and got a record out, there was a ready-made tour that would take you to the Bitter End in New York or the Chessmate in Detroit. I had my sights set on that goal, but in the meantime, I was playing wherever I could for whatever I could get. In this case, it was Bill Powell's club, the Ebony Knight over in Hamilton, and if I remember correctly, the gig paid sixty dollars for the two-day weekend, plus I could sleep in the performers' room at the club.

As I've mentioned, a lot of the coffeehouse clubs were social in nature, and a scene had grown up around them. They were often in big old houses, and a steady flow of transient people would crash where they could.

There was a girl in residence at the Ebony Knight. She was one of the first of the coming wave of flower children now that the "Summer of Love" was upon us. Bill, a generous and gregarious guy, was happy to shelter strays and had let her crash at the club for as long as she saw fit. She was a little waif, not much more than seventeen, and she was sleeping in what amounted to a closet in this big old building, with nothing more than her cat Muffin and what she could fit into an overstuffed shoulder bag.

After the first night's show, I got to talking to her. She was very curious about the scene that was beginning to develop in Yorkville. We got along really well, and without either of us asking or mentioning it, we wound up sharing her closet that night. She was sweet and as gentle in nature as anyone I'd ever met. We hung out most of the next day, and after the show was over, the next night as well. She didn't want anything from me. She didn't expect anything from me. Her head wasn't off somewhere in the future, nor was she trapped in the past.

When it was time for me to travel back to Toronto, she said she wanted to hitchhike in to see what was going on in Yorkville in a couple of days' time. She thought it would be too hard to carry her cat as well as her bag on the road, and she asked if it would be okay if I took Muffin back with me. Once she'd made her way to Toronto and found a place to crash, she'd pick up the cat. That was okay with me.

A couple of days later, I got a call from Bill Powell. Tressy (that was her name) had been hitching along the QEW after sundown and a car had gone out of control and hit her. It had been travelling at seventy miles an hour and knocked her a long way through the air, killing her instantly. I never even found out what her last name was.

And that was how we ended up with Muffin the cat.

Meanwhile, Patty's landlord had reacted predictably to the developing situation. He was trying to get some of Patty because he'd come to the conclusion that with all those men coming and going, she was a loose woman. When that proved to be a dead end, he accused her outright of being a whore and ordered her evicted from the building. As I was merely her guest, that meant me as well. I'm trying to imagine such a thing happening now, but I can't. Back then, there was no Landlord and Tenant Act, and leases had morals clauses. If you perceived yourself as powerless, which we did, you ran away.

So we got out. But now there was another matter to deal with. If we found a place together, that would change the message of the relationship from "Gee, it's nice staying here in your place and getting laid regular" to something perilously close to couplehood. I liked her well enough, and in all the important ways, we got along really well. She had a great sympathy for the creative life, and being from a showbiz family (her father and mother were both broadcasters), she had a romantic view of the realities of artistic poverty. She was well read and extremely intelligent, willing to stay up all night, and as committed as I to avoiding gainful employment in the conventional sense.

It seemed like the right thing to do at the time, so without any plans brewing for building white picket fences, I decided that moving in together would be alright. She seemed to feel the same way.

We found a little attic flat in a house on Brunswick Avenue, not far from Central Tech and still a reasonable walk over to Yorkville. It was just two rooms, really, with a tiny kitchenette crammed in between. We were up there under the dormers, so the ceiling took off at all kinds of crazy angles. The best thing about the place, though, was that beyond the door leading out of the back room, there was a little wooden deck. Out there, it felt like an eagle's nest. Up in the treetops, with a commanding view of the world, a person's thoughts could soar. It was funky and artistic and perfect for the likes of us. There was just the little matter of making the rent.

I was lucky to be pulling in a couple of weekend gigs a month at this time, but sometimes I'd do better. They never paid much more than a hundred and fifty or two hundred bucks, and the rent on the place alone was something like three hundred and fifty.

We were so close to the art school that it was just a short walk. I can't remember how it came up as an idea exactly, but one day when we were particularly short of cash, I remembered they used models for life-drawing classes at Central and I figured that might be a way to make ends meet. Of course, I wasn't thinking it should be me who'd march over there and take my clothes off! That never occurred to me. After all, I was a guy!

So Patty trooped over and listed herself as a model and pretty soon started getting calls from the school. Her first day was the worst. Figure on how people are generally so self-conscious about what they perceive as their flaws and then picture yourself stark naked in bright light with a bunch of pimply art students looking at your bum, and you might have some idea of how she felt.

She also became adept at finding the day-old breads and nearly spoiled, marked-down vegetables that we lived on while I laboured nobly on my artistic pursuits and generally took her efforts for granted. Sometimes, when our supplies were perilously low, friends like Myron Cooper or Noni Raitblatt would just seem to show up with a box of food, or we'd find ourselves invited to dinner at Billy and Barbie's place.

Billy was trying to hustle for me, with mixed success. Some of the gigs were tough ones. There was a place I got hired to play in called George's Kibitzeria, where I was the folk singer in the corner while the patrons filled their faces full of Italian food. I'd sit there in a complete funk, trying to sing while the dishes clanked and people talked away. Oddly enough, I got my first review there and it was a good one. I can't believe it under the circumstances, but god bless Sid Adilman, he always had an eye for quality.

Finally, though, Billy scored. He landed a major opportunity. There was a syndicated TV show called *Let's Sing Out*, hosted by well-known folk singer Oscar Brand. Oscar had a great reputation for singing the bawdiest and funniest songs—in fact, he'd released whole albums of them. He was very popular on the campuses at the time. The show was produced by a guy named Sid Banks, and it differed from its American counterpart *Hootenanny* significantly. The American show was devoted to only the most homogenized and commercial brand of music—the Limelighters, Kingston Trio, Peter, Paul & Mary kind. *Let's Sing Out* mixed a whole bunch of interesting music together: traditional, singer-songwriter, good-time and commie-controversial stuff. I haven't forgotten that this country put Bob Dylan on CBC national television when he was still a fringe artist in the U.S.

They were going to be shooting the show up at Laurentian University in Sudbury, and I was invited to be on it. I was excited on several fronts. Even though the money wasn't great, it was going to be a cash bonanza compared to what I usually earned. It was also going to be the first time I'd ever appeared on television, and that was such a substantial career step-up for me that I called my mother right away to let her know what was happening. I still went up occasionally to see my folks, even though things were strained with my father, and I reported any positive news to my mother so she'd be less inclined to worry about me.

One more thing was pretty exciting. Our transportation was going to be provided, and that meant we'd be flown up to Sudbury on Trans-Canada Airlines. It was going to be my first ever aeroplane ride!

On the day we were to go, I went out to Malton Airport. I found the waiting area for the flight and met the host and the other guests on the show. Oscar and Sid were very relaxed and gracious about making sure we all felt we were as important to the show as anyone else. I, for one, really appreciated that.

One of the guests was Jimmy Driftwood, who played a homemade Appalachian guitar fashioned out of barrel staves and had written the Johnny Horton hit song "The Battle of New Orleans." There was a duet called Fraser DeBolt. She went on later to a solo folk career as Daisy Debolt, and he wound up, so I heard, becoming a crane operator and helping build the CN Tower. Then there was a gorgeous blonde lady named Joni Mitchell.

She'd been in Toronto, playing a place called the Seven of Clubs, run by a guy named Mike Copas—at least I think that was his name. She'd been making a reputation on the American club scene after breaking up with the husband who had foolishly ridiculed her efforts at singing and writing, but she was yet to release her first record.

When it was flight time, we all trooped out onto the ramp—no security, no machines. You could walk right out and see the whole aeroplane you were going to travel in. I think the airlines thought of their planes in more affectionate terms then—not merely as sources of earned-revenue-per-seat-mile. They were proud of them, and rightly so in this case.

Waiting there for us was a British-built Vickers Viscount, one of the most beautiful small airliners ever made. It was graceful and sleek with its four turbo-prop engines hanging on the wings and its proud fuselage stripe that terminated in the shape of a lightning bolt piercing the bold circle with the maple leaf in it.

We climbed the airstairs and entered the cabin. I found myself in a window seat, and what a window! It went from just above your waist to about halfway up your forehead, and by today's airline standards, the view was panoramic. There was none of that sense of being cut off and claustrophobic that you so often feel in modern airliners.

It took off and flew northbound at an altitude where you could still see the rolling hills of southern Ontario suddenly give way to the rugged granite and many lakes of the Canadian Shield. You could make out the boats and the cottages and the towns and the trains that so recently had been my unpaid transport. I loved being in the aeroplane. It was a dream come true to be up in the air, and I had my nose pressed to the glass the whole time, watching the engines, the silver wings and the passing countryside.

The show went very well from the producer's point of view, and Sid seemed happy with what I had contributed. I was disheartened, though. I thought everyone on it was better than I was, and I felt self-conscious about playing and singing the whole time I was there.

I'd heard of Joni—people were talking about her—but I'd never heard her sing or been exposed to any of her songs. Judy Collins hadn't recorded "Both Sides Now" yet. I hadn't paid that much attention to her during the flight up, what with being so excited about the flight itself.

When she transformed herself into her full performing drag—sparkling little bum-freezer mini-dress, sparkling leotards, open-heeled shoes, nails, long straight Mary Travers–style blonde hair, a big Martin D-18 all topped off with those high Scandinavian cheekbones, she got my full attention!

She drew out two conflicting feelings in me at the same time because of the way she presented herself. On the one hand, I just wanted to throw her on her back, but at the same time, I wanted to put her on a pedestal and protect her.

I've always thought the most fascinating people or works of art are the ones that pull in different directions simultaneously. There's an inner tension that projects from them, and like it or not, you're drawn in by it. Joni seemed full of inner wars and conflicts. Certainly, there was a lot more at work in her than she was letting on.

Then there were the songs. She sang "Sisotowbell Lane" and "Song to a Sea-gull," both of which would find their way onto her first record, the one David Crosby would produce. They were done in these weird tunings on the guitar and sung in this impossibly pure high falsetto, and I had something of the same reaction I'd had the first time I heard Dylan—though not for the same reasons. She was the first woman I'd heard who was trying to blend contemporary poetic lyrics and folk music forms like the male writers I admired already. But she was different. She was exploring new territory, abstracting her relationships and using them as fuel, writing with wonderful sensitivity about how the insanities of the world affected her emotionally.

When we got on the plane to leave Sudbury, I had good memories of my first TV appearance—the flamboyant Jimmy Driftwood bellowing that now-famous battle song with the spirit of Grandpa Jones while flailing away on his improbable rough wood guitar; the warmth and welcoming of the fun-loving Oscar Brand; and Joni Mitchell, who made me feel like I was somebody tap dancing for the line-up outside the opera.

Not long after this, she came up to the flat to visit with us when she happened to be in Toronto. It might have been her first Riverboat gig, I can't remember. I do remember that we all hung out in the formal front room of the two-room flat and listened to the Beatles' *Sergeant Pepper* album, which had just come out. I had developed a bit of a crush and was trying hard not to let it show.

The Riverboat, which was owned and run by Bernie Fiedler, was now up and running and was rapidly becoming the premier folk club in Toronto. This was astonishing, considering it was so tiny, at only ninety or so seats, and given the fact it didn't sell booze—just coffee and strudel.

With its kitschy brass portholes, railings and varnished wood interior, it was run with military precision, and Fiedler had mastered the art of getting the crowds in and out fast. It was admission, sit down, six-buck espresso and sweet, forty-five-minute show, thank-you ladies and gentlemen, there's the door! Nobody had run a folk club in Canada like a show bar, and Bernie was making it work. He was also in contact with people like Paul Colby, who ran the Bitter End in New York, and Murray Weidenbaum of the Chessmate in Detroit—and he was acting as the Toronto date for top-line touring acts in package tours. His club was the place to come to if you wanted to catch Sonny and Brownie, Phil Ochs or Tom Rush. He was making contacts like crazy—artists, their managers, agents, other club owners, festival artistic directors. Bernie was gregarious and sociable. He loved to party, and usually had the performers over to his house. He liked the action and was rapidly becoming a force to be reckoned with on the Toronto music scene.

The people who organized the Mariposa Folk Festival used the Riverboat on Monday nights for an open-sing. They actually called it The Riverboat Hootenanny. It was usually well attended by aficionados of the form and acted as a talent-discovery mechanism for the festival. It was also a way to keep the club open and not have to pay the talent. Mariposa was an important festival at that time, along with Newport and Philadelphia, and it was a valuable place for a budding singer-songwriter to gain exposure. Each little leg-up you got could help in going further, so I went down and auditioned for the open-sing. These nights had a reputation for quality, and it wouldn't be seemly for them to let just anybody with a guitar walk onto the stage in case they stunk up the joint, so you pre-auditioned, and if you passed that, you were on. Fortunately, they saw something in me that I still didn't always see in myself, and I began to play Monday nights on a regular basis and started to work my way into the scene surrounding both the Riverboat and the Mariposa Festival.

Why, Because You Have to?

❧ I CAN'T REMEMBER THE REASON, but maybe it was just too hard getting together enough money for the rent every month. In any event, Patty and I had to move out of the little flat on Brunswick. After looking around for a while, we found a glorified room and kitchen at the back of a house at 48 Hayden Street, right by the intersection of Yonge and Bloor. Our home was on the main floor directly behind the offices of the Alvin Munch Talent Agency. It was terribly small, but at least it was also terribly cheap.

Patty set to making it liveable by artistic standards. She procured about a hundred orange crates. We scavenged a bunch of scrap lumber, bits of gyprock, plaster, chickenwire and paint, and went to work. When it was done, it was quite an achievement in miniature.

In the one room where we slept, there was now a raised platform loft bed with a ladder butted up against the wall, which now surrounded the sink, toilet and metal shower stall in the corner. This wall had been contrived by ingeniously stacking orange crates so that the open ends alternated in and out of the room. After being reinforced with the gyprock and chickenwire, the whole thing was plastered over. The end effect was a stack of alcoves for stashing knick-knacks, books and decorative lighting. At one end of the room was a faux fireplace, constructed of stacked-up bricks that had been liberated from a construction site and in it, depending on the season, was either one of those decorative fireplace units with the fake logs, the lightbulb and the rotating aluminum foil that provided the crackling fire sound effect or, if it was winter, we put in a badly needed space heater. The room was finished off with the usual stacked fleur-de-lis bricks and boards for bookshelves and a small work table. All in all, the effect was quite cosy, though there wasn't a whole lot of room left over for us!

The kitchen was a wooden add-on to the house and was uninsulated. It had a gas stove, a table and chairs and a door leading out to the tiny backyard. This room was barely habitable in winter unless the stove was on and you were cooking. The little yard had high wooden fences on both sides and at the end was the wall of a building made of grey concrete blocks. Nothing grew in it because it never got any sun.

We settled in for a continuing life of genteel poverty, supplemented by the good graces of our friends Noni and Myron, who were still taking it upon themselves to make sure we didn't starve.

I'd been readily accepted by Patty's mother, a very eccentric lady named Scottie-Belle Robertson. She'd been a teenaged beauty queen in her hometown of Silicauga, Alabama. It was a standing joke that the translation from the Cherokee word Silicauga was literally "place where the buzzards roost." She'd been married more than once. Her second husband, Patty's father, was named Herman Maurice Sockwell, but legend had it that the name had been Anglicized from the original French, de Sackville. Scottie-Belle thus made the connection in Patty's lineage straight to Vita Sackville-West. Her first marriage had been annulled after her new husband had taken another man along on the honeymoon. Her last marriage, though, had been to a man named Brad Crandall, who after divorcing Scottie-Belle, had gone on to become very wealthy as the "Voice of Chrysler" and a well-known broadcaster in the U.S. His alimony payments went a long way to making Scottie-Belle's life more comfortable.

It was a showbiz family, as I might have mentioned. Brad and Scottie had been run out of the south by the KKK for being a little too pro–civil rights in the fifties, so Patty and her brother Michael had literally grown up in various beat-up station wagons as their radio-gypsy parents went from town to town—wherever there was work. Scottie had introduced the kids to showbiz early, and Patty had been in kids' TV shows that her mother had cobbled together. They used to identify with that old song Judy Garland sang, the one that went: "I was born in a stage trunk of the (something or other) theatre in Pocatella, Idaho." Finally, they all wound up in Canada, where Scottie produced and Brad was the on-air host of a radio program which I think was called *Tempo Toronto*.

Scottie-Belle, with her refined Southern accent and her bright-orange-dyed hair, was now in the business, along with her live-in partner Lester Stanford, of organizing prizes from sponsors for a variety of game shows, as well as producing television. She was as eccentric as the day was long, so I was no shock to her. It was no secret that she much preferred artistic flamboyance to conservatism. In addition, as she was living in a common-law situation, she was hardly going to comment on her daughter's co-habitation with a scruffy folk singer.

She even helped us out financially—not by direct donation, but by hiring us for wages to paint the interior of the house she'd bought for the production offices of her company over on Birch Avenue. We busted our humps doing that job. Scottie also provided us with a car for a short while. It was a wonderful old English Morris Oxford station wagon with real leather seats and those little turn signals that come up out of the door pillars. We practically wore the thing out roaring off to New York and Ottawa before it fell apart. Later on, during one of our in-between periods, she even put us up in her big house up on Foxbar Road. She was very supportive and unlike any other mother I had ever met.

I was getting sporadic gigs—enough to keep things together and liberate Patty from any further need to do the modelling jobs at Central—but there would still be periods of desperate wanting in among the barely enoughs. I was getting very eccentric looking. I'd taken to stitching together weird additions to my clothing, like side-button jeans and canvas bell bottoms that completely covered the feet of my boots. I had two favourite outer garments—an old Mountie-issue buffalo-skin coat that had long before lost its sleeves and looked like a great shaggy brown ankle-length vest, and for warmer days, a green fake-plastic ankle-length python-skin woman's coat. Patty was beginning to look like she'd been dressed by a theatrical costumer on a three-day bender.

Curiously enough, however, even if things were desperate, we were happy at that point. It was a life free of expectations, so anything that came along that was good tasted twice as sweet. Our social sphere had expanded with my acceptance into the circle of the Mariposa Festival crowd, and I was going over to Yorkville pretty much every day, then hanging out in the gabfests at the back door of the Riverboat at night. There were always a bunch of people I knew, and on a summer evening, when the club became too hot, the door was opened so you could hear the music coming from the inside.

Bernie Fiedler, for all his interest in commerce, adhered to the unspoken policy that you didn't charge working performers admission to get into the club. We tended not to abuse that kindness by occupying a seat that might otherwise be filled by a paying customer, but if there was a spare seat in a booth, we'd sit in the club and catch the set, paying only for our drinks. One time, Patty and I sat for most of a night and watched Phil Ochs play everything from "Pleasures of the Harbour" to "I Ain't Marching Anymore" when I doubt we could have coughed up the cover charge if our lives had depended on it.

That summer of 1967, my brother Calvin came through for me again and co-signed a bank loan for the princely sum of five hundred dollars. I must have been a wild-eyed optimist to think I wouldn't default and leave him holding the bag, but luck was with me and I eventually paid it off. The money was for a motorcycle. I thought it would be the neatest thing in the world to drive around on a bike. There were plenty of them in Yorkville by that point—beautiful Triumph Bonnevilles, BSAs and the inevitable Harleys. I liked the British bikes and was determined to get a Triumph. The nearest I could come to my dream of a 650cc Bonneville, though, was a 500cc flat-head Triumph army bike that they were selling from surplus through Sun-Glo cycle down on Queen Street. It was still in its army drab paint with the big pannier racks on each side of the rear wheel.

I went down to the shop with a learner's permit and some money and drove the thing home with no lessons, no helmet and no insurance. What the hell, there weren't any helmet laws then, insurance wasn't required by law and cost more than the bike was worth, and the machine already had a licence plate on it. The guy in the store didn't give a shit if I drove out the front door and killed myself. I had a lifetime acquaintance with clutches and gears, and I'd a ridden a bicycle all my life. What was to know?

I learned the ropes by riding when there was very little traffic. Those were my normal hours, because I slept most of the day and stayed up all night anyway. Gradually, I got confident, and that gutless old motorcycle became my freedom machine. I just loved it. It cost nothing to fill the tank, and it ran all day at a steady sixty miles an hour, so I'd jump on and disappear for days at a time and decide where I was going when I was on the way. I even adapted it so there was a guitar rack custom-sized to fit Nick Hapanovitch's handmade case on one side, and I'd ride off to gigs on it.

That summer, Patty and I got the idea from somewhere to go down to Tillson-burg. Somebody'd told us you could make a fair bit of money in a short while priming tobacco. All you had to do was show up willing to work. We didn't have any idea what priming tobacco entailed, but I figured it couldn't be worse than stacking lumber in a sawmill.

We went to a farm that was hiring—a prosperous-looking place—and immediately found out that for starters, we'd live in segregated barracks while we were working there. After all, we were unmarried! Actually, they didn't even have any facilities for people who were. The next thing we found out was that priming meant walking the rows all day, bent over at the waist, yanking sucker leafs from the bases of the plants. They said it was easier if you stayed down rather than straightening up. I figured that after a week of this, we'd both be spending the rest of our lives in a wheelchair, so we got back on the motorcycle and came home.

Not long after our return, the Monday night open-sings at the Riverboat bore fruit. I was invited to play at the Mariposa Folk Festival, which was being held up at Innes Lake. The citizens of Orillia had kicked the festival out of Stephen Leacock country because they were frightened of drunken college students, subversion, sex and the ever-present danger that someone somewhere might be having a good time. I was only going to play a songwriters' workshop, not the mainstage, but it was a great opportunity, and it meant a lot to me just to get on the program at all.

I'd been working very hard on my songwriting and finally felt I was getting somewhere. One long night, I'd sat down in our little room and written "Child's Song" while feeling down after one of the infrequent and bittersweet visits to my parents' house. As soon as I finished that song, I recognized that for the first time, I'd really got it right. Through the Mariposa scene, I had also made the acquaintance of the members of a band called Three's a Crowd. At that time Trevor Veitch, Brent Titcomb and Donna Warner were a trio, but they would soon grow, with the addition of the very soulful, chronically troubled David Wiffen. I was beginning to make a small reputation for having some interesting tunes, and the band was looking for material for a new album they were working on. They were moving into a larger layered sound—more like the Mamas & the Papas and more pop than folk. I went around and played some stuff for them, and they decided to record one of my songs. I'd named it "More Than a While," but they changed the name on the record to "Coat of Colours" because that line was repeated most often in the song. I wasn't about to argue. I was as grateful as I could be that anybody anywhere would even consider singing one of my songs, never mind recording one. In the next couple of years, I spent an awful lot of time hanging out over at Brent's house near the village or at Trevor's apartment on Avenue Road.

There was another great gal who'd joined our ever-growing circle of friends. She was a regular entertainer at the Mousehole coffeehouse, the place down the other end of Yorkville from the Riverboat. It was a sister club, actually, because its owner-operator was now married to Bernie Fiedler. Anyway, Vicky Taylor was a high-energy whipped-cream-and-leopard-skin-bikini sort of gal. She'd learned the invented languages from John Lennon's book *In His Own Write* and had a near-manic love for Spike Jones records. She was fun loving and generously non-judgemental when it came to her friends.

Some of the most fun nights we had were just hanging out with her and a couple of other people and laughing our asses off. Mind you, it's hard not to when you've just smoked a little boo and you're listening to Spike play "You Always Hurt the One You Love." Yes, Virginia, we had discovered the joys of occasional recreational drug use by this time.

Vicky took up with a friend of ours on one occasion, and it had been rather a long time since she'd "done it." Shortly after things had begun in earnest, she and her beau panicked at the sight of great gouts of fresh blood, and they rushed her off to the hospital, thinking she'd had a haemorrhage of some kind. After she'd been in emergency for a while, the resident emerged shaking his head and looking at her male friend with some amazement. During her long hiatus, Vicky had grown a second maidenhead, and the doctor had never heard of this happening before. When he checked the books, he found it was rare but did occur. Vicky was elevated to the honoured position of being the only lady we knew, or knew of, who had been deflowered twice in a lifetime!

My range was expanding with each new opportunity, and I was now working a number of out-of-town clubs—not regularly, but at least my foot was in the door. I was still working the Ebony Knight. I'd added the Black Swan in Stratford, and I'd been hired to play at Café Le Hibou in Ottawa, which was run at that time by a man named Dennis Faulkner. I'd even got as far as Montreal, where I played a club whose name I'm not sure of anymore. Maybe it was the Totem Pole. It was owned and run by two people named Shimon and Niema Ash. Niema is well respected in poetic circles for her role in facilitating a certain contest between Irving Layton and Leonard Cohen having to do with time and distance evaluation.

Most everyone who had ever played at their folk club had stayed in their apartment, and their kitchen wall was a solid mass of some of the most prestigious graffiti you could imagine. It read like a virtual who's who of the world of folk. There was Dave Van Ronk, Patrick Sky, Sonny and Brownie, Bruce Murdoch and, of course, there was Dylan. Bob had played the club, but Shimon hated his music. He couldn't stand the way the guy sang, so he said. I can't remember for sure, but I seem to remember Shimon saying he'd terminated the engagement prematurely.

Niema was a tiny woman with masses of curly hair reaching way down past her waist. She looked like an exotic gypsy and had an old-soul sensuous warmth to her. After the first night in that apartment under her tender care, I was good for very little but scratching my ear with my leg.

Niema wanders around the world now. She put out a book a while ago called *Flight of the Wind Horse*, and she'll just show up somewhere after having spent some time with a Middle Eastern prince or some such person. Some people stick their toe into life and shiver. Niema did a half-gainer, and she's still swimming!

At the end of that summer of 1967, the idea of marriage came up. Given the fact that I seemed to be willing to hop in the sack without a shred of guilt with whomsoever seemed reasonably attractive and willing, I'm surprised I was the one who broached the subject. I sure can't have been sitting around one day thinking, "Hey, I'm a responsible guy, steady, reliable, faithful, good income. I'll make some lucky gal a wonderful husband!"

Interestingly enough, I'd had absolutely no instruction whatsoever on the subjects of sex, relationships, ethics, morality or marriage. Everything I'd figured out so far was as a result of floundering around on my own, plus what I'd picked up from my friends or from reading. There wasn't really any other voice of conscience at work in me to oppose the rapid shifts in popular behaviour that were beginning to occur. With the growing power of the counterculture and the sexual revolution, there was a kind of pressure brought to bear on people. If you weren't out there experiencing everything with everybody, you were off the bus. I was emerging in a milieu that generally applauded the kind of behaviour that came naturally to a moral vacuum like me.

Why did I make a proposal of marriage to Patty? I'm not sure to this day that I could really answer that. I was completely self-absorbed and consumed with my own dreams of making music. I did not have the emotional equipment to understand yet that if you just use people or betray them when they've opened up their defences to you, they can be terribly hurt. I think the dark side of the dreamer in me was an immature and needy man who wanted to ensure that someone was around to look after him. I also thought that Patty was needy and insecure and that an offer of marriage would make her feel happier. Love? I didn't know the meaning of the word!

There's an old saying, "If my aunt had balls, she'd be my uncle," which sums up the worth of trying to second guess the past. All I can say is that it seemed like a good idea at the time, and she said yes. She sure wasn't doing herself a favour when she did.

I rode up to the old homestead on the weekend to break the news. When I got there, my mother was out somewhere. I took my father off to the living room where we could talk quietly. We sat down uncomfortably. It was always a crap-shoot as to how one of our talks was going to go. I'm sure he wasn't looking forward to being bummed out or angry for the weekend on account of me.

"Dad, I'm going to get married," I said.

"Why, because you have to?" he replied, without missing a beat.

"No, not because I have to," I said reproachfully, then asked quietly, "Jesus Christ, can't you for once have something good to say?"

With that came the second bout of tears I'd ever seen from him and the revelation of a family secret.

Over the years, I'd always wondered why there seemed to be so much friction between my father and my oldest brother Ian. I could remember one particular New Year's Eve when Dad had had a few too many cocktails. I'd witnessed him stabbing Ian in the chest with his index finger and saying for all the world to hear, "You've always been a bum! You're always going to be a bum!"

"I married your mother because I had to," he said simply. "I've never regret-ted it, and it doesn't mean I loved you all any the less," he added.

Well, there it was. Another piece of the jigsaw puzzle fell into place. I could see in his eyes all the alternatives in his mind that life might have offered had he not felt compelled to adopt the path marked "The right thing to do."

I was only nineteen and filled with attitude. It was so easy for me to be judge-mental and self-righteous. I never said anything to him, but from that point on, I hardened in my mind an image of him as a role model for what not to do with my life.

When my mother learned of the plan, she professed to be happy for me, even if she wasn't. I know she had her reservations about Patty, but being the kind of person she was, she respected my decision and left the matter alone.

So Louise Patricia Joelle Hunt Sockwell and I went off to get a marriage licence, and on November 6, 1967, at the age of nineteen, as the first hints of winter began to make themselves felt in Ontario, we were married by a justice of the peace in a civil ceremony at Old City Hall in Toronto. The ceremony was attended by Patty's mother Scottie-Belle Robertson, my mother Margaret McLauchlan, and two of our friends. Conspicuously absent were any senior male representatives of either family.

❦

Yorkville

❧ WE WORKED OUR WAY UP TO a cozy little Christmas in 1967. As a matter of fact, a writer named Melinda McCracken did a feature piece on me in the *Toronto Star* that went on at great length about how Patty had transformed our little flat with lights and tinsel all over the place. Melinda lived with a former Montreal club owner and general rounder named Gary Eisencraft over in a communal house just north of Yorkville on Hazelton Avenue. One of the house's most illustrious occupants was Moses, the secretary-treasurer of the Vagabonds motorcycle club. They called him Moses because he was the first guy in the club who had really long hair and a beard.

Billy Fulghum had come to realize that he wasn't cut out for the job of artist's manager. He was a laid-back guy who had an easygoing gentility about him, and the kind of hustling involved in the job just wasn't in his nature. He was smart enough to realize he couldn't really do anything for me and had the good grace to bow out with no strings attached.

Onto the stage stepped Nick's mother, Hope. Hope Garber (whose son Victor most recently appeared in the movie *Titanic* as the ill-fated ship designer) was cut from much stiffer cloth than Billy. One of the first tasks she set for herself was to clean me up a little. It was a major struggle. She got me as far as tweed jackets, turtleneck sweaters and cords before I rebelled. You can see the results in my first professional publicity shot, taken in the backyard at 48 Hayden. I look completely miserable!

It turned out that most of the legwork was going to be done by Nick. I don't think he was happy about working for his mother or with me, though he tried not to let it show. He had his own dreams, and I think he felt he was in danger of settling for something else.

In the summer of 1968, I was invited to play Mariposa up at Innes Lake again. This time I was going to be on the mainstage, Saturday night concert bill, and all because of hanging out at the Riverboat.

I'd been introduced by B.C. Fiedler to Tom Rush. He's a very accessible guy, warm and friendly and as unpretentious as they come. Tom had been a big star on the folk circuit for a few years since his first efforts on Elektra records. His work had always tended to the bluesy and hard driving, interspersed with tender ballads that brought the girls around. "Galveston Flood" and "Statesborough Blues" were two of Tom's songs that really stuck with me. That was my kind of music!

Tom was becoming equally well known for discovering writers and being the first to record their work. He was already doing Joni's "Circle Game" and "Urge for Going" as beautifully as she had. Tom could take a tune that some might consider soft or "a girl's song" and be perfectly comfortable and natural singing it. It was an unusual quality at the time. He was the first person to discover Joni, James Taylor and Jackson Brown. He also discovered me!

Tom had changed labels and was now going to be recording for Columbia records, so he was looking for songs to put on the new disc. He asked me if I had any tunes I thought might be good for him. As nervous as any fledgling actor at the audition of a lifetime, I sang him "Child's Song" and "Old Man's Song," right there in the little back dressing room of the Riverboat. I just about had a heart attack a few days later when I found out he was going to cut both songs.

Tom is a very intelligent man. Legend has it that he has a degree in economics or business from Harvard. That could also be bullshit, but if you want to find out for yourself, he's living in Wyoming. In any event, Tom has done well by doing good, and early on realized that if you find young writers who need a leg up, they're generally willing to part with the publishing rights to their songs to get a good cut. I signed over the rights to both of the songs he was going to record, as part of the deal. If you're expecting me to say I regret that, I don't. Tom's recording was one of the most crucial breaks I had in my long career, and because of his reputation, the way I was regarded by people in the music scene changed completely.

So off I rode up to Innes Lake again on the back of my battle-drab Triumph motorcycle with the guitar strapped onto the side. Not only had I managed to work my way up to the mainstage, but lending my art school training to the cause, I'd designed the posters, brochures and cover program for the festival. I liked being involved. There was a sense of community that pervaded the festival in those days.

That Saturday night was a folk-blues fan's dream. I was sharing the stage with Bill Monroe, the daddy of bluegrass music, as well as blues legends Howlin' Wolf and Bukka White. "The Wolf" was particularly impressive because he was right out of the south side of Chicago and there was nothing tame or refined about the man. He just motored around in those size-fourteen triple-E high-top black running shoes and scared the hell out of anything that even *looked* white or liberal!

Joni Mitchell was back for her fourth year, but now there was a difference. She'd finally released the first album of her songs on Warner Reprise, and she'd hooked up with Elliott Roberts as her manager. Curiously, the album didn't have "Circle Game" on it, which was her best-loved song at the time, but it was a beautiful piece of work and she was really on her way.

Joni and I hosted the New Songwriters' Concert on the Sunday of that August weekend. A couple of pretty interesting people made an appearance. One was a twenty-eight-year-old man named Bill Hawkins, an evil-eyed sardonic poet from Ottawa. He'd shifted over to writing songs and had also been recorded by Three's a Crowd. His "Gnostic Serenade" remains one of the finest songs ever written. Bill was at Mariposa conducting the first poetry workshop ever held there. Legend had it that he'd taken his Canada Council poetry grant and gone off to Mexico with the money to occupy himself in the import-export business. He was deeply involved in all kinds of mysticism and had quite the little scene surrounding him in Ottawa.

One of the key players emerging from Bill's scene was a young man who'd played in Bill's rock 'n' roll band, The Heavenly Blue. He was taking part in the concert, and his name was Bruce Cockburn. Three's a Crowd had also done Bruce's beautiful song "Bird without Wings." All in all, it was a pretty stellar group if you were into singer-songwriters.

After that Mariposa, I felt like I was finally getting somewhere. I was hanging out with people who were starting to happen, and I was gaining some real legitimacy as a songwriter.

That summer of 1968 a lot of rapid change was coming to pass. Yes, the Riverboat line-up for that summer and fall looked like a who's who—Joni Mitchell, Eric Andersen, Richie Havens, Tom Rush, Tim Buckley, Doc Watson, John Lee Hooker—but there was a new kid on the block as well.

The quiet days of intellectual folk music were over. The "Summer of Love" had happened. There were hippies all over the place, in every nook and cranny, above every store. The kids were starting to come down from the suburbs in huge numbers, and carloads of gawkers were beginning to jam the streets at night. Rock 'n' roll had made its arrival. Clubs like Boris's and the El Patio were pumping out the volume. Several bands had emerged from the Yorkville scene. Two of the biggest of the bunch were the Paupers and the Kensington Market, and at the centre of these bands, driving the enterprise along, was Bernie Finkelstein.

Bernie had grown up as an Air Force gypsy. His dad was a quartermaster sergeant in the RCAF and had been stationed all over the place, from Downsview to Trenton to Germany. Bernie had acquired all the requisite skills, including, but not limited to, an uncanny knack with a pool cue and a natural savvy when it came to any kind of deal making. Along the line, he'd been gobsmacked by Dylan's poetry and attitude as much as I had and he'd become firmly committed to the counterculture.

Finkelstein had been drawn down to Yorkville by the intensifying energy of the scene and quickly found himself a make-ends-meet position as a dishwasher at the El Patio. He'd worked at Honest Ed's and gone from there to managing the Poor Alex Theatre, which really meant taking the tickets and sweeping the floor. Bernie was well versed in the intricacies of show business.

He emerged from the kitchen of the El Patio one night and announced to the band who happened to be playing that what they needed was a manager. The guys in the band apparently figured he was right.

Bernie quickly achieved almost legendary status around the scene for selling the Paupers to Albert Grossman, the manager of Dylan, Peter Paul & Mary and Janis Joplin. Bernie actually had a partnership with Albert, I believe. How he ever managed to keep the Paupers together, given the mercurial personalities of Adam Mitchell and Denny Gerrard, was beyond most people. A short time after the deal went down, the band blew up. Bernie came away with some cash and Albert wound up with not very much. It looked from the outside as if Bernie had run a number on the heaviest manager walking the planet at the time. So Bernie was generally regarded as an emerging mensch.

Bernie had a new band now, and they were the most musically challenging out-of-control dynamic collection of psychedelic cowboys the yard had yet produced. The name of the band was Kensington Market. The band's first album, *Avenue Road*, had broken a lot of new ground. It had about it a sense of being from right here, rather than from England or someplace else. The group had already played in the U.S. and was beginning to attract the attention of the major labels, who were hungry to sign every promising psychedelic rock band they could get their hands on. They'd also attracted the attention of Felix Pappalardi, a major New York producer, who with Leslie West would found the group Mountain. Felix was lined up to produce the band's second album. In the meantime, they'd been praised by Bill Graham and booked to play both Fillmore auditoriums. Kensington Market were the young princes of Yorkville!

But there was another guy around who thought of himself as royalty. He was known as Brazilian George. He and a skilled chemist named Ian had formed a partnership for the production and marketing of a next-generation quasi-psychedelic substance called MDA. It should be noted that MDA was not a controlled substance, so whatever you did with it was perfectly legal at the time. There is a certain fudging with reality inherent in that statement, though. The fact was that the FDA in the States and its equivalent in Canada couldn't move fast enough to add each new hallucinogenic drug to its list. There were new ones constantly emerging. While they'd been working on LSD, this new drug had slipped through the cracks. MDA was love in a bizarro world. It created a cruel parody of love, a passionate, desperate, "love on methamphetamine" sort of love, which spread its dark wings and enveloped you. But when the ride was over, your heart was a train wreck. The "love drug" was the drug of choice for Kensington Market.

The Upper Crust Café on the northwest corner at the intersection of Hazelton Avenue was the heart of the Yorkville social scene in 1968. Finkelstein used the pay phone inside the front door to conduct his business. He contacted everything and everyone from the café, with accounts payable in one back pocket and accounts receivable in the other. People would spend part of the day just hanging out at the sidewalk café. Sooner or later, anyone you wanted to find would come by. Kensington Market held court there, and you'd usually see Luke Gibson and Keith McKie killing time. Luke had been the leader of a high-energy soul band called Luke and the Apostles and had more experience than Keith at being adored by the usual group of curious girls. Alex Daroux, the bass player, was almost always there drinking endless cups of coffee and having long rambling conversations about the intricacies of existence. At thirty, he was practically an old man, and everyone listened to his wisdom on all matters. Gene Martynec, one of the greatest unsung guitar players of all time, had developed a high level of disdain for all the drug bullshit that was going on around the band and the craziness it was generating. He was there anyway. Gene was completely into music, particularly electronic music. He was learning a lot from John Mills-Cockell, who would contribute a great deal to the Market's second album with his mastery of the new sound synthesizer developed by Professor Moog. John had studied with Moog himself and was respected as the resident expert. He would soon found the band Sirynx, which would have a hit record with the theme music for a show called *Here Come the Seventies*. Gene went on to produce all the early Bruce Cockburn albums and also produced a number of mine. He was a charter member of my band, The Silver Tractors.

I'd started riding over to the Upper Crust on my motorcycle and parking it beside the fence. I had a pair of goggles that I'd perch up on a peaked cap, adding to my usual scruffy outfit. I already knew Moses from the Vagabonds because I'd been up to the house at 127 Hazelton where he lived. He and other members of the club might be sitting there. My old Triumph made a pretty sorry sight sitting next to Moses' shiny chopped Bonneville—he later got a Harley Sportster, of which he was justifiably proud—but Moses would acknowledge me anyway.

Later on, I found out that Luke Gibson used to see me coming on the bike and say, "Here comes that asshole who thinks he's Donovan!"

In contrast to the benign social scene of the Upper Crust was Webster's restaurant up on Avenue Road near Davenport. Webster's was an all-night greasy spoon that served as the brokerage depot for scoring drugs of all kinds. There were some fairly unsavoury people mixed in with the fast-fading flower children.

At this point, I wasn't really a druggie and I didn't drink much. Looking the way I looked—long-haired, weird and skinny—was reason enough not to go into bars, and I really didn't have the money. I'd smoked a little grass but I didn't like the taste much and found it just made me stupid. I'd eaten some hashish one night and spent the greater part of the next day huddled in the bathroom peering out from a little opening in a blanket. I'd taken LSD once.

While I was still living with Patty in the flat on Brunswick, Billy Fulghum came over with two hits of blotter acid. There wasn't a lot of the stuff around yet, and he was curious about what it would be like, but he didn't want to make the journey alone. We did it together, and it was the classic goofy trip.

We dropped and then sat there waiting for something to happen. Nothing happened right away, and we both just kind of sat there feeling that maybe he'd got ripped off but not saying it. I was idly looking out the glass door at the treetops that surrounded the deck. The day was windy and they were blowing around quite a bit, waving rhythmically with the gusts. I was drawn into the hypnotic movement, and it began to appear as though they were pressing against the glass of the door. They ceased to look like trees and became formless green amoebas with the jelly middles moving in sync with the wind. I looked over at Billy and realized he was seeing exactly the same thing.

"We didn't get the screens up any too early this year, did we," I said. And that was it! We laughed our asses off for about the next six hours.

I'd had a nice time but failed to understand what all the fuss was about. I was having a lot of trouble swallowing what I saw to be the huge amount of bullshit that surrounded the psychedelic movement. Intellectually, I thought there was a big difference between getting high and having a religious experience. For everything that was being said about acid changing your mind, all I was seeing was people staring at a soap bubble for twelve hours and going "Wow." I thought most of the people who were into it were just goofs. The stuff that was coming along in its wake, though, was much more dangerous.

What had started out as the sleepy pleasant little artistic enclave of my art school years had begun to blossom into something resembling Fort Lauderdale during March break. The press was turning a hard eye on the corruption of youth and the evils of the drug scene while endless cars with six guys hanging out the window cruised down the street at night, trying to get some of that free love everybody was talking about.

There was a permanent clinic on site for the continual stream of transient kids who were finding ways to bleach their brains. They were easy targets for the darker characters who were infecting the atmosphere.

On the music scene, there was a lot of ferment and transition. Neil Young had left his band the Mynah Birds and gone to L.A., where he'd form the Buffalo Springfield, granddaddy band of the California country sound that later evolved into the Eagles. His former bandmate Rick James was headed for an equally successful but more controversial career in funk/soul. Some of the top-line bands of just a few years earlier—what we called the "suit bands"—were quickly left behind by the emerging wave. It wasn't so long ago that four or five guys in matching sharkskin blue suits had been the norm, but now the look was long-haired and funky. Bands like David Clayton-Thomas and the Sheas had been the toast of the town, but now I'd walk by and see David sitting playing his acoustic guitar and nursing a bottle on the steps of the church near Webster's. He was playing incredible free concerts to a small knot of stoned-out freaks who didn't know he'd soon be riding around New York in a black limousine as the lead singer for Blood, Sweat and Tears.

On the strength of my growing number of cover recordings, Hope and Nick, acting on the encouragement of Elliott Roberts, decided to try getting a record deal for me in L.A. There was no CRTC back then, no content regulations and no level of support in Canada for homegrown music. You could walk into a top-forty radio station with a Canadian record and it didn't matter how good it was, they'd file it in the garbage. All the Canadian artists who'd made an impact had done so by going to the U.S. I was beginning to bump my head on the ceiling in Canada. Yes, I'd made it to a major festival and had a string of mid- to top-line clubs I could play, but that wouldn't translate into getting a record out and actually making some money. Poverty was a chronic problem—there'd be a modest amount of money, then a long desperate period of drought. I also knew very well that if things weren't perceived to be going someplace in this game, they were immediately perceived as going no place.

There was some interest at A&M, a new label started up by Herb Alpert of Tijuana Brass fame, and they agreed to fly us down for a look-see.

While Nick was trying to drum up interest in the Artist and Repertoire (A&R) department, I was placed in the custody of a really nice guy named Michael Vosse. It was his task to squire me around and show me the sights. Pretty much the first thing he did was stick a joint in my mouth, and we started driving around Hollywood. It turned out that he knew Joni, who'd recently moved down there permanently and bought herself a house in Laurel Canyon. She'd immersed herself in the psychedelic scene, got to work with Crosby on the *Song to a Seagull* album and realized that L.A. had replaced New York as the centre of the musical universe. It turned out that Michael was sort of babysitting Joni's house while she was out of town, so we drove up there to make sure it was still standing. It was a beautiful little place, sunlit and full of colourful artifacts she'd collected along the way. The living room was dominated by one of those huge votive candle holders you find in a Catholic church in front of a shrine or a statue of a saint. A high brass pedestal with a large ring-shaped top and a series of shelves held maybe sixty candles in little coloured glass jars. All I wanted to do was move in and never go back home.

I was supposed to do a guest set at the Troubador Coffee House that night. The idea was that I'd impress the record folks with my cutting-edge talent. We went over to the club in the early evening and stood outside for a while in the

153

warm fragrant air of Hollywood. It turned out I wouldn't get on stage for my little party piece until around one in the morning, which being still on Toronto time, meant more like 3:00 a.m. to me. It looked like we had some time to kill.

I strolled down the street a little ways and stopped in front of a storefront window where unusual clothes were displayed. There were rainbow-patched and embroidered pants, jackets, vests and shirts, but they weren't cheap or faux-psychedelic tourist artifacts; they were exquisite.

An extremely attractive young lady emerged from the store and said hi. She invited me in to look around and we got to talking. It turned out her name was Jeanie, better known in rock 'n' roll circles as "Jeanie the Tailor," because all the biggies in the rock game were coming to her for stage wear. She custom-made stuff for just about anybody you could think of who was big at the time, from Joplin to Hendrix. I told her what I was doing in town, and we got to talking. She was as nice and kind to me as if I'd been Jimi Hendrix instead of some bumpkin from Toronto. She gave me all kinds of encouragement and never mentioned that guys like me in this town were a dime a dozen. I passed a few happy hours just yakking with her, and then it was time to go over to the club.

It had been a long day and I was beat. There'd probably been one too many joints. The club had emptied out to the point where there was virtually no one left. Still, I was overawed to be there. I got up and sang without conviction or confidence to an empty place, and frankly, I wasn't very good.

The record label thought pure singer-songwriters were passé and weren't really that keen on anything but bands. My case hadn't been helped by my performance at the Troubador. There wasn't anybody from the company there by the end of my set. I went back to Toronto with my tail between my legs.

The Commune

PATTY DECIDED THAT SHE WASN'T going to pass up her chance for a white wedding after all. The trouble was that she came from a whole line of agnostics and atheists, and I wasn't exactly Mr. Religion. She fixed on the idea of having an affirmation ceremony that we'd write and produce ourselves. It would have no official or religious status whatsoever but would be an opportunity for the blowout we'd missed with the simple civil ceremony.

Patty's mother got into the act, and before too long, they'd chosen a date and a location, printed and sent the invitations and even gone so far as to register the faux-bride with the appropriate retail outlets.

I have no idea what transpired between my mother and father. I can only assume it was a titanic battle of wills. In the end, she prevailed, and my dad finally agreed to come.

The do was held in the Heliconian Club, a charming little board-and-batten church-like structure on Hazelton Avenue just north of Yorkville. I'd had a russet velvet Victorian jacket made, which I wore with a white shirt sporting a ruffled collar and cuffs. The outfit was completed with black bell-bottom pants, cowboy boots and a Wedgwood cameo brooch pinned at my throat. Patty wore an ornate wedding dress, complete with veil.

The ceremony was read by our friend Myron Cooper, who was taking full advantage of his resemblance to Pharaoh Ramses by dressing the part. The reading was about what you'd expect, given the times—a mix of pop philosophy liberally mixed with the writings of Kahlil Gibran.

The afternoon went astonishingly well. There was enough wine and champagne to oil the social slidings. My rather conservative family members seemed to get along with our friends and with Patty's decidedly un-conservative mother, and victory was won on several fronts.

My mother had convinced my father to publicly recognize my existence and swallow his embarrassment about what I was doing with my life. Scottie had produced another successful theatrical event. Patty had gotten her white wedding, and nobody had begun a conversation with the opener, "The trouble with *you* is . . ."

Yorkville was a crossroads. As soon as you knew somebody, sooner or later you'd meet everybody. Because of Melinda McCracken writing about me and Gary Eisencraft being around the club scene and the Upper Crust, and because of repeatedly running into Moses at the Village, Patty and I had been going over to 127 Hazelton, where they all lived, and we'd met the rest of the occupants of the house. There was Frank Perold, a bearded commercial artist, and his companion Karla Dickie, who was quite a talented painter. Moses lived there with his ladyfriend Polleen, a well-built freckled redhead with infectious good humour. There were Gary and Melinda and a couple of other ladies who came and went. They were a likeable bunch and even though the sparks flew, they seemed to make living together work. There were well understood rules about food and fridge and bathroom that ensured no one would step dangerously on anyone else's toes.

Through the folks in that house, I met a guy named Gord Jones, who introduced us to Joyce and Ian Hamilton. Ian was in advertising, and Joyce was a commercial artist. They had the ground floor of a nice house up on St. Clair Avenue. Their friends were all great music fans, and they'd developed the habit of having "house parties"—a sort of informal salon where someone would be invited over on the understanding that they'd sing for their supper. Tom McDonnell, one of their friends, was quite a good amateur guitar player and loved learning new songs.

Jones got us over there one evening to hang out. I played a few tunes, and that was the start of a regular thing. Joyce and Ian were incredibly generous people. I'm sure one look at the way we dressed and how much I weighed spoke volumes to them about our life. We'd go over there and swap songs and jam, then wind up having a great big spaghetti dinner with wine, bread and candles. They sort of adopted us, and we often had reason to be very grateful for their generosity.

I was now tolerated and even more or less accepted by the members of Kensington Market. I often found myself becoming involved in long conversations with Alex Daroux at the Upper Crust. I got to know Bernie Finkelstein, which was good because somewhere along the line, I'd targeted him as the person I wanted to be my manager. I took to following Bernie down Avenue Road saying things like "Let's work together, man! I'll make you a million bucks!" But Bernie had other fish to fry at the time.

As I was drawn more and more into Kensington Market's scene, I also got to know Brazilian George. George had a kind of princely arrogance. He disliked the street beggars who were constantly looking for spare change. They'd become a regular sight around Yorkville. When they asked George for money, he'd take whatever he had out of his pocket and throw it at them. Sometimes that was several thousand dollars. It was his way of saying that you were a piece of shit and that money meant nothing at all to him.

George was tough! He could kick-box and had demonstrated ample ability to take care of himself on many occasions. Everybody admired him, the same way we were drawn to the outlaw bikers. It was the prevailing myth that they were romantic figures giving the system the bird. And we saw them as being on our side. George was very generous with his resources and had a large group of sycophants surrounding him who were willing to do his bidding. He was probably more like Bugsy Seigal than anyone else. He was a free-spending flamboyant character who wasn't above buying loyalty; he saw himself as honourable but was largely amoral and had a temper you did not fuck with. At the time, his resources were for all intents and purposes limitless. He probably had a hundred grand in cash around at any given moment. George was in exactly the right business in a full cash economy.

I started going out to George's house in King City occasionally. Alex Daroux was often there. There were usually musical instruments just lying around to pick up and jam with, and I took the opportunity to wrap my hands around an electric guitar for the first time. There was a Japanese copy of a Gibson Flying Vee that I particularly liked the look of. One day I plugged into this tiny little amplifier, not quite as small as a Pignose but pretty close. I'd been smoking some hash and I was more than a little ripped, so I forgot what I was doing and managed to get the guitar and the amp turned up full at the same time. I was sitting there with one string sustaining away like crazy and every so often flailing on the chord it was part of. My eyes were screwed shut as I just listened to the way all the frequencies of sound were oscillating against each other. When I opened my eyes, Alex was sitting there smiling at me.

He'd been enjoying my little mental voyage of discovery. He didn't laugh at me.

"Yeah, it's alright to play loud!" was all he said.

There were always people hanging out at George's place. Bev, Don Baby, George's brother Tony. They were all great people to be with. They wouldn't screw you around or lie to you. They were living out on the crazy edge and I liked them. I didn't care what they did. Every so often, I'd dip my toe gently into the swimming pool of MDA, and when I did, I loved everybody.

The more I fixed on the idea of getting Bernie Finkelstein to be my manager, the more I felt that Hope Garber had no idea of how to get me where I wanted to go. I finally approached her about the idea of cutting me loose. My account was current and her out-of-pocket expenses were negligible. But Hope had it in her head that this was some kind of a manoeuvre. She thought Elliott Roberts wanted to work with me, which of course was the furthest thing from his mind. She decided to hold onto my contract. She sat on me as I stalled and went dead in the water. She wouldn't work for me and she wouldn't let me go. I didn't even know the phone number of a lawyer. If I had, I couldn't have paid the bill anyway!

Eventually, a compromise was reached and I was able to get out of the deal, but the damage had been done. Like I said, it's a fast-moving world, and if you ain't going someplace, you're going no place.

We moved into the colder months of 1968, and as the temperature dropped outside, it did the same in the little flat that Patty and I shared. Nothing had really changed. I was still getting booked into the same clubs, but so infrequently that we were still chronically short of money.

I'd been keeping myself occupied as winter approached by chopping and repainting my motorcycle in the kitchen. There were bits of the old beast all over the place. Patty, bless her creative little heart, thought it was charming to have a freshly painted deep-blue gas tank on the dining-room table.

One night, after sitting up reading for a while, I climbed up into the loft platform with her, got under the covers shivering and huddled off to sleep. Some little while later, we both stirred half awake and kicked the covers down because we were sweating with the heat. We rolled over in a semi-dream, thinking, "Great, they finally turned up the heat in the building!" and drifted back off into a fitful slumber.

The phone rang. I struggled awake, groggy, and answered it. It was Noni Raitblatt, just calling to see how we were doing. I was short tempered with her, I think. I hung up the phone and rolled over, facing away from the wall. Just as I was closing my eyes, I saw a spark jump. It arced across the floor down where all the books and papers were stacked.

"That's nice—a pretty spark," I thought, as I drifted back to sleep.

"No, no, no, that's not right!" a part of me insisted. "No, no, sparks mean fire, FIRE!"

I snapped awake and saw flames licking at the papers by the bookshelves. I leaped down the ladder and pulled everything away from the wall as I beat out the flames. Patty was now awake but groggy as she peered over the side of the loft.

"Is it out?" she said.

"Yeah, yeah! How the fuck did it get started?" I wondered out loud.

And then I felt the heat in the floor beneath my bare feet and heard an unmistakable roar and crackling right below me. I knew then and there that we had to get out fast. I was scared the floor might give way any second.

Patty scrambled down the ladder, and I went to the hall door to get us something to put on against the sub-zero night. Our winter coats were hanging on a hook on the other side of the door. When I opened it, I realized abruptly what a terrible mistake I'd made. The entrance to the downstairs was just outside our apartment, and the basement was where the fire was. I was hit with a blast of superheated air and smoke that scorched my face and singed my eyebrows. That was it! I slammed the door shut, and we ran out into the yard. Not knowing what else to do if we weren't to stand in the dark and freeze, we climbed the high fence out of the yard and made our way through an alley back to the front of the house on Hayden Street.

There we were, huddled in firemen's blankets in our sleep clothes on a freezing night while the fire department put out the blaze. But I wasn't grateful to be alive. All I could think of was "Shit! My motorcycle!"

Later, when I had time to reflect a bit, I shuddered as I realized how close we'd come to dying. We'd been warm and fuzzy and happy in our little cocoon because we were being asphyxiated by the toxic fumes from the fire. That was why I'd been so slow to react.

I know with absolute certainty that Patty and I and the little girl who would eventually be born to us all owe our lives to Noni Raitblatt. If she hadn't cared, if she hadn't phoned, we wouldn't be here.

The cause of the fire was predictable. There'd been a young man crashing in the basement. Pretty often the smell of grass would drift up from down there. On that night, he'd decided to go out, and he'd left incense burning in his rat's nest of bedding and draperies. The incense fell over and—poof! The sad thing for me was that I lost most of the things I'd liberated from my parents' house—pictures, copies of the magazine my drawings had first appeared in—boyhood stuff. I found my treasured fake-plastic python coat in a melted blob of goo by the front door of our flat next to my charred buffalo skin. But my motorcycle had survived!

We holed up at Patty's mother's house for a while until we could figure out where to go. Things were grim as Christmas approached in 1968. We still had a guitar, a motorcycle and each other, but not much else. We were living off the good graces of Scottie-Belle, and great as she was, that couldn't last. We had to get back on our own again.

As luck would have it, there was a vacancy in the communal house at 127 Hazelton. Patty wasn't keen on the idea at first, but not because she didn't like the inhabitants. It was going into a situation where there was a good deal less privacy that bothered her. She came around okay, though, and we moved into the main-floor front room. Though we didn't have much stuff left, there was even less room for us than we'd had at Hayden Street.

Life didn't get any more financially rewarding than it had been, but it was infinitely more interesting. We settled into the house routine (if you could call the chaos around the place routine) fairly easily. The allotted space in the fridge, the policy of cleaning up after yourself seemed to work out pretty well, and there were several features of the house that I really liked.

The kitchen was the best spot in the whole joint! Moses had installed a juke box, a big old Wurlitzer with the bubbles moving up the red-lit side panels. He was a music fan and was especially fond of blues. That machine was full of everybody named King except for Martin Luther. You'd pump some change into it and pull up Professor Albert singing "Born under a Bad Sign" or B.B.'s "The Thrill Is Gone." There was the requisite Steppenwolf track, "Born to Be Wild," and "Goin' Up the Country" by Canned Heat.

Moses was over six feet tall, with the aforementioned shoulder-length shaggy mane of hair and long reddish-brown beard; horn-rimmed glasses that made him look like one of the Hanson brothers in *Slapshot*; and old jeans and work boots that would come in the morning all by themselves if he just whistled! Moses also had his own vocabulary based around the word "lunch." It started out with the term "out to lunch," which referred to a person who did not grasp the intricacies of a given situation. From this came "lunchbag and lunchpail," which were derogatory terms for someone who was a complete idiot or beneath contempt due to double dealing or lying. Then there was the verb "lunch" in all its tenses, to indicate the destruction of some object or person, as in: "He totally lunched his scooter!" It could also be a description of extreme intoxication, as in: "He was totally lunched!"

All in all, Moses could be relied on for a colourful turn of phrase to suit any situation. I remember particularly well the occasion when at the "Peace Train" festival concert in Toronto at Varsity Stadium, Patty and I were up in the stands watching the show. We'd seen Gene Vincent, Alice Cooper (who was just getting started) and The Band. Now it was John Lennon on the stage with the new band Elephant's Memory. Yoko was there performing, and most people were still pissed off at her for breaking up the Beatles, so they weren't that pleased to see her in the first place. She began one of those performance art things she did at the time, where she crawled into a bag on the stage with a microphone, curled up in the foetal position and emitted a series of high-pitched nasal shrieks. She seemed to go on forever. The band was crashing away in the background. Suddenly, over the excruciating din of Yoko's art, came a voice from the crowd that rang out clear as a bell.

"Get that douchebag off the stage before I lose my fucking mind!"

It was the unmistakable voice of Moses.

I liked Moses a lot. He had an infectious good humour, at least most of the time. I do remember him coming down with a severe case of haemorrhoids. There is nothing more forlorn than a biker with this condition. Not only was riding out of the question, but he had to endure the indignity of sitting on a donut cushion to eat his hamburgers. I think all Moses ever ate was hamburgers and Coke.

He had tremendously strong opinions about everything and wasn't shy about expressing them. He had a pragmatic and fatalistic acceptance of what life threw at him, which carried over to his relationships with others. Whenever someone had a turn of bad luck, Moses would say, "That's life in the big city!" and shrug his shoulders. What can you do? No sense collapsing in a heap.

I remember the night we were all sitting in the big living room: Melinda, Gary, Karla, Frank, Helen Paulus, Patty, myself, Moses and Polleen. We were watching spellbound on the old black-and-white TV as Neil Armstrong stepped off the ladder and became the first man to walk on the surface of the moon. Moses didn't believe it. He thought they were faking the whole thing.

"This ain't real!" Moses claimed. "They've dummied it up inside a film studio or something!" Moses would not be convinced that the Apollo missions were genuine.

There were a lot of social events around the house and one of the most enjoyable was movie night. At the time, you could rent a projector and movie reels from the public library. Karla or Frank would usually arrange this. People would be invited over, and the show would begin after everyone had ingested their requisite psychedelics. There we'd be, a group of loonies lying about on the floor watching saucer-eyed as Disney's *Fantasia* played on a double-bill with a Mike Hailwood motorcycle-racing film. I no longer bothered with the LSD part of the entertainment, but I loved the movies!

Sometimes we had out-of-town visitors who were more than interesting. I remember dragging Jerry Jeff Walker over there from the Riverboat one night. Everybody thought he was a complete asshole, and they were right. He was drinking heavily at that time and was a major loudmouth. "Mr. Bojangles" had recently been a hit record and he was completely full of himself.

I'd been used to members of the Vagabonds hanging around. For the most part, they were reasonable, relatively normal guys. They weren't about to act up in Moses' place of residence. Anyway, I'd come to think of them as the template for the average biker! And then one weekend, a few members of the Detroit Renegades came over to visit while they were in the area. What they were doing in the area we didn't ask.

They were about the most frightening-looking human beings I'd ever seen, and by this point, I was used to a fair amount of variation in people. They'd pioneered the look of the outlaws in the movie *The Road Warrior* when Mel Gibson was still in knee-pants. We're talking big, battle-scarred, taciturn, mean, tattooed—the whole nine yards. I heaved a sigh of relief when they finally pushed off. For the whole time, I had that feeling you get sitting in a chair with a Rottweiler staring at you. You don't know whether it's going to lick your hand or tear off your arm.

There were occasional excursions over to the Rock Pile, which was the new name attached to the old Masonic temple at the corner of Davenport and Yonge. We all went over there to see the Mothers of Invention, who were heroes around the house, particularly after the classic album *America Drinks and Goes Home/ Brown Shoes Don't Make It*. Frank Zappa—always complex, funny, sarcastic—was brilliant and seemed to derive special pleasure from taking the piss out of the stoned-out acid heads that were all over the place.

127 Hazelton was the only commune I ever lived in. It was completely different in character from the way the press of the time liked to portray this way of living. For Patty and me, the people there became an extended family. We shared in each other's lives. We did things together. We had big fun. Frank and Karla adopted the role of being the responsible parents so the rest of us could act like goofy overgrown kids who had no expectations out of life. The only thing that finally put an end to living there was the need to have a little more personal space. But while it lasted, it was great. There was always somebody up when you came home—always someone to talk to.

Ghost Story

❦ I HAD BEEN OVER AT EASTERN SOUND while Felix Pappalardi was producing the new record for the Kensington Market. The band was now fully in residence on some other plane, and a large damage claim had to be settled with the studio after the project was completed. The sessions were twenty-four hours long, and it was an amazing experience for the brief time I was there. Felix was blown away by what John Mills-Cockell could do with the Moog. It was all high-energy incandescence, and there was a wide variety of fuel to keep the bulb burning. It always seems, though, that what burns brightest goes out quickest. The album was brilliant, but the band was over-revving and starting to fly off in different directions like human shrapnel.

I'd been accepted into the fold well enough to be invited along to open up for them at one of their shows—a high school gig somewhere near Toronto. I felt pretty stupid being out there with my acoustic guitar, all alone, singing folk songs to kids who were there to hear a psychedelic rock band. There wasn't a stage monitor system at the gig, so I was just flailing away and hoping that what came out the other end sounded okay.

Having no monitor wedges was normal for the time. The band had an impressive custom-made Wire sound system and huge amps for the instruments. They performed inside this huge wall of sound. Music stage production was different then. If music was incredibly loud, which it usually was, it was incredibly loud right on the stage. Your guitar amp was supposed to carry to the back of the house. The speaker system was just for vocals and drums.

Anyway, once I was done, the Market came onto the stage and began to play. It wasn't long before things went south. Keith McKie was about as interstellar as it's possible for someone to be whose body still walks the earth. Luke Gibson wasn't far behind. Gene Martynec was smoking mad. Jimmy Watson, the drummer, was going increasingly paranoid. Alex seemed to be the only one sailing along above it all.

Somewhere along the line, Keith simply stopped playing and stood there with his guitar feeding back and his arms outstretched as though he was Jesus on the cross. Gene, in complete disgust, kicked a bunch of stuff over and stalked off the stage as the whole thing just sort of lurched to a halt like a car crash.

Not long after that, the band ceased to be. It just burned itself out on intensity, drugs and arrogance.

Bernie Finkelstein had been living in a rat's nest of a warehouse loft up on Pears Avenue, just across Avenue Road from the old Village Corner Club. After the band dissolved, he was really spinning his wheels. I'd go up there to visit with him and spend hours rapping away, riffing improvisational comedy bits that were remarkable in their vulgarity. While doing this, we'd methodically shoot arrows at the wall with an archery set that he had lying around the place. By the time he left that warehouse, the wall looked like a piece of Swiss cheese, and Bernie needed sleep more than any human being I'd ever met.

He decided to flee the dark side of the force that was taking over Yorkville and check out the ever-growing "back-to-the-land" movement. He and Luke Gibson bought a farm together up in Killaloe, near the Madawaska Valley, and so my choice for a manager suddenly flew the coop.

While he was gone from town, Keith McKie got more orbital, Jimmy Watson refused to play the drums anymore because he thought they were made from dead animals; Gene Martynec devoted himself to the serious study of electronic music and production; Alex Daroux died.

Alex had long kind-of-reddish hair.

Alex had eyes like Rasputin.

Alex had a room upstairs from the Grab Bag on Yorkville.

One day, he decided to go up there and fast. He'd done this before as a way to clear and focus his consciousness. He began his fast. People would come by, friends . . . "Alex, how are you, man?" they would ask through the door. "Fine, go away."

Alex was fine and clear and conscious but getting weak. He kept on. Time passed and people stopped coming by because he was fine.

He was found in a very ripe condition by his brother.

I had a dream one night about Alex Daroux. In the dream, I went through a door into a room of the most unusual shade of blue—soothing and claustrophobic at the same time. If the music they play in elevators and supermarkets had a colour, it would have been this shade of blue.

The room had an intense overhead light source. Not sunlight, more like the first crack of a hydrogen bomb seen from a hundred miles away.

At the centre of the room, raised up in the middle of this intense light was an oblong slab the same colour as the rest of the room, and on it lay Alex.

Now even in my dream, I had the sure and certain knowledge that Alex was dead and the pale unmoving figure that lay before me gave no argument against that notion.

His eyes opened.

He sat up and swung his legs over the side and fixed me with a steady gaze. I noticed idly that he was naked, but this didn't register as unusual under the circumstances.

He began to speak very quietly.

"I made a mistake. This wasn't supposed to go down," he said. "I got too wasted and I couldn't get out of bed."

Alex talked for a long time. It seemed he'd found out we meet our end as the hapless victims of a cosmic practical joke. The gods amuse themselves playing a form of pinball with what remains of our consciousness.

"Oh, remember that fear-of-falling thing?" he asked. "No sweat, fall. This isn't such a bad space, actually. Are you still messing around with the flying vee?"

"No, I got a Fender Jazzmaster now," I replied.

"Shitty guitar. If you're not facing due east, the pick-ups howl. Don't be scared to play loud!"

"Oh." I guess it was going to be half of "okay," but only the first part got out before the sound of my reply woke me up. "Oh!" I sounded like Dorothy when her house landed on the witch.

I remember that morning so well because it's one of the few times in my life when I've wakened up feeling less puzzled than when I went to bed.

Trevor Veitch had met Tom Rush and moved out of the band Three's a Crowd to go on the road with him. Donna Warner had also left to pursue other interests. Now the band consisted of Brent Titcomb, Colleen Peterson, Dave Wiffen and the unusual addition of Bruce Cockburn, whom I'd run into quite a lot in Ottawa and at the festivals.

Brent's house over on Bishop Street near the village was the general hangout for everyone associated with that scene, and I wound up over there quite a lot. Brent's wife Maureen would occupy most of her time sitting there busily rolling joints while the jam session went on. There were always people coming and going, and whenever Bruce was in town, he'd usually end up there. I remember they had this awful little squirrel monkey that ran around all over the place, and if the little pest wasn't trying to get up on your shoulder and fuck your ear, it was as liable to bite it.

I heard a lot of Bruce's early songs around that table for the first time— "Together Alone," "Goin' to the Country," "One Day I Walk" were all songs I jammed on while I was there. I guess I got to know Bruce more than just to say hello to on a casual basis during those nights at Brent's house.

There was a close connection between that house and the whole Ottawa artistic scene led by Bill Hawkins; in fact, Bill would occasionally show up. He and Wiffen had already evolved into two halves of the same person. They drank together, doped together, played together and pretty much lived together. They had precious little time to devote to their significant others. I guess they were mates in the sense that word is understood in Australia.

Bruce wasn't planning on staying in what he considered to be a jobbing gig for long. He never said as much, but it was written all over him. He had his eye set on something more tailored to his personal taste. He was associated at the time with an Ottawa businessman named Harvey Glatt. He's a really nice guy and was acting in what he thought was Bruce's best interest, when to my amusement, he phoned me and asked if I could help him to convince Bruce not to go out on a solo career. He thought Bruce's place was to be in a band and he'd only hurt himself with unrealistic expectations of what he'd be able to accomplish on his own.

Bruce's wife Kitty had become pretty good friends with Patty while all this hanging out was going on. They went out and did stuff together and commiserated with each other, no doubt, about what assholes their husbands were.

Patty was getting pretty restless in the communal house, and at the same time, Bruce and Kitty had decided to move to Toronto. Rather informally, the plan came up to cut the cost of living, if the proper location could be found, by splitting a loft or an apartment between us.

Eventually, the ladies found a two-storey walk-up above a pawn shop down on Queen Street near McCaul. It looked perfect. From the front entrance, you walked up the stairs to the second floor, and there was a long apartment with a big front room overlooking the street, two rooms in the middle for whatever, a bathroom of substantial proportions, and in the back, there was a kitchen with a door leading to the fire escape. If you continued up the stairs, the same layout was duplicated one floor up. The rent was very cheap. The apartments were a bit funky and needed some cleaning and painting work because they'd been vacant for a while.

Outside, Queen Street was still in its old pre-gentrification glory—funky stores selling surplus, smoke shops, appliance stores. There was a dwarf, a rather nasty-looking, bad-tempered little man, who sold newspapers on the corner by the streetcar stop near Gold's Luggage. The neighbourhood was full of colour and atmosphere. It was perfect! There wasn't a hint of warning of what was to come.

Painting, scrubbing, scrounging bits of furniture, Patty went to work making a home again. She was happy to have Kitty around to go down and natter with. We settled into life. There were minor inconveniences. It was a long walk up to the village and home again. I would often be out all night and find the subway was closed when I wanted to return. Cabs were too expensive. We'd moved in smack in the middle of one of those times when I just wasn't getting anything more than occasional gigs, and the situation didn't promise to get any better in the immediate future. Things had stalled for me. I didn't feel any closer to getting a record out, the demand was all for bands and the one guy I'd thought could carry me out of the swamp had left town. We were scratching for the rent and trying to figure out which other bills we could get away without paying—the phone, for instance.

We were still going up to Joyce and Ian Hamilton's place on a regular basis. Their house and friends had become like our own. They were working very hard at trying to adopt a child and were sweating out the waiting process. Sometimes, maybe, we took their minds off the glacial passing of time.

I was run down from what was now going on four years of relentess hard living. I kept getting chest colds and bronchitis. I was smoking too much. I'd come home with a raging case of the clap from a gig I'd done in the U.S. I'd let it go and let it go, hoping that maybe it would just go away. I wish I'd at least had some fun acquiring it, but I hadn't.

I was staying on the couch of yet another bug-infested, dirty band house associated with the club I was playing. After the gig, I'd been sitting around with a few people, and we'd all smoked some fairly weighty hash. One of the people in the room was an overweight dirty blonde with enormous, pendulous breasts, who was far more stoned than she should have been. Eventually, things wound down and everyone split, much to my relief. I took off my jeans and lay down on the couch under a blanket and pretty much passed out.

I was having a dream. It started gently and then developed into a full-bore erotic wonder. I was in a sea of frothing bodies and there was a goddess riding me up and down and I felt myself rising and rising and getting closer and closer.

But I never seem to be able to come in a dream. That's one of the greatest disappointments in this life. (There's probably a website for people who can!) So as I neared the ultimate, I woke up. It was the trashy-looking blonde on top of me. I closed my eyes up tight and tried not to think of what was going on, then let go. A few days after, I started grinding my teeth when I peed.

So I was not in the best of health the night I went over to the Waldorf-Astoria Hotel (not the real one, the cheap one) to meet Trevor Veitch, who was in town playing with Tom Rush at the Riverboat. Trevor had moved down to the States with his wife Myra and had got a house in New Hampshire. He was moving in some pretty exalted circles now. Bennett Glotzer, Tom's manager, had gone into partnership with Albert Grossman, who was hitting the bigtime yet again with The Band. Trevor was now hanging out with Richard Manuel and other members of the Woodstock Royals.

Trevor wasn't planning on being a sideman forever, and I'd been looking more and more at the dead end I was in, so we began having speculative conversations about starting a band one of these days. We liked a lot of the same music, so the idea wasn't completely off the wall. In the meantime, though, Trevor was happy playing with Tom. They'd become good friends, they were both hip and smart, and there were plenty of Twinkies on the road.

On this particular night, however, Trevor had other plans than talking about the future. He'd procured a lot of MDA, and without giving the matter much forethought, I dropped a pile of it. I dropped more of the stuff than I'd previously even looked at.

I spent an amazing night. I fell in love with a chair, I think. I connected with the people there with an intensity I'd never felt before. There was so much love ripping through me it was almost painful. It lasted all through the night and well into the hours of daylight. Then, in the full glare of the bleaching sun, I crashed out of it.

I hadn't been feeling all that good about myself anyway. I was insecure about a lot of things, not the least of which being whether or not I was going to survive my own career choice. I was lost. I couldn't see my future—it was hidden behind a dark veil. But all that was nothing compared to this.

Heartbreak? What an insipid little word! Falling out of this love was like having your beating heart ripped out of your chest and smashed with a baseball bat. I couldn't bear it to be over. I came apart at the seams. It took several days before I could keep from bursting into tears whenever I was alone.

There was also something strange going on with the apartment. It started slowly at first—just a general unease, a feeling that even when you knew you were by yourself, you weren't. You'd walk by a doorway and as you'd pass, you'd look in because all your senses had registered that there was someone there, but there wasn't.

Bruce and Kitty had a great big cross-breed Irish wolfhound named Aroo who'd never had any problems with bravery. Yet at certain times, or when walking by a small closet that was tucked under the foot of the stairs, an odd little closet with a trapezoidal door that led way back into the darkness, Aroo would suddenly start whining, put his tail between his legs and slink away.

Then there were the dreams that started to come regularly—terrifying dreams, not surreal and disjointed but distressingly real and vivid, as though they were happening in real time.

In the dream, I would be floating disembodied through the apartment. As I moved about from place to place, I encountered our bodies, slaughtered in the most brutal way. There was blood everywhere—on the floor in pools, streaked along the walls. I would gasp awake, shocked and sweating.

No one was sleeping very well. At least Patty and Kitty weren't. Bruce was away a great deal of the time. One morning, after a particularly bad night, Patty and I were downstairs at the table having coffee when Kitty confessed to having had the most horrible dreams. She was becoming afraid to go to sleep. As she described the dream she was having, a chill ran up my spine. It was exactly the same dream I was having. Then Patty confessed she'd been having them too. Something was terribly wrong, and we didn't know what to do.

I might have attributed what was happening to my own fatigue, to being off balance from being sick or to the recent MDA blowout. I might have been happier with the rational explanation that I was going nuts. But I couldn't dismiss the fact that it wasn't only me. The atmosphere at the apartment on Queen Street became more and more oppressive.

In the meantime, Finkelstein had returned to Toronto and rented a small bungalow up in the north end of town near Yonge Street and the 401. Killaloe had gotten a bit small for his energies, and one night, he and Luke had had a blowout. Bernie got in his pick-up truck and started driving back to town. Somewhere along the line, he abandoned the truck and made his way back in a variety of ways that are still unclear in his memory.

He and Bruce had begun to move towards a working relationship during the time that Bruce and I had been sharing the flat. I was seeing Bernie regularly and was still hoping to induce him to work with me, but he seemed to think otherwise. Bruce had the perfect image for the time, and Bernie was smart to recognize that. Bruce had abandoned hard-edged rock and was now playing a kind of ethereal acoustic-based music that was perfectly in sync with the growing "back-to-the-land" movement. I was more than a little hurt because I was becoming more than a little desperate. I guess I was more than a little jealous too! Bernie, however, was too engaging and optimistic a guy to be upset with. He was also very encouraging and made a point of not closing the door on me.

The bad dreams continued and the situation at the apartment deteriorated rapidly. It felt like the minute you walked through the door, you couldn't breathe. There were no apparitions running around, no chains rattling in the night, no objects flying through the air, just this continual psychological water torture of nervousness and fear. None of us wanted to admit that we thought the place was inhabited by something evil.

A dramatic shifting occurred as the cold month of November came. Now the presence could be felt physically. I was sitting in the chair in our front room reading one evening, when suddenly I felt the fingers and thumb of a hand close around the back of my head. I nearly jumped out of my skin. Now I was really terrified and so was Patty. I was a rationalist and not prone to paying any attention to the supernatural. I was capable of detaching myself even from my own emotional aberrations and looking at them dispassionately. This thing, however, was scaring the shit out of me.

There was a pervasive drenching sense of something evil filling the apartment. It was there all the time now. I never heard voices or anything like that, yet I would suddenly be possessed by an overwhelming impulse to go to the kitchen and take out a butcher knife and kill Patty. I started to think I really was going crazy.

Late one night, Patty and I were together in the front room, trying to read. We avoided being in different parts of the apartment by this time. We both felt like drops of water on a hot skillet. It was a cold night outside, and it was raining a steady oppressive November drizzle. There was an open archway between the front room and the room where we slept, and as I sat there trying to read, my eyes were pulled reluctantly up from the book in my lap. As I looked through the arch into the dimness of the room beyond, I could see nothing, but something was there. I could feel it plainly, just as you know someone is in a room even when you have your eyes closed. Patty could feel it too. She was staring in that direction. Coming from that arch was the most indescribable feeling of rage and hostility. It hit us in waves.

"Do you want to go for a walk?" I asked Patty, my voice strangled in an effort to suppress the fear I was feeling.

She never even answered. We just grabbed whatever warm clothing we could and hurried down the stairs into the night.

We walked over to Yonge Street and started north. It was around midnight, I guess. We were wet and cold as we passed Wellesley, but we still hadn't said a word to each other. It was as though we were afraid to admit what had happened. Then Patty said, "What happens if it's followed us?"

That question broke the dam of my fear. It gushed out and ate me alive. The very thought that she'd just given this experience a personality and that it might be conscious precipitated in me a full-blown panic attack. I think Patty wasn't far behind. I was breathing fast and crying and couldn't think of what to do. Then, like a beacon in the night, the thought of a place where we would find shelter came to mind—friends who were stable, like parents, who wouldn't judge us, wouldn't ask a lot of questions that we couldn't answer and would protect us till we could figure out what to do.

From a phone booth on Yonge Street, there in the cold rain, we called Joyce and Ian Hamilton. We just said we'd had trouble and needed help. Without a moment's hesitation, even though their adopted son, Sandy, had just arrived, they urged us to come over and stay there as long as we needed to.

When we arrived at their house, which was now out near High Park, they were waiting up for us.

We were wet, shivering and frightened out of our wits. I'm sure the story we blurted out must have seemed incomprehensible to them, but they got us calmed down and warmed up enough to finally make some attempt at sleep.

Joyce and Ian, in an act of trust that still amazes me, put us to bed in the room where the new baby was sleeping. I think they thought the little guy would help calm me down or at least give me some reason to try to be quiet. I lay there all night awake, listening to the baby. I couldn't stop shivering convulsively.

How could I ever thank Joyce and Ian? They pulled us, drowning, out of the sea and protected us long enough that we found the courage to venture back out and face the world.

New York City

THERE IS A FOOTNOTE TO THE GHOST story. We needed to collect our things from the haunted apartment, so we mounted an expedition by daylight. It was difficult to return even when the sun was shining. We explored the dim recesses of the staircase closet and discovered an axe, a couple of old hickory golf clubs and a very weird-looking short cane. The cane was so small it would only suit a midget or a child. It was made of gnarled wood, with an oddly carved handle in the shape of a left-handed fist with the thumb stuck out between the index and middle finger. There was an inscription carved into it in a language that none of us could read. Kitty took it to a museum expert who said the inscription and the hand gesture would mean "Fuck you" if you were a Romany Gypsy.

Further research unearthed the disquieting news that the people who'd lived in the place before us had experienced a great deal more trouble than we had. They apparently moved in as a loving couple and wound up having violent arguments that culminated in his throwing her down the stairs.

Patty and I went up to visit Bernie in his house near the 401 and ended up crashing there. There were already a number of people in residence, so two more didn't make much of a difference. Bernie was a complete counterculture guy and seemed to enjoy the wide variety of people who came and went.

Some of Brazilian George's friends were around. Don Baby was there, sometimes with a sweet little girl who was finally put out on the street by a pimp who hung out down at the Brown Derby tavern. Bev was around a lot. There was a beautiful girl named Judy, tall and willowy, who just seemed to sail above everything like a sunny day in a summer breeze. Everybody was very understanding about what had happened to us. After all, they'd seen an awful lot of people go through all kinds of bad shit.

Patty and I were just crashing on a mattress in one of the rooms. There were several dogs in the house that were kept in the basement. No one ever cleaned up after them, so the basement was full of dog shit.

We spent Christmas of 1969 in that house. We couldn't face any of our relatives or even most of our friends in the state we were in. From a backlot dealer who'd given up the ghost on Christmas Eve, we liberated a tree that no one else wanted. We all decorated it with whatever was at hand, and all of us—misfits and waifs—celebrated Christmas. It was like Christmas in the trenches when the war stops for one night. It was emotional and poignant. We were at rock bottom.

Bernie watched me for a couple of weeks and then we had a talk. He was understanding and supportive, but he made it clear again that he wasn't in a position to do anything for me and that it wasn't in my best interests to hang around for the rest of my life figuring out what I was going to do. He suggested I try my hand in the United States. He convinced me that this was the only way, given the way the world worked, to achieve success in Canada, so I might as well go down to New York with the contacts I had through Tom Rush and try to see what I could get together.

I called up Tom and spoke to Trevor Veitch, who was staying at Tom's house in New Hampshire while they were woodshedding some songs. Tom suggested I come on down and we'd see what might happen.

So Patty and I decided to move to the States. We scrounged enough money from the folks around and from Bernie to buy a couple of bus tickets, and off we went.

We were ragged, tired, freaked out, broke and lost when we arrived at the border. Outside the bus was the cold dead grey of midwinter as we pulled up to customs and immigration. One of our suitcases was so worn out it was held together with a rope. I had a guitar. We were going down to get work if we could, so we were illegal. Paranoia started to rise in my gorge as I saw the burly Immigration man get on the bus. We'd never get through! They'd bust us for something. In the middle of the Vietnam War, hippies were about as popular as lice.

The big man in uniform worked his way down the aisle until he got to where we were sitting.

"Purpose of your visit?" he asked.

"Visiting friends," I tried to reply as casually as I could.

"Citizenship?"

"Canadian," I said.

"American," said Patty. (She'd been born in Alabama.)

I'd forgotten all about that. She had dual citizenship! We were cool. I was married to a Yank! The man seemed satisfied and moved on.

We finally arrived down at the station in the town near Tom's place and called over to get a ride to the house.

It didn't take long to get hip to the fact that Trevor had zero interest in starting up a band. He was happy where he was. Tom was kind but busy and seemed eager to have our situation resolved so we could move on. He made a phone call into New York to his manager, Bennett. When it was done, Tom pitched me a deal right there on the spot. Through the office of Albert Grossman/Bennett Glotzer, he was willing to purchase the publishing rights to my entire catalogue of existing songs if I was willing to go into New York to cut the deal with Bennett. What the hell, it wasn't like I had a choice. It was a little piece of something versus all of nothing! We picked up our rope-bound suitcase again and caught the first bus into the city.

Arriving at the Port Authority bus terminal and having no other place to go, we went straight over to the Grossman office, where we sat in the reception area like ragamuffins.

While we were waiting to see Bennett Glotzer, Albert himself walked in. He was in a grey jacket and jeans, with his long grey-white hair gathered back in a ponytail. I was awestruck to actually be in the same room and breathing the same air as Dylan's manager. He walked towards his office, and as he came abreast of us, he stopped for a second and peered over his little Ben Franklin glasses. He looked us up and down as though he was examining a specimen on a microscope slide, and without saying a word, went into his lair.

Finally, Glotzer was ready for me. He presented me with a contract that gave Tom Rush and him sole and exclusive control over the publishing copyrights for all the songs I'd written so far, plus those I would subsequently write until the end of the term. This included songs that would eventually appear on my first and second records and also meant that they (meaning Tom Rush now—he split with Bennett years ago) controlled and still control the rights to "The Farmer's Song," one of my biggest hit records.

In exchange, I was presented with a cheque for the sum of one thousand, four hundred U.S. dollars. If anyone's inclined to think sorrowfully of the goofy kid signing away his life, be comforted by the fact that I thought then, and I still think now, that it was the right thing to do. Suddenly, I was in New York, affiliated with one of the most powerful music companies on the planet, with a little money to live on and the opportunity to make a lot of contacts. I was already a lot further ahead than I'd been only a few days earlier, so whatever the cost, it was worth it.

We were taken in and introduced to Albert, now that we were officially in the fold. He was a good deal more friendly now that he owned me. I couldn't help but notice as I sat there that at least one of the stories I'd heard about him appeared to be true. Albert was a normal-sized man, but he'd rigged up his office so that his chair was a lot higher than the ones across his desk. When you were seated, you were automatically at a psychological disadvantage as he looked down at you from the elevated position of a judge.

So that was that. The deed was done and now we were moving forward, or *somewhere* at least! We left the office and moved to take care of the next pressing item on the agenda, which was where to lay our heads for the night. It was too late to do anything with the cheque. I didn't have a New York bank account and they were closed by now anyway, so we still had very little money.

We'd been given the name of someone to call when we'd left Toronto. We were told we'd probably be able to crash there until we got established. Tom knew the people and chuckled a bit at the prospect of us roosting there.

I called up Peter and Antonia Stamfel and introduced myself. Peter told us to come on over. They were a strange and interesting, very New York kind of couple. They had a grungy but homey loft on the Lower East Side. Peter had a band called the Holy Modal Rounders, which included among its personnel the future husband of Jessica Lange, playwright Sam Shepard. Antonia was a writer who at that time was making ends meet by creating erotic stories for Al Goldstein's *Screw* magazine. They welcomed us and were completely accepting. We told the story of how we'd come to the Big Apple, complete with the ghostly details.

The only wrinkle was that Peter, who was a twenty-four-hour kind of guy anyway, was working on music for the band and filling himself with crystal meth while he was at it. He was still on a stream of consciousness rap-fest at two in the morning while Patty and I were both drop-dead exhausted. I think we had a quiet huddle, and since she was the most tired and also a little sick, it was decided that I'd stay up with our hosts while she sacked out. So that was how I spent my first full night living in New York—listening to Peter rave on at Mach 2 and occasionally reading Antonia's smoking pages of steamy smut.

The next day, I went to one of the many banks that sprout up on New York streets like dandelions and deposited the cheque. I was worried about blowing the money, so I set it up that the bank would put the big amount into a special account and pay a weekly allowance into a chequing account that I could draw from for our survival expenses. I would have to jump through hoops to get to the big pile of dough, so there was a safeguard, I hoped, against foolish and precipitous acts.

Patty and I promptly headed down to the Village and got a room at the Albert

Hotel. This nondescript little downtown fleabag had the reputation of being a "musician's hotel." It was true. When you walked in the door, there were eight-by-ten photos hanging on the wall of all the bands who'd stayed there. There were the familiar faces of Zal Yanofsky and John Sebastian from the Lovin' Spoonful, among many others. The fact that it was an artistic hotel compensated for the fact that the rooms were tiny, dingy, dirty and thoroughly infested with cockroaches. They were tough as miniature rhinos, and existed at the Albert in numbers remarkable even by New York standards.

Our room was tiny, with only one window, which opened onto the dim inhospitable bricks of a light well at the centre of the building. Once we moved in, we examined our surroundings and found a clear plastic bag behind the radiator, full of multicoloured capsules left by the previous inhabitants. Not knowing what they were, we discreetly chucked them down the well in case we got busted for someone else's sins. The room came complete with a black-and-white TV on plastic rolling casters and an antique bathroom done in institutional sort-of-white tile.

Patty quickly went to work as only she could, figuring out ways to refrigerate food by using the cold outside the window and discovering means to cook meals in the room (which was verboten) on a sterno stove. There was a sort-of-phone made of antique black Bakelite with no dial! If you wanted to call out, you went through the patch cord switchboard down at the desk, which allowed the desk man to pay close attention to whatever was going on in your life. Patty put up a few personal things that she'd stashed to try and make the place at least a little homey.

One of Bennett Glotzer's suggestions was that I should come into the office to use the writing and rehearsal room, a tiny thing really, where I could work at trying to write songs for some of the bands and other artists that the office was handling. It wasn't as if I had a job with a lunch pail or anything, but I started going there fairly regularly. I was introduced to a bushy-bearded curly-haired young Jewish man named Barry Flast on the chance that we might hit it off and collaborate on some songs. We did get along very nicely, and not only did we soldier away in the office, but we hung out as well. He had a lot of connections in the New York music community, and because of him, I started getting the odd gig around town. One of the most astonishing things about him was that he'd never been out of New York. Anything he knew about the rest of the world was from books or TV. Barry eventually played piano on my first record.

One of the first gigs I did there was a concert at Cooper Union Great Hall with a who's who of the folk music community. Oscar Brand was hosting it, and it was great to say hello again. Theodore Bikel was playing ethnic Eastern European music, which was perfectly in character with his eventual role in *Fiddler on the Roof*. David Bromberg was on the bill, the man who would later gain fame working with Dylan, and who would eventually record "Child's Song." I was starting to feel good about being in New York!

One day, Barry and I got a gig playing at City College of New York. The campus was up on the west side in Harlem, which was becoming one of the less desirable places to be at the time. The campus and the area around it, though, were generally considered to be safe. It was a student union, cafeteria sort of affair. Barry pounded on their crummy piano and accompanied me on some of the songs I'd written. We were okay. We actually played pretty well, and people liked it.

Barry had to leave a little early, but by the time I'd finished playing, it was an hour before sunset. It was winter and the days were short, so even though it was late afternoon, night would be along soon. I walked out of the campus with my guitar, shivering against the cold. I'd figured I'd go out to the main thoroughfare and flag a cab going downtown. I was wrong. Every cab had something to do that was more important than stopping for me. All the drivers were black, and I began to wonder whether my whiteness was the problem. Maybe they didn't like hippies, or I was so skinny they thought I was a junkie. One thing was for sure. It was getting dark, and I was rapidly becoming the only honky around. Standing there with my guitar, I felt like there was a neon sign up on my head saying, "Mug the folk singer."

As the last light disappeared, a bus came along. It was going south, so I got on it. It went a couple of blocks, then turned left and started going crosstown. As the bus moved east into the Bronx, the landscape began to change. The streets started to resemble a battle zone. One in five buildings appeared to be derelict, and there were little knots of men standing around oil-drum fires. There was garbage everywhere. Cars had been abandoned by the side of the road, stripped down to frame and body. There were no people who looked like me at all, and I began to feel very uncomfortably white. I hadn't thought about it before, but now I became acutely aware that the inside of the bus was lit up with harsh neon, and as it went by the little knots of people, occasionally one or two of them would notice me looking out the window and their stares would follow me as the bus went by. I slid down in the seat.

Finally, the bus turned south again. When I got off, the parts of Manhattan that I usually haunted seemed kick-up-your-heels, whistle, walk-in-the-park friendly and safe compared to what I'd just seen.

New York City changed me forever. The place either makes you or breaks you. You either become isolated or you accept the fact that you're nobody special and you go out and meet people. There's nobody with more sense of who they are than the average New Yorker. I loved the fact that you could become involved in a conversation with complete strangers on any subject. It was a part of life. Maybe it's just that when life is nearly impossible, people do extraordinary things to hold onto their sense of humanity, and they're more honest with each other.

My best barometer for the state of life in New York was always the cops. They were so busy trying to keep a lid on the really serious bad stuff that you could walk down the road with a joint stuck in your mouth and they wouldn't even look at you twice. In Toronto, it seemed that the gendarmes had enough time on their hands to hassle people just for looking funny. I swam very happily in the anonymity of the big city, and started to move with its rhythms.

Patty and I were thinking about fleeing the Albert, so we started looking for apartments we might be able to afford. What a joke! We looked at one particularly crummy little apartment with dingy dirty windows looking out over the rooftops of the Lower East Side, home of the mugger and the junkie. With its police bar locks on the door, it felt more like a jail cell than a place to live, and it cost more than all the money I had in the bank just to get in the building. We realized we could stay in the Albert for a long time on that kind of dough.

Then I got sick. I didn't notice it coming on. I was in the habit of walking most everywhere, and I didn't have much more than a sweater and a light leather jacket. I travelled fast and ducked in someplace to warm up when it got too cold. But one day, when I came back to the room at the Albert, my chest felt tight and I had a raspy hacking cough.

Patty fed me hot tea from the sterno stove and went out to get Vicks and all the other stuff you use when you've got a cold or bronchitis. I stayed in bed with the covers drawn up, sweating and shivering. But I didn't get better.

One day when we were in midtown Manhattan, we'd had a surreal moment. We splurged and went into one of the movie theatres at Times Square to see John Voight and Dustin Hoffman in *Midnight Cowboy*. We were identifying like crazy, what with being two dreamers who'd come to the city in hopes of making something out of our lives. We had a lot in common with Voight's character Joe Buck. We were still naive and innocent and unaware of most of what could actually happen to us. It was a very sobering end when Ratzo died of pneumonia while riding the bus to Miami. When we emerged, blinking, into Times Square again, it was completely disorienting. We were walking out of the movie right into the movie!

I was thinking of that movie and its ending as I lay in the dimness of our dingy room, my fear growing as my fever rose. I began having short bouts of delirium when I wasn't passed out in an exhausted sleep.

As I lay there, my head rolled over and I stared at the TV just as the Beatles appeared on the screen. I became fully conscious when I saw them. I don't know what show it was, but they were in the recording studio, all of them sitting around in the flat calm aftermath of the terrible battles they'd been having. There was Yoko, the dragon lady, sitting with John. Paul was singing "Let It Be." I didn't make it halfway through the song before I was in tears. Some part of me sensed I was dying and the spirituality of the song tapped into that. As they say in the Bible, I became "sore afraid."

Patty hadn't realized yet quite how sick I was and tried to comfort me by making love, which was accomplished without much help from me. I was burning with fever and out of my head most of the time.

One of Patty's best qualities is a single-minded tenaciousness when the chips are down. She will not take no for an answer. She started trying to find a doctor to come and see me because she didn't think I was strong enough to get to a hospital. (I might have died in the waiting room before they got around to admitting me at Bellevue anyway.) She finally found a doctor who was willing to risk making a house call at a questionable hotel at night. I'll never know how she managed it. A doctor who was willing to make house calls was taking a huge risk, because at that time he'd be as likely as not to find some junkie and his friends lying in wait with a knife or gun to kill him and take the drugs in his bag. When the doctor arrived, he was visibly relieved to find a patient in the room. He was a relatively young guy, and I guess he still had some faith in the human race.

He took my temperature, raised an eyebrow, and without any hesitation, rolled me over and stuck a sharp hypodermic needle in my backside. He wrote a prescription, gave Patty some other instructions about what to watch for and left.

Within two days, I was out of bed and moving around, although I was still very weak. The antibiotics had done their work and headed off a very advanced case of pneumonia. The doctor had apparently remarked that we'd left treatment to the eleventh hour and fifty-ninth minute and that I'd come perilously close to "shuffling off this mortal coil."

Now I owed my life to three people. First the Scottish midwife, then Noni Raitblatt and now Louise Patricia Joelle Hunt Sockwell-McLauchlan had saved it again. If not for her level-headedness in crisis, they would have taken me out of the Albert in a bag.

IV

The Ship Isn't in, but You Can See the Land

❦ I ALWAYS THINK OF TORONTO AS flypaper. No matter where you go or what it is you've got going for yourself, you get drawn back to it and then you're trapped again.

After I recovered from the pneumonia, I got curious about how things were going back home. I made a call up to Bernie Finkelstein's place—just to say hello, mind you. Even though I was doing more and more things in New York, I wasn't any closer to my ultimate ambition of making a record of the songs I'd been writing, and I suppose I was testing the waters to see if he was any closer to putting something together with me.

It was springtime in the city. In New York, that's a drab grey dirty time until full bloom hits Central Park. Spring always makes me restless, and I was homesick. I missed the greenery and fresh air of Toronto. In my post-sickness state, I was hypersensitive to diesel exhaust and fumes of all kinds. I felt like I was wheezing half the time. It was time to get out!

The hard life had developed in me a harder ambition. I was sick of living like a rat! I'd seen pop stars riding around in limousines. I'd seen the people in the office kowtow when Janis Joplin arrived. I wanted to get some respect, and if not that, I at least wanted to make enough of a living to pay the rent.

Much to my surprise, Bernie had been really busy. The first Cockburn album was in the works, and his independent record label was up and running. He'd decided to call it True North Records, which I thought was a terrific name, especially since I was homesick for Canada. The most interesting twist to the scenario was that to get the financing to make the first record, Bernie had formed a business partnership with none other than Brazilian George! Bernie said it looked like time to start thinking about another artist for the label, and he thought I should come back home. There was a very good chance I might be that person! Bernie was about to do a bunch of records actually. Luke Gibson was starting to write beautiful acoustic songs. John Mills-Cockell had a project band called Syrinx and Bernie's old pal Jay Telfer had a solo project he wanted to do. Bernie was going to be a busy lad.

The chance to record was enough of a lure for me. Patty and I talked things over, and I think she was as happy as I was to leave New York. She missed her friends, and as difficult as their relationship could be sometimes, I think she missed the support of her zany mother.

We went back down to the Port Authority Terminal and caught a bus back home to Toronto. It was the summer of the new decade. The sixties were gone. Now I wouldn't have to fight acid rock to get heard—just disco and hair bands.

Patty and I took a modest two-room flat on Augusta Avenue in Kensington Market. We picked the area because I'd always liked the funk of it, and the best part was that it was close to Grossman's Tavern, the home of the blues jam and endless cheap draft beer.

I was so happy to be back that for the first little while we were home, I went overboard. I'd wander over to Grossman's in the late afternoon. Often, the band that was playing was led by Gerry McAdam, a guy I'd known slightly in art school. I'd just get wrapped up in the happenings and the music and keep getting draft poured for me until, suddenly, it was "Drink up, folks! Chairs on the tables! C'mon, drink up!" Then I'd stumble home in the best of moods, singing, "Good morning, little school girl" and usually fall over a fence into someone's front yard on the way home. I'd lie there on my back giggling, just happy to be drunk and alive. Toronto felt so safe to me. It felt like kindergarten!

I'd often run into Moses from the commune days at Grossman's, particularly if the Walsh brothers' band was playing. Downchild was a favourite of the Vagabonds. I remember one night when Rick Walsh, sometimes known as "The Hock," took his reputation as a hard-living blues guy to the max and walked into the bar with a small knife sticking out of his back. He was pissed drunk and I guess he just didn't notice it was there. The reputation Don and Rick Walsh enjoyed was always a bit of a chuckle really. Both of them are well spoken, well read and very intelligent.

In the mornings, when the sun was coming up, I'd sometimes go and sit on the flat roof of the Kensington apartment. I'd made a long pipe and I'd fill it full of sweet tobacco and have a bowl while I just looked up at the sky. I'd let my imagination fly up to where the seagulls were calling out as they made their way to the landfills for breakfast. This simple little ritual would recharge my soul. I need to dream the way some people need cornflakes!

We had a welcome home party, and the whole gang from 127 Hazelton came over. I got stinko and lay on my back on the floor, laughing like a hyena and trying to pull down Karla's knickers. Karla was a good sport, and I may also owe my life to her because she didn't just kick me one in the head at that party. A guy named Gary Ledrew showed up. He would later be in and out of my life a lot. He brought a large box to the party, filled to the brim with water guns. As soon as those things got into general distribution, all hell broke loose.

Our landlady was Portuguese and really didn't know what to make of us. She had a few strict rules, one of which was "No Pets." Somehow she became convinced that we were hiding a dog in the place, so she started snooping and trying to catch us out.

One of the first things I'd done to celebrate our return was to liberate a big Clairtone amp from one of those fly-eye stereo sets and hook it up to a set of mammoth wooden speakers. All that hotel living and moving around meant we hadn't had loud music for a long time, and I had really missed it. I'd be leaping around the house with Ramblin' Jack Elliot's album *Young Brigham*, the one he named after his horse, blasting away. Sometimes it would be *Blonde on Blonde* or *Are You Experienced?* or the ever-popular *Brown Shoes Don't Make It*.

I decided to have a little fun with the landlady. I'd found an album of wolf calls somewhere—one of those earnest nature series projects where they compare the calls of captive and wild wolves. I put on the record and cranked it to the max. It was one of my personal favourites, the solo song of an Arctic wolf.

A few minutes later, there was a horrendous banging at the door. I waited for a short while before answering. I noticed there were two sets of knocks. I turned off the stereo and went to the door. When I opened it, the landlady was standing there, red-faced, with a great big burly cop. He had a look on his face that said he'd rather be off chasing bandits than dealing with this.

The landlady was yelling, "They got big dog! They got big dog! No good! They gotta go! Get out! You go in, make them show!"

The cop was reasonably polite but he had his game face on. He asked to come in and inspect the premises with regard to the complaint he'd received. I smiled a big smile and invited him right in. I showed him the stereo. I showed him the record. He cracked up and started laughing, and he was still laughing as he walked out the door.

Bernie and I met up and started talks. I sang him some of the songs I wanted to record. By that point I'd written "Sixteen Lanes of Highway," about the destruction of my boyhood fields; I had "Child's Song" and "Old Man's Song" which had been recorded by Tom Rush. I'd written "Honky Red," about the winos I'd encountered when Nick and I were travelling, and "Back on the Street," my battle cry of freedom—and a lot of others that were really interesting. Bernie started to realize how hungry I really was. I was writing a lot of songs, and it was likely they wouldn't be heard if I didn't record them.

Without any contract being signed, Bernie and I just kind of evolved into an artist-and-manager relationship. We slapped hands on a deal to start work on a record as soon as the money was available for production. I was elated.

While I'd been soldiering away in New York and nearly dying, ironically enough, the perception in Toronto was that I was down there hanging out with Albert Grossman and The Band, being recorded by Tom Rush (which was true) and making a name for myself in America. This was pretty laughable. I knew better than anybody that I was but one of many down there. I believed in my talent and my art, but I wasn't stupid. There were any number of people who could write and perform as well as I could.

But that didn't matter in Toronto. Word got around that I was back and working with Finkelstein, and suddenly I was getting invited to parties at Gordon Lightfoot's house. He still had his old house on Blythwood, where he lived with his wife, Breda. It was on the night I first went over there with Patty that I met Ronnie Hawkins.

Ronnie was riding high at that point. He was taking full credit for being the mentor of Levon & the Hawks/The Band, and he was hanging out with John Lennon, who was staying at Ronnie's house when he came to town.

I knew who Ronnie was. I remembered the song "Mary Lou," but I also recalled he was considered to be one of those Yonge Street rounders. I knew his manager was some kind of gangster and I'd heard all the stories about Ronnie's hands not being able to open all the way because of all the fights he'd been in. It took me a while to find out what a sweet old puppy the guy really was.

I walked in the front door of Gordon's house with Patty, who had on about six pairs of eyelashes and was dressed in her usual costumer's fantasy kind of way. Ronnie took one look at her and made one of his now-classic remarks. He took her to be some sort of floozy, because in his experience I guess, women who dressed that way usually were.

I was still curiously old-fashioned about some things, and his tone hit me the wrong way. I went off like a little bantam rooster. There I was, red-faced and scrapping mad, beak to beak with Ronnie and saying, "That's my wife!"

He was only mildly embarrassed. I think he had a hard time not laughing his ass off at the sight of me!

Bernie Fiedler, being no fool, got wind that I was on the rise according to all the street indicators, and he hired me for my first gig at the Riverboat. That was a really big deal for me. I had now moved into the top echelon of the clubs.

The Riverboat was entering its golden age then. On a given night, you might walk in and there would be Neil Young, who was between Buffalo Springfield and realizing a great success with *After the Gold Rush*. In the meantime, he was just trying to pay his bills the best way he could. I doubt if any of the boys in his former band saw much money from it.

James Taylor had been recorded and discovered by Tom Rush and was coming up with all those wonderful songs like "Fire and Rain" and "Sweet Baby James." He was playing the Riverboat. James walked in there one night with this lady named Carole King, who was unknown by everyone except the industry insiders; they were aware of her songwriting successes with Gerry Goffin. Fiedler apparently offered her a gig, which she politely turned down. About a year later, she was making a zillion dollars a minute.

One of my favourite writers of all time and unfortunately one of the biggest pains in the ass was on the stage a lot at the time. Tim Hardin would show up barely coherent for his gig. He was a hard-core junkie on the methadone program and like most of them, he was overdoing his medication, then doing everything else he could get his hands on just to keep level. He'd be smoking hash, drinking, taking downers and be on methadone all at the same time. The man was a complete mess.

Yet he'd walk onto the stage and sing "Black Sheep Boy," "Reason to Believe" or the incredibly beautiful "How Can You Hang onto a Dream" and somehow pull it all together and transport the audience to some other place.

Ramblin' Jack Elliot worshipped the ground Hardin walked on and would practically follow him around like a puppy. In the short time I'd done some serious hanging around with Jack, I'd gotten to really love the guy. He was like an overgrown kid with a wonderful innocence about him, which existed side by side with the randiness of a satyr. Jack took a lot of flack for being a Jewish guy from New York pretending to be a cowboy, and that really pissed me off. If anybody doesn't like who they are and wants to reinvent themselves as somebody they like better, I say, God bless 'em! Besides, Jack had become a really good cowboy, and all those "real cowboys" out west all got there from somewhere else anyway.

One time Jack happened to be in town when Tim Hardin was playing the Riverboat, and when the show was over for the night, it was pretty obvious that Jack was looking for an opportunity to hang out for a while. I invited them over to the flat in Kensington.

When Hardin wasn't nodding off, he was openly abusive to Jack. He was a real asshole that night, and I could see that Jack was very hurt by it. We left Tim sitting on the couch weaving back and forth, trying to light a hash pipe, and went into the kitchen to get a drink. While we were in there shooting the breeze, I started to smell smoke. I ran into the other room, and there was Tim with his chin down on his chest, passed out. He'd mixed up the crumbled hash with tobacco and stuffed the combination haphazardly into the pipe he was trying to smoke. When he'd nodded out, the embers had fallen out of the pipe and got between his legs. They'd set fire to the couch and, it appeared, also to a delicate part of his anatomy.

I thought for just a second about seeing whether he'd burn himself awake, but Jack was kinder than I was, so we put out both the singer and the couch. Jack got him into a cab, and they went off into the night. I guess Jack was going to make sure Tim landed somewhere before he killed himself.

Tim Hardin eventually moved to Woodstock, where there was an abundant supply of heroin. He died there, but not before enjoying the singular distinction of being the only person who'd ever been such an asshole that he was 86'd permanently from the Joyous Lake Bar, the most popular watering hole at the time.

Nineteen seventy wound up being a good year, topped off by a cozy and happy Christmas. There was work, so for the very first time, there was a little left over once the bills were paid. We were eating regularly so we were generally healthier, and because of that, I felt tougher and more optimistic. We had a large bunch of good friends, and things were improving a bit between my father and me. I guess he'd finally come to terms with the fact that I was serious about all this and he'd better find a way to accept that.

In 1971, we got down to work on my first record. Bernie's company had made a good initial impact with Bruce's record, and there was a lot of buzz about this hot new little label. Bernie's wasn't the only indie label in town at that point, but it appeared to be the only one that was really avant-garde. The recording was to be done at Thunder Sound, a studio up on Davenport Road built by David Briggs, Neil Young's friend and tour manager, and an engineer named Henry Saskowski. The money for the studio was Neil's. For the time, it was a great little state-of-the-art facility, and Henry had built the board by himself. Henry began as the engineer on the album but was replaced before it was finished.

I called Barry Flast up from New York to play the piano, and he arrived all excited at finally seeing the world outside Manhattan. For drums, I hired Bernie's best friend and a guy I really liked a lot, Jay Telfer. Jay didn't really play the drums and was the first to admit it, but I was working on one of my wacko theories, and his lack of expertise didn't bother me. I thought most drummers played "too busy," and I just wanted a person who hit hard and kept good time without running all over the kit and playing flashy fills. Come to think of it, my idea wasn't that far off. As I learned more over the years, my favourite drummers were people like Barry Keane and Andy Newmark, who were simplicity personified.

Gene Martynec of Kensington Market was producing the record for me. (He'd already done the first Cockburn album for True North.) He was also lending his hand as a talented and lyrical guitarist. On bass was Dennis Pendrith, who remains one of the best all-round musicians I've ever met and one of the nicest guys. This was the beginning of a long and happy relationship with Dennis, during which I can never remember him having a bad word to say about anyone. Rounding out the band was Eric Robertson, a prodigy who was playing the pipe organ in church by the time he was in his teens. I guess Eric has produced about every Roger Whittaker album that was ever made. Eric played organ and arranged anything that needed charts.

And so we got down to business, with Chris Skein as our new engineer, to try and evolve a record album out of what I was seeing as a jam session in the studio.

I was so green. I was having a blast just playing music with my friends. I'd show up with a bunch of beer and a bit of this and that. We'd work out a song, and as it came together, we'd start putting down takes. I'd never really heard anything I'd ever done played back on a powerful studio system before, and I just wanted to play, listen and play some more, I was digging it so much. It must have been pretty hard for Finkelstein, who had a budget to think about, and Martynec, who had to think about a budget and making the act happy, to keep a rein on me.

We started the album on April 13, 1971, and by May 4, including some final mixing over at Eastern Sound studios, it was done. This must still stand as some kind of world record for multitrack recording. I thought the album was great. It was sloppy and rough, but it was bursting at the seams with the kind of raw energy I was feeling, now that I felt free to move forward as fast as I could.

We called the album *Song from the Street,* and the cover art, done by the mercurial Bart Schoales, featured some moody colour photos taken around my home in Kensington Market. The cover had me staring through the wire of a chicken cage at the birds as they waited for slaughter, unaware of what was about to happen to them. I think I was making a mental comparison between them and me when the shutter clicked.

Surprisingly, the record got good reviews. We had a particularly good collection of music critics at the time, who were fairminded, but more important, actually wrote about the ideas in the music and lyrics. They treated the new crop of records as though they were works of literature. Some of them, Jack Batten, for instance, were excellent writers, who happened to be working as critics to pay their bills. They latched onto the record's title and ran with it. In this way, the image of the hard uncompromising street kid that I carried around with me was born. It was a little strange for me because I'd put myself on the street; I hadn't been born to it. I was a working-class kid raised according to conservative values. Nobody pursued that avenue of inquiry, though, so I didn't bring it up.

Sometimes timing is everything. I think one really key element in the early success of my music, and Bruce's for that matter, was the fact that we came along with the advent of a new style of radio.

Top 40 was king, with its playlists and hit-parade charts. That was where the money was and the advertising that generated it. It was an impossible nut to crack for a Canadian record as a rule, although there were exceptions. Those that did break through were Canadian acts being released and promoted in the United States. Canadian top 40 program directors had a special file for submissions from Canadian record labels—on the floor!

But there was another kind of radio emerging. The new FM stations were just coming on line. There was little advertising revenue yet, and the stations were experimental. The station licences had been secured by the broadcast companies to have a spot on the FM dial "just in case." Nobody knew what their potential might be.

Naturally, because nobody was watching all that closely, the on-air slots were soon filled with counterculture hipsters who couldn't have cared less about playlists and Top 40. They'd sit there and rap for forty minutes on the air or play a whole side of a new album if they felt like it. Naturally, because the inevitable result was interesting and eccentric programming, it attracted a core audience of people who actually tuned in and listened for hours at a time, much in the way people listen to CBC today. These were listeners who would rather have put a bullet in their radio than listen to Top 40, and a lot of them were young.

So the FM jocks would just drop on a whole side of one of my new records, and people wouldn't know it was only a Canadian record and it wasn't supposed to be important. It would be up there alongside Jethro Tull or The Band and treated just the same as any other new release. Damned if people didn't come to the conclusion that it was important!

It was one of those lucky times that come along every so often when all the assumptions held dear by the masters of the old technology get shoved aside by something new. There was a blossoming in the music arts in this country that came with the freedom of FM radio, a freedom repeated again many years later with the emergence of *MuchMusic* on TV.

The attention of the press, combined with the radio exposure I was now receiving, meant I was getting a wider audience than I ever had before. I was working a lot more, and I was glad of it.

Goin' Back to New York City

BY 1972, THINGS WERE REALLY STARTING to change quickly. On the strength of that first Cockburn album, Bernie had signed a label distribution deal in late 1970 with Columbia records of Canada. The deal had an option clause allowing the company the rights to release records they selected in other markets—specifically, the United States. The U.S. parent company had picked up the option on the first of Bruce's discs, and they were very interested in what I was working on. They decided to pick up my second record, one that hadn't been made yet, but they wanted to become involved in its production. That was okay with us because they would get behind the project a lot more if they were involved from the get-go.

Bernie's relationship with Brazilian George suddenly got very complicated. Bernie had been running his business out of a house he'd rented on Scollard Street. His desk, from which he monitored his growing empire, was a junkyard table; two of the legs propped up with bricks. There was an alley cat named Claw that came and went and occasionally attacked the people it didn't like. Bernie slept in the house on an old mattress covered with a dingy sheet that hadn't been washed in a very long time. His nest was surrounded by months of old newspapers and magazines. With his long stringy hair and somewhat casual personal habits, Bernie was chronically short of money. He was managing two of the hottest new folk acts around, but that still didn't mean any of us were really making a lot of dough.

George and his cronies were around a lot. He'd taken something of a paternal interest in the label and its artists and had decided to become much more personally involved than Bernie would ever have wanted him to be. Sometimes, on the rare occasion when Bernie couldn't avoid having George attend a meeting at Columbia's offices, he proved somewhat difficult to have around. Frankly, he was getting to be a pain in the ass.

Then one day in late 1971, George's life changed forever. George had moved on to recreational heroin use. Combine that with the fact that, like all Brazilian males, he was convinced he was the greatest Grand Prix driver of all time, and the result was a truly toxic mix.

George always had Mercedes sedans, and he drove the wheels off them. It was a breathtaking experience to get in a car with him to go out to King City where the house was. He'd drive the King sideroad at straight-away speeds of over a hundred miles per hour—well over. He drove this way one-handed while carrying on a conversation with the back seat and occasionally glancing at the road. George applied the same arrogance and flouting of fear to driving a car that he did to everything else. I remember driving up Avenue Road with him one slushy winter day, trying to hide my face. He was taking great satisfaction in showering pedestrians as he tried to see how close he could run to the curb. Well, it all finally caught up with him.

One night, he was driving the King Road at breakneck speed with a nose full of smack and several people in the car, and his Grand Prix driving instincts deserted him long enough that he failed to negotiate one of the high-speed curves. The car left the road and impacted a very solid object made of hard wood. Everyone in the car was hurt, but George was the worst. When he was removed from the wreck, they nearly needed a second stretcher for his brain. He'd opened up his skull so effectively that a great portion of it was exposed.

He was in a coma for two months. He wasn't expected to live at all, but if he did, the doctors assumed he'd spend the rest of his days in a vegetative state. He did wake up, though, and amazingly, he was self-aware. He had motor skills and memories of who he was and who was close to him. But he was profoundly different. He was like George with a lobotomy. Many of the things he said just didn't make sense anymore. Most of George had come back, but the part that was smart, arrogant and on top was gone forever. Suddenly, Bernie had a guy showing up at the office who'd say things like, "One and one makes five, man! You know what I mean? Bongy, bongy!" Bernie ended the partnership.

So as we moved into 1972, Finkelstein was doing a dance with Bernie Fiedler of Riverboat fame, with a view to forming some kind of association. It was a logical step. Finkelstein was looking for a way to get Bruce and me out touring nationally in an organized fashion, and B.C. Fiedler was interested in promoting the shows. He was already running the most prestigious folk club in the country and had branched into major concert promotions by putting acts like Lightfoot and Joni into Massey Hall. Finkelstein's business was still a "run it out of your back pocket" sort of affair, and he needed and wanted an associate who could help him organize and expand and who might even be able to bring some capital into the company. After all, Elliott Roberts, Joni's manager, had just joined forces with the notorious David Geffen in what was being widely touted as a sort of good cop–bad cop merger.

There was one little wrinkle in the smooth fabric of events, however. During the time in which the two Bernies had been working out their deal, Fiedler had had a spot of tax trouble. The government determined that Herr Fiedler owed it a great deal of cash and offered the alternatives of immediate payment or having really bad things happen to him.

Fiedler got on the blower and had a conversation with Gordon Lightfoot, who had become his friend largely because Fiedler would sit up all night, babysitting him through his troubles. Lightfoot bailed poor Fiedler out of his dilemma and Fiedler began a special arrangement with Gordon regarding the promotion of the Lightfoot megaweeks at Massey Hall.

The cash infusion part of the deal between the two Bernies was no longer part of the play, but to Finkelstein, the rest of it still made sense. He was already working with me as the final stages of his negotiations were worked out, and he approached me one day and asked what I'd think about his forming a partnership with B.C. Fiedler. B.C. had a reputation for throwing great parties and moving easily with the stars. Socially, he was terribly charming, especially if he thought you were on the way up. Of course, the story about the tax problem was around, and people were unsure of where the chips were going to fall on that one. All things considered, I didn't think Finkelstein needed a partner, especially if there was no cash value in the deal. I told him I wasn't in favour of the partnership.

The deal went down anyway, and the partnership of the two Bernies was born. For simplicity's sake, I will henceforth refer to them as B.C. and Finkel. For a while, it got really confusing because our new attorney was a guy named Bernie Solomon, so now there were three guys named Bernie at meetings.

Meanwhile, Patty and I had moved out of the flat in Kensington Market and taken a loft that covered the entire second floor of Cadillac Johnny's fix-it-yourself garage down at the corner of Queen and Parliament. It was a promising space, but was what you'd call a handyman's special. The place was divided into two parts by a wall, and half of it was full of old junk that hadn't been moved in years.

Once the flat was cleared out, Bart Schoales came over to help with the initial demolition of the partition walls. (Bart had become a pretty constant fixture in my life by this time—he did all the True North art and mentored all of us with his strong opinions on all things creative and philosophical.) He was a bear of a guy with a tempestuous nature, who could be quite intimidating to those who didn't know him well. To those who did, he was a gentle and loyal friend.

He showed up with several quart bottles of sake, which we proceeded to heat up and drink in preparation for our labours. Bart had introduced me to Jimmy and Gus Kadonaga, who ran the Nikko Gardens restaurant down on Dundas Street near Spadina. They were two of the great original Toronto rounders, those guys—Gus with his trips to the Vegas casinos and Jimmy always at the Crest restaurant on Spadina Avenue reading the racing forms. I loved hanging out there and would often sit up with Jimmy well after closing time, which was how I acquired the taste for sake and all things Japanese.

After knocking off a couple of bottles of sake, Bart and I attacked the interior walls with crowbars and a sledge. There are few times in my life when I've let myself go and indulged in the complete joy of wanton destruction while orbiting the earth at the same time. We had a ball. We destroyed the place, and by the time we were done, I was so pissed I drank most of the last bottle of sake out of my cowboy boot while we laughed our asses off.

Once the place was opened up, we painted it white and built a bathroom with a shower. In the back part we installed dance mirrors and a barre because Patty was getting back into ballet. She had a keen interest and would eventually drag me into that world.

I loved the space of it. When I wanted to think, I'd sometimes ride a bicycle around the room. There were windows on both sides, so the place was always full of light. It also had a huge flat roof, which was accessible only from our back door, and there was no way to get up there from the street, so it was all ours. We put pine trees in tubs and a little deck out there, and that winter, I built a skating rink. The roof was held up with steel beams, so it was strong enough to hold the weight of the frozen water. I practised my slapshot against the outside wall of our loft to relax between bouts of writing. It was a great little scene. People were always coming and going. We had parties.

Our landlord, Johnny, had a bit of a street reputation as being "connected." I don't know. He never talked about that. He had a lot of business interests, among them a fleet of tow trucks. The towing business always provoked him into fits of rage. He was at war with a rival towing company, whose drivers were always arriving at police calls first and scooping up the business. Johnny was convinced that the cops were giving the competition an advantage. I do know that in a rough neighbourhood, where there was a lot of casual B&E and welfare-night skirmishes on the street, we were never broken into and no matter what time Patty was coming home, she never got hassled. Johnny liked us, and I think we were sort of off-limits. He certainly liked me enough that he bought a large number of my records and gave them to his friends.

There were some less than wonderful things about living there, however. One time when I came home late, Johnny was sitting in his office, nursing a bottle of rye.

"Murray!" he shouted as I tried to sneak past his office. "You come, have drink with me!"

"No thanks, Johnny. I'm really beat. I gotta get some sleep."

"Sit down."

"Okay, but just the one."

"This morning, you walk past my wife on the sidewalk like she's no even there. What, you think she's a pig?"

"Jeez, Johnny, I swear I didn't even see her. Of course not!"

I no sooner got that issue calmed down than he was off on some other tangent.

"You see these hands? All my life I work with these! Very strong. You take my hand, you see!"

"No, Johnny, I believe you!"

"Take hold of my hand!"

I put out my hand and what started out to be a firm handshake quickly became a bone-shattering vise-grip. I was beating on his forearm trying to get him to let go. I tried to avoid getting him upset, hoping something would distract him and take the focus away from me.

Then there were the fumes from the auto-body work being done below us, particularly the solvent and paint fumes. Some winter mornings, when the windows were buttoned up tight, we'd wake up with either splitting headaches or higher than kites. It was altogether totally artistic!

B.C., Finkel and I went down to New York to meet the movers and shakers from CBS who were going to make a big star out of me. We had lunch with Walter Yetnikoff, Ron Alexenburg and the head of A&R for Epic records, Don Ellis. Walter seemed like a nice middle-aged Jewish guy—paternal, kind. I guess I was naive. He's one of the toughest guys in the record business. Alexenburg seemed a little slippery to me, and I had a tendency not to trust what he said. Also wrong. Don Ellis I took an immediate shine to. He was a music guy, like Finkel. You sensed that his enthusiasm was genuine and unforced and based on a real understanding of what the whole game was about—making good work.

We went to lunch at the Russian Tearoom, and I didn't have a tie (naturally), so I had to wear one the restaurant provided. The talks began. It was agreed that the record would be done by a top-line producer and all the money issues regarding production costs were resolved. We'd begin to meet likely candidates for producer as soon as possible.

Now that Finkel and B.C. were partners, Fiedler felt that it was time my relationship with the management company was formalized by a contract—what with the serious nature of the negotiations we were engaging in with the U.S. company. Up to that point, Finkel and I had never had one. We all went next door with the documents, and my official signing to True North and Finkelstein Fiedler Management took place in a drugstore in midtown Manhattan. No gold pen, no pictures in the trades—hell, there weren't any trades in Canada except for the very, very fledgling *RPM* being run by Walt Grealis and Stan Klees.

Joni Mitchell was in town, returning to Carnegie Hall. We went to the concert and to the after-show reception at the Plaza Hotel. She gave a stunning performance and was dazzling at the party. I remember that a large number of the New York elite were there. Eric Andersen was much in evidence as he hovered around Joni for most of the evening. There were a lot of really good-looking well-dressed guys climbing all over themselves trying to get next to her. I felt like I'd walked into a formal dinner wearing a chicken suit.

At some point during the evening, I was introduced to David Geffen. He looked at me rather coldly and said, "I hear you're with Epic. Well, they won't do anything for you."

I was already feeling a little insecure, and his comment took me aback. I was crestfallen. I couldn't come up with a reply, and as I was trying to figure out what to say, he was whisked off somewhere else.

There was a young lady at the party, a folk singer well known for having a little container full of ups and downs and everything in between. She gave him something. Unfortunately for Mr. Geffen, it turned out to be the wrong something. He'd eaten from the side of the mushroom that makes you grow tall, not the one that makes you grow small. In minutes, he was on the floor with his heart racing, panicky, crying in his anxiety, surrounded by a bevy of concerned female attendants all clucking and soothing. I looked down at him, and I must confess the thought that crossed my mind, "There is a god who avenges unnecessary cruelty."

The producer we all finally agreed on was a man named Ed Freeman. He was currently on the A-list, having just completed Don MacLean's mega-hit "American Pie."

Ed was about the most laid-back guy I'd ever met—lots of curly hair, thick beard—and he smoked more grass than anyone I'd ever seen. He kept a shoebox full of herb by the studio console, and as he listened to takes, he would absent-mindedly tilt the box and shovel its contents up to one end with a playing card—to separate the seeds. Ed smoked more dope than Bob Marley. I don't know how the guy could complete a thought, never mind walk around. We got along really well because he was extremely easy to get along with. Screw conflict resolution—conflict wasn't even possible!

Ed had a wide variety of interesting friends in the session game around the city, and most of them came in and out of the studio at one time or another. There was Jake Jacobs from a band locally known as Jake and the Family Jewels, who was an absolute sweetheart and a disaster as far as his life went. There was Ruan MacKinnon, who had one of the most beautiful voices I'd ever heard and used it to full advantage on the cut we did of Warren Zevon's song "Carmelita."

I'd picked up that song earlier in the year when I'd done a tour of western Canada and the Pacific Northwest, opening up for the Everly Brothers. Some of the gigs were just the Everlys and me, while others included a band called Commander Cody and the Lost Planet Airmen. Fresh off a hit version of the old tune "Hot Rod Lincoln," they were a boogie-woogie-style novelty act. A couple of the dates I did were with them alone.

I'd brought my pal and bassist Dennis Pendrith, and Finkel was on the tour as well. Those were the days when he needed no excuse to get out on the road if there was some action.

The Everlys had, as usual, the most fabulous band there ever was. Any music aficionado would be familiar with the names. They had Waddy Wachtel, familiar to Jackson Browne fans, playing guitar. Rusty Young was doing the honours on steel, and on the piano there was Warren Zevon, who was just about the maddest bastard I'd ever met up to that point in my life. I took to Warren like a duck to water and ended up burning the midnight oil and a lot of other stuff with him. We ended up swapping songs on the tour, and I traded him "Honky Red" for "Carmelita," a song he'd written that chronicled the life of a burned-out junkie in East Los Angeles.

I guess the biggest episode of bonding on the whole tour was when I found the Danny Dope of Prince George, B.C., and bought a bunch of MDA, which Don Everly had never had before. Neither had any of the rest of those good ol' boys, for that matter. Well, we did about all of it and then tucked into a bunch of forty ouncers of ouzo while we screamed along with every Beach Boys and Jan and Dean record that had ever been made. That was what we did for the whole bus ride from Prince George into Edmonton, and I don't think I've had as much fun since. By the time we got to Edmonton, poor Don Everly was so far gone that he had to be carried off the bus by the hands and feet and placed in his bed in the Corona Hotel.

In Edmonton, I met a little cute blonde-haired hippie girl and she wound up tagging along for a while. She was heading out to B.C. and we were moving back that way. She was a really sweet and pleasant little road muffin but she helped demonstrate that the Commander Cody band wasn't nearly as much fun as they let on. There was one tour leg where I was, for convenience sake, going to catch a ride on Cody's bus instead of the one Don Everly was using. It was one of the dates the Everlys weren't doing, so it was easier to travel with the other band than to make a bunch of alternate arrangements.

At the appointed hour in the morning, I showed up outside the bus with the little girl in tow and walked up the stairs to the inside. Two things met us. The first was an incredible stench of old socks and B.O., like these guys had been living in this thing for months without having a shower or stopping at a laundromat. The second was a wave of protest that quickly enveloped the bus about bringing my companion into their midst. Cody took me aside and said "Man, you can't bring her in here. Some of these guys haven't seen their wives and sweethearts for months. Everybody's trying to handle it the best way they can, but we got an iron-clad rule: No women on the bus!"

Well, I was a little pissed but—what the hell—it was their bus and they could do what they wanted. I made other arrangements, and we got to the next town okay and did the show that night. Of course, after the gig was done, it was party time and I had to laugh. After all that sanctimonious "wives and sweethearts" horseshit, didn't Cody show up with two of the trashiest-looking split-up-the-leg shantung-silk-dressed hookers you ever saw. Their job was going to be to make all those boys miss their wives and sweethearts a little bit less.

My temporary friend had nothing more on her mind than finding a quiet little place out in the Gulf Islands where she could raise goats. I considered myself fortunate to be in her company until we said goodbye the next day.

There were a lot of amazing things about that tour, but perhaps one of the most telling was my reaction to Don and Phil's music. If you've ever opened for anybody, you know that once you've seen the show once or twice, you usually split when your bit is done, in search of more interesting pursuits. Not on this one! I went out front every night and sat as close as I could get to the stage just to hear that band play and those guys sing. Even if you've heard the records, you've got no idea just how good they are until you've heard them live. Every night I'd let those perfect close harmonies wash over me. Every night "Bye Bye Love" and "Cathy's Clown" sounded just as fresh as if I was hearing them for the first time.

I didn't really get to know Phil at all. He was reclusive and didn't travel with his brother or stay in the same hotel. They had had a falling-out of major proportions some years earlier. It was rumoured to have been over a woman. In any event, by this time, Phil wasn't even talking to Don. But you would never have known it when they stepped on the stage.

I had one of the best times of my life on that tour. A nice footnote is that on the rare occasions when I run into Don Everly, usually in Nashville, his face still lights up in a big smile when he sees me. Maybe it has to do with that bus ride.

So that was how "Carmelita" found its way onto the record as we soldiered away in the summer of 1972 in the bowels of The Record Plant in Manhattan.

I was living in the Gorham Hotel on Fifty-fifth Street, just a short walk from the Carnegie delicatessen of *Broadway Danny Rose* fame. That became my regular hangout for breakfast, lunch and often dinner too. One thing they didn't have, though, was fresh stuff—you know, fruit! In that area of town, it wasn't easy to find an apple or an orange, and every so often I'd just get one of those cravings for something that wasn't boiled, fried or steamed and sliced with mustard between two pieces of bread.

I finally did find a pitiful little all-night store that had a limited supply, but everything was in styrofoam trays and shrink-wrapped. I used to go in there and buy some apples and feel like I was liberating the fruit from some kind of prison.

One night, I was having thoughts about just how far Manhattan really was from everything that sustained it. Watching the produce trucks delivering to the restaurants in the wee small hours I was thinking that, Jeez, it's likely a guy like my pal Barry Flast wouldn't have known that apples grew on trees unless he read it in a book. I wandered back over to the Gorham Hotel, and without much effort, wrote a little poem of thanks for all the people who grew the stuff that came into Manhattan, or anywhere else for that matter. Then I put it to a simple tune, and the result was "Farmer's Song." Once it was finished, I sang it a couple of times. I thought it was simplistic and kind of goofy, and I didn't really know if it was any good.

The next day, I walked into The Record Plant and found Ed with the shoebox in his lap, sorting out the seeds with the playing card, and I told him I'd written this goofy little song the night before. Did he want to hear it?

It was just Ed and me with our engineer, Tom Flye (who'd just completed a live record for the Rolling Stones), sitting around in the control room. I took out the guitar and played the song and I was almost apologetic when I finished. I didn't think Ed was going to like it.

Ed wanted to cut it right then and there! I was so surprised I didn't know whether to shit or wind my watch. I went out into the room and so did Tom. We cut a basic track with just me, and him playing the drums. Then Ed came in and laid down a bass-and-rhythm track played on an old bellows-driven pump organ. The only other thing on the record was me yodelling through the reeds of my harmonica on a number of tracks for a special sound effect. Forty-five minutes to write it. Four hours to record it. And twenty-three years later, it's still on jukeboxes in farflung regions of Canada. It would never have got on the record if Ed Freeman hadn't been such a chance-taking dope-smoking looney! Thanks, Ed.

Nineteen seventy-two was the year I went to Montreal to play a benefit for the legal fund dedicated to putting a halt to the James Bay power project. This government project with Hydro-Québec was slated to flood an enormous area in northern Quebec that just happened to include the homes and hunting grounds of the James Bay Cree. Much of the power produced by the damming and flooding was to be sold to New York State. The show was in the Paul Sauvé Arena, and Joni Mitchell was flying in to play it as well, against the advice of her manager.

I'd been in the Riverboat one night a few months before the benefit, hanging out, when B.C. Fiedler had announced he was going to Vancouver the next day to see Joni. I think she was playing at the Queen Elizabeth Theatre, but I can't remember for sure why she was there. In any event, she was in the early stages of building the house she'd designed up near Halfmoon Bay, so she was planning on going up to stay for a while and supervise the work while relaxing at Lord Jim's resort.

I think Fiedler was well aware of my rather casual attitude towards marriage when he looked at me and nonchalantly said, "Why don't you come along?" I also think he was aware that I had a bit of a crush on the lady, and in typical Fiedler fashion, wanted to throw all the ingredients into the pot and see what happened.

I announced to Patty that I was flying out to the coast the next day and wasn't quite sure when I'd be back. Patty, probably realizing I was up to no good, didn't question me. At that point in my life, I reacted badly to anyone getting between me and whatever I wanted to do. I'm not sure of what was actually in my mind at the time, but I can guess. I think it was some variation of the pathetic fantasy that I was going to become so successful and I was so artistic that Joni would somehow find me irresistible and I would run off to California with her.

Fiedler and I flew out there, and after a day at the Bayshore, headed up to Lord Jim's. At the time, Joni and Fiedler were great friends. He was a very relaxed kind of confidant-therapist who could be relied on not to take her too seriously at a time when practically everyone else was. The three of us had a great time hanging out and talking—having dinner, drinking wine. Joni was the same then as she is now. Wind her up and let her go! Once she's awake, the woman never goes back to sleep. She's a stream-of-consciousness, free-associative monologist who makes wonderful sense of the world. She makes it up as she goes along.

There was a strange moment I remember. We were playing pool in a little roadside bar not far from Lord Jim's, just having fun knocking the balls around really. Joni was concentrating hard, lining up her shots, doing the geometry. Suddenly, for no apparent reason, she burst into tears.

I was gobsmacked! Fiedler calmly said something like, "Joni, darling, what the fuck is wrong?" He got her calmed down after a while, and it emerged that there was a bit of a war going on inside her. It was a lot of masculine-feminine stuff about wanting to win but hating the fact that she wanted to win and then feeling that her feelings of competitiveness were too masculine. I'm not drawing conclusions here, this is just some of the stuff that came out.

I remember thinking back to the impression I'd had the first time I'd met her in Sudbury, that there was intense inner turmoil that wasn't completely hidden by the serene blonde goddess exterior. Anyway, the storm blew over, and all was sweetness and light once more.

I think she was coming to terms at the time with the real impact of her fame—with being stalked and hounded, with the prurient interest in her romantic life (made more poignant by the fact that the bulk of her writing was inspired by precisely this). I was learning a little about the consequences of fame by watching her handle it.

Being around her for that time and seeing the depths of her character emerge put a person behind the romantic image for me. The person had ambitions and flaws, but that just made her all the more interesting. By the time I flew back to Toronto, I had more than a crush on her.

So I was looking forward to doing this weird benefit for the Cree cause in Quebec—not just because it was a good idea but also because she'd be there.

The show itself was macabre. The arena acoustics were about what you'd expect—terrible! Bernie Finkelstein was there with me, and I went through my songs with Dennis Pendrith playing bass. We were given a lukewarm response. I hadn't had my big hit yet, and I wasn't very well known in Quebec.

When Joni got up to play, she was, of course, solo. There was a fair amount of din in the arena from the people who were there just to be there. A common characteristic all audiences exhibit when they are served something up for free is that they tend not to pay any respect to what they are seeing. Maybe the mind makes the connection that if it didn't cost anything, it isn't worth anything. There was a hard core of tough Québécois girls in the arena who were not impressed by her at all—to the point where several of them could be heard quite plainly yelling, "Fuck you, English blonde bitch!" It was a tough and seemingly ungrateful crowd. And, of course, the first stage of the James Bay project eventually went ahead.

At some point in 1972, cocaine had made an appearance on the scene. It wasn't commonplace, but it was around and I just loved it. Rather than making me feel stupid, like hash or grass did, it made me feel smart and on top of things. It also acted as a bit of an emotional anaesthetic, particularly for any feelings of guilt. What it was really doing, if I'd had the objectivity to notice it, was making it possible for me to be a complete asshole while simultaneously thinking I was fine.

It was with a bit of coke-inspired courage mixed with good scotch that I decided to call Joni in her room that night, after the concert was over. She was by herself when I called and said to come on up and hang out.

For a while, it was talk, talk, talk, and being a bit coked, I was fairly intense, I suppose. I did a sketch of her, which I still have in a book of loose creative stuff. It's a drawing of her with my old mailman's peaked cap perched on her head at a jaunty angle. At some point, I just blurted out, "Joni, I think I'm in love with you!"

She looked at me for a short while. Not much was written on her face.

"Is it hanging you up?" she asked.

I had a male acquaintance once who described something that had happened to him when he was being prepped for a hernia operation. A nurse had come in with the equipment for shaving the area where the operation was to take place. Try as he might to suppress the hydraulic reaction, when she began the process, he got a hard-on. She matter-of-factly gave the swelling appendage a well-placed light slap and rinsed him off with cold water, effectively putting an end to the incident.

The way Joni asked her simple question had precisely the same effect on me. There was no mistaking it was the end of the issue.

"Nope!" I answered.

I then went back downstairs to my room and wrote a desperate song about death and resurrection called "Revelations." It was a pretty good song actually.

Farmer's Song and Beyond

BACK IN TORONTO, I RAN INTO Brian Ahearn one day, and he was beginning a new production project. Brian was an all-star producer who'd already worked with a lot of big acts and would eventually wind up married to Emmylou Harris for a while. He was doing an album with a guy who was known only for writing one hit song, even though he was a legend in Maritime Canada. The song was "Snowbird," which had been the career starter for Anne Murray, and the project was the collected songs of Gene MacLellan.

Brian liked the way I played rhythm guitar and asked me if I'd like to come down to Woodstock, New York, to the Bearsville studios that Albert Grossman and The Band had built, to play on Gene's record. It took me about a second to say yes.

The other players on the session were to be Amos Garrett on electric guitar; Chris Parker, from Paul Butterfield's Better Days band, on drums; Ben Keith, who was a stalwart member of Neil Young's band; Skip Beckwith from Halifax on bass; and Rat Rizzo on keys. Dropping in would be Bobby Charles, who wrote "See You Later, Alligator" to sing backgrounds, and probably Butterfield himself, because Amos was playing in his band at the time. What was to turn down? I would have done it for free, and I nearly did!

I wound up staying at Amos's house on the outskirts of Woodstock, where he was living with Carol Robinson. Amos had a well-earned reputation as a wild man, and Carol, who had known him so long, seemed intent on getting him to calm down enough to ensure his future survival. I got down there and just wanted to roar, so I suppose I undid some of her efforts. We partied pretty hard the whole time.

The music was fun. It was a gas to be sitting jamming in the studio and working out stuff with such a bunch of stellar players. Gene was a fluid and beautiful singer with an astounding collection of great songs that owed more to R&B or gospel than to folk music. This was right up everyone else's alley, but it took a little educating for me to get into the groove.

Even then, Gene was a quiet and somewhat troubled man. I didn't know him and didn't realize how deeply religious he was because he was quiet about it. He wasn't interested in coming out and ratting around after the sessions, and I just put it down to shyness. I did wonder what Brian was going to do with the record after it was done because it didn't look likely that Gene was going to last long in the post-production publicity mode.

In the meantime, once the daily grind was over, usually in the smaller hours, Amos and I would retire to the Joyous Lake Bar and I would indulge a taste for straight bourbon washed down with beer. Amos eventually persuaded me to try his drink of choice, which was amber Bacardi mixed with tonic water and a slice of lime. I switched over because I was in a tropical kind of mood. We got monumentally tight and had a swell time with the happy-go-lucky young women who frequented the establishment. Sometimes it went a little over the edge, and we were lucky not to wind up in jail or dead.

One night, we were in the place drinking with a couple of gals and I, full of fun, was attempting to auction one of them off to all and sundry for the right price. I had this blonde girl's shirt undone and spread open to expose her rather nice breasts to a grateful world as I yelled, "Who'llagonnagimmefifty!"

Now Amos was in the beginnings of his "Famous Amos" phase and had this Panama hat that he was very attached to. It may have been tilted back on occasion at a rakish angle, but it never came off his head. Well, this girl I'd been auctioning suddenly decided that the funniest thing in the world would be to grab Amos's hat and stick it on her head and bolt for the door, which is precisely what she did, with her friend in tow. They raced to the parking lot and jumped into their car. The chase was on as Amos and I headed out in hot pursuit. He wasn't about to lose that hat.

We hit Amos's car at about the same time that the girls' car, tires smoking and squealing, roared out of the parking lot. What followed was one of the wilder car chases through the back roads around Woodstock. For a substantial portion of it, one of the doors on our car was hanging open as we shrieked around bends. I have substantial holes in my memory of what followed, but we did get Amos's hat back, and everyone wound up safely back in the bar. That night, when we returned to the house, I gave Amos a tour of the whole place by towing him around on his back, pulling him by the feet. Carol, normally good humoured, was not amused.

We finally finished the record, and I thought the results were amazing. I'd made some fast friends, and a couple would play on my next record. I regret that the MacLellan project never found its way into release.

Gene's dead now. Sadly, whatever was inside him ate him up and he hanged himself. But somewhere out there, there's a hell of a master tape with his songs on it.

"Farmer's Song" surprised the shit out of everybody. I was the most surprised of all. It was no doubt the most improbable song there was to become a hit record, given what was charting at the time. It started small when a country programmer named Ted Daigle went on the record just because he liked what it said. Then other programmers picked up on it. After that, it crossed over onto pop charts and adult radio everywhere. Within a short while, it sold seventy thousand singles in Canada. Single—you know, 45 RPM vinyl with the big hole in the middle! It was a bona fide smash, and it was the popular support of ordinary people phoning in to radio stations that created it.

This song changed the gears of my life once more. I won three RPM Gold Leaf awards for it. That was what they called the JUNOS before they became the JUNOS. I won best country single, best folk single, and the most meaningful of all for me, composer of the year! The record was out in the States, I had the Tom Rush credibility down there and I was making enough of a reputation to start getting invited to play the Philadelphia Folk Festival, run by Paula Ballon. I had a strong U.S. club tour, where I was now headlining in most places. They were starting to be top clubs, like Paul Colby's Bitter End in New York, and the Main Point in Bryn Mawr, just outside Philadelphia. There was the Exit Inn in Nashville, where I met Paul Davis (composer of "Ride 'Em Cowboy") and Mylon LeFevre, with whom we all went out to the country for a studio jam. There was the Earl of Old

Town in Chicago, where I met John Prine and really got to know Steve Goodman (one of the great and really courageous ones). We'd all congregate at Philly or Mariposa, which by this point was held on the Toronto Islands and had grown so big it had freaked out the people who were running it.

The folk festivals had grown and changed. They were really more like major pop festivals with an ethnic bent that attracted the cream of the emerging singer-songwriters. Some of them were handling this transition comfortably; others weren't. Philadelphia was cool and fun to hang at. It was routine for me to wind up in a room with Prine, Goodman, Loudon Wainwright III and even Jim Croce, who was cutting his teeth on the folk club circuit. A regular crowd went down there from Toronto and helped with the event. There was a lot of crosstalk between music events, and the same people could often be found soldiering away in Winnipeg, Toronto or Philadelphia. The irrepressible Richard Flohil, to name one, had been drawn into the whole thing because, like many Englishmen, he had a deep and abiding love for blues. He had made many pilgrimages to the clubs on the south side of Chicago when it was still quite a dangerous thing to do. Richard was great friends with Dick Waterman, Bonnie Raitt's manager and fellow blues lover. It was his devotion to music that got Richard involved in labour-of-love concert promotions, where he invariably lost his shirt. Richard would give his whole heart to keep real music alive.

At one point, a Maoist group who were convinced that all music should be free arrived en masse at the gates of the Mariposa Festival screaming and yelling as they tried to crash through. There was Richard, manning the barricades! Richard had taken me down to Arkansas twice: once in '71 and once in '72, the first time with Luke Gibson, the second time with Tannis Neiman to play a concert at a theological college in Conway. We'd had some great adventures, roaring down there all packed into Richard's tiny little Japanese car.

There was a regular contingent of girls who followed the festival circuit. I don't mean like camp followers but more like volunteers and helpers, although some of them weren't averse to comforting a lonely songwriter. Dick had a friend named Cathy Miller who was not only helpful and really nice but also incredibly well endowed. I remember one old boy in a bluegrass band nearly having a heart attack when she showed up at the motel pool in a makeshift bathing suit made of brief denim cut-offs and two handkerchiefs.

Mariposa wasn't handling the transition too well though, and I kind of got caught up in the middle of it. I guess the whole thing came to a head when Joni Mitchell, Neil Young and Bob Dylan decided to get back to their roots and drop by to hang out and maybe jam a bit. There were some berserk fan stampedes.

I gave over half of a special little mini-concert that I was doing so Joni could play, and Bruce Cockburn did the same thing for Neil. It was a natural thing to want to do. Our managers were all friends; B.C. had booked Neil at the Riverboat and promoted Joni at Massey Hall. Bruce and I were sympathetic to the idea that these two artists just wanted to play some informal music. It seemed like a good idea at the time.

There were several thousand people out in front at each of these afternoon shows, and they all wanted to hear. The workshop sound systems had to get cranked up to keep the fans happy, and there was some spillover into other areas. Estelle Klein, the artistic director of the festival, got pretty out of shape. She felt that people were pulling "star trips" and ruining the nature of the festival. An ideological conflict was beginning to happen. There was a core group running the event, and I think they felt they were losing control of it, that it was being turned into a rock festival. They had a history of turning a cold shoulder on people who got "too famous." Joni, who'd played the thing from the beginning when she was starving and had always been very supportive of it, was rather hurt.

It wasn't long before it was my turn. The circumstances were just about the same except now it was only me. I was getting pretty hot, and a ton of people showed up to hear an afternoon concert I was doing. The system got turned up so they could hear in the back. Estelle came storming over and got into an argument with Finkelstein. Locking horns with Finkelstein when he is defending the interests of his act is not a wise thing to do. I was not invited back to play the festival again until the nineties, when it was a radically different affair (Lightfoot and I both played on the same stage, the same day—to no one).

I was sorry about being banished. I had always supported the festival and had done a lot for it in return. I felt it should be about expanding the boundaries of art; it should not act merely as some kind of cultural museum.

In the meantime, life on the club circuit out there in the U.S.A. was a blast! I had some very funny moments. Some of them were eye openers. I remember being booked into the Main Point on one occasion. I was the headliner, and the opening act was a local Philadelphia band that couldn't seem to break out nationally. The band was Hall and Oates.

I arrived at the club early enough to hear their sound check, grabbed a coffee and sat down. I was there doing my singer-songwriter thing with Dennis Pendrith playing bass. What was up on stage was a full-blown white soul R&B band, complete with a very new innovation called the Mellotron, a presynthesizer string machine that used chain drives and taped loops of sampled string sounds. They cranked up this giant ensemble and launched into their first song of the sound check. They played "She's Gone," and it sounded incredible. I just wished the earth would swallow me up!

Eventually, I got big enough on the Eastern Seaboard that I finally appeared at the Main Point with Eric Andersen opening up for me! It was a weird feeling because I respected him and thought the billing should have been the other way around. Eric was a smooth creature, though. He just sat down there in the basement dressing room between sets and had girls bring him drinks, and other girls bring him roses, and other girls give him kisses on the cheek, and Eric just smiled.

The Main Point was a paradise for girls, or more specifically, those who were fond of girls. Being out in one of the tonier areas of Philadelphia and close to Bryn Mawr, it had no shortage of well-heeled highly intelligent young goddesses new to freedom. Many of them took jobs slinging drinks at the club. For me, it was a smorgasbord. Usually, all you needed to do was smile politely and say, "Excuse me, but I'm lonely and far from home. Would you like to come and sleep with me tonight?" Just a simple question, nothing creepy about it, nothing fake. She'd think about it, weigh the entertainment value against the consequences, and more often than not, say okay. Sometimes they'd do the asking, which would mean happy times because of the special enthusiasm implicit in that forwardness.

New York was always a great gig. I really enjoyed playing at the Bitter End. It had tons of history, and when the night was over, there was lots of other stuff to do: wander around to the Kettle of Fish to hear the next Bob Dylan or have a natter with Eric Franzden; go over to Rienzi's where usually one member or the other of the New York Dolls would show up; hang out at Wendy Winstead's apartment and play with her pet skunks (on the cover of the *Day to Day Dust* album, there's a picture of Dennis and me with one of Wendy's skunks, taken while we were sitting in the Dugout Bar next to the Bitter End). I always loved just walking around in New York City. Something would always stop you that would turn out to be interesting.

I was playing the Bitter End one time, and the opening act, a young lady whose name I can't remember, got sick or took the wrong pill and called in to say she couldn't play. Paul Colby called around to find a substitute for the evening and announced to me that the opener for the night was going to be a band called LaBelle. The name didn't immediately ring one—no pun intended—but when they arrived, I quickly figured out what had happened. Patti LaBelle walked in the door with Nona Hendrix in tow, both of them done up to the nines. Patti had just formed the group, and they were playing in it while recording the album that would eventually result in the smash hit "Lady Marmalade"—you know, "Voulez-vous couchez avec moi, ce soir?"

That night was hilarious. The club was virtually hijacked by black gay screamers in Mylar space suits. None of my fans could get in the door. So after LaBelle had worked the joint into an insane frenzy, I went out and did my little "Good-bye Mama, good-bye to you too, Pa" thing. The audience was very polite actually. I don't think they'd ever seen a real folk singer before and they thought I was quaint. You know what else? Patti LaBelle was as nice and sweet and polite to me as though I was the president of the United States, even though for her this was slumming.

In Ottawa, there was a really interesting scene surrounding Bill Hawkins, Café le Hibou and the house on Somerset Street belonging to Dr. Ted Schaeffer and his wife, Penelope. Penelope had been Joni's travelling companion for a time while she was having her romantic adventures in Greece. Joni actually wrote a poem for Penelope which I have in a book of stuff she gave me. The poem is called "Penelope Wants to Fuck the Sea." It's a great piece of erotic poetry too, right up there with D.H. Lawrence's "The Elephant Is Slow to Mate."

Dr. Ted was doing research projects on brain function for I don't know who. I took part in one of them, as a matter of fact. I had my head all wired up with electrodes, and then a series of rhythmic pulses was played. After the pattern had been established, the machine was programmed to omit pulses at random to see what the brain would do. It turned out that regular people (who aren't musicians) have no reaction at all to the pulses that aren't there. The musician's brain, on the other hand, goes off the scale with electrical activity as it replaces the tone pulse that isn't there.

Ted and Penny's place was the artist's mecca at the time in Ottawa. They ran a sort of psychedelic circus and made interesting home movies starring themselves and some of their closer friends.

Through Bill Hawkins, I met Alison Gordon. She'd been going around with him for a while. Alison's friend, a lady named Jennifer Rae, was dating Trudeau at the time, and they'd all go out to Harrington Lake where the prime ministerial retreat was and hang out. It was an odd assortment the RCMP were guarding—a strange collection of personalities rowing around the lake blowing smoke rings.

I eventually became Alison's boy-toy for a while. I asked her and she doesn't mind my telling anybody. She says I was her young lover, which is funny because I'm not very much younger than she is. She broke the mould and eventually became a sports writer of repute who documented the travels of the Toronto Blue Jays through several seasons, and she is a well-regarded author of mystery novels (she writes the Kate Henry books). She's a great lady too, and I recently helped to celebrate her fifty-fifth.

So I was having the time of my life—travelling a lot, playing a lot, writing like crazy, finding ample opportunities to fuck my brains out and making enough money to afford the occasional gram of coke. Life was good, or at least a damn sight better than it ever had been since I'd left home.

In 1973, I wasn't ready for the concert market yet, although we were packing the clubs wherever I went. "Farmer's Song" had been a hit but that hadn't translated into a big concert audience yet. B.C. and Finkel were looking for ways to introduce me to the bigger venues, but not unless it was the right thing.

In the meantime, I called up Amos Garrett and Chris Parker, with whom I'd had such a great time on the MacLellan record and asked them to come up to Toronto to play on my next effort.

The result was an album called *Day to Day Dust*. The cover was a black-and-white photo, done by Bart Schoales, of me sitting in a chair. Everything in the picture is white except for me. I'm wearing a black leather motorcycle jacket, black boots and black jeans. There is a chrome samovar perched on a stool next to me, with a white-painted dead tree sticking out of it and white ping-pong balls pouring from the spigot. The cover was a great send-up, referring as it did to the amount of nose powder we'd been consuming while we did the record. When we got out of Eastern Sound, the lid of the piano had a street value of ten thousand dollars.

The first single from the record was a song called "Linda, Won't You Take Me In." I'd written the song while I was in a fit of high good humour one night above

Cadillac Johnny's. I had just seen the classic Linda Lovelace porn movie *Deep Throat*, and I was trying to write a song asking her to do to me what she does best, without actually saying it. The song was a complete scream, but of course I never mentioned what it was about. It climbed a substantial way up a lot of charts before some geezer out west in either Calgary or Edmonton finally twigged to what the score was and yanked the song off the air. Other stations quickly followed suit, and that was the end of my gentle tribute to Miss Lovelace.

The concert-circuit opportunity the management team had been looking for came along in the person of Neil Young. Neil had embarked on his "Tonight's the Night" tour, based on a whole lot of songs he'd written after the heroin-induced death of a friend. The tour was to be done in smaller venues instead of stadiums and arenas, and Elliott Roberts, who was managing Neil, was not in favour of the idea to say the least. Let's just say that Elliott didn't see this as a career-enhancing move.

Neil was making a swing through Ontario, and it was suggested that I open up a couple of the shows for him. I was doing well regionally, and I might add something to the bill. It was a weird kind of set-up because Nils Lofgren was already opening up with his band Grin, as well as playing in Neil's band, so I was a little mystified as to why they needed me. The band he was touring with had Ralph Molina and Billy Talbot as the rhythm section, Nils and Neil playing guitars and my old pal from the Gene MacLellan Bearsville studio sessions, Ben Keith, on steel. It would prove to be a sensational band—searing and angry and loud, loud, loud!

The first gig was over at one of the southern Ontario universities. I can't remember anymore whether it was Western or Guelph. Anyway, I got out there and did my opening set as a surprise special guest, and to my astonishment, the joint went nuts. I guess my *enfant terrible* reputation was catching on with the college crowd. The reaction wasn't lost on Neil either, because he promptly asked me to do the whole tour of the U.S. with the show.

The tour was surreal. A small venue for Neil Young at that time in the United States was still more people than I'd ever seen in one building in my life. The opening date was at Boston Symphony Hall, which is enormous—balcony after balcony stretching up to the distant ceiling. The high of choice at the time for the American college student hippie–radical–Buffalo Springfield fan was a wicked combination of Quaaludes and wine, which served to make them both stupid and loud. The audience at that gig was loaded for bear.

Nils went out with his power trio Grin and cranked up the decibels enough to drown out the incessant screams of "Neil Young, Neil Young!"

When I went out there, you could hear them just fine—no problem! It was really noisy and really hostile. Dennis and I were doing our two-man folk thing in the middle of a rolling crescendo of catcalls.

I finally got totally pissed off, stopped in the middle of what I was playing and yelled, "Go fuck yourselves!" at the top of my lungs. To my surprise, the audience cheered! We were actually able to finish our short set.

When we were walking off, there was a guy at the side. I didn't know him from Adam. He walked up to me and said, "You shouldn't talk to an audience that way!" I looked at him and said, "Go fuck yourself!" He turned out to be the reviewer from *Billboard* magazine.

We began the tour riding on the bus with Neil and the band. David Briggs went along as the tour manager, but Elliott Roberts was conspicuously absent. I developed the impression the whole effort had been orphaned by the management company.

It was a pretty happy-go-lucky group at first. The mood was rebellious and buoyant (lots of rock 'n' roll attitude). It was interesting when the bus would pull up to a Denny's restaurant or some other highway stop. The waitress would go absolutely apeshit when she found she was serving a grilled cheese and fries to Neil Young! Neil, with that black sense of humour he's got, would toy with the girls like food while he spun their heads around.

Neil's stubborn insistence on playing a bunch of songs that were dark, angry and unknown, instead of a diet of hits was taking its toll. Nils and I were still getting booed while we listened to people chanting "Neil, Neil!" The situation got so absurd sometimes that it defied reason. Some of the crowd members were so stoned that when Neil did come on and started playing "Tonight's the Night" they didn't realize it was him because they didn't recognize the song. They started yelling "Neil Young! Cinnamon Girl!" even when Neil was on the stage playing. The band was awesome, but the reviews were mixed and the audiences were ranging between impatient and hostile until they got what they wanted to hear. Perhaps because of the mixed response and the lack of support from management, tensions were growing. Bernie, Dennis and I were asked to leave the bus and make our own way up to Chicago. We never were invited back on the tour bus again. That was the first indication I had that there might be two classes of people on this adventure, and even though I respected everybody's right to do their thing, my feelings were hurt.

We were compelled to fly up to Chicago at a time when airline security had just been introduced (burn in hell forever, you terrorists). I was paranoid about the airport authorities finding my plastic bag of goodies, so I gave my stash to a certain band member and wondered why it was that a few people were chuckling behind their hands. I found out when I met the guy in Chicago and he sheepishly presented me with about 10 percent of what I'd left with him! He had a prodigious appetite.

The venue in Chicago was massive, like the one in Boston had been. The top balcony had clouds forming around it. By this time, as I was more than a little baked from travelling and I'd seen the show enough to figure out what was going to happen, I decided to split early and go back to the hotel.

When we opened the stage door to go outside and get our lowly taxi (poor man's rock star limo), I was confronted by a sight that I'll never forget. There, standing in the dismal steady rain, was a girl. She had long hair hanging down like wet rope over the shoulders of the dirty cotton dress she was wearing. Her face was marked by the kind of complexion you get from doing a lot of methamphetamine. She was bedraggled, soaking and obviously wasted. The rivulets of rainwater flowed down and fell from a brown cardboard sign that hung around her neck on a piece of binder twine. The sign, written in black crayon, said simply "Where's the band staying?" There, in a nutshell, was the rock 'n' roll business— the new religion for the feeble-minded.

One night, while I was out on the road with Neil, my mother went to get some fried chicken from the Colonel Sanders place around the corner from the apartment she and my father were now living in. It was a new place they'd moved into after selling the house up on Stayner Avenue. Once my sister Sandy had moved out, there wasn't much reason for my mom and dad to keep a large house anymore. The new place had two big bedrooms, a good view of the sunset and no maintenance. They'd liberated enough money to do a little travelling and were having a better time than they'd ever had in their lives.

Anyway, there was my mom, standing in line for a bucket of chicken, when she realized that she recognized the guy in front of her.

"Excuse me," she said to him in her polite Scottish accent. "We have something in common. I think my son's out playing with your son."

It took a few seconds of looking at her before it dawned on him what she was talking about.

"You must be Mrs. McLauchlan!" he said.

They had a lovely chat about their problematic children, and to my mother's amazement, he wrote an article in the paper about their meeting a few days later. For any of you who may not know, Neil's dad is Canadian writer Scott Young. He wrote one of my most influential boyhood books, *Scrubs on Skates*.

The tour wound up in Berkeley. That was the best date of all. Some music acquaintances had recommended a Japanese-style hotel called the Miyako in San Francisco, and we tried it out. It had tatami rooms, full neck-deep Japanese baths and a complete menu of all the foods I was accustomed to eating at Nikko Gardens back in Toronto.

The concert was great. Even for me, an unknown, the California crowd were open-minded and enthusiastic. I met Bill Graham, the great man himself, when he showed up backstage to hang out. In spite of his reputation for breathing fire, I found him to be very polite and respectful. He was extremely nice to me, even going so far as to mention that he was familiar with Tom Rush's version of "Child's Song".

The "Tonight's the Night" tour ended, for the most part, on a positive note for me. Still, I couldn't help but reflect on how big "big" really was and wonder if it was worth the cost to chase the brass ring all the way to stardom's stratosphere. As far as I could see, all that money made people more inclined to edit the truth when they were around you. You were the star. No one treated you as a normal person anymore because they wanted to keep you happy and up for the show. After all, they depended on you for their paycheques. Privacy became a memory. These drawbacks were generally accepted as the price of fame, but I'd begun to notice how crazy the whole phenomenon could make people.

I began to think that maybe fame itself was an undesirable thing—something that smart people endured in order to beat a path to riches a little quicker. I knew I had a compulsion to write songs and because I wrote 'em, I had to sing 'em. Who else would? I had real doubts, though, about whether I wanted to be at the centre of some Looney-Tunes showbiz circus! The music business seemed more confusing and dangerous than before. I figured I'd concentrate on what I could do best and leave it to Finkelstein and Fiedler to deal with the sharks. Mind you, they were pretty good swimmers themselves.

Massey Hall Debut

&. MY FATHER WAS SICK. HE HAD something called aplastic anaemia. I didn't even know how to spell it. All I knew was that when the doctors were checking him out for some kind of surgery, they discovered that his blood wasn't thick enough to handle it. He'd also had a minor heart attack when he and my mother had been travelling. The blood thing that he had was a form of leukaemia apparently, and the net result was that he had to start going to the hospital more and more frequently for medications and transfusions. I knew the indicators were not good because he'd begun to mellow. For the first time in my life, we were actually talking about things. He was beginning to accept the fact that I might do alright, even though he still thought I was putting my eggs in the wrong basket.

Patty and I had moved out of Cadillac Johnny's and into an apartment in the round building at 50 Alexander Street, down behind Maple Leaf Gardens. There was a regular little colony in the place. At the time, B.C. Fiedler, Gordon Lightfoot and Finkelstein all had apartments there. The management company and True North Records office were also on the premises. All we had to do was open up a store in the joint and we'd never have to go outside!

Patty did her thing, and pretty soon she had it worked out so she had the bedroom for a dance and exercise studio and most of our living got done in the main room and the kitchen. We had a sofa-bed and shared the space with a hydroponic tomato garden and a ten-gallon tank full of fish.

She'd started taking dance classes down at Lois Smith's school on Front Street in the old walk-ups just west of the St. Lawrence Market. She'd introduced me to the ballet, and I'd gotten so hooked on the magic of it that pretty soon she talked me into taking lessons as well. It was easy to get drawn in, given the quality of the dancers I'd been seeing as my introduction. I'd seen Nureyev in his prime, Erik Bruhn and the very fledgling Karen Kain just stretching her wings as a principal soloist, then moving on to partner with Frank Augustyn. Patty and I were in the audience at the O'Keefe Centre sitting near the crowd from Lois's school on the night the Bolshoi B-team was performing. The company was a snore. Half of them had tensor bandages visible beneath their tights, and their performances were half-hearted—that is, until an unknown young man burst forth from the wings. He somehow created the illusion that he was twelve feet off the stage. His performance was fiery and fluid and passionate, and when he was done, I couldn't help myself. I stood up on my chair along with the rest of the cheering crowd and screamed at the top of my lungs "Defect! Defect!" I noticed that a couple of the teachers from the school were looking at me with alarm, but I didn't think anything of it and the moment passed. I went home wondering about the young man I'd just seen.

The next day I was in Philadelphia, having breakfast with Finkelstein. He was reading the paper and said in an offhand way, "What's this here? Ballet dancer runs off with wife of well-known Canadian folk singer!" I jerked my head up and he was grinning. Bernie had a bit of trouble accepting the fact that I was taking ballet lessons and lost no opportunity to let me have it. He passed the paper over.

There it was in large headlines: "Bolshoi dancer defects!" As I read the story of his twenty-four hours of running from the KGB and suddenly realized that Lois Smith's gang had hidden the young dancer, it dawned on me why I'd gotten the panicky looks at the performance. The young dancer was Mikhail Baryshnikov.

People came and went at our apartment on a regular basis. Jay Telfer, Bernie Finkelstein's friend and my first drummer, was dating a gal named Liz Braun, who worked as a receptionist for Finkelstein Fiedler and would later go on to become a newspaper writer.

One of our longstanding acquaintances, a folk singer named Dee Higgins, was around a lot at this point, and one day she showed up with an unexpected guest in tow. He was the scruffiest kid I'd ever seen and that was saying something. He had a mat of tangled woolly hair that made him look like a thatched roof on two feet—literally: he wasn't wearing any shoes. He was very shy and I was very gruff. I wasn't real easy with people I didn't know or who hadn't been introduced just showing up without being invited. Well, the guy stuck around anyway and he did alright. It was Dan Hill!

Another regular drop-in was Cathy Smith. She was living upstairs with Gordon Lightfoot, and she'd occasionally come downstairs to hang out. Cathy was really smart and also fall-down gorgeous with a lot of curly chestnut hair. She was funny as hell, and she liked and understood musicians. Patty didn't like her coming down, although she never said much about it. I guess she was having a wifely moment and saw Cathy as a potential threat. Oddly enough, she wasn't. I certainly never got the impression that Cathy had any part of her hat set for me, and taking a run at Gordon Lightfoot's girlfriend was not something I was inclined to do anyway. If anything, I got the sense that she was a bit lonely. I felt like there was a sadness in her because she was a good singer who could have done something with herself, and it seemed she was making a career of hanging out with people who did what she wanted to do. Sometimes I think she came down to get some relief from Gordon, who was, as they say in the biographical euphemisms, "wrestling with his personal demons." He could get awfully serious.

Fiedler's apartment was always hangout and party headquarters. He had what seemed to be a mission in life to screw every attractive woman he could get his hands on, and in that regard he was both single-minded and dedicated. He would sometimes meet and seduce more than one in the same evening. We made jokes about replacing his front door with a turnstile. Interestingly enough, most of the girls who were around seemed to enjoy his company, found him funny and charming and didn't mind one bit that the only thing forthcoming from Fiedler was a fast slap and tickle and a good supply of nose-candy.

There was also a plentiful supply of great opportunities for jamming and hanging out. The Riverboat was in full swing, Fiedler's concert promotions business was really taking off, and anyone who was playing anything that Fiedler was promoting would wind up at his place partying. It was an illustrious roll call. I probably spent more time up in Fiedler's apartment than I did in mine.

I had the first car I'd ever bought myself. It's hard to believe, but even though I was working a lot more, I wasn't making that much money. I might make a thousand and a half U.S. for working the Main Point in Philly for a long weekend, but once I paid Dennis, transport, accommodation, management commissions, rent, phone, food, cleaning, the coke dealer and the government there was nothing left. So putting together nine hundred dollars in one lump to buy my old '67 black Pontiac Parisienne fastback with the crunch marks on the fenders, the oil-belching small-block v8 and the three on the column manual transmission was a major accomplishment. But that was just the beginning!

It wasn't a car, it was something to bond with. I drove it around for a while and then, probably because I'd been such a great fan of Robert Mitchum in the movie *Thunder Road*, I decided to make a street rod out of it.

I went to Crankshaft Specialty Company and bought an engine, a 327 cu. in. V8, polished and ported with a three-quarter cam installed with solid valve lifters. To top it off, the crank was dynamically balanced so the whole assembly would pull some serious revs!

While the engine was being finished, I had the rest of the car taken over to Hogan Pontiac, where the suspension was done with stiffer springs and shocks and anti-sway bars. The steering was rebuilt with new tie-rods, and the whole thing was topped off with a set of wide rims and high-performance radial tires. I didn't do a thing to the body work or the upholstery. To the untrained eye, it looked like a piece of junk, but once it was put together that car was some piece of work.

I'd pull up to a Sunoco station, where they custom-blended gas at the pumps, and I'd say to the gas jockey, "Fill it up with 260."

"What for?" he'd reply.

I'd get out and calmly lift the hood to check the oil and he'd just say, "Oh!"

My poor long-suffering parents! When I had the "honour" of driving my dad to the hospital, he and my mom would come down the elevator from the apartment where they now lived and try their best not to let me think they were embarrassed to be picked up in something that sounded like the front row of a NASCAR race and looked like the back row at an auto wrecker's.

My dad was getting weaker and losing weight. My poor mom had started to show signs of strain. She knew the death watch had begun. She wasn't sleeping well at night. Every time my father got up to go to the bathroom, she'd hold her breath with anxiety, for fear that he might fall and hurt himself.

I began work back at Thunder Sound on a new collection of songs. The title of the new album was *Sweeping the Spotlight Away* after the song by that name. It used the image of Emmett Kelly, the circus clown, as a metaphor for my life, and I still think it's one of the best songs I've ever written. There was a lovely guitar solo in it that Bruce Cockburn came in and played.

I was beginning to hit my stride as a songwriter, and there were a number of powerful songs on the record. "Down by the Henry Moore"—named after the English sculptor—captured the energy I soaked up rambling around Toronto or midnight skating at the City Hall ice rink where "The Archer" was located. I locked in a great unison solo, which became the song's signature hook, with my new friend Ben Mink on mandolin and me on harmonica.

There were a lot of really good players on this record. Chris Parker was brought back in to play drums except for one song. On that one, I borrowed Barry Keane from Gordon Lightfoot's band. He played on "Shoeshine Workin' Song," which I wrote after a young shoeshine kid on Yonge Street named Emanuel Jaques was murdered.

Mike McKenna from the band McKenna–Mendelson Mainline played a beautiful slide solo on "Maybe Tonight," a song about the life of a travelling sales-man inspired by my oldest brother Ian. Ian passed away in January '98 while I was writing this book, worn out by emphysema.

In perhaps one of the more poignant appearances on the record, Cathryn Smith sang on "Do You Dream of Being Somebody," a song I'd written after watching an exhausted Judy Garland on TV belting out "Somewhere over the Rainbow" one last time. Lightfoot took an especially dim view of her appearance on the record, and they had a pretty big fight about it, according to Cathy. I guess there was an irony, given the title of the song. After moving to steadily rising levels of notoriety in her travels with Hoyt Axton, and in her association with Keith Richards, she became a permanent somebody in the eyes of the media after she stuck in the needle that killed John Belushi. Sometimes I listen to that song and just shake my head.

Also appearing with me for the first time was Ron Dann on steel guitar, fresh out of Jesse Winchester's band. Ron would provide me with a lifetime's worth of good memories and a big collection of laughs in the all-too-short time he was around. He died of cancer not too long after playing beautifully on my first record for Capitol, *Swinging on a Star*.

Sweeping the Spotlight Away was the second production effort by the comedy team of McLauchlan and Finkelstein. We had great fun making records together. We were both arrogant, which gave us great confidence, and we weren't afraid to go with our instincts and just do what felt right. We were both inclined to put making music first and think about its commercial applications later. Maybe we caught some of the magic touch from one of our frequent drop-ins, Moses Znaimer (he'd bought the studio recently and was making plans to go into television). As a matter of fact, Moses pitched Bernie at the time about expanding out of the piddling record business and joining him in the television game, but Bernie didn't pursue the suggestion.

It sure looked like we did something right because when the record was eventually released, the first single, which was "Henry Moore," went to radio and immediately hit paydirt. We got saturation play on that song. We got strong country radio airplay on "Shoeshine." We got big time FM play on "Do You Dream of Being Somebody" in Quebec. This record really hammered home the success I'd had with "Farmer's Song" by expanding people's perceptions of what I was all about as a songwriter.

In the meantime, I was ready to do something that only a few short years earlier I would never even have dreamed of. I was scheduled to play my first show at Massey Hall. To me, Massey was like a church. The idea of standing up and singing in exactly the same spot where I'd watched Dylan in his buckskin jacket was overwhelming.

The old building on Shuter Street was steeped in atmosphere. There had been numerous moves to tear it down and replace it because of the fears that huge numbers of people would be killed or injured if a fire broke out. But it survived to nurture fresh generations of young performers into the big time.

In the hours before I was to play, I sneaked away and walked the high steep balconies with their black lacquered pillars. The red plush seats, made for times when people were smaller, lay waiting under the vaulted ceiling. I looked down at the old wooden stage with its simple sound baffles and thought of the great artists who had played on it. I was sick with apprehension for a moment as the thought crossed my mind, "I don't belong up there!" The full promotional onslaught of Finkelstein and Fiedler had worked its magic, however. The people had voted with their dollars, and it was too late to run away now.

I'd been using the services of a very eccentric limousine driver by the name of Jack Cunningham, better known as J.T., for various and sundry purposes. Now we were planning a concert series for central Canada, and had decided to use his car as a tour bus. It was an enormous Lincoln—a duplicate of the one used in motorcades by the president of the United States.

Jack was a gentleman's gentleman. He wore white gloves and was always quiet and impeccably groomed. He'd been a mortician, so he understood show business pretty well and had naturally been drawn into driving rock 'n' roll people around after being contracted to haul Elton John.

The night of my debut at Massey Hall, I dispatched Jack in his splendid car—complete with chilled bucket of champagne—to fetch my mother and father from their apartment. It was an especially sweet moment for my mother, who had championed me so vigorously.

My father had never seen me perform. At first he was too angry. Then the kind of places I was playing in weren't his cup of tea. Now he was getting too tired and weak to go out much.

When I took the stage that night to a sold-out house, there were my parents, sitting in the front row. My hard-core fans gave me a triumphal welcome. But I was also faced with one of the most difficult things I've ever had to do in my life: I had to keep from losing control while I sang "Child's Song," because I could see that my father was in tears. It was a cathartic moment. Our fences were mended. He finally understood why I had fought him so hard. He had come to respect who I had become, and in return, I had developed a great sympathy for who he was. There have been few moments in my life that were as satisfying spiritually, creatively and emotionally as that first concert at Massey Hall. My walking onto that stage said to my parents, "Look! I'm your kid and I did it!"

Goodbye to You Too, Pa

SOME DAYS I'D GO OVER TO MY mom and dad's apartment and my dad would be sleeping in his chair with his feet up on the footstool, his package of Export A beside him. As he got sicker, he hadn't quit smoking. I guess he figured, What's the point?

I would look at his working man's hands with their tobacco-stained nails curving slightly around the ends of his fingers and think of the many things they'd done to help make a life for all of us. I looked at the outline of his thin legs under his gabardine slacks and thought of the miles they had carried him in his fruitless searches for work. I looked at his worn-out sleeping face and thought of the laughs he'd had with his mates, the laughter and tears he'd had with my mother. I looked at his body sleeping there and thought of all the sadness inside me over the years as I wished for some sign of approval or support from him. Yes, we had reconciled, but I had a whole lifetime full of questions.

One day, after sitting around on a Sunday watching television, it was time for me to leave.

"See you next week!" I said to him.

"By next week, I'll be playing centre forward for St. Mirren," he replied with a weak smile.

St. Mirren was his favourite Scottish football club, and I thought he was indulging in black humour. But those were the last words I ever heard from my father. It was his way of letting me know what he already knew, but I didn't catch the clue.

He was taken to the hospital. He'd been experiencing difficulties, and they kept him in. He was fitted out with all the terrible hospital tubes that everyone fears.

My mother was keeping watch, but the staff at the hospital assured her he was stable for the time being and told her to go home and try to get some rest.

I guess my father had gotten tired of his growing weakness and the indignities being visited on him, for during the early hours of the morning he pulled out all the hospital stuff invading his body and rang for the nurse. When she arrived, he held out his hand for her to hold and, looking into her eyes, he died.

I got a phone call from my brother Bill in the early hours of the morning darkness. I felt a stab of emotion as he told me what had happened. It was a hard shot of everything all at once—stomach-turning nausea, fear, loss, anger, futility, uncertainty. Who am I now if I don't have him to set myself against?

I had a concert to do that night. I could have cancelled it, I guess, but then what? There was nothing I could do about anything. My father's body was somewhere between an autopsy and a funeral. There was no role for me to fill immediately and I got the feeling from somewhere deep inside that my father would have wanted me to do the show.

Finkelstein was very kind in offering to help postpone the show, and I guess he was a little surprised when I decided to go ahead with it. Everybody was very soft on me, and I appreciated that a lot.

No announcement was made to the crowd about what had happened. I would have felt that was grandstanding, and my father would have agreed. Instead, with Dennis, I went out and played the best concert I'd ever done. I was raw, emotional and vulnerable. Every song seemed to connect with me in some new and special way. I don't know how I managed to sing "Child's Song," but I got through it.

When I returned home at two or three in the morning, I cracked a bottle of scotch, poured myself a very large tumbler and sat down at the piano. I sat and played improvisational melodies that sounded like every Scottish air that had ever been written until the tears came. Then I just sat there with my head down and wept silently until morning.

We had a good funeral for him. A lot of people came, and it made me feel better to see how many lives he had touched. It's funny, the directions that your out-of-control emotions will take you. I remember becoming highly incensed with the minister's comments about my father being a poor weak sinner or something to that effect. The minister was quickly forgotten, though, when Wing Commander William Kensitt took the floor.

The Wingco, as I called him, had flown Hurricanes in the battle of Britain for the RAF and distinguished himself in the war as a fighter pilot. After Germany surrendered, as he was waiting to be transferred into the RCAF, he had a car accident in a London taxicab. His neck was broken, and he was left a quadriplegic for the rest of his life. He had one of the finest classical educations you could encounter and had the courage to get on with his life, marry and face his future squarely with surprisingly little bitterness. He was my father's best friend.

The Wingco sat there in his wheelchair and, with quiet dignity, began to speak. He began to tell the story of "Wullie," as he called my father. As he spoke, a picture of a man I'd never met began to emerge. It was someone emotional and sentimental. Someone who could have a scotch and sing "My Love Is Like a Red Red Rose" for his wife with all his heart because he loved her. He described a courageous and loyal friend, and as I listened, I cried without shame. My loss was in knowing that here was a guy I would really have liked to know, and now I would never have the chance.

My task was to rally to the side of my mother. She had loved her husband, and they'd been through so much together that she wasn't used to thinking of herself except in terms of being part of a couple. She was wrestling with difficult feelings and was horrified at the things that were going through her mind.

I had lunch with her shortly after the funeral and induced her to actually have a drink of Tio Pepe and light up a cigarette (she'd given them up a long time ago), just so she could relax. Then I asked her indirectly about how she was feeling inside.

She finally admitted that she was shocked to find that she was glad he was dead. I wasn't shocked. I knew exactly what she meant. First of all, she was feeling a great sense of relief that the tension of the death watch was finally over. Once she was able to sleep again, she had slept and slept and slept, as though catching up on a lifetime.

It wasn't just that, though. All the years of diplomacy and manoeuvring to bring my father around, of putting everyone else's needs above her own, of being a hard-working and dutiful wife were finally over. My mom was an independent thinker with strong opinions, and I think she was surprised at how good it felt to suddenly be able to take a deep breath and actually contemplate the freedom of doing whatever took her fancy.

Of course, she hadn't wished for her husband's death—everybody understood that! But now, as a family, it was up to us to assure her that it was okay to feel good about being freed of her burdens, and that she wasn't a bad person for having all those feelings.

In the aftermath of my father's death, my mother slowly began to blossom and become a friend to me. I began to know her in a way I never had before. She would shoot straight with me without being overly judgemental, and I felt there was little or nothing that I couldn't talk to her about.

A few years later, she took up golf. I think she got into it mostly because her friends laughed at her for thinking an old broad like herself could learn how. That was a red flag for Peg McLauchlan. She joined Flemingdon Park Golf Club on a seniors' membership and started punting her way around the course after taking a few lessons. She wasn't a long hitter and often didn't count her whiffs, but after a while, she was getting around the course in a reasonable number of strokes for an older girl.

She was always looking for someone to play with, preferably someone who could also provide transportation to the course. I'd played a lot in my youth, so I just naturally fell into taking her out and playing golf with her.

Those were some of the best times with my mom. We'd pot around the course and talk easily about this and that. We'd sit on the terrace outside the clubhouse watching people duff their drives down the first fairway and try to pretend they were invisible.

One day she said idly, "You know, your dad had a chance for a career on the stage."

"Really?"

"Yes, he was offered a chance to go down to London and audition for a musical stage production."

"Did he go?"

"No. We had a long heart-to-heart about it. He wanted to know how I'd feel about packing the kids up and going to London, and I told him, Bill, whatever you need to do, I'll stand behind you a hundred percent."

"What happened?"

"He decided against it. He felt it wasn't fair to put the family at risk on the chance of something that might not work out. He felt duty bound to work at his trade because it was steady and provided a living."

I looked at her for a long time.

"Are you meaning to say that he was afraid he might fail?"

She paused for a while, thinking about what she was going to say. Then her face relaxed.

"I think so, yes." My mom was trying to help me put more pieces into the jigsaw puzzle.

Bars, Boats and Limousines

THE TOUR I DID WITH BERNIE and Dennis Pendrith in Jack Cunningham's limo was probably one of the more surreal experiences of my life. The albums of choice were Bob Dylan's *Blood on the Tracks* and that Rolling Stones album—the one with the song "Memory Motel." We were totally self-contained in that big long Lincoln car. It was our travelling womb. We had all kinds of reading material from comic books to novels. There was a good sound system. There was a radio-phone with an ornate silver cover for the handset. There was a complete bar and a TV set.

Having taken the precaution of procuring a quarter-ounce of blow as a hedge against the alienation of the hinterlands, we set off on a great swing up through North Bay, Sudbury, Sault Ste. Marie and Thunder Bay. Eventually, we'd wind up back over in Montreal, but we'd cover a lot of miles first.

We wound ourselves up singing, "She got a mind of her own and she uuuuu-use it weell, yeah! She's mighty fine. She's one of a kind" as we watched the winter landscape roll by through the tinted windows. We maintained an even strain by pacing and balancing our abuses.

It wasn't the tourist season, so no one was on the Trans-Canada apart from long-distance truckers and locals. Half the highway pit stops were boarded up for the season, and in the rest, no more than a few people would be huddled over their coffee. A sanding crew or a mine supervisor might be sitting there, sucking on an Export A as we pulled up in the big battle cruiser.

Wherever we'd pull up, all activities ceased from the moment we were sighted. From the outside, that car was so impressive and respectable and conservative that people just naturally assumed it was carrying the prime minister or somebody else of great importance. Jack would get out with his conservative three-piece pin-striped suit and his white gloves, walk to the rear door and open it. People expected to see the chauffeur. Then we three ragamuffins would tumble out into the snow and stagger into the restaurant. You could almost hear the collective clunk as their jaws hit the tabletops. I don't think they'd ever seen anything quite like us in anything quite like that ever before. Sooner or later, someone would twig to the fact that it was the guy who'd written "Farmer's Song," and that would explain the whole thing to their satisfaction.

"Oh, Jeez! They're a bunch o' rock stars, eh?"

We developed absolute trust in J.T. Cunningham. We felt that nothing bad could happen to us when he was in control. He was calm, quiet and trustworthy. He drove sedately and confidently and never attracted any attention that would cause the cops to dare interfere with our progress. Thank god you couldn't see through the windows.

One night, we were working our way back east through the dark and brooding low mountains north of Lake Superior. Visibility was low and a fine-grain snow was falling in an icy fog. There were two black tracks in the snow-covered highway where trucks had recently passed. There's a curious thing that can happen as you wind your way up and down the long hills in conditions like that. You can lose track of whether you're climbing or descending.

We were all asleep in the back, whacked out from the gig. Something made me wake up. When I opened my eyes, I could see guard-rail posts flicking by just inches from the side of the car. I raised my head and watched in fascination as Jack fought with it. I guess he'd been tired and had fallen prey to the illusion that he was going up when he was actually going down. He must have quickly realized his mistake because he was immediately off the throttle. As the weight of the long car shifted forward, the back wanted to push the front wheels straight ahead, regardless of which direction the wheel was turned. If it was unable to do that, the back end settled for second best by wanting to race down the hill ahead of the front end. Jack steered out the oscillations calmly and quietly as the rear of the car fishtailed back and forth—no overcontrolling or panicky applications of the brakes. Like a skilled Grand Prix driver, he nursed that monster back to docility and proceeded on as though nothing had happened. He never mentioned the incident to anyone, which was very consistent with his personality and professionalism. I think that if anyone else had been in that seat, the three of us in the back would have met our end at the bottom of a tree-studded cliff. Thanks, Jack.

My favourite memory of J.T. occurred one morning in a hotel somewhere in the north. Bernie and I had been up all night discussing the meaning of meaning. We hadn't slept a wink, and it was time to hit the road. We were a couple of

French-fried basket cases. There we were, sort of bleaching in the morning light, when there was a gentle tap-tap on the door of my room.

It was Jack, immaculately dressed as usual, and fresh as a daisy by our standards.

"Good morning, Mr. McLauchlan. I have a question," he said.

"Sure J.T., what is it?"

"I'm afraid I rather overslept, and I was wondering if you would object to my not shaving this morning."

"Of course not. No problem."

Jack quietly left the room, and when he was gone, Bernie and I stared at each other in disbelief. When they made this guy, they broke the mould!

The final destination was Montreal, as I mentioned. I was scheduled to play Théâtre Maisonneuve in Place des Arts, and we would be staying at Mordecai Richler's favourite haunt, the Ritz-Carlton Hotel. This was some pretty toney stuff for a guy like me. I remembered Montreal as the kind of town where they wouldn't admit you to the average bar on Mountain Street if you were wearing jeans. I was wondering how we'd be received at the Ritz.

We were pulling into downtown. Jack had washed and polished the car that morning, and it looked immaculate. We were confident that we'd make as good an arrival as any premier American musical act or film star. The big Lincoln pulled up to the curb by the familiar black iron canopy of the hotel, and just as the doorman moved towards the car, a major radiator hose blew. There was Jack's pride and joy in front of the finest hotel in Montreal in a cloud of steam, hissing out its life blood in a great green pool. The doorman opened the door for us, and out we piled. While J.T. attended to the car, we went through the doors towards the desk to check in.

On our way across the lobby, we were intercepted by the bell captain, who had begun walking towards us as soon as we entered. "Uh-oh," I thought to myself "here it comes." We began bracing for trouble and preparing our attitude.

"You look like a couple of sports fans!" the bell captain burst out. We were taken aback.

"You like the hockey?"

"Well, yeah, sure we do!"

"Well, I got a couple of tickets for the game tonight at the Forum. You want them?"

"How much?" Bernie asked, immediately suspicious.

"I give 'em to you face value—I can't use 'em myself. I just like to make the guest happy!"

So we checked in, had a fabulous meal and then took ourselves off to the Montreal Forum, cathedral of the national sport, to watch the mighty Habs in action. Actually, Bernie and I often went to games when we were on the road if we could swing it. We always tried to catch the Flyers when I was playing in Philadelphia. We were major fans of Bobby Clark.

Going to the forum was a perfect entrance to what was then Canada's most vibrant city. The only down side was that the Habs lost that night, so the streets were a bit of a danger zone for a while after the contest was over. Henri Richard was once asked what was the worst possible thing that could happen to him in his career, and he replied, "To lose a game at the Forum!"

It was one of the screwier things I ever did, doing a whole tour in a big limousine, but it sure pointed up the way the world changes its face towards you when you seem to have the trappings of wealth and power. They sure will forgive a lot of eccentricities. The Ritz? It remains high on my list of great places to stay. I once heard a Southern lady define hospitality this way. If a guest shows up at your formal dinner party in a yellow rubber raincoat and boots, you quietly slip off and put on your yellow rubber raincoat and boots so they won't feel uncomfortable. The Ritz always lived up to that standard of graciousness!

I guess the first of the after-hours bars I frequented in Toronto was over an art gallery on Yonge Street. It was the place to go and hang after I played the Riverboat during the later stages of my tenure there. It was run by a Toronto painter, and there was always a poker game going on in the place. I started going over because Fiedler and Finkel did. They got involved in the card games, but the pots were too rich for me. Professional gamblers would sometimes insinuate themselves into the game. When that happened, things would tend to get out of hand. Besides, I was much more interested in cruising the bar and striking up conversation with attractive young ladies who would often play a part in my not showing up at home until the sun was up.

The owner's wife was about six-foot-five and very beautiful. She introduced me to her friend Sarah, who was from Philadelphia. Sarah was six-foot-four and the sight of them together was really something. I would hang out with Sarah when I was down in Philly sometimes. She was a blue-jeans-and-combat-boots kind of gal who liked to smoke up a lot of reefer, then pile me into her vw microbus and drive through South Philly in the middle of the night. She got an adrenaline rush by pulling up to a stop sign and waiting till all the black guys hanging out on the corner would notice the white chick sitting in the bus and start to come towards us. Then she'd start laughing and boot it out of there. This was not a safe thing to do in Philadelphia at that time.

I guess the king of all the booze-can operators of all time was Gary Ledrew. Gary was the patron saint of all the hard-drinking painters in Toronto. They'd drink themselves out of money, or show up broke and then pay their bar bills in art. Needless to say, Gary soon acquired a substantial collection by noted painters.

I saw a lot of Peter Gzowski in Gary's around the time he was anaesthetizing himself after the horrific experience of having done *Ninety Minutes Live*. Ian Tyson was sometimes there as well, during his post-Sylvia period of adjustment. Pretty well everybody of any note in town would pass through Gary's of an evening. Hell, even the cops who'd busted him the week before would show up and drink for free when they were off duty. They were people you had to give a wide berth. When they got jolly, they tended to get a little aggressive.

Oddly enough, although I had by now developed a second career as a rounder, it wasn't drinking, gambling and chasing women all night that were the biggest influences in my association with Gary. His most profound effect on me was introducing me to the world of sailing.

Gary was a Nova Scotia boy. His mother was from Lunenburg, and his daddy was from the Rock. For a while, when Gary and his sister Gail were kids, his parents were the keepers of the Louisbourg lighthouse.

Maritimers have a different way of looking at the world. Gary took a natural pleasure in providing a social service that was equally important to the mighty and the meek, and he didn't play any favourites based on wealth or fame. In fact, if he sensed any signs of anybody thinking they were hot shit, he'd work diligently to deflate that particular balloon.

He'd done a year of hard time in Kingston Pen for simple possession of marijuana. It's hard to imagine that now, but the Dark Ages weren't that long ago. (Don't hold your breath, they're always just around the corner.) Anyway, his mom and dad had accepted his bust as just a part of life and never judged him harshly for it.

Gary had been in the Navy and knew pretty well everything there was to know about nautical lore, particularly as it pertained to sailing ships. He knew all the knots and could tell you the difference between a hermaphrodite brig and a topsail schooner.

Now it was a fact of the times that some people who were utopian at heart had gone a different route from going back to the land. Instead, they had decided to build great big trimarans (yachts with three hulls) and run away to live a romantic life sailing the warm tropic seas, surviving on fish and sea beans.

Gary knew a whole tribe of these people; one of them was a guy he'd become friends with after his parents moved to Uxbridge, Ontario. This man, Gary Hodgkins, had been one of the first people ever to have his leg surgically reattached after an accident. He'd been driving an old Harley down in California and got T-boned by a car. His girlfriend, who was on the back, was killed outright, and Hodgkins had his leg amputated by the impact, except for a flap of connecting tissue. But he was fortunate enough to be close to a surgical centre that was developing reconnective techniques and to be attended by a police officer who had the sense to put the leg on ice and send the ambulance to the right place. They did remarkable work, and in addition to the connective surgery, reduced the length of his remaining leg. He'd be a little shorter, but he'd be able to walk more normally. Eventually, after a long stint of physiotherapy, Hodgkins returned to Canada, and with the money from the insurance settlement, built a forty-six-foot Cross trimaran in a barn out at Whitby.

Eventually, the boat was launched, and Hodgkins and his wife, Diane, went down to the Bahamas. Sooner or later, you have to buy things for boats. You have to buy food. You have to buy rum. There are expenses. No one who started out with the idealistic dream of living a free existence on the ocean ever wound up realizing it. They all wound up in the chartering business instead. And Gary Ledrew acted as an informal travel agent to feed prospective charter customers to his friends.

Gary worked on me for a while, and finally convinced me that the absolute best thing in the world to do in the winter was to get on a sailing boat in the Bahamas and anchor in some remote cove under the stars every night. We finally made a date, and just for good measure, Gary decided to come too. We flew down to Miami, caught the Chalk Airways Grumman flying boat into Nassau harbour by way of Bimini, and then connected with a charter aircraft down to George Town on Great Exuma to meet the boat at the Hotel Peace and Plenty.

What a beautiful spot! I'd never been to this part of the world before, and the hotel was one of the most gracious small hotels in the islands. Its dining room and bar surrounded a courtyard overlooking the turquoise waters of George Town harbour. There, bobbing gently at anchor just a few yards off shore was *Isla*. That was the name of the boat Hodgkins had built, and she was a beauty! She was ketch rigged, meaning she had two masts: a large main and a smaller mizzen at the back. With her bright white superstructure and varnished wood masts over her light grey hull, she sparkled in the tropical sunlight. First impressions are everything, and this one was so positive that I was immediately in love with the boat.

We settled in, Patty and I, in a small private cabin, Gary in a wing berth, and Hodgkins and Diane in their usual digs. Once we settled down and found out where everything was, we went back ashore to the hotel as the sun was going down to relax and have a drink manufactured for us by Lermon, the bartender—a man who was nearly legendary for his skill in these parts.

There was a dance on the patio that night, so we stuck around for the music. Hodgkins liked his rum and was always up for a good time. I was like a caged animal let loose in a sea of pina coladas and proceeded to get fairly stiff with Patty. We practised trying to set the floor on fire while she taught me the finer points of the merengue. We danced and laughed and leaped and screamed and drank until two or three in the morning and had a fantastic blowout.

The next morning—only a few hours later, actually—I was feeling the effects of the previous night as we all chowed down on a big breakfast of bacon and eggs fried in New Zealand tinned butter. I ate like a hog and felt much better after that. I guess I'd forgotten the drinker's first rule. If you feel okay after a night like that, you haven't sobered up yet!

After everything had been stowed, we weighed anchor, and the boat began to make its way up the harbour towards the northern cut. We were going to anchor out this first night and then continue north up to Staniel Cay, then up to New Providence Island and Nassau Harbour. It was a perfectly beautiful day with steady trades and bright sunshine, and I was straddling the mizzen-mast boom like a cowboy, singing sea shanties badly at the top of my lungs.

We got to the north end of the harbour and proceeded through the cut and out onto the rolling waters of the Exuma Sound. The boat began to pitch and roll on the long swells with that peculiar pause and lurch common to trimarans, and suddenly, I no longer felt like singing heroic sea shanties. Holding on carefully, I abandoned my position astride the mizzen boom and made my way on my hands and knees up to the webbing, which was strung between the bows of the multiple hulls. I lay down on my stomach with my face poking through the gaps in the web-weave and retched heartily. I retched and retched and retched until there was nothing left and then I retched some more. Someone brought up a sheet and wrapped it tightly around me so I wouldn't add third-degree sunburn to my woes. They picked my head up by the hair and poured some watered-down juice through my lips, but I chucked that up too.

I stayed in that position all day until the boat pulled through a cut and anchored in a quiet backwater cove on the protected side of a small key. I got up and gingerly sipped down a glass of plain water mixed with a little rum and began to feel a little better.

Hodgkins and Ledrew announced that they were going to get the hand spears, masks and flippers and swim over to a small mushroom-shaped coral head to see if they could find a couple of spiny lobsters for dinner. I decided to go along, so I donned some gear and jumped in with them. The water was incredibly clear and so much like my dreams of what it would be like that I was amazed. I felt like I was flying as I paddled leisurely along, tagging behind the two others as they poked around in the crevasses and caves that riddled the coral head. I was preoccupied by the riot of colour offered by the little wrasses as they dashed about and by the rhythmic crunching of the parrot fish as they fed on the coral. I was so enraptured that I forgot all about how ill I'd been, and when my two companions finally shot a pair of good-sized lobsters, I was almost reluctant to go back to the boat. Once back on board, I was completely recovered and was never seasick again in all the years I sailed. Gary looked at me and offered this piece of advice: "Only a fool goes to sea sober!"

Over the next little while, I began to gradually learn the ropes. The next time the boat anchored, I was eager to get back in the water. It was a little deeper this time with a sandy bottom about thirty feet down and the edges of my world disappearing into the blue haze. Ledrew was already in the water heading off down to a coral head, swimming away in the general direction of the outstretched anchor chain. I hadn't really given much thought to the other creatures that inhabited the ocean, and I was absently turning in gentle circles, admiring the hull of the boat from underneath, when, all of a sudden, I was no longer by myself. As if from nowhere, there was a black-tipped reef shark swimming by! My eyes went wide as saucers as I watched it swimming calmly towards Gary's position. I went to the surface, and forgetting that I had a snorkel between my teeth, I made the sound "Znnoooooo!" with great force. Noticing the blank stares that greeted this warning, I spat out the snorkel and yelled, "Shark!"

"How big?" shouted Hodgkins.

"I don't know. Six feet maybe! It's heading for Gary!" I replied.

At that moment, Ledrew stuck his head out of the water and yelled, "There's a little dinky shark up here, maybe a foot and a half or two feet. Should I shoot it for dinner?"

Ledrew dined out on this story for a long time after that.

There was a rule on the boat that you had to eat what you shoot. This was to discourage the gung-ho individual who, in the full blood of the chase, wanted to go down there and shoot everything that moved. It's exciting to use your body's energy to swim down hard and with only a hand spear or a Hawaiian sling (a kind of underwater bow and arrow) stalk a grouper or a lobster through a labyrinth of coral. It's easy to get carried away.

By the time *Isla* had made it up to Nassau, I'd already developed some rudimentary skills at spearfishing. We were anchoring out at Rose Island when I got the lobster of the century (my first). It was about a five pounder, and I was so proud of myself I was fit to bust. Nothing ever tasted better!

One day while we were there, Hodgkins and Ledrew were poking around a reef while I hovered on the surface with a handspear, observing what they were doing. Hodgkins was making quite a commotion down there clinking on the hard coral and moving around to different holes. He was actually on the track of a large Nassau grouper that kept evading him. The trouble was, every time Hodgkins would get a bead on the fish, a whopping great green moray eel would stick its big toothy head in the way and smile at him. Finally, becoming frustrated, Hodgkins shot the moray. It was out of character for him to do a thing like that, but I guess he was having a bad day.

There was a great boiling of sediment, and Hodge realized he had a real problem on his hands. He had shot the eel rather far back from the head and not fatally, so he was now attached to a very large, very pissed-off moray that was trying to get up the spear to him. Ledrew came over, and sizing up the situation, put another spear into the eel, but they still couldn't control it. Ledrew headed up to the surface towards me. When we stuck our heads out of the water, he breathlessly said, "Come on down and put another spear in this thing so we can get it to the surface!"

234

I still didn't know what was going on. I thought Hodge had a large fish on the spear and couldn't get it out of the hole it was in. I barrelled down after Gary with the handspear, and when I got to the scene of the turmoil, all I could see through the boiling murk was a large green head with a great number of sharp pointy teeth. I went back to the surface immediately!

Gary Ledrew came up again and yelled, "Come on, we need you to put another spear in it!"

"Fuck you! You put a fucking spear in it!" I yelled back.

Ledrew also dined out on this story for a long time.

He took the handspear from me and went down and shot the eel again, this time near the tail. Now, with a spear in the front and one in the back, they could manoeuvre the unfortunate creature to the surface and wrestle it on board *Isla*.

So there it sat on the deck—a very large, very tough, very dead, not very appetizing and rarely eaten nondelicacy covered in green algae, which Hodgkins was now obliged to incorporate into his diet.

He got out his filleting knife and attempted to dissect a steak from the corpse. It was so tough, he had trouble even cutting it. After going to get a more robust cutting implement, Hodge was making his way back to the scene of the crime, when he sort of kind of stumbled on his short leg and sort of accidentally knocked the eel, which slipped off the side of the deck and sank without a trace into the depths.

"Too bad!"

"Yeah, too bad!"

"Shame about that!"

"Yep."

We didn't have eel for dinner, and no further mention was made of Hodgkins' crime against nature.

Patty took to the life like a duck to water. She even went to the trouble of having prescription lenses mounted in her face mask so she could see underwater. Normally a physically reticent person who stayed out of the sun, she changed a lot during our two weeks aboard *Isla*. In fact, we had such a good time that when we had to leave the boat because a new charter party was due, we couldn't bear the thought of going back home to face the winter, so we signed on for two more weeks on another trimaran, a beautiful yellow-hulled boat called *La Paz*, and went back out again! I started to understand the old sailors like Sir Francis

Chichester who, after winning the round-the-world race for solo sailors decided that he was having so much fun, he went 'round again!

On and off, I sailed the waters of the Bahamas for the next ten years in the winters, and relationships were born and died on the boats. Eventually, bounce diving for conch at forty-five feet became as natural to me as walking down the street.

V

A Very Good Year

𝕝 I GUESS 1976 WAS THE YEAR IT all really came together—so much so that I wonder how it all fit into such a short time span.

In 1975 I had laid the groundwork for the release of a set of two live recordings I'd made at the Rebecca Cohn Auditorium in Halifax called *Only the Silence Remains*. I'd continued to sell out Massey Hall and a lot of other places besides. My hard touring in the U.S. had resulted in a full-page article in *Rolling Stone* magazine by a guy named Steve Weitzman, who caught me at the Philadelphia Festival and became a fan.

Bernie Finkelstein had changed things around as his deal with Columbia Records of Canada expired. He allowed Columbia to keep the rights for the True North line of fine entertainment products for Canada, but in the U.S. I would now be released on Chris Blackwell's Island Records. Blackwell had brought Bob Marley and reggae music to the world through his British company and was now opening an office in Los Angeles. They were particularly interested in what I was doing because I was starting to sell a meaningful number of records in Canada and they thought the music I was making would travel well. I had built up a solid reputation in the U.S., and Island looked likely to be able to move that up to a higher level.

The success I was beginning to enjoy was having an effect on my music. I was suspicious of it. This was showing up in pieces like "Train Song," which had me sitting in the dining car of a fast-moving train and staring out the window looking for someone who used to be me.

I was less worried about sticking to a story line in my songs, and they were becoming more impressionistic as I began to hit my stride. I began to use imagery much more freely and to enjoy bouncing around through time. In "La Guerre, C'est Fini Pour Moi" I used that device. Standing in an abandoned World War II gun emplacement and letting the past be painted onto the present to make an antiwar statement, I used the images of children playing and teenagers making innocent love in the ruins of the bunker to form a contrast with the sinister artifacts of state-sponsored death.

In "On the Boulevard," I took a good-humoured and rather accurate look at who really holds the power and what they eventually do with it. I really liked the lines from the last verse that went, "Keepin' up the cash flow. Keep the corporate taxes low. They say Switzerland is where the money goes!" What I was shooting at was the notion that democracy is an illusion fed to North Americans to keep them from finding out what's really going on.

I'd been introducing these songs in concert for a while, and they'd been hitting the mark, so as I worked hard in January 1976 on a new album to be called *On the Boulevard*, I felt a lot of confidence in what I was doing. I had a terrific core of musicians with whom I'd done a lot of work by this point. The only new guy was Jørn Andersen, who'd called up the office one day and asked to talk with me. He'd been playing with a Toronto rock band and had become disillusioned. When I finally met him at the True North offices, he got right to the point and simply said, "I'd like to play with you."

Jørn was not a good drummer; he was a great one (he still is). I realized once the recording sessions had begun that what we had here was a band. It was the best kind of band because it had grown up naturally out of playing music together. We'd begun to think as a unit and respond to each other's ideas without having to engage in a lot of discussion. Everybody brought something unique to the ensemble, and everybody respected the other guy's ability.

The band was now Gene Martynec, an awesome guitarist and musical mind; Ben Mink, equally awesome on the violin and mandolin; the absolutely rock-solid Dennis Pendrith on bass; and the pyrotechnic Jørn on drums.

As in all bands, nicknames were assigned as everyone relaxed and got to know one another. Ben became "The Fidget" because of his habit of always bending down to fiddle around with settings or cables or knobs or pedals. Gene was dubbed "Moose Martynec," principally because of his wonderful Ukrainian nature. He had a great taste for beer and would often smile after doing something brilliant and say, "Smart like streetcar!" Dennis became Luther Pendragon after the Arthurian legends or some such thing. Jørn Andersen was immediately dubbed "Sven." His presence caused an eruption of bad Danish accents and jokes about marinated herring. If they gave me one at all, they kept it to themselves.

We knew we were a band, and we knew bands had to have names, so we held a sort of ad hoc name-the-band campaign. The winner was Dennis Pendrith, who pointed out that the original name for the Beatles had been the Silver Beatles. On the strength of the imagery from my first big-hit record, Dennis offered the suggestion Silver Tractors. The name stuck. Everybody liked it, so we became Murray McLauchlan and the Silver Tractors.

We were back at Eastern Sound with a new engineer named Ken Friesen behind the board. He was the perfect guy to work with a bunch of loonies like us because he was just as looney. He could match anybody, abuse for abuse. He'd been a Junior A hockey player, so he was completely understanding when we would stop working to go into the lounge and watch the all-important Stanley Cup playoffs. He never put the time on the books, even though we were occupying the studio to the exclusion of any others. When the situation called for staying up all night because we were on a roll, Kenny would do it without complaint. He was on the bus.

I guess it was around February or March of that year that Gordon Lightfoot decided to put on a benefit concert for the Canadian Olympic Team. To his credit, Gordon really is and always was an ardent nationalist. He wrote about Canada, and even though he had worldwide hit records, he remained here as well. So when the fundraisers came to him, I guess he was cornered by his own best instincts. I expect that his close relationship with Fiedler had something to do with my being asked to participate in the show. I was selling out Massey Hall, but that was a long way from filling the Concert Bowl at Maple Leaf Gardens. Finkelstein and Fiedler thought it was a really important thing to do, as I would be premiering a new band and it would set the stage for the release of the *Boulevard* album. I don't think Gordie really needed anyone else on the bill at that point because he had the mega-hit "If You Could Read My Mind" and could probably have filled the place himself. I was looking forward to playing the Gardens under any circumstances, and by the time Sylvia Tyson, Liona Boyd, Gordon and I posed for a publicity shot in the backyard of his Rosedale house, I'd worked up to a pretty good peak of excitement.

The Bernies, as they had come to be known in the industry, had also cemented plans for the first-ever feature television special to be made with me, and by that summer, we were hard at work with another mad Ukrainian named Ron Meraska, who'd been assigned to direct the show for CBC TV. He was a major character— very innovative and fun loving.

One of the first things we established about the show was that simply pointing the camera at a guy doing a concert was not the way to go. Yes, it was going to be a one-hour featuring me playing my music with the Silver Tractors, but we came up with the idea of drawing the parallel between the music business and sports. The idea originated with Finkelstein.

I'd grown up with the "Scrubs on Skates" image of sports, while Bernie Finkelstein had a far more pragmatic view of the world. There was a great moment during a game between the Soviet hockey team and the Philadelphia Flyers (the Russians were over playing a series of exhibition games) when the Soviet team got pissed off about something or other and left the ice en masse during the game. They got Bobby Clark up into the press room and the announcer, looking all concerned, asked Bobby breathlessly if he thought this was a serious international incident and whether he thought the Russians would come back to resume the game. "They'll be back. They need the money!" was all Bobby said. That put everything in perspective.

So that was the idea. Sports and show business—they were interchangeable. It was all about putting bums in seats in the long run. What we did on the show was to treat the concert as if it was a hockey game. We got Howie Meeker to come in and do the between-periods commentary. I sat there with a towel around my neck all covered in sweat while Howie moved little models of us around on a tiny stage and did a faux-critique of our play-making skills. The skit worked really well and made the point perfectly. We even got a surprise appearance from Eddie Shack, which Meraska set up without telling me it was going to happen. The show was fun to make. We all pulled in the same direction, and when it was finally released, it was very well received.

In early June, the day finally arrived for the benefit, and I don't think I've ever been more nervous. Everything was new. It was the biggest place I'd ever played. I'd never done a live show with the band in its present form. I'd never played the electric guitar on stage before, and I wondered how that would go over with my folk fans (memories of Dylan).

During the sound check, I was less than reassured by the fact that the sound just seemed to roll all over the place in that big old hockey arena, to the point where it ran right over the monitors and made it very hard to hear what we were playing. We got it semi-sorted out before showtime. I sure felt for Liona Boyd who was going to get up in front of ten thousand people in this barn and play Villa Lobos on a gut-string guitar. Well, she'd opened for Gordie many times before, so I assumed she knew what she was getting into.

Sylvia and Liona were scheduled to play first that evening, and as I listened to the muffled sound of the performances from backstage, I was so nervous that I get nervous now just thinking of how nervous I was.

Finally, it was our turn. There was a brief flurry of activity as the roadies changed the stage around to accommodate me and the Silver Tractors. Then there was a flurry of tuning. I plugged in my guitar and stepped up to the microphone. On the footstool next to the mike stand was my collection of harmonicas and capos, my cheat sheet of songs and a bottle of cold Heineken beer for the thirst. We were announced, and the band blasted into the opening breakdown chords of "On the Boulevard." I stepped up to the mike to sing and—nothing! There was no sound. I turned around to give a sign to the monitor man or to receive some signal about whether the front of the house was also off, and as I turned, the neck of my guitar caught the bottle of Heineken square on and spilled it all over my harps and pedals and pretty much everything else around. Everything just sort of crashed to a halt, and for a second, I just stood there. I felt like a paper bag full of shit had just landed on my head.

I guess there is a patron saint for folk singers. I stood there in my bright blue Toronto Maple Leafs hockey sweater that I'd worn for this occasion, and instead of collapsing in a heap, something made me see how funny the situation was. I broke out in a big shit-eating grin, looked at the crowd and held my arms out in a shrug. There was a cheer, and the ice broke just about the same time that the sound system came back on line. We hit the chords for the first song and never looked back. It would be an understatement to say that show was a triumph. We played our asses off. We lit each other up, one guy feeding off the next guy's energy. For me it was the right thing at the right time in the right place, and everything just came together with a curious kind of powerful ease. We got sensational reviews for that show, and it really did the job as far as setting the stage for the album release. The show made almost $100,000 for the Olympic team and enhanced Gordie's reputation as a great Canadian, so it worked on every level. The Bernies were delirious with joy.

About a week later, another event occurred that was controversial but fortunate for me as far as free publicity was concerned. A guy named Howard Tate, who was assistant general manager of the CNE (Canadian National Exhibition), was on a CBC show called 24 *Hours* being grilled about why, given the quality of Canadian acts available, so few of them were invited to headline at the grandstand show. Cornered, Tate demanded examples of just who the interviewer thought might be appropriate.

To the suggestion of Bruce Cockburn, he replied, "Who's Bruce Cockburn?"

When my name was suggested, he said, "No way! We will not have him on the stage because this is a family affair! I don't want that kind of show on the grandstand. His language, his story, his show, the whole darn thing. I don't care if he is the greatest thing that ever happened. Do you want your eight-year-old kid sitting in the stands and listening to that stuff?"

As soon as the story hit the papers, I thought Finkelstein was gonna bust open he was so happy! Tate had truly stuck his foot in it, and pretty soon, the whole music industry, which was becoming very nationalistic at that time, was buzzing like a hornet's nest.

Later in the week, in answer to questions on the story by another reporter, Tate stubbornly stuck to his opinion. He even repeated his remarks, but when pressed, admitted that he couldn't remember the last time he'd actually seen me perform. Poor Howard phoned the reporter back to try to cover his tracks and get himself off the hook by confessing that he'd confused me with a comedy act called McLean and McLean. I knew those guys really well. They were Maritimers who did an adult show in bars and night clubs, and they were good friends of Gary Ledrew. The fact that they barely had any music in their act with the exception of a couple of novelty songs made Tate look even worse. We had a laugh wondering if his wife knew what kind of joints he was hanging out in. Of course, he just dug himself in even deeper and went from provoking anger to inspiring ridicule.

Finkelstein and I should have got down on our hands and knees and kissed the guy's feet. At the expense of his reputation, he gave us a million bucks' worth of free publicity. There's nothing like a good scandal to help launch a record, particularly one in which you are painted as the underdog.

After threatening lawyers and eternal damnation, we decided not to seek damages. We didn't want it to appear that our self-respect could be bought. In lieu of compensation for damage to my reputation and career, the CNE and Howard Tate had to make a very public apology not only to me but to the entire Canadian music industry. It was a sweet moment!

One day, after all the dust had cleared, Bernie Finkelstein and I were delighted to receive a lovely note and a free case of Freddy Heineken's finest brew. Apparently, the company reps were happy to learn from the extensive coverage of my onstage accident at the Olympic benefit that I favoured their product. They too enjoyed the free publicity. We were on a roll!

On July 18, 1976, I did something else that would effectively change my life forever. It would change the way I looked at myself, although that would take awhile. It would change the way I looked at the world right away. On that day, I walked into the small terminal at the Buttonville airport, met a tall stringbean of a guy with thick glasses named Ian Shimmin and began the process of learning how to fly.

Ever since the day in the yard at Danesbury when I saw the Arrow, I had dreamed of doing this. Now that for the first time in my life I had a little extra money at the end of the month, it was possible to finally do it. Besides, it was the one thing in my life that required you to show up with a really clear head, and as I had just turned twenty-eight, I was beginning to realize that having a clear head some of the time was good for me.

I love aeroplanes. No—not like or admire, love. An aeroplane, even if it was made for a sinister purpose, is a beautiful thing in the same way a sailboat is. It must cooperate with natural laws in order to do what it does. Even the most brutal ones must seduce the air into doing their bidding in order to fly. Each aeroplane has the qualities of the designer who conceived it, and the character of the many individuals who constructed it. A plane is working sculpture, a fully realized piece of moving art. No two aeroplanes, even of exactly the same type, are ever alike. Each one has a personality all its own. I loved that little hundred-horsepower, two-seat Cessna 150 that Shimmin and I packed ourselves into as much as any aeroplane I have ever flown. As I became more confident, that little craft taught me more and more. It let me have fun with it. I never came down from a flight feeling anything less than completely exhilarated. Eventually, it carried me safely through the ordeal of courage every fledgling pilot has to face— my first solo.

My progress in the world of flight was painfully slow. *On the Boulevard* was released at the end of that summer and immediately began to get a lot of attention. I was gearing up for a fall and winter tour with the Silver Tractors, the TV special was coming to air and I was about to get busier than a one-armed paperhanger!

The tour was the first coast-to-coast, fully produced series I had ever done. We were in all the major concert halls, and they were all sellouts. We had two shows booked at Massey Hall on October 28 and 29. That was five and a half thousand people in Toronto alone before we moved on to Hamilton Place.

We had sound and lights travelling with us, but the queen of the tour fleet was the band vehicle. We'd rented a huge GM motor home from an RV company out in Kitchener. It was state-of-the-art modern and really more like a tour bus than a Winnebago. It had double-airbag suspension, which made for a smooth and very stable ride. There was a kitchen, tables, a shower, couches and a sort of little stateroom in the back for me to hang out in when I wanted to sleep.

I got Bart Schoales to be the driver for the tour. Bart was the artist who did all the True North graphic work, but basically was a hard-core rock 'n' roll kind of guy. He really just wanted to hang out, and giving him the job of driving made that possible. Besides, I wanted everybody who was along on our merry little quest to be "one of the family." Things can get pretty weird when you're out on a long tour, and it's better to have people around who don't require you to explain yourself.

What can you really say about the business end of a tour that hasn't been written about in the papers? We played sellout houses from the Rebecca Cohn in Halifax to the Jubilees in Calgary and Edmonton and the Orpheum in Vancouver. We were golden. The reviews were raves. We were newly arrived, and we were really, really loud. The Silver Tractors was a country rock fusion band that at times seemed closer to Mountain than Bob Dylan. We blew them away!

I remember other images from that frantic fall and winter, all jumbled up together. In between the concert halls, there were the less-than-comfortable venues. I remember sitting in the cinder-block dressing room of the Sudbury Wolves Hockey Club, sick as a dog with the flu. We'd just finished the show, and I was a wreck. Two really rough-looking girls who said they were sisters had gotten into the room somehow and were quite insistent that I party with both of them for the night. I replied that they were just irresistible, but I was in no mood for any partying, given my state. I remember being surprised at how suddenly abusive they became. One of them said rather shrilly, "I *figured* you were a fucking fag!"

I remember one day out in the Prairies when Bart was exhausted and at the end of his tether. Everybody was tired. Gene, Ben and Jørn were sitting at the little table behind the driver's area. One of the eccentricities of our bus, which slowly fell apart as we travelled the country, was a fridge door that would suddenly fly open whenever there was a right-hand bend in the road. Somebody who was sitting nearby would automatically hold the damn thing shut when we encountered one, but on this particular day, no one did. A bunch of shit came out and somebody grabbed a sandwich from the mess and chucked it up in the air. It promptly got batted about like a volleyball until it got batted straight at the back of Bart's head. Infuriated, Bart grabbed and fired it back over his shoulder. It hit Gene Martynec square in the kisser and before anybody knew it, he was up on his feet, red-faced and yelling at Bart, "Step outside, man, right now!"

It was such a ridiculous situation. Here was Gene, yelling at Bart (who could break him in half) to step outside while Bart was in the driver's seat of a ten-ton vehicle going seventy miles an hour. Absolutely—step outside, right now! We all just cracked up. Eventually, they cooled down.

There was the ongoing table hockey tournament. Someone procured a set at one of the towns we played, and it became a major feature of our recreation while we drove. It was such a laugh. Finkelstein and Dennis, with the assistance of Ben Mink, developed rosters for all-Jewish hockey teams and would call the play as they competed. "And it's Bobby Gold streaking past the blue line with a quick drop pass to Phil Epstein!"

A lot of my memories revolve around various bus breakdowns. By the time we were in eastern Canada, the thing was 25 percent gaffer's tape and Crazy Glue. There was tape holding all the cupboard doors shut. There was tape wrapped around electrical connections and pressure hoses of various kinds. One cold night on the road between St. John's and Cornerbrook in Newfoundland, the heater packed it in. It got cold pretty fast. I'll never forget the spectacle of Finkelstein, looking every bit like a dog's breakfast, as he woke up some terrified motel owner in the middle of nowhere to try and buy extra blankets. God knows what the poor man must have thought!

Perhaps one of the sweetest memories is of a night when we were heading into

Fredericton, New Brunswick, to do the Playhouse. There was a problem with the suspension on the bus. The pneumatic pump that regulated the pressure in the airbags had packed it in and the soft-ride suspension had suddenly become the no-ride suspension. Bart got on the blower and found a truck repair depot that could handle the job, but it would take some hours to accomplish. On the way to the repair place, we passed a small town fair with the lights from the revolving rides beckoning the rubes to congregate in the gathering twilight. We had Bart drop us all off there while he went off to get the bus fixed.

Walking into that fair was like entering a time warp and going back to a more innocent age. I swear there were girls in kick-pleat skirts walking with guys who had their cigarettes rolled up in their T-shirt sleeves. The smells in the air were of candy floss and corn dogs on a stick, the rich smells of waffles and ice cream and French fries with vinegar. The sounds were of shooting galleries, ring tosses and barkers trying to get the stroll-bys to play whack-a-mole. The pulsing diesel motors of the Zipper and the Tilt-a-whirl competed with the mixed cacophony of the blended rock 'n' roll music from the Dodge-'em cars.

We ate the place up. It was the perfect escape from what we'd been doing for so long. We were anonymous in the darkness of the carnival. The crowning point of the evening was when somebody sized up the operator of the Dodge-'em cars correctly and offered the guy a few joints. We rode for free all the rest of the time we were there. Finkelstein still talks about that night at the carnival somewhere in New Brunswick as though it was his field of dreams.

It was a hell of a year, 1976. We never put a foot wrong. We worked our asses off. We had a lot of good luck, and to top it all off, as a result of the above, I earned my first certified gold record album. "Farmer's Song" had been a gold single, but this was for the whole shootin' match.

Crash and Burn

BY JANUARY OF 1977, I WAS ALREADY at work on my next record. I was literally off the road and into the studio. I was burned out from touring *On the Boulevard*, but the prevailing wisdom was to strike while the iron was hot. I'd been trying to write on the road, but it was very hard to do. There were constant demands, no time, no privacy and when I did achieve something, it was often very bleak because of the way I was feeling.

I had never done that kind of touring, where you keep going on one-nighters relentlessly. You never meet anyone except superficially, and the only people you talk to at any length are the people you're travelling with. It was the complete opposite of the kind of freedom I'd been used to. I'd always enjoyed my several days at clubs like the Earl of Old Town or the Cellar Door in Washington. During my time off there, I could wander through the Smithsonian to my heart's content and indulge my passion for history. I'd enjoyed my collection of gals in every port. This was different. I felt more than a little trapped by it. I felt caged by the relentless necessity to be somewhere all the time and to perform whether I felt like it or not.

I was also beginning to put more effort into having as good a time as I could, and learning how to fly, than I was putting into creating music. I thought I was at the top of my game and that everything I touched was just naturally going to work out alright.

The Silver Tractors and I went back into Eastern Sound with Kenny Friesen, and when we came out, the result was *Hard Rock Town*. It was a much tougher album than *Boulevard*. Gone were the sweet acoustic-centred folk-rock stylings, replaced with something a lot more in keeping with the title. The feature track was a hard look at life in a company town—namely Sudbury, and it was by far the best song on the record. There was "Poor Boys," where I looked somewhat autobiographically at rock 'n' roll being the only way up if you were working class. In "Immigrant," one of the gentlest songs on the record, I looked at the homesick foreigner trying to adjust to Canada and watching as his children become either strangers to their parents or ashamed of them. "Well, Well, Well" was written for Patty, who had now changed her name to Marguerite de Sackville-Hunt. She was becoming angry and restless and trying to assert herself. Who could blame her? Life with me wouldn't have done anything for her sense of security. In the song, I wrote, "I caught you at the window, just looking for any little piece of the sky."

When Germaine Greer's book *The Female Eunuch* came out, Marguerite was heavily influenced by it and by the flow of feminist literature and thought that followed. When she examined her life in this way of thinking, she was shocked to realize that she didn't have much of a life of her own, independent of her relationship with me. During disputes with her, I began to hear her say things like, "All our friends are your friends" or "I'm a non-person!"

I was a feminist's nightmare. As I mentioned before, I was self-absorbed and selfish. It wasn't that I didn't care about Marguerite. I did, in fact, care very much about what happened to her. For me, though, being married was a convenience. It kept aspects of life that I didn't want to worry about from overwhelming me because there was somebody around to take care of the everyday shit.

I'd made no secret of the fact that I was sleeping with anyone I found attractive and receptive to the idea. Marguerite didn't like this, but I gave her only two options. Put up with it or fuck off. She never could get up the head of steam that would have let her do what she should have done long before—leave me! Complicating things was the fact that although she was incredibly bright, she didn't really know how to do anything that could earn her a living if she did leave. So she seemed to have adopted the view that my philandering could be tolerated as long as I didn't fall in love and threaten to destroy the whole house of cards.

I too had stayed married far longer than I should have, perhaps because of my guilty little secret. I had broken rule number one in the code of human behaviour. You should never say the words "I love you" just because someone says them to you. When I was nineteen and we were married, I had no idea what the meaning or the impact of those words was. I was twenty-nine now, and if I didn't fully understand, at least I knew enough to realize that I didn't have that depth of feeling for the person to whom I was married. I think I was trying to hurt Marguerite into making the first move towards setting us both free without really being aware that that's what I was doing.

So Marguerite was taking steps to reclaim her self-respect. She'd gotten her teeth capped and was going to dance classes, trying to earn her Cecchetti certificate so she could eventually teach dance. She had begun to write occasional dance reviews for one of the Toronto papers when the regular columnist couldn't. She demanded and got a salary for conducting life around the house. I had no problem with any of this. My attitude was basically, "You want a life? Have a fucking life!"

We had a house now, by the way. We'd been living in a rented main-floor flat at Michael Hayden's house. Michael is a well known sculptor in neon and other industrial media. I'd met him through Bart Schoales, who knew just about everybody there was. Michael had been a great landlord, and a close friendship had developed between us. He would eventually wind up doing the cover for one of my biggest albums, *Whispering Rain*. At that time, he was splitting his time between Canada and the U.S. as he developed megaproject sculptures for the corporate world. His heart had been shattered when his young wife had developed a distinct preference for cowboys who weren't him, so when he was in town, Michael would often come up to our place and hang out with his latest stray date in tow. Heck, one night he got a cab home and the driver was a girl. Needless to say, the cab was parked in the driveway all night!

The success that followed the *Boulevard* album finally allowed me to take the plunge and stop being a renter, so we left Michael's place and bought a small semidetached house on Withrow Avenue in the Broadview-Danforth area of Toronto. It was a wreck. It had been occupied by an old Latvian man who'd had about a hundred cats. The smell of the place was unbelievable, but it sure kept the price down. I was surprised at how good it felt to be the owner of even a modest little house. It was a great feeling after all this time to know that you could knock out a wall without asking anybody, and no one could make you leave. In short order, and once again with Marguerite's skilled hand at making something out of nothing, the place was rendered livable.

There was a crime problem in the area. It hadn't been gentrified the way it is now, and there was a mix of different classes of people. There were still a lot of houses around with rusting appliances in the backyard.

The house was a three-storey affair perched on a hill, so that from the rooftop you could see the whole of Toronto and a lot of Lake Ontario. There was a back-yard that sloped down to a garage with a little walkway running alongside, which gave access to the laneway behind. There were two exits to the yard. One led out of the basement, which was partly finished in a sort of postindustrial Latvian manner. There was a toilet and shower cubicle down there, and it was high and dry enough for various forms of recreation and storage. The other exit was out of the kitchen onto a wooden porch, with stairs leading down to the grass. We were already making plans for rooftop decks and such to take advantage of the natural view, but we hadn't got around to that yet.

One night, I had just come back from a gig in the southern states. It was a warm evening in the early summer, and the kitchen door was open, although the metal screen door was closed and locked. I had thrown my carry bag, which had passport, camera and a couple of thousand U.S. dollars in it, on the kitchen table and gone down to the basement for a shower. (I had manfully taken that bath-room as my own—another concession to the new regime.)

I had just come out of the shower and was towelling off when I heard a scratching noise at the back door from up the stairs. I didn't think much of it because we still had a lot of cats coming around who used to freeload from the previous owner. Then I heard the screen rip and the door latch click open. You always wonder what you're going to do in a situation like this. I can tell you for a fact that the last thing you do is think!

My eye fell onto a Crossman Co-2 cartridge pistol I had that was a perfect replica of a long-barrelled Smith & Wesson .38. I kept the thing down there because I had a target range set up in the basement where I would amuse myself by putting holes in beer cans and such. Without hesitation, I picked it up, and stark naked, began to climb up the stairs to the kitchen.

As I climbed, I picked up speed and my adrenalin started to kick in. Halfway up the stairs, the guttural growl coming from deep in my throat became a roar. I hit the top of the stairs, waving this pistol, starkers and screaming my lungs out!

I got only a glimpse of the guy in the kitchen. He turned saucer-eyed at the sight of me and took the back door right off the hinges trying to get out. He'd been holding my bag and he was so frightened that he dropped it right outside the door as he fled through the yard and down the footpath beside the garage.

I was so pumped up by this point that I followed him right out the door and chased him into the laneway. I was running past the other garages, screaming at this guy, when I came to my senses and realized what I was doing. I looked around and thought, "Jesus Christ! I'm naked, running down an alley in the middle of the night waving a gun! If the police come, they're going to shoot me!" I turned tail and scuttled back up to my house. Then I called the police, who turned up in moments and actually caught the man. He was walking down the next street, calmly sizing up another house after going through all that! I had to call the police again the next day to come back because the fellow had filled my garage with stolen goods from houses he'd hit before he got to mine.

Nineteen seventy-seven was already proving to be an exciting year because, in addition to working on the new record, which would be simultaneously released in the U.S. on Island, I had managed to fly my first solo on February 19.

I'd been fitting in as many flying lessons as I could, but it was hard because there were so many interruptions. I had slowly been learning how not to over-control the little aeroplane, which was so sensitive that the pushing and pulling of a novice like me had it porpoising all over the place. I occasionally despaired of ever getting it right. But at last I'd learned under the skilful instruction of Ian

Shimmin to fly using the light touch of just a thumb and the first two fingers of my left hand to work the yoke.

No flight instructor worth his salt will ever tell you that you are about to go solo. You are out one day practising takeoffs and landings in the circuit around the airport, working on your radio procedures, and he just says something like, "Make this one a full-stop landing and pull off onto the taxi way." You immediately think "Christ, what did I do wrong?" You pull up and stop the aeroplane with the parking brake on, just waiting for the lecture to begin when, suddenly, he opens the door and climbs out, cheerfully remarking, "Okay, take it around on your own!" That is precisely what happened to me.

Ian shut the door to the little Cessna 150, and Romeo Fox Bravo and I were on our own. Rivulets of sweat began to run freely down the centre of my back as I taxied down to the holding bay at the end of the runway. I thought to myself, "He's got to be out of his fucking mind! I don't know what I'm doing!" My body kept doing these automatic things, though, as if it didn't really care about what was going through my brain.

My body said, "Buttonville tower—Romeo Foxtrot Bravo, ready to go when able, in the circuit." I watched in detached horror as my body taxied the little craft onto the runway and lined up on the centre. Then the two halves joined together again. I had a brief debate with myself about whether I should do this and realized that if I didn't, I would be dead anyway because I would have shown by my actions that I was afraid to live. I pushed the throttle in, and the aeroplane began to pick up speed rapidly without the added weight of an instructor on board.

Oddly enough, even though he wasn't in the cockpit with me, I could hear Ian's voice going, "Hold the attitude steady, let it climb naturally, back on the power now, okay, left climbing turn onto the crosswind leg, turn to the downwind leg now level out at 1650 feet, throttle back, fifteen degrees of flap, okay, call the tower, turning base leg, throttle back, descend at five hundred feet per minute, that's it, trim for hands off, carb heat on full flap, trim."

"Romeo Fox Bravo cleared to land, full stop," crackles the radio. Chirp, bounce, chirp, bounce chirp, chirp, chirp—rolling now, brakes, pull off at the second taxiway-stop.

"Buttonville ground, Romeo Fox Bravo."

"Fox Bravo, go ahead."

"Fox Bravo, clearance to the tie-down."

"Fox Bravo, cleared to the ramp."

I am soaked to the skin with perspiration. It is dripping off my upper lip, and I can taste the salt of it in my mouth. I am exhilarated as the reality of what I have just done sinks in. I have just flown an aeroplane for the first time in my life all by myself! I have faced a test of courage that was part of a dream for me, and I have passed. I am alive and I didn't run away. I am not only living, I am alive. Thank you, Ian!

I had high hopes for the new album. It felt like a step up again, and we were going to promote its release in the U.S. by doing a showcase gig with the Silver Tractors at the Bottom Line in New York City. It felt to me as if the folks at Island in the U.S. were really behind the record, and in fact, they were. I thought, quite naturally, that the attention being paid to what I was doing in the U.S. would only add gloss to the whole picture in Canada. There was no reason to think otherwise. That had always been the case. In fact, Bernie Finkelstein had leaned on me more than once to think seriously about moving to Los Angeles. He felt that sooner or later, if I remained in Canada, I would lose critical momentum and we'd all fall back to earth.

He was right! Nationalism aside, if you didn't make some kind of footprint outside of Canada for the media to get all breathless about, sooner or later they'd just dismiss you as being no good. I didn't want to leave Canada, though! I was stubborn and didn't want to feel that I was being driven from my home. I had also been up close to big-time American show biz by this point, and I was very disturbed by how ego-ed out and crazy it seemed to make people. I had the classic ambiguity. I wanted to be well known and respected by the whole world for what I did, but I didn't want to be famous.

So we found ourselves in the Big Apple, waiting to go on stage with May Pang hanging around (a notorious John Lennon flame). We kicked ass! The revues were good on the record, and back in Canada, the critics voted *Hard Rock Town* as their pick for one of the top ten rock albums for 1977. On the day the signal for Toronto's new powerhouse rock station Q-107 came on the air, "Hard Rock Town" was the first song they played. The Tractors and I did the first-ever television FM radio simulcast for CityTV/CHUM-FM at the El Mocambo nightclub on Spadina Avenue. Things were starting to roll nicely as the band and I headed out on tour in October to do all the same concert halls we'd done on the *Boulevard* tour. The only difference was that this time out, we'd built up the production. We had a real bus this time. We were carrying sound and lights in a tractor-trailer and crew to run things. By Canadian standards, it was a very expensive show to take on the road. I was committed in a big way. That's when luck deserted me for the first time and things started to come off the rails.

The first development was that for reasons unknown to me, Chris Blackwell, the multimillionaire Englishman who had a good deal of control over my destiny, decided without any warning to pull the plug on the American operation. I suddenly had an orphan record in the U.S., and all the promotional support that would have been directed my way disappeared overnight. I'd never met Blackwell, and I suppose my dilemma was nothing compared to the hopeful people in his organization who suddenly found themselves out on the street without a parachute in the hard town of Los Angeles.

The next thing that happened was that some, but not all, of the radio momentum on the record came to a halt. It was enough, though. Sales were soft compared to the record that had preceded this one. Worse than that, it became evident as we were touring that ticket sales on the tour were soft as well. It looked as if people just didn't like the tougher sound of this record, and they were voting with their dollars and their feet.

Things began to get really bad by the time the tour was out on the west coast. After a less than stellar night in Victoria, I woke up to find myself—band, tour bus and tractor-trailer—trapped on Vancouver Island in the middle of a B.C. ferry workers' strike, which had been in danger of erupting for several days and chose this moment to do so.

Finkelstein, who was burned out himself because of the numerous blows he'd had to absorb with the collapse of the record deal and from the effort of trying to keep the promoters from freaking in the venues we were coming to (they were already smelling losses) announced to me that he'd had enough and he was quitting the business right then and there! I guess he must have felt like he was trying to stop the ocean with a slice of Swiss cheese!

So it was left up to the tour manager and the west coast promoter to find a way to get us and all the gear off the island, bond it, get it into the U.S. by American ferry (they weren't on strike), then get it back into Canada for the show in Vancouver the next night. It was a logistical nightmare, but we got it done.

So the "Hard Rock Town" tour limped back to Toronto haemorrhaging money all the way. I needed 75 percent of houses in most cases just to break even, and we weren't even close. By the time we got home, I was personally on the hook for about thirty-five thousand dollars. But there was more. I was only halfway through.

Poor Finkelstein, who had by this point semi-recovered his wits and was back in the office, still couldn't face me directly on this one, so he got Fiedler to do it. Fiedler had a lot more experience saying unpleasant things to people that they needed to hear. Fiedler sat me down and patiently explained to me that if I continued with what I was doing and did the second half of the tour the way I'd planned, it would take me three lifetimes to dig myself out of the financial hole I would create. The only solution was to reduce expenses by letting the band go and finishing the tour as a solo artist. I went through all the standard reactions to having a death in the family—denial, rage. But as much as I might want to throw my spoon and kick my feet on the ground, I couldn't escape the certain knowledge that Fiedler was right.

Fiedler was kind enough to offer the service of making the calls to everyone in the band, but I couldn't let anybody do that for me. It was one of the most difficult things I've ever had to do, to sit down with each of those guys and explain what had happened. To tell them I couldn't pay them the money they had a right to expect from the coming dates. I felt like everything was my fault. I felt like I was letting friends down.

I left it to the office to downsize all the other logistical odds and ends that had accumulated. We changed from carrying our own production to relying on theatre or contract sound and lights and all the uncertainty that that entails. Every night, you're teaching the job to someone new.

The rest of that tour is a blur. I've rarely been more depressed about anything other than matters of love or death. I had all the wind completely knocked out of my sails, and my basic belief in the rightness of my instincts was shattered. After all the work of mounting the album and the tour, after the high of playing the Bottom Line and the optimism of making a mark in America, I wasn't prepared for how rapidly everything crashed and burned in a few short weeks. Finances were suddenly precarious again. I was in shock.

The Comeback Kid

I DIDN'T STAY MOPEY FOR LONG. I brood, but I realize after a while that it doesn't do any good. I always hear my mother's voice saying, "Stop feeling sorry for yourself!"

I've always found that moving creates movement. Even though I may be just watching the pictures go by, I can still generate enough juice to start thinking about what the next move is.

I was pretty angry. I felt rejected. I'd never really failed at anything I'd tried before, and I was happy to say "Fuck you!" to the music business. I was acting like a jilted lover.

The first thing I did was to throw myself wholeheartedly into finishing my flight training. I wrote the exams for the ministry of transport, and on February 23 of 1978 I was sitting in a four-passenger Cessna 172 at the end of the runway at Buttonville airport with my examiner in the right seat. Ian Shimmin had worked me hard to get me to this point and I was keyed up. I didn't want to let him down!

The examiner, whose name was Bent, was a good man. He was a career aviator who'd fetched up at Buttonville working as a flying instructor and flight test examiner after having a terrible incident in his last flying job. He'd been flying a great big Canso flying boat (same as the American Consolidated PBY-Catalina), working for a surveying company. One day he was coming in for a routine landing on a lake. The big plane touched down and planed along on the keel until it lost enough momentum to settle down farther into the water. As it did so, a failure in the mechanism that kept the nose-gear doors shut tight during water operations caused the doors to burst open. The force of the water entering burst the bulkheads in the flotation compartments of the hull and the Canso sank to the wing roots in seconds. There were a number of people travelling in the rear passenger compartment, and as Bent and his co-pilot went through the cockpit overhead escape hatches and frantically ran along the fuselage to open the emergency hatch in the rear, they were drowning. No one got out.

Bent had made a couple of subsequent flights and then, on final approach to a lake, he found he couldn't do it anymore. He'd put himself on a sabbatical until he could face the job again.

I was lucky in my student days to fly with guys like him. The people I flew with were anything but green twenty-year-olds filling in time until they could find a job with an airline.

I took off down the runway with Bent and began the exercises in flying and navigation that were required for the private pilot's licence. It wasn't a great day. Like so many winter days around the Great Lakes, there was reduced visibility and cloud was plentiful. The forward visibility was down to maybe five miles at the best of times.

We came to the part of the test which called for a diversion from the planned course. The theory is that, due to weather or mechanical problems, you may have to reinvent your flight plan as you go. You are shown a point on the map and told to fly there. Bent pointed to a spot where there was a little town but there was nothing to refer to on the way—no roads, rivers, railroad tracks—nothing to hang your hat on from a navigation perspective. I was down to figuring a course line, guesstimating the wind drift and groundspeed and flying a heading until I ran out of elapsed time on my watch, at which point I should be over the destination. While Bent looked on silently, I made the necessary calculations and then struck off into the murk.

As the aeroplane bored on into the gloom, my face inched closer and closer to the wind screen, looking for anything I could relate to the map on my lap. My elapsed time passed by and there was still no town. Five more minutes went by, and I began to get the sweat on my upper lip that signifies that imminent brain meltdown is near.

"Where are you?" Bent yelled over the noise of the engine.

"Stand by!" I shouted back—a standard aviation stall, which immediately alerted a seasoned veteran like him to the fact that I was already hopelessly disoriented.

I was already unconsciously S-turning gently and looking from side to side, hoping to pick something up. I was ten minutes past ETA when I spotted a town about five miles to the left. There was no way it could be the one I was supposed to find, and I had no idea which one it was. I was now sweating profusely and my heart was sinking as I realized that I had blown the ride.

There is a time problem attached to all flights in a powered aeroplane. If you stay up long enough, you'll run out of fuel, and then you'll come down someplace you hadn't planned on. Bent knew that I was dithering around and that I didn't know where I was and started to load on the pressure. He knew that in a real situation, I might not have the time to be indecisive.

"What are you gonna do?" he yelled at me.

"Stand by!" I tried again.

"Don't give me fucking stand by! What are you gonna do?"

I got angry, and when I did, I started thinking again. "I'll tell you what I'm going to do!" I yelled back.

Without hesitation, I put on the carb heat, throttled back to reduce airspeed, popped on thirty degrees of flap and dove the aeroplane straight for the town.

*In the backyard in
Paisley, Scotland, with Sandra*

First fish at Wood Lake

William McLauchlan (right) and Margaret Fisken, Windsor, 1920s— still dating

William and Margaret McLauchlan at 5 Stayner Avenue around 1954

Daydreaming in my brother Bill's 1959 "bug-eye" Sprite

*Back at 11 Drums Avenue
with Mrs. Docherty*

*At Central Tech
art school, age seventeen*

*Early PR shot, at
about twenty years*
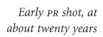

At the Mariposa Folk Festival, early 70s

*Back room at the
Riverboat with Dennis
Pendrith, early 70s*

Getting louder, 1980s

PR *shot that was supposed to impress the Americans, 1987*

With B.C. Fiedler

"Swinging on a Star"
taping with Dan Hill

*"Swinging on a Star" with
Gary Fjellgaard*

*"Swinging on a Star" with
Andrew Cash*

*With Denise Donlon,
Tom Cochrane and
Paul Hyde recording
"Let the Good Guys Win"*

Wall o' Folk: with Danny Greenspoon and Kit Johnson

Floating over Canada: with Gordon Lightfoot

Some old fart with this pretty lady from Saskatchewan

Bathurst Inlet Lodge, "Floating"

Standing on the high ridge over Bathurst Inlet, "Floating"

CG-TGN—*a great old gal*

Intrepid jet pilot, Germany

With Kevin Welch,
writing at Stoney Lake

Karin Ucci with Corsair

*Gord Price at Red Deer, Alberta,
doing the biplane dance*

*Partying with Vezi Tayyeb,
Joanne Perica and Kit Johnson*

Michèle Williams

A happy foursome at the Peter Gzowski Invitational Golf Tournament for Literacy

Calvin McLauchlan

*Mugging with Denise at
some industry "thing"*

Sarah Sackville-McLauchlan (formerly Amy) done up for a musical presentation

Duncan and his dad

The end of the beginning

When I was at a safe altitude, I levelled out, flew slowly past the watertower and read the name on it—Tottenham! Now I knew where I was, and it was close to where I was supposed to be going, so I found the right place in short order.

"That was good—very good!" shouted Bent. "You were thinking. You use whatever you've got, to find out where you are. Don't waste time! Fly out of your way if you can follow a road or a railway rather than going direct over unknown country. Let's go back to the airport. You're okay!"

I was dumbfounded. I thought I'd washed out. Bent was already sure I could fly before he went out with me. He just wanted to teach me a good lesson as part of the process. It's saved my bacon a few times. Now I could add Licensed Pilot to my cv.

The next therapeutic act I performed was to collect Marguerite, load us into the car with basic supplies and hit the road. We had a loose plan to drive Route 66 and no particular time frame. I'd been doing the things I was supposed to do— writing, recording, then touring, doing publicity, TV—and frankly I was just sick of having to be somewhere. I was in desperate need of time to recharge my batteries. Yes, we had been doing sailing trips, but they were still to some degree structured. Other people's interests were involved, and it was never completely spontaneous. I need spontaneity in my life the way a fish needs water.

It was no trouble convincing Marguerite to go. She didn't have all that much to drop at the time, and we both loved vagabondage. Whenever we felt boxed in, we'd just jump in the car, or in the old days, hop on the motorcycle and go off to the Gaspé or Vermont, or down to Florida to visit Grandma Hallie-Belle and then go to Sanibel Island to hunt seashells. Things had grown stale between us. She was rightfully mad at me, and everything had changed so much and so quickly in the last few years that there had been no time to catch our breath. We were both looking for something, and neither of us really knew what.

So we set off for the lure of the southwestern desert, worn out by the long Canadian winter. We'd no sooner made it across the U.S. border at Buffalo and turned west along the south side of Lake Erie towards Pennsylvania than we hit one of the worst early spring blizzards on record. I bored on through the driving snow until things just got too scary. There was zero visibility in the vicinity of transport trucks, and cars were pulled off and stuck everywhere. I wanted to pull off too, but I was honestly afraid we'd be snowbound and asphyxiate in the car trying to keep warm or be hit by a snowplough. Finally, an exit appeared. After creeping off the thruway, we could see a Holiday Inn sign looming out from behind the white veil. We pulled in and went into the lobby, where we were confronted with a scene from a disaster movie. There were people everywhere, trying to make themselves as comfortable as possible on whatever surface they could use to spread out a blanket or put down a pillow. There were crying children. There was general pandemonium. The thruway had just been closed, and everyone was trapped wherever they were. There were no rooms left anywhere. Rescue teams were going out to fetch people trapped in their cars.

Here we were, trying to make an escape to the romance of the southwestern desert, and now we were trapped in the God-forsaken outskirts of Erie, Pennsylvania. It took a day and a half for them to open up the road again, and it was two bleary-eyed and exhausted people who gratefully hit the modest lane of clear pavement between the mountains of snow. I wound up writing about this incident in the collection of songs that would grow from the trip. I hadn't realized it, but I was on an odyssey, and the result would be the album *Whispering Rain.*

We headed southwest on 66 and found our deserts and high plateaus and the brooding emptinesses that made us quiet down inside. We wandered through the Petrified Forest and saw the Grand Canyon. We gazed on the Grand Coulee Dam, and I remembered the songs of Woody Guthrie. We stayed in a pueblo way up on top of a mesa in the Hopi Indian reservation—no phone, no TV, just a million stars at night and crows flying down below in the daytime. We went to El Paso and ate spicy food next to the suit of lights in which Manoleto, the bullfighter, was gored to death. We savoured the Mojave and the myriad scents of the night-time desert. We drove through the furnace of Death Valley, a case of ice-chilled beer in a cooler in the back for survival's sake. I was beginning to forget there ever had been a music business.

Finally, we came out of the desert and down the long hill leading into Los Angeles. We figured on venturing into civilization for a few days to see how it felt again.

Jimmy McCarthy (ex Dirty Shames), after quitting the music game, had developed into a very successful sound recordist for film. While on location, he had become romantically involved with one of the stars, an actress named Elizabeth Ashley. She was divorced from George Peppard, adored Tennessee Williams and was generally larger than life, in the mould of Tallulah Bankhead.

Jimmy had been a denizen of Gary Ledrew's bar and had exhibited an extraordinary talent for shooting craps. "Never bet against me. I'm just naturally lucky!" he'd admonished me one fateful night when I did precisely that and promptly lost all the expense cash in my pocket—cash earmarked for a forth-coming tour leg. It's true, I've never seen anybody who could shoot craps like McCarthy.

Jimmy had moved down to L.A. and was comfortably ensconced in Elizabeth's house in Santa Monica. He was in the process of doing something about an excessive fondness for either alcohol or being Irish. You can take your pick! He was also trying to figure out his next move because he had grown disenchanted with the film industry and regretted leaving music behind.

I called Jimmy, and we went over for a visit. We never left. Elizabeth seemed to find it cute having the folkie vagabond-as-resident-writer hanging about her patio. She really was a genteel Southern lady at heart, even to the point of hav-ing the same black lady who'd been her nanny still working as her housekeeper. She kept a lively house full of interesting people who came and went at all hours. The actors James Farentino and Jimmy Caan were regulars, as well as a motley assortment of technical people—directors of photography and stunt coordinators. Mary Martin (manager of Leonard Cohen and others) was in town then, and she and Elizabeth were good friends. She and Jim went back a long way as well.

While labouring away on Elizabeth's patio, I wrote the first little bit of the song "Whispering Rain." I didn't quite know what I was getting at with it yet.

We drove north out of L.A., following Highway 1 along the ocean. It may well be the best highway in the world outside of Europe. It hugs the steep cliffs along the Pacific and only occasionally dives inland for some relief through a run of beautiful shaded valleys. We visited Big Sur and Monterey. We stopped off in San Francisco and visited briefly with Amos Garrett, who was now living across the bridge in Oakland. Then we went back towards Canada, out of California into the rugged reaches of the Oregon coast.

I've seen few places more beautiful than the joining of Oregon and the Pacific Ocean. One day I sat for hours watching the waves crashing over the rocky head-lands that bordered the driftwood-studded beach. The west wind picked up the spray from the breakers and spun it into gold in the slanting sunlight. I became hypnotized by the surging rhythm and something happened in my head. I guess you'd call it an epiphany.

I've tried to describe it, and this is the best I can do. It's as though you are peacefully watching the world and suddenly there is a little tear in the fabric of reality. You are able to look through for a microsecond and see that everything is perfect. It all takes place so fast, though, that you don't really *see* anything. It's as though something incredibly beautiful passed by and you only know it happened because of the smoke trail it left when it passed. In the deepest level of my being, I knew after that moment that everything was alright! After that, I was able to finish "Whispering Rain."

Marguerite and I finally arrived in Vancouver, where we promptly had a fight. I don't remember what it was about. Probably nothing more than having been cooped up together in a car for too long. She stayed on to visit with my friend Anne Garber (formerly Hershoran), and I went back to Toronto.

Bernie Finkelstein had not been idle. We owed one more album to Columbia under the existing agreement, which Bernie was eager to negotiate anew. I had all the songs for a new album, but he felt we could put the new one out under better terms, so we opted to complete the term of the deal with a *Greatest Hits* package. I felt a little awkward about doing such a thing, as I didn't exactly have a lifetime of giant radio hits behind me, and I was worried the thing might be more than a little sparse. We recorded a couple of new tracks for it and included an unreleased song from the *Sweeping the Spotlight Away* album to sweeten the package. Ironically, though it took a little longer, *Greatest Hits* became another of my gold records.

By August of 1978, I had begun work on my multi-engine rating. I began training in a Piper Aztec, a six-passenger twin with two 250-horsepower Lycoming engines hung on it. It was quite a step up from what I'd been flying. It was a two-hundred-plus mile per hour aeroplane with a range of over a thousand nautical miles. Once I'd gotten this rating, the world was definitely going to open up.

I wish I'd developed at least half the consideration and caution in the rest of my life that I was devoting to flying. I was no longer even thinking of myself as a married person, and had even begun an affair with someone who worked in our organization. So as I began work at Eastern with Kenny Friesen again, life was on the verge of getting extremely complicated and messy.

There was an all-star cast of musicians assembled to do *Whispering Rain:* Ben Mink; Dennis; Eric Robertson doing keys and arranging and conducting string parts; David Wilcox, who'd done such a brilliant job on "Honky Red" when we'd put together *Greatest Hits;* and Ron Dann on steel guitar for one tune. The rest of the contributors were American.

It was Friesen who came up with the idea of going to Nashville to work on the record after we'd done the basic tracks. It started because I was looking for a special kind of background vocal sound on the title track. I had written "Whispering Rain" with the sound in my head of Gogi Grant's classic "Wayward Wind." I was looking for rich, blended background vocals but not something as square as the Anita Kerr Singers. Kenny suggested the Jordanaires, Elvis Presley's old backup group. I immediately remembered "Don't be cruel-oooh wah oooooh" and realized it was the perfect sound. "Those guys wouldn't want to work with me!" I told Kenny.

Kenny said they'd work with anybody who paid them, just like anybody else, and the only question was how much they were going to cost. So he called down to Nashville and set up a massive week-long session at Woodland studios. He not only lined up the Jordanaires, but also Lloyd Green, an all-star session player on steel guitar, as well as the Buddy Skipper horn section, which was widely touted at the time to be stealing thunder from the Memphis Horns. Oddly enough, the whole thing was planned so efficiently and everybody was so professional and worked so quickly that the sessions didn't wind up costing us that much money.

I'll never forget the moment I first had the Jordanaires in the recording studio. I was afraid to mention Elvis. The King had recently died and I wasn't sure if they'd want to talk about it, but as soon as they were in the room, it was wall-to-wall Elvis anecdotes. They talked about the way he'd changed after he came out of the army and had gotten into speed and pain killers, ups and downs. They were very saddened by what the pills had done to him.

When they got down to work, I'd never seen anything like it. They listened to the song once. While they were listening, they wrote out a little coded number chart of the song structure. Then they went out into the studio and gathered around one microphone. They didn't wear any earphones. They monitored the song on a little bitty Auratone speaker and blended their sound by moving in and out on the one mike. They ran the song through once to check the parts. The next one was a take!

The very second I heard that rich wonderful vocal sound come out of the studio monitors, I couldn't help myself. I just broke out in a big wide grin. It was a sound as familiar as my own face in the mirror and as distinctive as a snowflake.

We set the songs up, they knocked them down. They did everything in one three-hour session. I'd never seen anybody work that professionally before. They were real gentlemen, and they kicked the whole record up a big notch in quality with their presence.

Once *Whispering Rain* was finished, it was apparent to me that it was far and away the best and most polished record I had yet been able to accomplish. The only thing remaining was to get the cover shoot done with Michael Hayden, who made a special piece of sculpture incorporating the title and my name out of mirror-backed Mylar. The idea was that there would be no graphic add-ons. One photograph would be the whole cover. It was spectacular. In fact, the idea worked so well that he decided to flip the sculpture backwards, turn me around and use the reverse for the back cover.

I had one last hurdle to overcome on the way to finishing up my multi-engine endorsement in the Aztec—a cross-country flight of not less than five hundred nautical miles. I was quick to notice that there was a minimum requirement but no maximum. My flight instructor Ian Shimmin and I put our heads together and decided to go on a nice long flight and dial in some fun. As November approached, the weather was cooling down, and the south was starting to look attractive again. The government of Canada allowed a tax deduction for flight training in those days, but I didn't think we could stretch their good will too far. I settled on Key West, Florida, for a destination.

Now I thought it was silly to take a great big aeroplane south empty, so we figured on filling up the seats. I called up my brother Calvin and told him what was up, and the idea of heading down to the Keys for a few days' R&R caught his fancy. He filled one more seat by suggesting he'd like to bring along a friend.

A couple of years before, Calvin had been over at Michael Hayden's house when we still lived there, at one of our dinner parties. There'd been about eight people there, including him. At that dinner party, he loosed what I call a "Drink Spitter."

Marguerite was giving a rather tiresome and somewhat strident speech: love is a sham and a cynical fabrication of sentiment geared to luring women into unequal relationships in which there is no hope of self-realization—that sort of thing.

Calvin, who had consumed more than a little cognac at the time, had listened to it long enough, and when she finally stopped to take a breath, he rose up on his hind end and stated: "As a practising homosexual for the last thirteen years, sister, let me tell you a thing or two about love!" I spat out a fine spray of cognac and concealed it with a cough. I said absolutely nothing and tried to hide any reaction that would indicate that this was news to me. I was absolutely astounded. As worldly as I thought myself to be, I'd had absolutely no idea!

By the time I was planning the Florida trip, however, the shock had long subsided, and I had become completely comfortable with whatever my brother chose to do with his life.

I decided to take along my current affair and didn't say anything to Marguerite about guests on our flight. Ian Shimmin invited a young lady named Karin Ucci, who at that time was a student pilot at Buttonville.

And so it was that on November 25, 1978, Aztec CF-BBD took off from Buttonville airport with myself at the controls, bound initially for Charlotte, North Carolina, where we would take on fuel and clear customs. The weather was excellent and the view was spectacular as we moved past the rolling mountains and over the urban stacks of the industrial heartland, finally landing in Charlotte, where in true American style, a red carpet was rolled up to the plane by the fuel supplier and the customs man tipped his hat when he said, "Hi, y'all! Welcome to the U.S."

We flew on down to St. Petersburg, Florida, to fill the plane up to the brim with fuel. Prices were notoriously high in Key West for aviation gasoline, and the Aztec holds 140 U.S. gallons, so the extra money could add up if we had to refuel there. We planned to carry enough from St. Pete's to tanker the aeroplane halfway back up the U.S.

After topping off the tanks, the Aztec was at 5,200 pounds, which was its maximum gross weight. With Ian in the left seat, this time we taxied out to the end of the runway for our flight down to Key West.

It was hot, and as anyone who has done any flying knows, the hotter it gets, the less dense the air is and the more the performance of an aeroplane deteriorates. The runway in use ended at the waters of the Gulf and had adequate length, so there wasn't much of a problem with obstacles except for some low bushes at the end. Ian stood on the brakes and moved the manifold pressure levers up to the stops. With the prop levers full forward and the RPMs at max, the engines howled as they developed all the power they were capable of. The plane began to accelerate lethargically down the pavement as the brakes were released. We'd done our homework and figured on a takeoff distance of about 2,500 feet to reach an altitude of 50 feet. We'd lift off at about 80 mph and set up to climb initially at about 120.

It must have been a lot hotter directly over the runway with the sun beating down on it. We were about halfway down the centre-line and had just lifted off with a positive rate of climb on the vertical speed indicator when Ian sucked up the landing gear to allow the plane to accelerate. As soon as we were out of ground effect (an area of higher lift about one and a half wingspans above the surface), the big Aztec settled back alarmingly, and for one horrible second, we thought we might hear the props strike the runway now that there were no wheels down there. The reliable twin did as it promised in the book, however, and recovered its poise, but Ian held it straight and level all the way down the remainder of the runway until we were likely doing 150 mph and staring straight at those rapidly growing bushes at the end. Then he pulled the nose up and climbed right smartly. Everyone in the back thought he was hot dogging but they liked the ride.

We climbed up and over the water to about 2,500 feet and were just settling into the early flight routine in cruise climb when the right engine burped and stopped cold for a brief second. The plane yawed slightly as our hearts leapt into our mouths, then the engine coughed back to life on the windmilling prop and never missed a beat again. Obviously, there had been a brief interruption in the fuel supply, perhaps air in the line, but once the air was sucked through, the engine was free to resume its normal work. We listened to every beat of both engines very carefully for the rest of the flight.

Once in Key West, we bedded down the plane and checked in to our accommodations, a not particularly glamorous motel resort which did, however, have a reasonably nice pool. We got down to the serious business of exploring the bars and restaurants and visiting the sights—going down to the wharf for the nightly sunset ceremony, watching the arriving boatloads of Cubans, counting the toes on the many descendants of Hemingway's cats.

We organized a day of reef diving with an outfit called Reef Raiders. I was quite keen to get out on the ocean as well as in it. I was an avid and adept snorkeller and spear fisherman by this point, and even if it wouldn't be much of a challenge, it would be great just to go out for a dunk.

My date came along, as well as Ian and Karin. We caught up with the dive boat, and it was a fair-sized motor launch, specially fitted out with a large platform at the back for easy access in and out of the water. They had a mascot on board—a wiry man who appeared to be somewhere around eighty years old. It turned out he was the safety man, who would shepherd the inexperienced back when they strayed too far from the boat. He was one of those cackling old characters for which the Key is notorious, but the old boy was full of good humour and tough as nails. I took an immediate shine to him, as did Karin, who was all teeth and smiles as he flirted with her outrageously but not seriously. A tall Budweiser cooled my fist as the boat headed out to sea.

There had been a series of storms during the few days preceding our arrival, and the waters of the Gulf and the Straits of Florida were still a bit choppy. There was a nice big sloppy swell running, and it wasn't too long before a number of the people who'd come out to snorkel were feeling the effects. Nobody was hurling exactly, but most of them were content to sit very still in the boat and watch the horizon intently to stave off the unpleasant feelings that were growing within. A few of them were turning green.

Karin was one of the first people in the water, and I idly looked over the side and watched her. With her hair slicked back by the wet ocean, she was all flashing eyes as she enjoyed herself in the brilliant blue water. She swam like a dolphin. It was the first time I'd really focused on her, and I found myself taking a long time to unfocus.

I thought to myself, "What's with you, man? You're already down here screwing somebody you shouldn't be, and that isn't enough? Already you're thinking Variety Pack?" I shook it off and jumped in.

I found myself swimming with her and the old man. We were the strongest swimmers there, and it was easy to bounce down to the bottom for coral viewing. We were having a ball and I was beginning to forget about my date. We'd have a rest and swill down a beer to wash away the salt, and I'd find myself stealing long looks at Karin as she sat there. There was just something about her. Yes, she was beautiful—dark-eyed and sleek, fit, great ass—but it was something more. I felt drawn to her.

The boat arrived back at the dock as the sun grew low and the air turned to the pinks and golds of early evening. I was still on the boat, but Karin was up on the wooden dock standing by a piling. She looked as if she was in her own world standing there. The light did something to her, and she looked golden. She caught me staring, flashed a smile and gave me a conspiratorial wave, just the tiniest movement of her hand. For a moment, all the world disappeared beyond the edges of her. A feverish plan began to form in my head.

I was organizing a trip on *Tao*, a twenty-eight-ton trimaran owned by a man named Dave Matthews. It was to be a two-week trip around the outer islands of the Bahamas. Mike Hayden, who had broken up with his wife and been seriously wounded in the process, would be going. Ian Shimmin was going. Marguerite had opted out of the trip this time, though. She was attending dance classes and had things on the go that she didn't want to take time away from. Maybe she was fed up with being on boats, I'm not sure. It was a perfect opportunity for me to pull a Murray.

There was just something about this Karin girl. Right there, in front of the person I'd taken down to Key West, I asked Karin if she'd like to go on a sailing trip. She had a boyfriend at the time, but I'd learned that things were not all they could be, so I casually added that she was free to bring him if she thought that would be a good idea.

I turned around and my current affair was looking daggers. If looks could kill, I would have been stabbed through the heart for all eternity. This may have been among the top ten rat-like things I have done in my life, but I just couldn't seem to help it.

Karin said she'd like to go, and she probably wouldn't bring the boyfriend.

Life Gets Really Complicated

☙ THE FIRST THING I DID AFTER returning from Key West was to go and do the flight test for my multi-engine rating. I flew the Aztec CF-PUX, with the chief flying instructor for Toronto Airways, an ex-wartime Lancaster driver by the name of Gordon Craig, as the examiner. He was the terror of all initial students because he had the gruffest of manners, but I found him very much like my old art teacher Bob Ross—hard but very fair. He had once failed me on the check-out ride prior to my first solo flight after I committed the error of landing with the brake pedals depressed. Tires make terrible noises when you do that!

I can forgive myself the state of distraction I was in before that particular ride, as I had just had my very first aerobatic experience riding in a Pitts S-2B biplane only moments before jumping into the little Cessna 150 with Mr. Craig. I was still ten feet off the ground and upside down.

This time, though, I was very much up to speed in the big Aztec and went through the ordeal with flying colours. Gord didn't spare the pressure and pretty well did simulated failures on everything that could fail. He put his head in his hands, though, when he signed my logbook and saw that I'd gone to Key West for the cross-country. He didn't want to see his name on the tax receipt!

A week later, I was on an airliner headed down to Fort Lauderdale with Ian Shimmin. Mike Hayden was flying in from L.A. to meet us, and Karin Ucci was already there, as her father had a house in the Canal District by the marinas, where she was staying with her sister. We were all meeting in Lauderdale because Captain Dave Matthews of the sailboat *Tao* had a transportation link set up with a local charter operator who would fly us over to meet the boat wherever it happened to be.

It was a brilliant sunny Florida morning when we all met outside our pilot's office at the Fort Lauderdale Executive Airport. Karin looked every bit as good to me as she had the last time I'd seen her. Her sister Andrea had come along to see her off and, I suspect, to ascertain what the kid sister was getting herself into. Andrea took one look at the newly thin, tanned, rather California-looking Michael Hayden, and you could almost see her wheels whirring in appraisal. It seemed to me she viewed him as the likely sexual prospect for the trip. For a moment, it looked like she regretted not going herself.

We took off for the Bahamas from Lauderdale in the chartered Piper Navajo and headed out over the Straits of Florida. I noticed idly how the cloud shadows on the water looked like land in the distance. That illusion had lured many a lost pilot into chasing his tail.

We landed and cleared customs in Bimini before heading over towards Long Island. The pilot used the reliable method of placing a U.S. twenty under the forms, and we were quickly on our way.

By that night, we were bobbing happily at anchor, listening to the slap of the wavelets on the hull of the big trimaran. With the brilliant canopy of the Milky Way and all the other stars in the heavens, I could see perfectly well up on deck, even with no moon. Unless rain threatened, I slept there under the stars. It may be the best feeling there is, tumbling off into sleep and spiralling off into the heavens at the same time.

Within a couple of nights, after an evening of playing guitar, Karin was up on the deck with me under the stars. I thought, "No, *this* is definitely the best feeling there is!" I assumed this was merely going to be the beginning of another affair with a very desirable young lady (she was only nineteen). I felt a certain sense of accomplishment, given that Michael had been in really hot pursuit ever since we'd got on the boat. But something was different this time. I had feelings toward Michael as a rival that I had never experienced before. I would have been quite ready to dump him over the side and drown him, even though he was a good friend, just to get at her. What was it about this girl?

We were a ship of fools anyway. Relationships were being born and dying daily, as so often happens on small boat voyages. There was another couple on board, and they were already in trouble when we got on. He was a lawyer and a bit of an asshole. He made a habit of belittling his wife, and it wasn't long before Michael and she were getting along very well indeed.

Even Ian Shimmin, who was one of the world's shyest men, found love in the person of a very sweet red-headed girl when we anchored at San Salvador.

I knew something different was happening with me for sure when we anchored off Conception Island, a small uninhabited piece of land occupied by nesting ospreys and the occasional wrecked or abandoned aeroplane, the jetsam of the drug trade. Maybe Karin was aware that I was losing my head over her before I was. I'm not sure. Whatever the case, she made a point of spending most of the day walking around the island with Michael.

It was a rough half-day's walk to circumnavigate the little island. It was wild, and often you had to wade into the ocean to clear the outcropping of a limestone headland or find your way through thick bush or mangrove. At one of the little coves, we came upon a brand-new Cessna 210 that had landed on the beach, probably early that very morning, and been abandoned after whatever cargo it carried was off-loaded to a boat. There it sat, waiting for the incoming tide to drown the value out of the instruments and fittings that were still in it. There were a lot of valuable bits there, and me without so much as a screwdriver!

I kept noticing that Karin and Michael were disappearing around headlands, and when they were in view, there was a lot of laughing going on. I found myself getting upset. I found myself getting sulky and morose. I found myself wondering, "What the hell is going on with me here?" I was jealous. I had never before felt the deep and subtle wellings of homicidal anger that were stirring in me, and I suddenly realized that I was falling in love with Karin Ucci. It was also beginning to dawn on me that this was the big one, the one that changes your life forever.

I know what she thought, because in the angry aftermath of my jealous fit, she told me. She thought I was a major asshole when she met me in Key West—just another guy out screwing around on his wife. She thought I was arrogant and had an overinflated opinion of myself. She made it clear that she had no intention of screwing anyone else on the boat because she did not want to become the shipboard slut, but she would spend her time talking or hanging out with whoever she felt like, and if I had a problem with that, I knew where to stick it.

I told her I was already in love with her and that I'd never felt like this about anybody before and I was sorry for the way I'd acted but I couldn't seem to help it. Things smoothed over and we paired off. Everybody let us move together the way people do when they see that something really intense is starting to happen between two incipient lovers.

Tao carried us like a world unto herself. Her twin trails of glowing phosphorescence stretched behind like a surreal rocket trail as we sailed through the starlit night back over to the Exumas. I was happier than I had ever been in my life as I began to feel that things might just be the same with Karin as they were for me. I slowly learned about her life—how she had lived in India, up in the remote hills. I learned about her wealthy Italian-Canadian father and her brother, who was wasting his life as an addict. We talked about dreams and music and her love of horses. We talked about when she was little, and I could see the optimistic spunky girl behind the armour she'd built up over the years. I saw the flame in her that never died, and it melted me.

Karin had to go back earlier than the rest of us, so we took *Tao* up to Nassau. Ian and I walked back across the bridge that crosses to Paradise Island after putting her onto the Chalk's Seaplane Service flight back to Miami. We stopped in the middle of the bridge to watch the old flying boat take off from the turquoise water of Nassau harbour. As I looked on while it climbed into the lowering sun, the spray streaming from its hull in a glistening trail, I was glad to be wearing the sunglasses I had with me. I had never felt such longing for anyone. I felt like the heart was being torn out of me.

There were tears rolling down my face from underneath the shades. Ian, being a good man and a good friend, looked anywhere but at me and said nothing. After a while, we walked down to one of the many waterfront bars and had entirely too much to drink.

On January 5, 1979, to celebrate the earning of my multi-engine rating, I decided to try in some small way to pay back someone who had given me so much. I enlisted the help of Ian Shimmin and Doug Campbell, one of the other flying instructors up at Toronto Airways, and booked Aztec CF-PUX. It was time to thank Wing Commander William Kensitt—Wingco, my father's friend. There was no way to adequately thank him for all he had done and represented throughout his life. He had made sense of my father's death. For four and a half years he had got into a Hurricane fighter, through the battle of Britain, Dunkirk, D-Day, all of it, scared to death but going anyway—never glorying in the men he had to kill but instead saddened by the horror and necessity of it. Rendered a quadriplegic by a senseless accident after going through the war without so much as a scratch, he never collapsed into bitterness. Possessed of a fine classical education and a patrician bearing, he still gave a lifetime of service helping ordinary working people. When he was unexpectedly blessed with a little girl child, he became a devoted father. He loved poetry and he loved the poetry of flight. Many people know a line or two of "High Flight." The Wing Commander could recite it by heart in its entirety. But the last time he'd been in an aeroplane, it was a Hurricane and that was over thirty years ago. It was time to take the Wing Commander flying.

I arranged to have him brought up to Buttonville Airport on that bright sunny January morning. He was wheeled out to the ramp in his chair. Ian got into the seat behind the co-pilot's chair; and I slid into the left front pilot's seat. Doug Campbell and a couple of the ramp lads then wrestled the not inconsiderable frame of Mr. Kensitt out of his wheelchair and up onto the wing, so he was seated by the access door with his legs facing the rear of the aeroplane. All this time, he had to be carefully propped up because he couldn't sit up on his own. Then, with me dragging him by the shoulders and arms and the others working his legs around, we finally manoeuvred him into the co-pilot's seat and strapped him in. There was only a lap belt and shoulder harness—not a five-point restraint system—so Ian's job was to act as a safety man to stop the Wing Commander from slumping over, by holding his shoulders back into the seat whenever necessary.

With everything secured, I started the engines and noted that Mr. Kensitt was paying close attention to every item on the pre-flight checklist. Thirty years hadn't dulled his instincts. Once I'd done the run-up on the engines, I called ground and taxied down to the button of Runway 33. Another call to the tower, this time after the pre-takeoff checks were done, and soon we were rocketing off down the runway with five hundred horsepower in full cry. Gear up, positive rate of climb, let her accelerate nicely, cowl flaps trail, manifold pressure 24 in., RPM 2400, call clear of the zone northbound. We headed north towards the south shore of Lake Simcoe near Jackson's Point. The Wing Commander was obviously enjoying being back in the front seat of an aeroplane again, and the chatter was lively, but he had no idea yet what the plan was. He was busy asking a lot of very intelligent questions about operations of various systems in the plane as I trimmed it out for level flight with the overhead crank (never did like electric trim much).

Once the Aztec was flying straight and level, I looked over at the Wing Commander and said simply, "It's your aeroplane." There was a moment's hesitation and he looked straight ahead. Then he put his withered hands up on the yoke. Within minutes, he'd figured out how to do coordinated turns by using one hand on the yoke and the other to lift his useless leg onto the appropriate rudder pedal. He would then press the leg down with his hand until he got the desired degree of rudder input to correct the adverse yaw. Soon, he was executing 180-degree turns and then 360s without gaining or losing a foot of altitude.

The Wing Commander flew the aeroplane for quite some time without saying a word. I looked over at him surreptitiously at one point, and I could see his eyes glittering with the sheen of excess moisture. Some of it ran down his cheek. To see that what I had done meant so much to him meant more to me than I could ever say. Even though my father was dead now, I had never felt closer to him than at this moment.

It hurt for that flight to be over because when we landed, I could see the burden of life falling back on the Wing Commander's shoulders. The resignation in his eyes contrasted so clearly with the all-too-brief time during which he'd been carried back to freedom.

Almost as soon as it had been released, the single *Whispering Rain* was all over the radio. By raw instinct and luck and refusing to die, I had put the puck in the net again. Finkelstein also had a lot to do with the record's success. He was working it like a Rottweiler, and as it started to make waves, we were well into touring plans. I had decided to fly the tour and really put that new rating to good use. Finkelstein archly remarked at one point that it would be a good promotional gambit. If I rolled the plane up into a ball, all my records would sell like hot cakes, and at the very least, we'd get lots of press coverage because they'd all come out to airports along the way just in case I crashed. This turned out to be true. There was always a small group of vultures waiting for me to screw up.

I worked out a deal for an extended rental with Toronto Airways for CF-BBD, another Aztec and the best of all the examples of the breed I ever flew. It was a good aeroplane, made on a Friday by happy workers.

You might laugh at that observation, but I had already experienced rogue aeroplanes. Every pilot has. They are planes in which many things, great and small, are always going wrong, always at the worst of times. You get a feeling when you're flying her that she's out to kill you. Pilots quietly avoid these machines. But BBD was a sweetheart, without vices of any kind: steady, reliable, honest, like a good trail horse.

Ian Shimmin was willing to take a sabbatical from his flight instructor position, and together we would fly the length and breadth of Canada on the "Whispering Rain" tour.

I hadn't yet seen Karin since coming back from the Bahamas. She was still down in Florida, but I was talking to her on the phone with great frequency. She was occupying a lot of my brain time, and I was very distracted by anticipating when I might see her again. I had confessed to Finkelstein that I had fallen in love, and his reaction was pretty noncommittal. He remarked that the unhappier I got, the more songs I would write, and that sufficed as his blessing.

Don't get me wrong. I think Finkel was right about a tremendous amount of stuff. He lifted his thoughts on songwriting directly from Lao Tzu. "When the road to the mountains is rocky, it's best to follow the ruts!" There has never been a more pithy summation of all that is the music business. He certainly turned out to be right about your best songs often being fuelled by profound misery.

On February 19, 1979, Ian and I pointed the Aztec BBD east towards Fredericton, New Brunswick, with Dennis Pendrith and my sound and lights–road manager–all-purpose neat guy Dave Scace happily ensconced in the back seat. We had a hot album, a good aeroplane and the prospect of a string of sold-out shows in beautiful theatres to look forward to. It was doubly satisfying, given that only a year before, there had been rumours regarding my imminent career death.

The show at the Playhouse in Fredericton was a smash. I'd gone back to basics with just Dennis and me on stage. I'd learned my Canadian economics lessons hard. Nobody seemed to feel the music was lacking in impact—band or no band!

Premier Richard Hatfield came to the show. He was a fan and had been coming since I'd started playing the nicest theatre Fredericton had to offer. It was also evident that Richard had a little bit of interest in my road manager. It was no secret except in the press, who tended toward greater restraint in those days, that the good premier swung that way. He kept an interesting house and was a lively and entertaining conversationalist, particularly after a couple of joints and a snort of overproof rum. I liked him a great deal and thought he was more like the Deep South model of a politician—expansive, generous, larger than life.

On this occasion, he cracked me up. The conversation had turned to the controversy in the news at the time regarding some comments he'd made about the spring seal hunt. Richard, who by that point was very much off-duty, put his head in his hands and declared in a most pitiable tone of voice, "All they ever want to talk about is the seals. Fuck the seals!" It was a good barometer of just how slap-happy extreme political fatigue can make you. Premiers aren't so different from pop stars! I don't feel bad about recounting these things now because, regrettably, Mr. Hatfield is no longer among us and I think the world is a less colourful place for his passing.

We played the Confederation Centre in Charlottetown and then, loaded up to the max with gas, made the long hop over the frigid waters of the Gulf of St. Lawrence, its grey face dotted with the white dishes of the ice pans. The St. John's show was a love-in and had been sold out for weeks. I had more energy to do the shows, and I was playing better than I ever had. There were two principal reasons for this. First, the flying was good for me. Of all the rules I'd broken in my life, I never ever broke the cardinal rule of flying. I never mixed drinking (or anything else for that matter) with flying an aeroplane. Because I was flying every day, it was keeping me off the sauce. I felt better than I ever had before on the road. The second reason was that I was in love and suddenly found I had absolutely no interest in staying up all night courting someone I would never see again. I was getting lots of sleep. I never meant to get healthy, it just happened.

I'd taken the precaution of leaving a day on either side of the gig in St. John's because of the notoriously bad weather at Torbay. In a typical example of government planning, they'd placed the airport precisely where the greatest number of socked-in days could be wrung out of a calendar year.

On the morning of the twenty-fifth, Ian and I woke up and looked out the window to find a carpet of dense fog and a coating of ice on everything. February in the Maritimes bodes ill for weather at the best of times, but we were in the black hole of aircraft movements and we knew it!

We went out to the airport anyway to hang around the meteorological office and try to gauge the trends. The forecast was grim for the foreseeable future. A persistent light easterly flow had brought the cold wet air from the ocean onto the even colder land, where it condensed into thick fog that gradually froze when it came into contact with objects like railings, guy wires, masts and aeroplanes.

We had limited de-icing capability, but lacking heated fuel vents, we were not legal or safe for flight into known icing conditions. We were stuck on two counts, so we headed back to the hotel and hoped the next day would bring an improvement.

I was beginning to think hard about the unpleasant reality of cancelling and rescheduling the show at the Rebecca Cohn in Halifax if we couldn't get our aeroplane out of St. John's. As we woke up again on the twenty-sixth, there was absolutely no change in the situation. We went out to the meteorological office again, where the specialist helpfully showed us a log from a couple of years before when there had been no movement of aircraft for two weeks! I was feeling kinda grim as we gave up and went back downtown.

Finally, on the twenty-seventh, it warmed up a bit, and even though there was still fog, the ice melted away. There was a change in the light character of the fog also, which suggested that even though it was thick on the ground, just a few hundred feet up there would be beautiful clear air. The forecaster confirmed this. We convinced ourselves that there was three-quarters of a mile's worth of visibility down the runway so we could at least look seriously at the option of a departure.

Halifax had a good forecast for the period it would take to fly there, given the winds. The only snag was, if we went out of St. John's IFR (instrument flight rules), the weather there was below minimums for shooting an approach and landing again if we had a serious problem, and there were precious few options of any kind for a long way. It was a sucker situation. Just good enough to get you going, just bad enough to kill you if anything went really wrong. Fuelled by the strong desire not to cancel the Halifax show and risk losing the money, I opted for departure, and we filed our flight plan for Halifax using either Fredericton or Moncton for an alternate. We had enough reserves of fuel for the flight. It seemed do-able, providing everything went according to plan.

But nothing went according to plan. Shortly after convincing ourselves that we could actually see three-quarters of a mile down the runway at Torbay, we took off. The tower kept a watchful eye on our departure with the precision-approach radar, just to assure themselves that we weren't blundering into any of the nearby hills. Shortly after we'd become airborne, we suddenly broke into the brilliance of the clear air above the ground layer of fog. The world was a flat, bright, uniform feather bed as far as the eye could see.

The first sign anything was amiss was when we started to notice that we weren't getting the kind of ground speeds we'd expected. We quickly confirmed unforeseen and greatly increased headwinds. The system that wasn't supposed to beat us into Halifax had pressed the accelerator pedal and intensified at the same time. We were going to spend a great deal more time over the cold Gulf of St. Lawrence than we had figured on. After some hasty calculations on the circular slide rule and an appraisal of the available fuel, the situation began to capture our complete attention.

It got quiet in the cockpit as we began to fly into the cloud layers and the slight turbulence that marked the advancing front. We were still a long way off shore. We droned on. The ground speed was dismal. It felt like the aeroplane was flying backwards. As we made the Nova Scotia coast, there was no great sigh of relief. We had used up our fuel reserves for our alternate and were now chewing on the forty-five-minute reserve and the half-hour contingency supply for approaches. That meant we could still get over to New Brunswick if Halifax went down, but we'd have precious little when we got there to do anything with. In practical terms, it meant that we were going to attempt landing in Halifax no matter what.

Thirty miles out from Halifax International, things were truly dismal. We were in pelting rain and it was getting very choppy. Suddenly the Aztec didn't seem so big. Certainly not when we heard a Boeing 727 commercial jet in front of us for the approach report "moderate turbulence." That meant we were going to get the shit kicked out of us. The weather at the airport was a mile and a half in rain, ceiling just under a thousand feet (which was the only good thing going for us), but there was a crosswind gusting to thirty-five knots.

On final approach, we were getting bounced around so much that I was having difficulty seeing the panel. It was all I could do to keep the wings level and the airspeed and rate of descent within some reasonable parameters as we went through wind shear.

When BBD finally broke out of the clouds, I was looking down the left wing tip at the trees after being upset by yet another gust. Once on the runway, it took every bit of skill I had to hold it straight. Brakes were out of the question on the rain-soaked surface until the plane had rolled off most of the energy. Taxiing in, I could barely stop the yoke from whipping back and forth and rapping us on the knees. I don't want to think about how much fuel we had left.

I think I was very lucky that we didn't get into serious trouble. If a couple more things had not worked out, or there had been an equipment failure to add to our woes, things could have ended very differently and Bernie Finkelstein would have sold a lot more records.

Ian and I buttoned down the reliable old Aztec and went straight to the bar of the hotel where we were staying and had a triple straight rum each. We'd developed the habit of gauging our approaches and landings that way—one rum, two rum or three.

You Thought That Was Complicated

ℬ ONCE THE EASTERN LEG OF THE tour was finished and I was back in Toronto, I was quick to get in touch with Karin. By a strange coincidence, she was living only two blocks away from the house I had bought on Withrow Avenue. She had a little top-floor garret in a house that she was splitting with friends.

I started spending whole nights over at Karin's place and walking back home in the morning to start the next day's activities. We'd hardly get any sleep at all, and I was in a daze with being love-struck and feeling guilty at the same time.

Marguerite had understandably gone orbital when she found out I had broken our unspoken agreement. Anything that didn't threaten our marriage she could turn a blind eye to, but it was obvious that this was something more. She fought back with everything at her disposal. She got Karin's number and called her to confront her without my knowing about it. She as much as told her that she was just another screw and that as soon as she'd been around long enough, I'd get tired of her. Marguerite gave Karin a fairly graphic account of the number of times and the number of friends and acquaintances of ours with whom I'd been unfaithful and implied that things wouldn't be any different for her.

Ironically, one of the reasons I was sure about Karin was because my looking around had stopped completely after meeting her, and I'm sure she was aware of that. She took Marguerite's fright tactics for no more than what they were. Karin was a pretty tough kid who had been through the wringer as far as betrayals were concerned. She was upset, though, at finding herself being characterized as a home wrecker.

Marguerite had long been very fearful of aeroplanes and thunderstorms and many other things, but she went up to Buttonville and enrolled in a ground-school course to try to learn more about my consuming passion for aviation. I felt terrible when confronted by this attempt to build a bridge when there wasn't even a river to cross anymore. I couldn't help falling in love! I couldn't help it any more than I could help breathing. I knew I might have avoided it, though, if I hadn't put myself in a position where it could happen, and this added to the guilt I felt about betraying the promises I'd made to Marguerite long ago, back when she was just Patty.

It had surprised me when initially Marguerite reacted like a woman scorned. I was still too dumb to figure out that often what people say has nothing to do with how they actually feel.

We were renovating the house at the time and had established a bedroom in the basement while the upper two floors of the house were being done. We were opening it up and putting in decks and skylights—the usual stuff. I would come back in the morning after a night at Karin's place, and as soon as I walked in the back door, I'd hear Marguerite down there crying her eyes out in rage and frustration. Even though I knew I was acting cruelly towards her, I couldn't seem to help what I was doing!

It was clear to me that I had to end my marriage. There were no children to consider. I was more than willing to help Marguerite financially and continue to do so. She'd been making more and more noises in the last few years about wanting her independence, even to the point of suggesting that we should buy a house that had two self-contained apartments so that we could have a more "European-style" relationship.

One wrung-out night, as the strains of Van Morrison's "Into the Mystic" played in the background, Marguerite and I made love. It was an act saying "I'm sorry" while drowning in sorrow. It was a goodbye, or so I thought.

Ian and I flew the Aztec over to Kingston on the last couple of days in March to do a concert. The show was routine and successful, but as we flew back that night to Toronto, I began to feel really crummy. I had a fever and swollen glands and broke out in a rosy sort of rash all over my body the next day. It looked like measles, but I'd had them when I was a kid. We called the doctor to come over and have a look at me. She looked at the remnants of the rosy rash, poked me a bit, and based on the fact that I'd already had measles, diagnosed my condition as "psychoneurotic dermatosis," whatever that was. As near as I could tell, it meant that I was a flake and couldn't handle the pressures of my crazy life, so I was manifesting a sickness that she couldn't accurately diagnose. She prescribed some kind of horse tranquillizer that was supposed to calm me down. I took one and immediately felt like I'd been stuffed into a sack full of gauze with no air in it. That was the only one I took. I resolved to have little more to do with doctors as long as I was able to walk around.

Not too long after this happened, Marguerite came down with the same condition. The same doctor was called and what again looked exactly like measles to me was diagnosed as a nonspecific viral infection. Marguerite had also had measles when she was a kid. For some reason, the word rubella never came up.

After flying down to Chatham, Ontario, in mid-April to play a flood-relief benefit I'd organized for the area farmers, it was time to start the western leg of the tour. I had asked Dan Hill, who was now a major star after the mega-hit "Sometimes When We Touch" to play the benefit, and he was the only person of all the stars I asked who didn't even hesitate to say yes. He paid for his generosity by being pitifully motion sick all the way down and back in the aeroplane. He's a good man!

Ian and I took BBD west by way of concerts at Sault Ste. Marie, Thunder Bay, Winnipeg and Brandon, gradually making our way out to Alberta, where I'd arranged for Karin to join me on the tour, flying around in the aeroplane for a couple of dates. It made me forget the turmoil I'd left at home, having her there and doing all these energy-charged, sold-out shows. When she went back home after a few days, it was all I could do to keep going west and not turn the aeroplane around to follow her.

After the Orpheum in Vancouver, we turned around to capture dates we hadn't done yet. When we hit Lethbridge, I got the phone call. It was an urgent message to call Marguerite at home. I didn't know what the hell to think as I dialed. It turned out that after eleven years without so much as a suggestion of the light going on, she had been to the doctor and found out that the missing ingredient in her fertility and mine had been Van Morrison. At the eleventh hour and fifty-ninth minute of separation, she was pregnant!

I was devastated by the news. I felt like the jaws of a trap had just closed around me. Of all the fucking times in the world for a thing like this to happen, why now? There was also the issue of us having both been recently sick with we didn't know what to further darken the future. I had thought we'd be able to work things out and an equitable freedom would be had by both of us, but now things were very uncertain indeed.

Ian was the best of friends as always and sat down to drink with me and listen to my endless self-pitying bullshit without comment or criticism.

By the middle of May when I got back to Toronto, the first order of business was to try and find out what the hell Marguerite had caught from me. If it turned out to be German measles, there was a strong risk of serious complications in the development of the baby, as she had fallen ill in the first trimester of her pregnancy. The tests pointed out only that she had been exposed to the rubella virus at some point but weren't specific as to when. The doctor who had made the initial nondiagnosis refused to commit to an opinion that might eventually lead to a termination of the pregnancy.

Marguerite and I sat down to try to discuss what to do, and it followed the usual pattern of our discourse. She refused to consider the option of termination and flatly stated that she intended to have the baby whatever I might think about it. She also informed me that she wanted her life back and that she didn't want to raise the child. That would be my role. It's hard now to imagine the state of mind I was in that allowed me to see any sense in what began to evolve in the way of a plan.

Marguerite found a nice little apartment up on Avenue Road and moved in. I was paying her rent and expenses, and we began to cobble together a separation agreement that would eventually allow us to divorce as amicably as possible. I accepted her at her word and began to make the necessary alterations in my life. First I re-renovated the renovated house, creating a nanny's room and a nursery. I found a nanny who satisfied me that she knew everything there was to know about babies, and I moved her into the house. I leased a car for the nanny. We bought all the stuff you get when you're expecting a baby—little clothes, booties, a crib—all the shit that you put up on the wall. Then we waited.

With Marguerite out of the house, Karin was around a lot and would often stay over, but we were lovers, not living together. She was perfectly content with the status quo. Sometimes we would sleep under the stars out on the deck. I had rigged up an outdoor shower with the total privacy the rooftop afforded. It was hedonistic and sensual, luxuriating in the wash of hot water while watching all of the lake to the south. The top floor was strictly off limits to nannies and other intruders of any kind. It was my retreat, my castle in the clouds.

I had no intention of causing any trouble for Marguerite or denying her any kind of access to the baby anyhow, any time. I was actually fairly content with the idea of trying to raise a child. I never thought about my qualifications as a father. I just looked on it as another hand I'd been dealt, and I would do the best I could with it. I was very happy to be separated. I was happy to be done with the horrible day-to-day tension and pain of our life together.

The nanny kept telling me I was out of my mind. She said she shouldn't talk this way to me but she could see nothing but heartbreak ahead, and that even though it meant her job in the long run, she felt obliged to let me know that she thought I should try another plan—any other plan. "She is never going to give up that baby!" said the nanny. Most all the women I knew who had the nerve to talk to me that way, including my mother, agreed with the nanny.

"She's set on this. She won't change her mind. I know her, and she'll keep her word," was my standard reply.

I waited and waited. I worked hard. I got back on course for yet more flight training, and by July I'd written my exam and passed the flight test for my commercial pilot's licence.

I got very productive and started writing some pretty interesting songs towards a new album. I wrote the title track for *Into a Mystery* that summer after staring up at the stars one particular night. I kept feeling as I looked out on the arm of the Milky Way that we were all on some backward sidetrack in the great glow of the galaxy and that all the real excitement was out there somewhere. I kept wondering about all the "might be" civilizations in the universe. I wondered, if they showed up, whether I would get on a ship and go with them if I had the chance.

That fall, while Marguerite swelled with the life growing in her, Shimmin and I took an Aztec down into the Bahamas. Both Karin and her sister Andrea were along as we flew through the States and over the Straits of Florida to Nassau. The eventual destination was a small fly-in resort at Pittstown Point on Crooked Island, at the southern end of the young country. The resort had a compacted coral landing strip, just long enough to get the Aztec out of as long as you didn't wait 'til the day got too hot.

It was a really nice little out-of-the-way place with cabins on the edge of the ocean and all the waters around teeming with fish and full of bright and beautiful coral heads.

One day, Karin and I went out diving with one of the local Bahamian guides. We were just snorkelling around, enjoying ourselves. Once he assured himself that we were comfortable and weren't going to drown, he began to poke around in the holes and crevasses of a coral reef, looking, no doubt, for a free lobster dinner. The guy had blown himself up a bit as "the best diver and fisherman around these waters, Mon!" so I was more than amused, as I watched him hard at work, with his head buried in the reef, probing with his spear and making a big racket, to see a very large nurse shark slowly making its way towards him, attracted by the noise. The shark, which is a harmless type, was probably eight or nine feet long. As it reached our guide, it did a vertical pull-up and swam right up the length of his back without actually touching him. It was at this point that the unfortunate man finally realized something was behind him. The big shark was just kind of hovering there when the man turned around, and from twenty feet away, I heard the gurgle of his scream as the snorkel came out of his mouth and he began thrashing and flailing. Of course, the shark quickly swam away, thoroughly alarmed as our friend, choking out bubbles, fought his way to the surface. Once up there, he gasped and sputtered until he regained his composure.

We were down there for Guy Fawkes Day, which is still celebrated in many remote areas of the Bahamas, even though the origins of the holiday have long faded away from local memory. We went to a big beach party, attended by all the people from the local village, where they hung effigies in the trees with the names of people who had done various misdeeds in the last year attached to them. Once the sun had gone down and it was suitably dark, they were set on fire. Being stuffed with fireworks and such, they made a hell of a racket once they got going. I tried to imagine what any passengers would be thinking on a boat going by offshore as they looked through their binoculars at all those bodies burning in the trees while people danced around them yelling and carrying on.

When it was time to leave, we paced off the distance and did some very accurate calculations just to make sure, before we loaded up, that we weren't going to find ourselves a little short of runway. It took every bit there was to get off.

We made our way via Nassau back to Florida and on up the Carolinas. The Aztec we were flying, cf-gfl, had no de-icing gear at all. We had to avoid any icing that was forecast, or if we encountered unforeseen ice with more than a light catch rate, we had to get out of it as quickly as possible.

We had filed from Charlotte, North Carolina, right to Toronto, and most of the flight would be at night. The forecast for Toronto was variable overcast to broken in stratus but with a good ceiling underneath the cloud and no precipitation. En route there was layered stratus cloud forming up in the flow from the

Great Lakes as the air moved from the northwest to the southeast. We filed for nine thousand feet, which we figured would keep us well above the tops.

Things were perfectly normal and the scenery was spectacular, the lights of one American town flowing into the next. Then, as we got up southeast of the Shenandoah Mountains, things started to change. We kept running into a persistent cloud layer that would bust through our altitude, and when we did, we would start to accumulate some rime icing. The clouds were full of moisture from the lakes, and it was November. At that altitude, it should have been too cold to pick it up, but we kept frosting up anyway. I would call up the area control facility that we were assigned to and request a different altitude to get us out of the cloud. It wouldn't take much, just a little bit higher, and we'd be back in the clear looking at the stars while the ice sublimated away. Then suddenly we'd be back in cloud again and accumulating more ice. We weren't getting enough to really compromise the performance of the aircraft. It was more of a pain in the ass than really dangerous. The cloud layers were thicker and more numerous than indicated in the forecast but Toronto was still good and so was the alternate. We hadn't twigged yet to what was actually happening.

This is what was occurring: as the air mass moved down into the countryside of Pennsylvania and past Pittsburgh, it was pushed up by the rolling ridges of the Shenandoahs. Then it started to undulate in waves as it alternated between mountain ridge and valley. The effect was being felt much higher up in the atmosphere than predicted, so the freezing level was moving around. If we just flew a constant altitude, sooner or later we'd run into one of those waves again and be in cloud and picking up ice.

We ran into a long patch of the stuff and started to accumulate a fair amount of rime. As I shone the flashlight out the window at the wing leading edges, I could see the milky ugliness slowly beginning to compromise our ability to fly. There was no way to get rid of the stuff. It wasn't really serious yet, but we had to decide on a course of action—and soon.

Ian was flying, and I started to check with flight service about what available airports we might divert to if the situation became worse. The news was not good. Everything on the south shore of Lake Erie was experiencing freezing rain at the surface. We immediately called centre and advised them that we needed a higher altitude due to ice accumulation. After adding all the power we had, the aeroplane carried us up slowly but gamely—two hundred feet per minute and getting worse at full power. There were occasional little airframe tremors as the ice affected the balance of spinning props and disrupted the smooth flow of air, and a feeling of sluggishness as the non-turbocharged engines gasped for the air they needed to develop power at this altitude. Where were we? Approaching eleven thousand—Jesus, we shouldn't be this high with no oxygen on board.

The Aztec was barely climbing at all when suddenly we punched out the side of the wave we'd been trapped in. Intensely grateful to the gods of aviation, we could plainly see the glow of Toronto and Buffalo lighting up the clouds from underneath in the far distance. Odd that we couldn't pick up Erie the same way. We had already started to lose the ice we were picking up, but in the flashlight's beam, it still looked a little ugly out there as we descended back to a more reasonable flight level. There was no moon, but I could clearly see the Big Dipper to reassure me that we were heading north to home. It appeared that there were no more nasty surprises between us and the airport at Toronto. It was still very dark. Then I noticed I couldn't see the Big Dipper anymore. I couldn't see the comforting glow of the distant cities anymore.

I barely had time to say, "I think we're about to fly into something" to Ian on the intercom when we were in it. We ran smack into some kind of convective build-up in the pitch dark, smack dab over Erie, Pennsylvania. There was suddenly a lot of turbulence, and a lot of slushy ice hit the aeroplane as though someone had thrown a bucket of the stuff at us. Shortly after we hit the second violent updraft, I heard Ian on the intercom calmly say the words no pilot wants to hear from the guy in the left seat. "I've lost control."

I looked over, and he was making large control inputs on the yoke and absolutely nothing was happening. The big twin dropped a wing and shuddered.

I'm not sure how we saved the aeroplane. Ian and I had flown so much together by this point that when something happened, we almost acted like one person. We just went into survival mode, I guess.

The Aztec's performance had been so degraded by the ice that when hit by the violent updraft, it had stalled, dropped off and begun to enter into a spin. I was on the engine controls immediately and brought the manifold pressure levers back to idle and props and mixture controls full forward while Ian instinctively kicked the rudder that would move the ball away from where it was pinned on the side of the turn and slip indicator. At the same time, he shoved the yoke full forward. The Aztec recovered from the spin it was entering and instead entered a steep dive, from which Ian skilfully rescued it, pulling hard, but not hard enough to break the wings. All this time I was only vaguely aware of an intensely loud high-pitched scream coming from the rear.

Then we flew out the other side into clear smooth air, and there were the lights again. Everything was normal except for being in an aeroplane that was staggering along with ice smacking the side of the fuselage as it came off the still windmilling props. We quickly added power, trimmed and called centre to explain why we had just abruptly lost several thousand feet of altitude. Ironically, when I told the guy in Toronto Centre that there was a build-up in the area of Erie that had almost knocked us out of the sky, he just said laconically, "We're not painting anything out there on the primary radar." "Well, I guess it just fucking well doesn't exist then!" I thought to myself darkly.

We landed at Toronto International fast and long and taxied up to the customs area. When I got out of the aeroplane, there were still big clumps of ice falling off from underneath and melting on the tarmac.

Interestingly enough, we found a souvenir of the incident in old GFL. Karin's sister Andrea had long well-manicured fingernails that were her pride and joy. We found a couple of them imbedded in the seat back, directly in front of where she'd been sitting. Now I knew who'd been making all that noise.

The Beautiful Girl Child

MARGUERITE WANTED TO HAVE A natural childbirth, so in the middle of all this heartache and acrimony, incredible as it may seem, we started going to Mothercraft classes, together with another friend who would be assisting at the birth. There we'd be, practising her breathing with her, carrying on as though all this was completely normal. We had the socks and the tennis balls and the music and all the other stuff you were supposed to need for the siege of birthing.

For the short time before she was actually due, just a couple of days, Marguerite stayed at the house. It wasn't wise for her to be by herself at this time.

Finally, on the fifth of January, she went into labour. She stayed home as long as was comfortable, and then we called our friend and went off to the hospital.

Several hours later, it was already apparent that things were not going as planned, and it would not be an easy birth. Marguerite was having a lot of pain and finally gave in to having an epidural. The prospect of having a needle stuck into her spine was frightening, but the pain outweighed the anxiety. Hours passed. She was becoming stressed and tired. The baby was becoming distressed. Dilation was not occurring fast enough, and the baby was in the wrong position.

The obstetrician gave us the straight goods. We had passed the point where carrying on with the status quo was a good idea. It was becoming dangerous to continue and he recommended that Marguerite be prepped immediately for a C-section. She was very frightened, and we were all tired and drained.

The hospital was progressive, and in answer to Marguerite's request, they allowed me to suit up and accompany her into the operating room. She would be conscious during the procedure although completely numb from the waist down, and it would be my role to comfort her in her anxiety as much as I could.

I was standing beside her holding her hand when the incision was made. I couldn't see it but I felt it immediately. There was a fluttering tremor in her hand and a sharp drop in temperature as it went cold and clammy with the shock her body had registered. The baby was removed and carried over to the side, where she was quickly suctioned, cleaned and tight-swaddled. Then they handed my new girl child to me while they attended to Marguerite and finished closing the incision.

I just stood there in my ridiculous plastic shower cap and my green suit with the oversized sock booties and stared down at this little being. Then, simply over-whelmed, I started to cry. She was so beautiful. I was broken-hearted to be the cause of her being born into all this ugliness and dissolution. Her arrival should have been an occasion of unrestrained joy. I was torn by conflicting emotions. I was deeply drawn to this new person and felt a strong love instantly. I hated myself!

Slowly, over the next few days, I recovered my equilibrium as Marguerite regained her strength and winced through the post-surgical pain. I found I was excited at the prospect of living with the little girl child, whom we'd named Scottie Amelia. The Scottie was after the ladies of Marguerite's family. Amelia was my choice, after Amelia Earhart.

I was back and forth to the hospital every day, and I'd started making light-hearted comparisons between myself and the guy in *The Courtship of Eddie's Father*, a popular show about a single dad. The nursery was ready. All the little goofy things were on the wall with the bright yellow paint.

I went over the night before Marguerite's release. The new baby was sound asleep in her little bassinet when I got there. Almost immediately, with no preamble,

Marguerite started into it. "I'm not giving up this baby. I don't want that woman [the nanny] laying a hand on her. I'll take you to court. I'll fight you if you try and keep her."

She went on in this strange tight emotional rant, but I had stopped hearing her. I had stopped hearing anything. I don't remember being angry. I remember going numb. It was as though my brain just shut down, and for a little while, I just went away. It was Amy making a little noise that roused me out of wherever I'd been, and when I came to my senses, I was almost surprised to realize that Marguerite was standing there with a frightened expression on her face. I had advanced on her and was in the process of slipping my hands around her neck to throttle the life out of her. I left the room and the hospital and then my senses.

I did the foolish things that most men do when they are consumed with emotional anger. First, I let the nanny go. Then I got in touch with Marguerite and said I was moving out of the house. She could have it. She could have everything—the money in the bank, the leased car—everything! I just didn't want to deal with her anymore. Then I called up Karin, who had moved into an apartment building over in Cabbagetown owned by our renovator, and asked her if I could stay there with her for a while. I packed some things, grabbed my guitar, locked the door and just walked away.

But you never get to just walk away. That only happens in the movies. In real life, there is unrelenting continuance. There is involvement from which there is no escape.

Karin was living in the apartment with her girlfriend. It was a big enough two bedroom, but it was made rather smaller by the conditions in which they maintained it. Karin had been spending most of the time over at my house, and I was a bit unprepared for the way they were living. There were several days' worth of dishes in the kitchen sink, cockroaches running around the countertops and an overflowing cat litter box badly in need of refreshing. The fridge was growing cultures of microbes, and the place hadn't seen a vacuum in a while. Karin's roommate, also named Karen, but with an "e" instead of an "i," was the daughter of a well-to-do plastic surgeon. They had both grown up not having to do much in the way of housekeeping.

I immediately set to work to impose some civilization on the place. I was happy to roll up my sleeves and make it more liveable because it took my mind off the emotional roller coaster I was riding.

I knew that Karin wasn't ready for us to live together, at least not yet. I was eleven years older than she was and carrying a suitcase full of newly acquired problems. I had landed on her doorstep because, at least in the short run, I couldn't think of any place else where there would be some comfort for me. She was too young for life to suddenly get so serious.

One afternoon, when I thought they were both out, I was in the bathroom swearing a blue streak, venting all the rage and frustration I was feeling. When I walked into the living room, Karin was sitting there looking uneasy. She had come in and I hadn't heard her. She had heard the whole emotional vomit I had just gone through and was torn between quietly leaving and pretending she hadn't or staying and admitting she had.

I was afraid of a lot of things. I was afraid that Marguerite was playing head games with me at the expense of a child. I was afraid she was using our daughter to maintain an influence in my life that was geared to my undoing. I was afraid that the intensity of the love I had for Karin, coupled with all the problems I had now, would frighten her away. In short order, I had lost my child. (Once the mother was in the house with the baby in those days, there was no going back. The courts never awarded custody to a father.) I had lost the house I had worked for (possession is nine-tenths). The love affair that had precipitated the situation was threatened, and just to top things off, even though I was making a good income from the recent success of *Whispering Rain*, I was beginning to haemorrhage money.

Karin and I would talk a lot into the wee small hours about what we were going to do. She had problems of her own. She hadn't completed her education. She had run off to India after majoring in marijuana through high school and lived there for a year. She had hit a point in life where at the age of twenty she realized she didn't really know how to do anything. She burned inside with a desire for her life to take on some meaning, for something to do that would involve her considerable intelligence. That was the irony. I recognized immediately on meeting her the first time that she was highly intelligent, intuitive in her understanding of what makes people like me want to create things and quite capable of doing anything she wanted.

But she felt insecure, tending to avoid discussions that she thought were over her head. She was under the impression that because she'd smoked away her schooling, she was stupid. That wasn't about to change when her chief pre-occupation at the time seemed to be going out with her friend, the other Karen, scoring grass and getting high, or spending her time running around clubs. It sounds crazy, but I felt like there was someone inside Karin's complex web of surface camouflage struggling to get out. It was that person deep inside her that I was in love with. Or maybe I was in love with some idea I had in my head of who she was.

One night we were talking about her life, and she began to reminisce about how happy she'd been around horses. She'd had a lot of that as a younger girl. Somehow, the information came to light that they were hiring people for practically nothing to look after the racehorses over at Greenwood Racetrack. They were still running thoroughbreds there at the time, as well as the trotters. The job would entail a lot of mucking and grooming, but eventually there was the opportunity to be an exercise rider as well. A couple of days later, Karin went out and put her hat in and landed a job.

She was game. She got up while it was dark and made her way out there, working until she dropped. Karin was never one to shirk hard work as long as her heart was in it. It wasn't the greatest job in the world, but it was around horses. Even though it didn't last all that long, it got the ball rolling, and the change in her was immediate and evident.

Another problem in her life was her brother. Practically her twin in appearance (they were both very much their father's children), Peter had been reeled in by the Danny Dope guy down in Fort Lauderdale and become a junkie. He was on and off methadone programs, but he chipped, ran credit card scams and stole, even to the point of robbing his grandmother of her pain medication. It was hard for Karin to watch him slowly unravel.

Karin came from a rich family, but a troubled one. As kids, they had been witness to painful conflicts between their parents and finally an ugly divorce. There had been affairs, ill-concealed from them. The money had served to make them dependent as children. They had all become adept at survival stratagems as they grew.

Peter just went away—period. Andrea was all feminine wiles. Karin had developed thick emotional armour, a hot temper, a sharp tongue and an unwillingness to trust anybody or anything that got too close.

Somehow Karin and I survived that first highly volatile period in the immediate aftermath of Amy's birth. We moved into a house together. It was a modest little renter near Pape and Danforth, just up the road from a little Greek Orthodox church. Life developed a bit of stability, although there were almost constant phone calls from Marguerite about one crisis or another.

I had to watch the dollars, but I still had enough to keep flying, and at the end of that May, I went up to Lake St. John near Orillia after convincing Ian Shimmin to come with me for the sheer fun of it. After two days of hard flying, I earned my seaplane endorsement on my pilot's licence. I had an easier time than most because I had bags of sailing experience. It was challenging and fun, especially given the fact that when you put an aeroplane up on floats, what you get is a lousy aeroplane and an even lousier boat.

I started to work on a new album. I'd written a great little song for Amy before she was born called "Don't Put Your Faith in Men," and I was putting that on the record. I had the title track "Into a Mystery." I had a bunch of other songs, ranging from things I'd written when Karin and I had been separated by circumstance to sailing songs like "Rockin' on the Sea" that were tributes to life on *Tao*. On reflection, I thought several of those songs were better at the time than they actually were. Probably the best song other than the one for Amy was the one I wrote for Marguerite. It was called "Try Walkin' Away" and would prove to be the most effective radio single.

I had also lined up Carole Pope from the band Rough Trade to sing background vocals, and she in turn lined up three other great ladies, Shawn Jackson, Sharon Lee Williams and Colina Phillips. They really got their teeth into "Don't Put Your Faith in Men." Carole had her own eccentric kind of followers, and they were rabidly devoted to her. One day at a university concert, a young lady asked me, "Is it true that Carole Pope is singing on your record?" I said that it was. She screwed her face up in a most unpleasant way and asked, "What's she singing with *you* for?" This was the first intimation I had that I might not be as hip as I once was.

Somewhere around launch time for this record, I got a call from Marguerite. She needed to speak to me. It was urgent. I had got used to "urgent," and I was in a bit of a funk as I made my way over.

There was something wrong with Amy's eye. Marguerite had been tending to her and noticed something in it. It didn't look normal.

It wasn't normal. Soon our worst fears came true when the Hospital for Sick Children confirmed that Amy had live rubella virus in her system and that it had begun to cause cataracts to grow in the lenses of both her eyes. Gradually they

went opaque and unseeing. At only six months, little Amy endured her first operation as the lenses were removed so that, with the aid of thick corrective glasses,
she might have a chance to see.

A Smoking Hole Where I Used to Be

❧ KARIN WAS AN ANIMAL LOVER and was always taking in some old alley cat
or other. I wasn't much of a cat person, so when she started making noises about
wanting to have a pet, I bought a dog from a breeder network. He was a pedi-
greed Alaskan Malamute pup, who was going to be imported for us from the
States. When he finally arrived, he was just a little pot-bellied ball of fur who was
so fearful from being weaned too early that he spent most of the first day hiding
under a chair. He quickly grew into a game and confident adolescent, and I built
him a big house out in the backyard. Karin had the habit of just opening the sliding door in the back and letting him out, instead of taking him out herself. I had
arguments with her about this. He was a young male dog, and he wasn't going to
hang around if there was some kind of mischief to get into.

One day, I walked into the kitchen and noticed that the door was open. Karin
had let Corsair (that was his name—after the famous aeroplane) out on his own
again. I was just about to start swearing when I heard the screech of tires and the
unmistakable scream of a dog being hit. I recognized that voice.

It took about an hour to find him. He had crawled under a porch shocked and
in pain. It was barely possible to pick him up, he whimpered and howled so pitifully. Naturally, it was a weekend and the vet was closed, and so was the Secord
Animal Hospital. Karin, who was feeling pretty terrible by this point, got in touch
with an organization called the Animal Rescue Mission, which ran an ambulance
service that administered to animals at any time, day or night, and had a twenty-
four-hour network of treatment facilities. The hospital performed emergency
surgery on Corsair. He had a fractured pelvis and a smashed leg, with internal
injuries to boot. He came back home eventually with an artificial hip joint and
one short rear leg, with a permanent limp. Over the years, it never seemed to
bother him much, and he could still run all day, although we were advised that
his sled-pulling days were over.

Karin was so grateful to the Animal Rescue Mission that she wanted to go out
to their facility and make a donation in person. Eventually, one day, we found the

time to go. It was out in the east end of the city. When we arrived, they offered to take us on a tour of the adoption areas so we could see how their operation compared to the Toronto Humane Society.

We were going by the cages in which stray cats were kept when Karin stopped short in front of a rough-looking coal-black alley cat. "That's Nikina!" she exclaimed. She was referring to a cat that had sensibly run away for greener pastures some time ago from the previous apartment. This cat was no fool, and as soon as it sensed attention was being paid to it, went into the whole affection dog-and-pony show! Every time she said "Nikina," this ball of mange would do back flips and rub its sorry muzzle against the bars. Karin, being strong willed, was not taking no for an answer. She was convinced that this was her long-lost cat. There was no debate on the issue. We were taking the animal home.

The handler removed the cat from its cage and handed it to Karin. It was green-eyed and had a slightly demented look to it as its tail twitched back and forth.

We went back out to the reception area to fill out the forms and pay the ransom for this creature. As the clerk was processing the paperwork, the cat was restlessly shifting around in Karin's arms, with its tail still twitching back and forth rapidly.

I pointed towards its belly and said, "We'll have to clip all that matted hair or it'll get skin sores." Just as the words were leaving my mouth, the cat, suddenly finding footing, launched itself out of Karin's arms and planted the claws of both its forepaws firmly in the flesh above the wrist of my left hand. That being accomplished, it buried its fangs in the soft flesh of my hand, perforating the area between my thumb and first finger completely and scraping the bone of my thumb as it went clean through. Then it hung there chewing and wouldn't let go. The thing had moved like lightning and had caught me completely by surprise.

I grabbed it around its neck behind the ears and squeezed hard with my right hand until it finally opened its mouth. I got the handler to help unhook its claws, then stood there and bled while they took the animal away. "Don't kill it!" I shouted. I wanted it quarantined.

They took me in the back, where we washed the wound out with soap and water. "Okay, take me to Mount Sinai," I said to Karin. "What for?" she replied. I could have throttled her. I was scheduled to play Massey Hall in two days, and I knew that the only thing worse than a cat bite as far as infection goes was a bite from a human. My hand was already beginning to swell.

We went down to Emergency, and the admitting surgeon knew the score. He shot me full of a wide-ranging antibiotic as well as a tetanus booster, thoroughly cleaned the wound and said, "If you get a lot of pain and throbbing and start to notice any blue colouration tracking up the veins in your lower arm, get back down here right away!"

By two o'clock in the morning, I woke up feeling as if my lower arm and hand were being hit with a sledgehammer every time my heart beat. When I put the light on, I could see the telltale tracks of the budding infection. I already had a fever and was feeling really bad.

Karin drove me back down to Mount Sinai, and they admitted me right away. I was barely into a ward bed with the curtain pulled around me, feeling like death, with drainage tubes stuck into my arm on one side and an IV drip full of antibiotic stuck in the other, when the curtain was abruptly pulled aside. It was a photographer from the Toronto *Sun,* who promptly flashed off several exposures right in my face. The next day my mug was in the paper. The headline said: "McLauchlan sidelined by cat scratch." Gee, it's great to be famous!

I eventually recovered and about a week later was released from the hospital after fighting through a generalized case of blood poisoning. For many months after that, every time I tried to play guitar, my hand would swell up like a sausage because of the damage that cat had done to the veins that normally carried the blood and lymph away. During the recording sessions in New York for the album I would make with Bob Ezrin, I had to seek the services of a surgeon to lance my hand just to bring the swelling down! Fucking cat scratch indeed!

We lost the Massey Hall dates to promote *Into a Mystery,* and I never played that big hall again. Finkelstein always said that this episode marked a turning point in my career. The album didn't pick up any real momentum.

As had so often been the case for me, the record that followed a successful one produced disappointing results. *Into a Mystery* didn't exactly stiff—it sold respectably well—but it didn't go into the gold range. It hit around thirty-five thousand sales in Canada and stopped going, even though "Try Walkin' Away" was a pretty solid turntable hit. Finkelstein was disappointed and so was I, but rather than rolling with it and trusting our instincts as we always had, we looked around for a more active solution. Bernie was a strong believer in the old saw that if you're not active in the U.S., pretty soon your star in Canada will start to dim. That seemed to be happening to me. We'd made a good record, but there just didn't seem to be the level of excitement about it that we'd been used to. I had forgotten my pattern of recording ups and downs. The record we'd just made was a bit more of a rocker than *Whispering Rain,* and generally speaking, my fans didn't like those records as much. This had happened before when I made *Hard Rock Town* on the heels of the *Boulevard* album. I'd developed a solid style and a definite sound over the years and it had weathered the test of time reasonably well. But now we began to doubt it.

By a coincidence of fate, Bob Ezrin, who had achieved early fame as the producer of Alice Cooper and most recently had had a mega-hit with Pink Floyd's album *The Wall,* was in town working on some sides over at Nimbus Nine studios. Jack Richardson, who was Bob's mentor, had built the place into a shrine, and Bob liked to work there. I can't recall exactly how it came about, but Bob invited me over to work on the sessions playing acoustic guitar. There were charts to read, and it was all fairly challenging. But it was fun hanging out, and Bob and I struck up an acquaintanceship.

When Finkelstein and I came to the conclusion that the "save" for my career situation would be a solid American production deal with a high-profile producer, we got in touch with Bob. On the day of our first meeting over at the True North offices, we got our first case of "sticker shock." Bob's going-in-the-door price, just to secure his services as producer and induce him to negotiate a deal, was pretty much our entire Canadian recording budget. It was going to cost us fifty grand before Bob even poured himself a coffee. The record, when it did get made, would have to be done with whatever money was raised through the U.S. production deal. This was very rich for our blood but we wanted to play in the pen with the big boys, so we agreed. We ponied up the dough, and Bob went off to L.A. to work his special magic on Joe Smith, who was, at the time, president of Asylum Records, the company started by David Geffen and recently sold to Warner Brothers.

While all this was going on, Marguerite was beginning divorce proceedings against me, and with lawyers now in the picture on both sides, things were getting ugly. Baby Amy had turned out to have a wide range of complications from the rubella virus. She had a hole in her heart that the doctors said would close with time. She had pulmonary stenosis, a roughening of the interior lining of the heart and the major arteries, which made her highly susceptible to bacterial infections. (The roughening gave the microbes a ready home in which to breed.) In addition to all that, she had developed pediatric glaucoma, almost a certainty when there is any invasive eye surgery in infants. She was going to need medications to control rising ocular pressures and periodic eye operations to relieve the pressures when the medications failed. There was a whole list of other stuff to be watched out for down the road.

One thing was for certain. There was no chance of a normal upbringing for Amy. She would initially require full-time care, which meant a full-time mother. That meant the full-time mother would be unable to work to help support herself. There would be extraordinary medical expenses to consider and the likelihood of special schooling to plan for. Money was always going to be a problem.

Bob Ezrin was as good as his word and came back from L.A. with a deal worth an additional one hundred and seventy-five thousand U.S. in production money. I felt this was a coup, and one day, as I was sitting in the True North offices, I was busy being pretty excited about the prospects of doing this record. Carole Pope of Rough Trade happened to be sitting there as I was telling someone about Ezrin's all-star production record and about his last effort with Pink Floyd. "Don't forget! He also produced The Babies," Carole said dryly.

Bob set up a demo session over at Kensington Sound studios down in the market off Spadina Avenue, and it was at that session that I first met Vezi Tayyeb, who would become a long-time friend and the best man at my second wedding. He was one of the owners and the chief engineer at the studio.

The first song we put on tape was "If the Wind Could Blow My Troubles Away," a simple song I'd written almost like a little haiku prayer to light one of my dark nights. It just said, "If the wind could blow my troubles away, I would stand in a hurricane." The rest of the song was just variations on a theme. It was a sweet little thing, but almost as soon as I was finished, Bob, in his flamboyant style, shouted through the intercom, "Don't think about that song anymore! Don't sing it at all! It's great, but I'm hearing something with it and I can't explain. I just don't want you to lock your head into something else with it." So until we actually cut it, I dutifully never sang or thought about the song. Bob was a Phil Spector kind of producer, and the idea was that I would surrender all my preconceived notions about what I did and not be afraid to try new things. I went along with this and put my own thoughts on hold to see where this would lead me.

When we finally started production, it was at The Record Plant in New York

City in December of 1980. I felt good about being back there; after all, I'd cut "Farmer's Song" in that very spot. I felt that I was going somewhere again.

On the first day of recording, I met the band. The drummer was Andy Newmark, the most laid-back guy on the two and the four beat that was ever created. He'd just finished making John and Yoko's *Double Fantasy* and was completely jet-lagged from having to switch over from being in the all-night groove. The bass player was the ultrafriendly and very cool Neil Jason. These two were the primo New York session guys at the time, so we were off to a good start.

Karin came down to New York with me. She was usually willing to pick up and go hang out at the drop of a hat! It made life more fun to have someone to play with when the work was done.

Karin, and Neil's significant other—a very cool, tough and funny black lady named Maxine—got along like a house on fire, and pretty soon they weren't bothering to do anything as mundane as hanging around the studio—they were off shopping or terrorizing the night clubs.

Bob had a Winchester rifle and a baseball bat leaning against the studio wall by the side of the console. "That's for when the act gets out of hand," he announced. He refused to call the people he produced "artists."

There always seemed to be a plentiful supply of evil nose powder on hand, and its abundance contributed to the character of the sessions. Sometimes Bob would ask me to leave the room in a half-joking manner because he had his lawyer on the phone. Bob too was in the middle of an ugly divorce, and by a quirk of fate, the lawyer representing Bob—Jeffrey Wilson, an advocate of children's rights—was also representing Marguerite against me! Sometimes I imagined I heard Jeffrey saying, "Is he there? I can't talk if he's there!"

The weirdest thing was, we'd roared off into production on this record, and for the first time in my life, I didn't think I had enough songs. No problem, according to Bob. We laid down grooves and rhythm tracks in the studio, the idea being that I or he or all of us would supply the song to fit the groove as we went along. This is exactly how "Tell Your Mother She Wants You," a sort of *West Side Story*–style rant, came into being. Bob wasn't worried about something as basic as songs. He'd been doing records this way for years. Hell, he razored together every drum track on the Floyd album.

We got into a really nice loping groove on "Wouldn't Take Another Chance on Love," which stated simply that if things went south between Karin and me, I'd take a pass on the affliction called love for the rest of my natural life.

When Bob started building up the anthemic track for "If the Wind Could Blow My Troubles Away," he left me behind. It was as different as it was possible to get from how I had conceived the song. It sounded like it was being produced by Leo Tolstoy. We were talking big here! And Bob had plans to make it even bigger.

We went back to Toronto, and in February of 1981 got to work on building more layers onto the tracks down at Manta Sound. Numerous guests came in to play or sing. Dom Troiano played guitar. Bruce Cockburn guested. Greg Godovitz played, as well as Zero from the band the Kings. Slowly, the tracks began to flesh out.

One of the most intriguing songs we worked on was "Falling Off a High Wire." It was a portrait of a street junkie and was the closest I'd ever gotten to the work of Lou Reed. Because Neil, Andy and Bob had cobbled together the music in a way I normally would not have done, I was free to write a less structured lyric. I was moving away from strictly folk forms.

Bob was really stressed! He was troubled a lot with post-nasal drip, but then again, so was I. The strain of his divorce and trying to keep up with a punishing schedule for my album, as well as vetting forthcoming projects, must have been difficult for him. He terrorized engineers. He drove one of his own assistants to the point of a breakdown. Still, Bob sailed over it all like a true rock 'n' roll prince. Even with all the stress, he could still go to the CNE and get a kick out of the music blasting out of the speakers near the midway rides. He never lost that sense of being just an overgrown kid who was crazy about music.

After Bob had recorded and conducted the string parts at Manta, we headed off down to Nashville for a couple of days. We were returning to Woodland Studios, where I'd had so much success with the Jordanaires. This was going to be a pretty ambitious session as well.

Bob was looking for a particular massed vocal sound for his grand project song and, to that end, had a local scout find him the best black gospel choir that was to be had. When we arrived at the studio, they were in full cry, rehearsing for church. They were testifying! They were rocking out so it felt like the roof was raising up in time to the hand clapping that underpinned the singing. What a sound! That must be the only kind of music God really hears, you can hear so much God in it!

Bob was enthusing about how he'd like to come down here and do a special project. Maybe get the best white and the best black choir together and record them singing in unison right here in Woodland. One of the studio assistants, a bit of a cracker, muttered, not quite under his breath, "I don't think that'd be such a good idea."

Finally, in March, we took the project to Producer's Workshop down in L.A. for mixing and a little additional recording. Some of us had done too much coke over the last three months, but the supply was yet to taper off. Things were becoming edgy as I began to get the uncomfortable feeling that while I'd been in my state of surrender, we'd manufactured a suit of clothes here that, while interesting and a bit gaudy, didn't fit the person who was going to be wearing them— me! I was already wondering how I was going to tour this record.

Karin was down with me again in L.A. and she was having a great time. Maxine Dixon was around again and they were hanging out a lot. Karin was extremely vivacious and always provoked a lot of attention, particularly from men.

One night, after mixing, Bob looked at me and said, "She's just a little cock teaser, you know! She's gonna break your heart!" I actually suggested that we go out to the parking lot, I was so pissed off. It was the wrong thing to say to a guy like me. I guess he was just pissing on my turf for some reason that night. I don't know why he bothered. He was already in a league I was unlikely to ever approach. I wish his appraisal about her breaking my heart hadn't turned out to be so accurate.

When the album was finally released, it was immediately evident that the marketing department at Asylum didn't know what to do with it. There was no easy handle on it. As a product, it was all over the place—from hard rock to R&B to novelty to ballad. It just didn't hang together. It never even made a ripple in the water stateside. Bob gave me a gold Dunhill lighter and moved on. I didn't!

We got a bunch of airplay on the big anthemic song in Canada. It was even selected as the theme for the International Year of Disabled Persons. But that was the only song that got played and that was only on one type of radio—MOR. The album still sold reasonably well on the strength of "If the Wind," but it didn't even outshine *Into a Mystery*. People just didn't like it, and I found it hard to blame them because, at the end of the day, I didn't really like it much myself. Somewhere between basic tracks and mixing, the album had lost its rudder and sailed off to somewhere that just wasn't me.

The results didn't show up really clearly until I put out the next album, *Windows*, in 1982. Sales on that one were down by about twenty thousand.

Finkelstein and I had rolled the dice and lost. I hadn't had the sense to keep faith and control in and over my music. At a critical time, my body was there, my appetite for coke was there and my ego was there, but the parts of me that mattered were sadly absent. I had a real chance to step up to the plate and I, personally, had let it fizzle! I stood by and let it happen. It wasn't Finkelstein's fault and it wasn't Ezrin's fault either. They did everything they were supposed to do.

That was the end of my being a force to reckon with in the recording industry. I'd had a ten-year run, but the writing was on the wall. There was a new British invasion. Punk and New Wave had arrived. The era of the singer-songwriter in the sense of what that used to mean was over, and I would now be spun gradually out to the margins, although I would continue to make records.

VI

Love's Bubble Springs a Leak

🎵 I SNAPPED BACK PRETTY QUICKLY from the setback of *Storm Warning*. I accepted the fact that I was going to be working at a certain level and began to realize that the lunacy of the upper echelons of the music business wasn't, perhaps, a goal I had really desired in the long run. I had started out sneering at the idea of writing and recording to get hits and had wound up coming perilously close to doing just that. I wanted to get back into a more basic mode and write for the sake of it with no agenda attached. That was always what I'd done best. Maybe Bob Ezrin and I had lost the short game, but he might just have saved me for the long one. Hell, I wanted to be an artist, not a dancing bear. I settled down and got to work again.

I was also shielded from the effects on my self-confidence by the fact that life with Karin was really good. We had moved into a new house, a lovely spot up in Moore Park, and she seemed very happy there. She was showing signs of wanting to end the ups and downs of dependency on her father's money, and of becoming reconciled to the fact that I really did love her and wasn't going to run away or betray her.

It was difficult for me sometimes when I did think about finances. I was carrying two households from soup to nuts. Karin had her own investment income, but it wasn't used for our expenses. At one point, she was driving around in a Porsche while I was getting advances on performance royalties to pay my taxes. I really think she didn't know what the score was, though. I don't think I ever confronted her with the matter of finances, and I figured, "What the hell, I'd be covering the same expenses if I lived on my own anyway!"

As difficult as it was, Marguerite and I were nearing the point where there was a time line for the end of divorce proceedings. The deal was pretty simple. She would get everything we'd held together and I would get my guitar. The stumbling blocks had involved her lawyer inducing her to go after things like my publishing, based on the intriguing idea that without her inspiration and support, I would never have written the many songs I had produced. Lawyers! All I had to do was point out the several albums of songs I had made since we separated, but the process took up the court's time anyway.

So in spite of the problems that little Amy was having, and the endless divorce proceedings, there was light at the end of the tunnel. I began to think about asking Karin to marry me.

She had by this point jumped back into the world of horses in a meaningful way. Her father's new wife, a wealthy Danish lady, was keen on equestrian sports and proved a convincing ally in swinging Karin's father around to supporting her in her efforts.

Karin had begun training with a well-respected three-day-event rider-trainer, and it wasn't long before she was good enough at it to go down to the United States and compete. Eventing was not her thing, though. The strict discipline of the dressage element in the competition was not really her style. Karin was more a hell-rider at heart; she loved the cross-country galloping part.

Gradually, she had moved over to show jumping, and she was becoming extremely busy with commuting back and forth to the country nearly every day in order to work with her horse and trainer. All summer there were competitions in Canada, and then in the winter months or early spring, there were various American competition circuits to take part in.

I fit in fairly well at the show-jumping events. I quickly learned that boyfriends and husbands weren't supposed to help with the horses. That was a job for the lower classes. The old money types tolerated me the way they'd tolerate any "new money" and the *nouveau-riche* types were tickled to have me around because I was well known. They likely thought I was rich. What a joke. I was completely comfortable because the people were easy to read, and there was more coke around than there had ever been in the music business. There were also some people that I liked a great deal—funny and genuine people like Olympic rider Jim Elder.

The shooting of John Lennon had provided me with the inspiration and anger needed to write an uncompromisingly bitter song about the man who'd killed him. It was evident to me that he had shot John to achieve his moment of fame, and I wrote a song saying I hated everything that motivated him and I hoped his name would be forgotten for all eternity. It was called "I Hate Your Gun."

I wrote a song called "Hiroshima," which was both a reaction to the horror of the bombing and a celebration of the fact that things were once again growing there and that people laughed in the streets once more.

I was amassing a collection of songs that weren't standard pop fare.

During this period, Andrea, Karin's sister, got married. At the wedding, Karin looked breathtaking in her bridesmaid's gown. I walked up to her father during a quiet moment and did the traditional manly thing. He was an Italian gentleman, and I wanted to do things right. I quietly took him aside and asked, "Would you approve of my marrying your other daughter?" He looked at me directly and laughed. "If you can talk her into it!" was all he said, then walked away.

One evening, Karin and I were having dinner with Bruce Cockburn and his girl-friend, Judy. Karin was back in town for a short while after being down in Florida with the horse. She would be returning to Florida soon. I'd been missing her a lot and was happy to have her back. It was tough dealing with the long periods of separation. I got the heartaches when she wasn't around. I don't remember how it came up, but during the conversation, it was revealed that Karin was not only sleeping in the same trailer as a member of the male persuasion, but due to space limitations ostensibly, she was sleeping on the same two person bunk—fully clothed, of course. I tried hard to cover up how shocked I was by being lively and laughing it off, but it was terribly embarrassing that I hadn't been aware of the situation.

That night, we had it out. It wasn't the work or the separation. In fact, I encouraged Karin to have a life and to work hard, whatever the cost. It was that I suddenly felt insecure about what else she might not have told me. Then she dropped the bomb.

There are moments in every relationship when you say something and it's like jumping over a precipice. You can never take it back, and everything changes from that point on.

She said, "I don't think I love you the same way you love me."

I just stood there and looked at her dumbly. I could see that she meant it.

Something went out inside me. Way off in my head, I heard a sound like shattering glass. It was the last of my confidence breaking the door panes as it left the house.

Nothing was the same after that, and we began a long downhill slide towards separation.

As time passed, there weren't many ways that Karin acted that were guaranteed to make me feel secure. The first place a woman always makes her feelings known is in bed. She took to retiring with a joint and her Walkman phones on, off in her own world. We fought more about little things. She made the rounds of the clubs at night. I was still very much in love with her, and now I didn't know what to do with it. It was starting to eat at me instead of lifting me up.

I had an idea for touring *Windows* that was like nothing I'd ever attempted before. My road manager and tech Dave Scace and I cooked up a sort of one-man show using tapes and rear-projected slides of illustrations that I'd created for the songs. I guess it was my version of "performance art." Nobody got it. Half the time, the stuff we were presenting was miscued or just didn't work. After a few dates in the Maritimes, I abandoned the technology and just started singing the songs with guitar or piano. The reviews were unanimous in their disapproval of everything. I was really floundering.

As if things weren't bad enough, the people who owned the house that Karin and I had been living in, the one she actually felt at home in, decided to move back from out west. We were going to have to move.

My friend Gary Ledrew helped me find a house in the country, at Sunderland, just north of Toronto. I convinced Karin that living out there would be a good idea because it would shorten the time spent commuting to the horse, and it would be quieter and more pleasant. I guess I thought that if I got her away from the city and all its distractions and temptations, we could somehow calm things down and find our way back together.

She hated it from the word go. She hated that in the springtime you could smell the fertilizer from the farmer's fields in the breeze. She didn't want to have anything to do with the small-town people. Basically, she didn't want to be stuck out there in the middle of nowhere with me. She'd formed an opinion of who I was by this point, and it wasn't very flattering. She thought I was angry and moody too often. I never wanted to have fun. I wanted to keep her at home, and then when she was home, I would criticize her for not being around more often. I guess she was accurate. I know I was acting like a jerk some of the time, but I didn't know what to do with the fact that I thought the person I loved didn't love me back.

The kicker was when she finally rented a room downtown so there'd be a place to stay in the city and then presented this to me as though it was a terrific idea. I felt great wandering around out there in Sunderland on my own after she effectively moved back to Toronto.

I still worked, though. Thank God for that, because writing has always taken me either away from what's going on or helped me, in some way, to make sense of it. I started soldiering away on a bunch of new songs that were about something more than just me. For the first time, I started looking at the miracle of the place I lived in and I became preoccupied with how all-consuming an experience it was just to try and cope with being Canadian. I was now fully into looking at songwriting as an art rather than a job.

The songs I began to create were among the best I'd ever done. The album I made with them was one of the best I'd ever created and predated the so-called "New Country" movement by a decade. They were things like "Red River Flood," which explored the fragility of the works of human beings in the face of nature. "Never Did Like That Train" hearkened back to the yearning for adventure any kid felt when he heard the call of a train's whistle keening through the sleepless night—going somewhere, anywhere. "Trying to Stop the Sun from Going Down" was one of the best things I ever wrote about the hard realities of the migratory Maritimers. But the most passionate of all was "Out Past the Timberline," an unblushing love song for Canada.

Maybe the desolation I was feeling inside spurred me to look for a greater attachment for my soul. I know that can happen. I had begun to understand that romantic love or "falling in love" could be obsessive and needy and destructive. I had begun to understand that my love had been so needy that I'd been smothering the person I loved and driving her away. I was beginning to realize that I had to put fear and arrogance aside if I was ever going to be worth anything as an artist. That realization helped me enter a new phase where my work might possibly be good by intention, not just by accident. I had begun to realize that if I ever hoped to keep Karin, I must stop holding on so tightly.

When *Timberline* came out, it got more respect than anything I'd done in a long time. It was gritty. It was real. It was uncompromisingly me. For the first time, Finkelstein and I made a video (the song was "Never Did Like That Train"). It was done on a shoestring budget by an unknown filmmaker named Brad

LeMay, but it turned out to be a little classic. It caught the attention of a guy named Bob Burwell who worked for the Jim Halsey company down in Nashville. He happened to see it on Canadian TV when he was up visiting his folks in Buffalo. Bob and I would connect later in a bigger way.

'Floating over Canada'

{@ THE MOVE OUT TO THE COUNTRY had been a noble experiment but a great failure. I found a house in the city again. It was a charming little Georgian overlooking the whole sweep of the Don Valley and had a backyard for Corsair. Karin liked the house and agreed to give up the room. We'd try to make things work.

It was clear that if I was going to become a recording artist selling only artistic numbers, I would have to find other things to do. Otherwise, I and everyone around me that I was feeding, would soon be panhandling on the street. Yes, I was touring and doing concerts, but once the bills got paid and the band got paid and the manager got paid and the agent got paid, there was nothing left except what might take care of the bare necessities, and as I mentioned before, I had two sets of bare necessities.

I thought hard, and an idea began to form, based in part on the feelings I had while composing "Out Past the Timberline." I loved to fly, and I especially loved flying floatplanes. What if I took a whole period of time and just flew around Canada, documenting the characters who peopled the vanishing edges of our country. Then I could make a project out of writing songs about them. Maybe it could be a film documentary. Maybe I could tie it in with a radio series and an album that would be like a special project. The more I thought about this cockeyed scheme, the more plausible it seemed.

It just so happened that cable services were coming on line in Canada at that time and one of the new services being brought to a grateful nation was called First Choice Pay TV. The trail of people I'd been talking to informally about my idea led to a slightly more formal meeting with a very smart lady named Joan Shafer. She'd agreed to meet me for lunch to hear what I had in mind.

She was in charge of developing and financing new program production for the service. As part of their licence agreement, they were under mandate to develop indigenous programming, and Joan was sitting on top of a lot of money that had been earmarked for this purpose and needed to be spent.

She was absolutely charming, and I liked her immediately. She listened attentively while I laid out my ideas about spontaneously documenting the margins of Canada in film and original song. I was honest with her about the crossover potential for the other projects that could piggyback. When I was finished, without preamble she said she liked the idea and committed on the spot to thirty-two short film inserts to be carried between feature films and concerts on First Choice with a budget of about $1.2 million to do them. I was flabbergasted! This was more than I had dreamed of.

On the strength of the deal with Joan, I went to see Matt Blajer at the CBC. He'd gotten in touch with me when he'd found out what I was up to. He thought the idea for making a radio series where I would interview notable Canadians (not necessarily famous ones) and then write songs about them was a good one and right up CBC's alley. He wanted to be the guy to produce the series, so he went upstairs with the plan and got the budget to do it. It looked like everything was coming down better than I'd ever imagined it could. I started crunching numbers, looking for aeroplanes, doing trial flight plans and researching which areas to go to and who I might want to seek out when I wasn't just looking for spontaneity.

Then, what was becoming a pattern of questionable luck began to kick in. I'm not sure exactly what the sequence of events was at First Choice, but it went something like this. A large investment backer got a bit panicky at the amount of money going out the door in start-up and development when very little was coming in the door in revenues. I guess there were meetings at the board level and all the players decided to put an indefinite freeze on all new project development. The net result of all this was that Joan had a very powerful title and absolutely no money to spend, even on things she'd committed to—my project, for instance. I didn't take it hard and wished her well—after all, I thought the whole thing had sounded too good to be true!

Matt Blajer already had approval for his end of things, though. The budget was in place, as modest as it was, and he wanted to go ahead anyway with the show, even if it was a scaled-down version. I could still go out and interview Canadians and write songs about them. I just wouldn't be doing it by aeroplane.

I started travelling around Canada to meet people we'd found through researching a story or people who represented a special area of endeavour. Some of them were already part of my life and had had a great influence on me—like Jan Zurakowski, the pilot I'd seen so long ago flying the AVRO *Arrow*, or Max

Ward, one of the original great bush pilots and the founder of Wardair International. There was Margaret Trudeau, who'd taken a lot of undeserved hits from a cynical media and a couple of bone crushers from her ex–old man.

So it went—fur trappers, tugboat captains, friends of mine like painter Robert Markle and concert promoter Ron Sakimoto. The songs were completed, the editing was done and the radio series hit the air. But Joan Shafer hadn't been idle all this time.

She and her companion, a documentary filmmaker by the name of Peter Thurling, had been chewing on my original idea and talking it around. They'd taken a revised treatment to CBC television and met with the new head of variety programming, Ivan Fecan. After a lot of back and forth, they'd arrived at a concept that was mutually agreeable.

After that, they got in touch with me to see if I would agree to do it. It sure didn't have much to do with my original idea, but the good news was that I would still be able to take an aeroplane around Canada, and that alone was enough for me to want to be in the game. Also, there would still be a fair-sized whack of cash for a performance fee and a considerable amount of my music would be used in the show, which was to be called "Floating over Canada." The bad news was that any thoughts I had about going out and documenting spontaneously, in original song, all that was gritty and real about the frontiers and people of Canada was no longer part of anyone's thinking.

The plan now was to do a series of high-gloss music videos in the context of a trans-Canada travelogue. Murray flies his floatplane to Alberta, drops down and by a remarkable coincidence, there is Buffy Saint-Marie in full Native regalia singing "Star Walker" and taking part in a drum dance.

A few months earlier, a writer named Mike Tenzen had got word through the aviation grapevine of what I was attempting to do. I'd been looking around for aeroplane brokers who might be able to help me find a good Cessna 185 on amphibious floats that wouldn't break the bank, and I suppose the word had leaked over to Mike. He decided to do a profile on me for a cover story in *Canadian Aviation* magazine.

I didn't have a floatplane yet for the cover shot, so Mike made a few phone calls and located one that was down at the Niagara Regional Airport at St. Catharines. It was a nice clean 185, and even though it wasn't the one I'd be flying, it would do for the shoot.

I'd returned to the float base at Lake St. John near Orillia and done a bunch of recurrency training through April, so by the time the shoot came up on May 1, I was current and eager to try the larger 185. I'd be checking out on it for the first time.

The airplane was CF-SEC, and we had a super time with it. We stooged around the area and did water landings over on the Niagara River. I slowly got used to its characteristics—the importance of having some takeoff flap, the knuckle-skinning water-rudder control lever, the necessity of carrying some power on approach. It was a little bigger, but as all Cessna aircraft are, it was docile and a joy to fly. The cover shot we took was a bit of a gag and got a lot of comments in the flying community. It showed me trying to paddle the big amphibian back to shore.

Now it was time to go back over to the airport and do my first landing on amphibious floats. For those who don't know what I mean, they are conventional-looking floats attached to an aircraft by struts and bracing wires but with a major difference. They have two double-wheel main-gear struts and two single-wheel nose-gear struts that extend from and retract into the floats hydraulically. This enables the aeroplane to land and take off from either water or land, depending on the pilot's preference.

I set the aeroplane up for a nice long final approach with power on to control the rate of descent and committed this first landing without incident and smooth as glass. The major difference I immediately noticed was the curious sensation of landing while still seated so high above the runway. It was more like landing a DC-3.

Once we'd buttoned up the aeroplane, Mike and I went over to another hangar, and he introduced me to a slight, intense-looking young man. His name was Angus Gordon, and he ran an aerobatic instruction business out of the airport in addition to working as a corporate pilot for a local firm. It didn't take long before I was in the front seat of Angus's Bellanca Decathlon and he was talking me through some basic aerobatic manoeuvres. By the beginning of 1984, I was coming down to St. Catharines once or twice a week to take instruction in aerobatics with Angus.

The Decathlon was a lovely little aeroplane. Bright yellow with contrasting blue sunburst strips, it had a symmetrical wing that flew as well upside down as the other way. It had fuel and oil systems that allowed the engine to run and be lubricated while inverted. It had a 150-horsepower fuel-injected Lycoming engine and a constant-speed propeller. This is a nice addition to an aerobatic plane, as it prevents the engine from over-revving in diving manoeuvres. It also allows for good climb performance while still achieving a reasonable speed in cruise.

Some people have remarked that they find it strange that I wanted to fly "stunts" (how I hate that term). They seem to think it's terribly dangerous. Nothing could be further from the truth. For one thing, nothing is safer than flying aerobatics in an aeroplane meant to do the job, when you are directly above an airport. There is no danger of collision, as other traffic is either much higher, or low down and far out approaching a runway. You are alone in the mid-altitudes over the airport. In the event that anything goes wrong, such as an engine stoppage, you simply land.

I was attracted to aerobatics for a whole set of reasons. First, I wanted to try to master a set of skills that few pilots ever acquire. Second, it was difficult, and I had begun to realize that unless I have challenges in my life of a positive nature, I will quickly create negative ones. Third, for better or for worse, I was and am a conscientious pilot, and I thought that acquiring these skills would make me a safer aviator if there was any kind of emergency requiring abrupt or extreme handling of an aeroplane. Fourth, and most important by far, it is absolutely guaranteed the most fun it's possible to have with your clothes on!

We all tend not to live in the moment. We're always thinking about what we've done or what we're going to do. When I pulled over the top of the loop section of a half Cuban eight, caught my ground reference upside down heading for the terrain at a forty-five-degree angle, then rolled the lovely little aeroplane upright and pulled back to level flight, I was absolutely smack dab in the middle of right now! I had never felt so alive!

It was natural that as my relationship with Angus developed into friendship, and my respect for his abilities as a pilot deepened, I approached him about coming on board the *Floating* project as a second pilot. I was looking at the job of moving a slow noisy uncomfortable single-engined aeroplane with a limited but legal IFR (blind-flying) capability all the way around Canada against a tight shooting schedule and through a lot of potentially bad weather. The crew would be operating in and out of remote locations with challenging landing facilities in many cases. This was clearly not a one-man job. I was to star in the show, so I'd have to be reasonably alert for shooting. There would be occasions when the plane would have to be doing air-to-air filming while I was working at a ground location. The hard slogging of long flights to get to all the shooting locations would have been enough work for two guys. But there were also the so-called shit jobs: the little things like keeping logs and paperwork and inspection schedules up to date—time consuming but necessary.

Angus had a very adventuresome spirit. Ernie Gann was his favourite writer. His dream was to break the last big aviation record and fly around the world without refuelling. It took him about ten seconds to agree to going along on the job I was offering.

Meanwhile, Joan Shafer and Peter Thurling had put the other financing elements in place—the usual sources, Telefilm, OFDC—all accessible because CBC had agreed to buy the show. CBC was in for a very modest amount of actual money, but they were the key to the whole deal.

Slowly but surely, an office had been set up and production people and researchers had come on board. There was now a route plan, a time frame, a director of photography, a graphics company and promotions people. All this time, Angus and I were looking around for the perfect aeroplane. Time was of the essence because it would have to be taken apart, inspected and painted before we could begin.

I could be a little testy on occasion, partly because I'd seen my original concept go so far off the rails and partly because of the pressure of just getting on with it. Occasionally, I was invited to production meetings at Ivan Fecan's office when there was nothing too dangerous to be discussed.

I had gone over the top on several occasions. One of the first times was when the production company announced that I wouldn't be allowed to fly the aeroplane. The idea was that if I got myself killed, the show couldn't be completed and it would drive up the insurance costs. The only reason I was doing the fucking show was so I could fly the aeroplane, so you can imagine what my reaction was.

We had just received the design for the aeroplane paint scheme back from Supergraphics of New York, the firm that had been hired by Shafer Thurling Productions. Everyone was ecstatic about it, including me. It began with a sunrise on the spinner and gradually went through all the colours of a day as it progressed to full night at the tail, with the stars and moon on a dark blue background. It just looked spectacular. If the object was to use the aeroplane for a promotional tool and get it noticed, this design would certainly do that!

Peter and I trooped down to Fecan's office, Peter with the schematics under his arm. I guess the purpose of the meeting was to allow Ivan to *ooh* and *aah* over the look of the design, and Peter thought it would be safe for me to attend.

We had no sooner unrolled the drawings when Fecan abruptly said, "Too American!"

"What do you mean, too American?" said Peter, caught by surprise.

"All the little stars on the tail there. Too American. It looks like the American flag! You should replace them with little maple leafs instead," said Ivan.

"But, Ivan, there aren't any maple leafs in the sky, only stars. I mean the thing is supposed to represent a day in the life, you know?" said Peter, with a sick look on his face.

This was one of those little send-it-back items that makes film budgets go crazy, but Ivan kept on that these stars had to be replaced with little maple leafs.

I finally lost my temper and said rather hotly, "The only place you're going to see a maple leaf in this show is on a fucking tree!" That was the last production meeting I was invited to attend. The stars remained on the tail of the aeroplane!

In May of 1984, I got to work on the album part of the project. I started a CBC-True North coproduction featuring the songs written for the radio series Matt Blajer had produced. The album was to be called *Heroes*. There was some urgency in finishing it, as several of the tracks featured on the record would also be in the TV special and they would have to be done in time to be synced up for the film shooting.

Angus and I finally found the right floatplane. We flew up to Collingwood, Ontario, to have a look at our prospective mount. The aeroplane was a good Cessna 185 with the call sign CG-TGN, and after looking it over, Angus flew it. This was in part to satisfy the broker who was going to do the deal with us that Angus could be insured. I didn't have enough time yet on that particular type of plane to make the insurance company happy about me soloing it. It wouldn't take long, though.

Once the paperwork on the aircraft lease was done with the film production company, TGN was taken off to the paint shop to be reborn as a film star. Ian Shimmin and I took an Aztec down to St. Catharines in the first week of August, picked up Angus and went up to Collingwood to inspect the work in progress. She was already looking spectacular, even without some of the control surfaces hung back on the airframe. By the second week in August, TGN was ready and test flown. The album *Heroes* was done and mixed. Home life with Karin was as stable as it could be, and I was ready to begin one of my greatest adventures.

On August 15, 1984, Angus and I picked up the colourfully painted Cessna 185 at Collingwood and flew it back down to Toronto Island Airport. He dropped me off and took it over to St. Catharines overnight. It was just like having a new pet. We listened to all its little idiosyncratic noises and read its personality while we learned its habits, both good and bad.

The next morning, Angus was back at the Island airport to pick me up, and off we went, back up north to Lake St. John, where a day's shooting was already planned. They wanted to get footage of the plane for promos and also to test out whether the camera mounts and the methods we'd devised for doing things like routing cables and installing monitors were going to work. There was a long day's shakedown, and miraculously, not a single snag. Angus and David O'Keefe, the DOP (Director of Photography) on the shoot, were particularly proud of their invention for mounting a big Arriflex 16mm movie camera, complete with magazine, well forward on the toe of the left-hand float so that it had an uninterrupted panoramic view. This allowed us to get expensive-looking $700-an-hour helicopter shots for the $150 or so it cost to operate TGN. Saving money was important, and it really was a nice piece of work.

Angus and I left the bay by the seaplane base at Lake St. John the next day and headed over to Wiarton at the bottom of the Bruce Peninsula, where, fuelled up and loaded with everything we could reasonably carry, we set off for our first destination. It was an ambitious one for the first time out. We were headed up to the northernmost shores of continental North America to Bathurst Inlet for the first round of filming with a group of local Inuit people who had a settlement there.

As soon as we got en route, we were off in our own little world. There is nothing better than flying long cross-countries over Canada, low and slow. Once we got to the point where we really didn't have to talk to anyone on the radio anymore, we just monitored the emergency frequency at low volume and talked on the intercom about everything. We told war stories and swapped opinions. We talked about the works of writers we'd enjoyed, while munching away on a box of homemade cookies that Angus's girlfriend, soon to be his wife, Marlene, had made for him. She was an old-fashioned girl who never sent him off without some little reminder of her love. Her devotion to him was enviable.

We made our way over the sacred lands of Manitoulin Island and on into Sault Ste. Marie. The flight service guys, normally fairly reserved on frequency, noticed our wild paint job as soon as we appeared; they were full of questions about what we were up to. We had a great time with all the nuts and bolts people at the airport, without whom nothing would run. Within fifteen minutes of arriving, we were well known, and the word was already travelling down the line to our next destination. Aviation is full of generous and caring people who take their jobs very seriously, and our first experience in the Sault set a pattern that was unbroken across Canada. Airport personnel, ramp rats, meteorologists at flight service, tower and ground controllers—all of them were willing to bend over backwards to help us in any way they could.

We pushed on and wound up our flight for the day in exhausted sleep, sharing a tiny room in a truckers' motel in Terrace Bay. The scent of industry wafted by and tickled our noses while we dreamed.

We pushed hard the next day. The production crew were going to meet us in Yellowknife, and they were expecting us to be there. One day's delay meant another big chunk of cash would be sucked out of an all-too-meagre budget. After all, we were going to make a TV special with a bunch of stars, fly around the entire circumference of Canada, move a film crew around, pay for logistics, food, insurance, gas, whatever, as well as do post-production, for the princely sum of $750,000. That may seem like a lot of money, but consider this: the CBC was spending over a million to do an Anne Murray concert in London, England, and she was staying in one place!

We headed northwest over the pickerel-rich lakes around Sioux Lookout, then watched the ruggedness of the Shield disappear as the land flattened out towards Winnipeg. The endless vista of Saskatchewan was broken by curtains of dark rain falling from distant thunderstorms as we made our way from Yorkton to Prince Albert and La Ronge. We picked up the Athabasca River at Fort Smith and followed its banks, sandbars, snags and mud north through the unbroken expanse of the boreal forest to Lake Athabasca. Only the occasional glimpse of a trapper's cabin gave any indication that humans had ever been there. On past Fort Smith we flew, until we finally arrived at Great Slave Lake and the stomping grounds of Max Ward, the town of Yellowknife.

Yellowknife is a government town—two towns, really. There is an older, less civilized section, where the houses are built willy-nilly and the roar of radial engines still breaks the silence. That part is where all the colour is; it is by far my favourite part to visit. That's where the seaplane port is. Max Ward's blue single-engine

Otter was bobbing at the dock the day we arrived. It still did service carrying family and friends to his well-appointed fishing camp out on the big lake.

We parked TGN over at the infinitely less funky dry-land airport. There was maintenance to be done, and we needed dry areas to do various and sundry things. Most of the docking facilities over at the seaplane base were owned by private operators anyway, although I'm sure they would never have begrudged us a spot to tie up.

The film crew had arrived, and Peter Thurling was in the final stages of hiring the charter that would get all the other people and the equipment up to Bathurst Inlet Lodge. There were a thousand small details to be taken care of.

As far as Angus and I were concerned, the principal reason for remaining in Yellowknife for the two days we did was weather. The weather was unpredictable and changeable in the vicinity of the Arctic Ocean. Sea fogs and low stratus with rain could roll off the icy water and linger for a long time. There was only the briefest of windows in the Arctic summer to get the job done, and we wanted to make sure the forecast would allow us sufficient time to get in there, do the shoot and get back out without getting stuck.

It was also going to be a challenging flight. There was nothing along our route in the way of navigational aids. There was a relatively new industrial strip at Lupin, the high-security site of a new gold mine. We were going to have to stop somewhere and refuel from the five-gallon jerry cans we were carrying in the float compartments. We couldn't carry enough in the tanks to ensure that if we missed the settlement at Bathurst Inlet due to weather, we could still continue across to Cambridge Bay, where there was an instrument approach. So we planned to get permission to stop at Lupin to refuel with our funnel and chamois method.

We had LORAN (a low-frequency navigation system), but there was no coverage in the Arctic region then, and the Global Positioning Satellite (GPS) system didn't exist yet (not for civilians anyway). There were a lot fewer satellites orbiting the earth in 1984 for spotting weather and none for helping you find your way around. We didn't have an astro compass and we didn't have a slaved directional gyro, so we were back to using the basic methods from the golden age of aviation to find our way there. We would read a map, check off ground reference points, use a watch, calculate groundspeeds as best we could based on observation, and if we lost sight of the terrain in cloud, hold the last heading until we got another fix. In short, we would be dead reckoning.

The difficulty in this was that most of the landmarks on the map, except for the abrupt transition zone when you left the treeline just north of Yellowknife, were things like small lakes or eskers. But there are about a zillion small lakes, ponds and puddles out there, and an esker is nothing more than a pile of glacial rubble, indistinguishable from every other pile of glacial rubble. Add to this that we were constantly in and out of stratus cloud, and you can understand how navigation was a bit of a worry.

We were more than a little relieved to find our navigation skills vindicated when the big tower of the mine at Lupin loomed on the horizon. You could see it for miles. We got in touch on the company frequency, and they gave us permission to land and refuel, but they instructed us to taxi to, and remain at, the end of the runway farthest from the mine. A truck with a couple of guys in it drove out to supervise us while we serviced the aeroplane. They sat there and watched us silently, never greeting us directly. Maybe the company thought we were suddenly going to take out UZI submachine guns and rob the mine or something. Anyway, they eyed us suspiciously until we boarded, taxied, turned into the wind and took off.

The weather was good by Arctic standards as we made our way ever northward. We were in cloud quite a lot, and it became increasingly difficult to get ground references. Finally, the watch said we should be over Bathurst Inlet. The first hole in the stratus we found, we circled down and came out looking directly at it. Now the only problem was figuring out exactly where we were. We could turn right or left to look for the lodge settlement, but the inlet was a big body of water; if we went the wrong way, we might not find our destination. We set a time limit for looking based on available fuel and determined that once that limit was reached, we would proceed on to Cambridge Bay. We knew roughly where we were, but the settlement was really small and easy to miss. They had a low-powered Non-Directional Beacon (NDB) located there, and if you were very close by, you could use it to home in on. Just as we were in the process of making up our minds which way to turn, the needle on the Automatic Direction Finder (ADF) waggled to life. We found the settlement, and after a brief reconnoitre, landed without incident and taxied up to the dock.

We would be staying in the Bathurst Inlet Lodge, where Pierre Trudeau often took his sons to experience the Arctic. It was a fantastic place. The surrounding barrens were unspoiled by anything for hundreds of kilometres. There were caribou and muskox—and the river running nearby was full of char. There was a small community of Inuit people at the inlet, as I mentioned before. They were doubly interesting because they'd abandoned the corruption of towns and industry to return to the subsistence life that was their birthright. They had taken what they needed from modern technology and abandoned the rest. They used outboard motors to get across the water but used dogs instead of snowmobiles. They lived in geodesic domes by the water's edge.

Once we'd eaten and rested, Angus and David O'Keefe rigged up the Arriflex and all the cables and gear on TGN, a very complicated and time-consuming procedure, and then began to use the aeroplane as a camera platform to shoot the breathtaking aerials that eventually found their way into the show. This was Angus's job.

While they were doing that, I had some time to look around, so I decided to go for a hike. I walked for hours and hours, up and up, until I crossed over the ridge above the settlement. The buildings were completely out of sight. I walked for hours along the ridge saddle paralleling the inlet. When I became tired, I sat down on a hummock of tundra to rest. It was so unbelievably quiet! The only sound I could hear was the rustling of the wind blowing through a riot of colourful low vegetation. I realized they were all stunted versions of plants I was familiar with. I wondered at the fact that when you looked at the ground that appeared so colourful at your feet from a distance, it appeared to be uniformly brown.

For the second time in my life, I had one of those moments they call an epiphany. I felt that the whole world was revolving around this very spot where I sat—not around me, but around this place on the earth. I felt as if I was the only person in the whole universe, but instead of feeling frightened and alone, I felt complete. I lay my head down on the fragrant softness of the tundra and went to sleep.

I don't know how long I slept, because the daylight was almost constant at that time of year, except for a brief dusk. I was awakened by a large, loud, rodent. I had one eye open and was staring into the face of a very irate Arctic ground squirrel. This plucky foot-high fighter was not in the slightest intimidated by my size and was bent in no uncertain terms on letting me know that I had been sleeping entirely too close to its place of residence. I rose, bowed, apologized profusely for the intrusion, and began to make my way back across the ridge. I was feeling more refreshed and renewed than I had in years.

Eventually, the settlement appeared again, and after several more hours, I was among my own. One of the Inuit men, Robert, came up and asked me where I'd been. I told him about everything that had happened. He looked at me for a little while, then burst into a huge smile and said, "Next time you want to go for a walk, I will go with you and I will bring a gun." Robert patiently explained to me that what I had done was extremely foolish. The Eastern Slope grizzly bears were in the area feeding on the char, and being opportunistic feeders, they weren't above taking a free meal where they could find it, whether caribou or human. Out in the open, there was no chance of outrunning a grizzly. I, who had digested *A Field Guide to the Mammals* at an early age, had forgotten that these large bears ranged freely throughout the area. Maybe the lumbering giants had an agreement not to eat guys who were having spiritual awakenings.

The presence of the film crew sparked the social event of the season, and pretty soon, Inuit people started arriving from different settlements in the area. Who knows how they'd heard about the movie, but across the icy cold water they came. Whole families loaded into a big aluminum open boat with a seventy-five-horse Johnson on the back, bashing through the water, and not a one of them could swim a stroke. Swimming wasn't much use in the Inuit lifestyle, I suppose. Even in the summertime, any exposure to the water would quickly incapacitate a person. If the boat capsized out on the ocean, nobody would be able to hang onto it for very long in that frigid sea. And who would come to rescue you anyway?

Still, the Inuit made these amazing epic journeys just to visit, without a second thought. They are among the most good-humoured and resilient people I have ever encountered. They treat their children with a kind of good-natured indulgence and just let them run wild. So their offspring are always getting soaked falling in the water around shore, running around in shorts when the temperature is a chilly six degrees Celsius in the sun. They will be found simultaneously pulling the ears and the tail of a long-suffering dog, who bows his head and indulges their youth. Life will get hard soon enough! The funny thing is, when one of the parents makes a low quiet sound of warning, all these exuberant kids stand in line and salute while they await further orders.

The day of the shoot for the song "Into a Mystery" was a huge treat for all the Inuit, since in their eyes, Robert was exhibiting great bravery. He was the only member of the community who would dare to go out on the water in a skin kayak. The craft had been procured by Peter Thurling from a museum of some sort. The local Inuit didn't use them anymore because they were tippy and dangerous and uncomfortable when they leaked, which was often. When things aren't part of everyday life, sooner or later the skill is lost, and that is what had happened. Peter and the CBC had wanted to portray a scenic fantasy of the noble northern Native in a sealskin parka, paddling his kayak through the tranquil waters of the Arctic. Unfortunately, the kayak had to be brought in, as well as the parka, and the only guy brave enough to actually get in the small boat had to be taught how to paddle it. Television!

I thought, and I still think, that what the Inuit are actually doing up there—combining technology with traditional practices as they pick and choose from our world and their culture—is infinitely more interesting than anything we portrayed as fantasy with our silly little music video.

Robert was a local hero after accomplishing his movie mission, and when the shooting was done, there was a spontaneous party right on the rocky beach, which was much more fun than the one at the lodge. By the time we were ready to leave, some of the Inuit men were talking about using caribou skins, wood and bone and—just for fun, mind you—building a kayak and paddling it around. They thought Robert looked pretty good in his role as a traditional Inuit.

Angus and I took off from Bathurst Inlet on August 26 for the next big leg of travel. We'd be working our way down to the coastal waters around Vancouver.

It was a lot easier finding our way back to Yellowknife with its multiple approach aids that could be sensed from a long way off. We refuelled and kept going, working our way to High Level, Alberta, where we picked up the Peace River. As we flew along its course towards Fort St. John, the sobering realities of modern industry were evident below. We were back in the trees now, but these were the ones the pulp industry feeds on. It was dismaying to see the whole country north and south of the Peace dissected into logging-road grids, with smoking fires from brush burning everywhere. There was nowhere to look without seeing vast rectangles of denuded forest.

We made our way into Fort St. John and settled down for another night sharing a room in a cheap motel. We woke up the next day, looked out the window and knew right away we were going nowhere. Who would have believed it? Two inches of wet snow had landed on the ground—in August, for crying out loud! The weather had been better in the Arctic!

As thrilling as the prospect might have been to spend another night in the Fort, we left the next morning to continue west until the Peace ran into the depths of Williston Lake, where we turned south and picked up the Fraser towards Williams Lake. We were a floatplane. We weren't about to go mountain hopping. The weather in the passes could be instantly changeable, and it was always a comfort to have landable water close by. Once we were flying the Fraser, though, that comfort was gone. I wondered more than once what course of action we should take if the engine stopped while we were looking down at sheer canyon walls and a raging torrent.

Down to the delta and on into the big city we went, finally landing at Vancouver International.

We spent two days in the coastal area and very little of the time was anything but hard work. I was shooting the sequence for "Song for Captain Keast" over at the log-boom areas around Gambier Island. Not only were we doing aerials, I was crawling around boats and even got to drive one of those mini-tugs that bashes logs around while they're being made up into rafts.

We left early on the morning of August 31. We climbed and climbed through solid cloud to a safe altitude to begin the first leg of the trip through the Crowsnest Pass. The weather wasn't cooperating, and we had to move, so we added a little more risk to the flight and did single-engine IFR over the mountains. I still remember the tone of voice of the Vancouver controller who kept inquiring after our progress in tones of disbelief as we crawled along through his airspace. We were chugging along at a hundred and ten knots, and his normal traffic (jets and turboprops) was considerably faster than that.

Things cleared out once we'd refuelled at Cranbrook and taken off again. This time we were able to see the Kootenay. As we flew through the Venturi funnel of the Crowsnest Pass, we picked up the most unbelievable tailwind. It was just smoking—all that air being forced through the mountains by a moving front, with no place to go. We were showing 150- and 160-knot groundspeeds coming out of the mountains and back into the high rolling hills of western Alberta.

We had two shoots to do in this area, three if you count my song. We flew over to Waterton Dam and filmed in the area around the reservoir. We shot the sequence where the plane flies out of the blue and encounters the mystical Buffy St. Marie on horseback. Angus and I spent the whole day up to our asses in mud!

After that sequence was done, the whole crew went over to the Blood Indian Reserve to film the sequence involving Buffy's song "Starwalker." When we honkies got there, it was a pretty dispirited and sullen group that met us. They figured they were doing the tourist bullshit thing for the CBC and were more interested in when the pay would come and what was for dinner. Within moments of Buffy's arrival, she had galvanized them into one of the most astonishing displays of Native pride I have ever witnessed. The boy slouching on a horse in the heat suddenly became a proud warrior with a great heritage. The women, whose lives weren't great at the best of times, stood straight and tall in admiration of Buffy, who was a woman like them but exhibited great presence and power. Call it what you will, she is a natural leader and has such passion and knowledge that no one who meets her is unaffected by it.

We went over to Pincher Creek and shot the sequence for "Honky Red," then went over to Ian Tyson's ranch, where he and his wife, Twyla, graciously entertained us all, and Ian put on an impressive display of cutting-horse expertise. Then he trailered some horses up into the foothills, the plan being to shoot Ian and me riding Old Paint up through God's country. We forded a river and rode up the ridges to the area where Ian kept a wilderness teepee for campouts, and we had a terrific time enjoying the scenery and riding around while the film crew got what they needed.

When it was done, Ian and I were walking the horses down through a meadow back to where the trailer was parked when he looked over and said, "Race you to the trailer!" Then he took off hell for leather. I had ridden a bit by this point, but it was all English style and all in a ring, and I had done little more high-speed stuff than cantering around in a circle. This was one of those shit-or-get-off-the-pot moments.

Ian had given me a smart, beautiful quarter horse, with a winning personality. Sure-footed and experienced, she wanted to go. I stood up in the stirrups, bridged the reigns and let her. Holy shit! I was terrified! If I ever fell off this horse, I was convinced I'd break my fool neck. I sure was awake, though! We just galloped flat out through the meadow, and I think my whooping must have passed for exuberance instead of fear. Finally, my hat came off, and I had to stop her to go back and get it. I sat back and sawed gently at her mouth, and she stopped on a dime, turned ever so nicely and waited patiently while I dismounted and retrieved my chapeau. Well, I felt like I could walk ten feet tall when I got back to the trailer, even though I'd finished last in a race of two. I think Ian expected to be home in bed before I made it back. I was happy to have survived, and I regretted not being able to stay long enough to really learn how to ride.

Angus and I moved TGN up into the midlands of Saskatchewan, where we spent a couple of days filming the sequence for "Farmer's Song," and then it was time to be taking the reliable Cessna back to Ontario for the second leg of the shoot.

Floating, Part II

✒ I WAS STILL VERY MUCH IN love with Karin, but I was beginning to surface out of the kind of goofy-eyed trance that had kept me from seeing that our relationship was dysfunctional and, at least from my side of the fence, self-destructive.

We had had three wonderful years when I was happier than I'd ever been. We'd shared sailing and flying trips, and in many important ways, understood each other's needs extraordinarily well. Things had been wonderful until she had begun to feel pressure from me to deepen her commitment. Things had been wonderful as long as I remained successful and therefore secure. Things had been wonderful as long as I didn't have too many problems. As she'd begun to feel forced to take a position when she wasn't sure I was the right guy, she'd pushed me away. The harder I'd tried and the more insecure I'd felt, the worse she'd acted in response.

Things were in this state when I returned to Toronto for a brief six days' respite from *Floating*. She seemed pissed off at me for being away so much, but at the same time she didn't seem that happy to see me come home.

The house was a mess. The former roommate from the apartment was around all the time, practically camped in the living room. Karin's brother was a black hole of depression as he played endless Rolling Stones records on the stereo. There was nothing to eat in the fridge and not so much as a cold beer to drink. I found myself sitting around thinking, "What the fuck is going on here?" as I rattled around the place in fatigue while the girls went out to score some grass.

Marguerite was constantly calling, and it was usually about money. It wasn't money for frivolous things. It was for expenses relating to Amy's medications or transportation help to get them back and forth to an eye clinic at a university outside Toronto. I was angry anyway, but never at Amy. I was angry at life, feeling that it had trapped me.

I felt like a hornet stuck on flypaper. I was angry because I'd convinced myself that Marguerite had done everything in a manner calculated to maintain control of my life. Mostly, I was angry because way down deep, I was beginning to realize that what I thought about Marguerite wasn't true.

I was guilty of using the combat of divorce as an excuse for avoiding the responsibility of maintaining a growing relationship with my daughter. I knew I was emotionally immature, that I was just running away from taking responsibility for my actions. I was using the moral high ground of making the big monthly payment as a sanctuary to hide the shame of not being able to come up with any emotional support as a father. I thought I had to choose—I thought my past had to go if I was going to have any chance at my one big love. I was beginning to wonder if I'd made the wrong choice.

It was with a sense of relief to be away from my day-to-day life again that I got into TGN once more and headed, along with Angus, for the airport at St. Hubert, just south of Montreal.

We were going to be shooting with a Québécoise *chanteuse* named Sylvie Tremblay. The production company had found a farmhouse over on the south shore of the St. Lawrence, and the plan was that I'd land on the river to explore the house and discover that it was haunted. I was then to chase the spectre throughout the house while the ghost/Sylvie sang her song, "Passage."

The shore at the location was a weed-choked mess of snags and power lines, and I flat-out refused to land the aeroplane there. Angus took over and found a way in. To be shown up in this way didn't put me in the best of moods anyway, but as the day wore on, and I watched this fantasy scenario unfold with me in it, I felt completely foolish. I felt like a jerk running around up and down the stairs feigning surprise while the acrid smell of the castor-oil effects smoke turned my stomach. I descended deeper into a funk.

I hadn't touched a drop of alcohol during the entire flight and filming so far, but on this day I swan-dived off the wagon. I started swigging from a bottle of red wine, then another, until by the end of the afternoon, I was completely shit-faced. I don't even know how they carted me to a hotel, but as far as my taking part in moving TGN from the location, that wasn't in the cards anymore.

It wasn't just that my role in this particular concept made me feel ridiculous, it was my growing discomfort with a lot of the concepts, coupled with the unhappiness and financial stress I was feeling in the rest of my life, that probably caught up with me that day. I certainly paid for my sins on the next one.

Angus and I were to take the plane to Moncton the next day, but there was no question of my being moved. I didn't even start throwing up until morning. Anyone with a terminal red-wine hangover knows how I felt. I would have welcomed death! While I retched my shame away, Angus took our beautiful bird on to Moncton with David O'Keefe, the director of photography, sitting in my seat.

There was strain on the crew as well, and it was beginning to show. We were so low budget that everything we were shooting was being done with only one camera. That meant that everything we wanted to shoot from a different point of view had to be reset and done over again. It made for exhausting days for poor David O'Keefe and his assistant. Things would soon come to a head.

In the meantime, I caught a commercial flight to Moncton once I'd recovered, and made my way over to the Marshlands Inn in Sackville. We were going to be filming "Acadian Driftwood," the classic Band song about the dispossession of the Acadians and their migration to Louisiana. Levon Helm and I were going to play Acadians fleeing the British while Levon lip-synched the words. We had a great time, charging through the reeds of the Tantramar Marshes, blasting away with flintlock rifles.

Levon was a great character and had tons of acting experience already, so he was easy to work with. There was one particular scene in which Levon, his wife (whom he'd brought along to the shoot), a young child and myself were all supposed to be in a small boat, fleeing to the ocean. His wife didn't want to get in the boat at all because she said she was terribly prone to seasickness. She was very funny, a real flower-child type of lady. We assured her that the boat wouldn't actually be out on the water. It would be sitting on the bottom by the beach so it would be stable enough to shoot. She was reluctantly coaxed on board.

There we were, not thirty seconds into Levon's noble close-up with him singing the song, in a boat lodged firmly on the beach, when his wife suddenly emptied the contents of several days' meals over the side. It's probably an outtake somewhere on the cutting-room floor. Now that's what I call seasick!

I got kicked out of my room at the Marshlands Inn for half a day because Queen Elizabeth, who was on a tour of the colonies, was going to be stopping by to freshen up between functions. My room was the nicest they had. The folks at the inn were wonderful and treated me very well in compensation for the minor inconvenience—free drinks, that sort of thing. For security reasons, we were forbidden to be near the place while she was actually there, but as soon as the royal party had moved on, I couldn't resist going straight up to my room, which I had now reclaimed, and going into the washroom. I stared down at the commode in awe and thought fondly of the royal presence. The vessel seemed to glow with a newly acquired, sanctified light!

I flew the next leg with Angus over to the airport at Halifax, where we were to split up again. Angus was going to ferry TGN across the cold Gulf of St. Lawrence to Newfoundland. Without the extra weight, the trip was a lot safer because he could carry maximum fuel. Even so, it was not an enviable trip in a single-engined floatplane. In the big rolling swells out there, landing on the water, even if it could be accomplished, would have no better result than landing with no floats at all.

I was to be helicoptered out to an oil-drilling platform named SEDCO 709, which was located near Sable Island. There we would be filming the song "Ten Thousand Miles from Shore," which I'd written after a previous visit to the rig during the making of the CBC radio series with Matt Blajer.

It was in the preparations for this shoot that the problem with David O'Keefe came up. David had a full British navy-style beard, of which he was justifiably proud. Imagine his reaction when he was told he'd have to shave it off in order to be granted permission to board the rig. This was not a matter of dress code, it was a safety issue, and the company had strict rules about it. The oil rig was an extremely dangerous environment, with the ever-present possibility of toxic gases being released. Everyone who came on board had to be familiar with the location of their escape equipment and how to use it. We were assigned cold-water survival suits and breathing masks to put on in the event of a blowout. The problem with the facial hair was that it stopped the breathing mask from sealing properly against the face. There was no convincing David. He flatly refused to go.

That was too bad, because he missed out on a fun experience. His assistant was attached to the open door of a helicopter and flown dizzily around the site for spectacular aerials. He was lowered by crane to the heaving ocean in a sort of bosun's chair–web basket and onto the deck of a lurching, rolling supply tug. I did all that stuff too, and it was a blast.

Peter Thurling was actually very uneasy about the noise and danger of the rig itself. It was always a real possibility that if one of these things had a gas blowout just when old Ernie was doing some structural welding, we'd all be sitting on clouds playing our harps shortly thereafter. Peter seemed quite distracted and had trouble making decisions, so I just kind of took over for this brief time and really rather liked it.

I organized members of the crew into an ad hoc dance troupe and got them all to do a choreographed jig for the camera, topped off by throwing their hard hats up in the air. This was made easier because the group I picked were going off shift and were waiting for the helicopter to take them back to shore. They all knew the helicopter wouldn't leave until they did their thing.

After we flew back to Halifax, Peter and I and the rest of the crew took a flight over to St. John's, where we did several days' worth of filming. On one particularly memorable day, I was in a small cove riding back and forth in a fishing boat, tossing fish up into the air to attract hordes of seagulls for the effect. That was the day I drank the screech and kissed the cod on the lips, as is the custom.

Then it was time to take TGN back to Ontario for the last round of filming. We left St. John's on a bright perfect morning, figuring to make a destination on the north shore of the Gulf of St. Lawrence at Blanc-Sablon, after stopping in Deer Lake for fuel. There was a good wind out of the west that day, but the visibility was great and the scenery was fabulous, particularly as we made our way up the west side of the Avalon Peninsula towards the Strait of Belle Isle. We were going to do the smart thing and cut our distance for overflying the rough water to the absolute minimum. One look down at the breaking waves and the whitecaps confirmed the wisdom in that idea. I also noted that the peninsula wasn't a good place to have an engine problem: the land side of the aeroplane was rugged and rocky, with little level ground and no water bigger than a puddle to make a landing. There was no safety in floats around these parts. It was while having these thoughts that I noticed the windshield was turning brown. It was accumulating a fine mist of oil!

I got that prickly feeling in the back of my hands as my eyes darted to the engine instruments. They were all normal. Oil pressure was good, temperature okay. The propeller, however, was slowly gaining RPM. Angus and I had a brief talk, and I agreed with his view that it was the seal on the propeller governor mechanism. We were sure the engine would keep running, but we weren't sure we wouldn't have a runaway propeller. One thing was certain, it was becoming difficult to see out of the windshield.

After some experimentation, we determined that we could control the RPM effectively and hold it with a reduction in power, but that meant we were running rather more slowly. It was time to abandon the flight plan and head for the nearest place of safety.

We headed for the airport at St. Anthony at the very top of the peninsula and gave flight service a call to alert them of the change. Fifteen miles out to the south, we called up the tower and alerted them to our presence and to our mechanical problem. They asked the standard, "Do you wish to declare an emergency?"

"Negative," we replied. Declaring an emergency is something you do when you really have one; otherwise, it makes too much paperwork for everybody.

I found I could get an abstract impression of the world through the windshield, and if I stuck my head over far enough left into the pilot's side bubble window, I could see ahead—sort of. It was still a better view than Charles Lindbergh got in the *Spirit of St. Louis*!

Two miles back, I selected the gear-down switch and waited the long hydraulic cycle out, watching the four little annunciator lights that told me when the gear was locked safely into place. Clunk, went the main gear, and I watched the little light turn green, then another one for the nose wheel right side, then—nothing more. Two of the little green lights remained stubbornly dark. Suddenly, we weren't sure if the gear would collapse when we landed because we couldn't confirm it as locked. We called up the tower and advised them that we'd be going out over the water to the north to check something out. They asked if we had further problems and we just advised them to stand by. We went out to cycle the gear up and down, but when we selected down, we kept getting the same result. We tried diving the aeroplane a bit and pulling up as the gear was cycling down—same thing again. It would indicate up and locked alright, but not down. We sucked up the wheels and called the tower.

He didn't want us screeching to a halt on the keels and tying up his runway if he could avoid it, so he advised us that as long as it appeared we could make a water landing, there was a pond (as they call a lake in Newfoundland) over to the east about ten miles. There was, he said, a local guy who flew turbo-Beaver in and out of it all the time. What he failed to mention was that the guy went in and out of there really light.

We went over there, found the place and circled it for a look. There was nothing on it but a dock and a little shack of some kind. It was in the middle of nowhere and it was really small—really, really small!

I came as close as I've ever got to slapping the floats on the foliage when we were coming in over the trees on approach. TGN splashed down about a hundred and fifty yards from the dock. We taxied over and tied her up firmly after shutting down. After cleaning up the oil, Angus started up the aeroplane while it was still tied up and gave it a little power for the hydraulic pump's benefit, while he hit the gear-down switch. I watched the wheels cycle down into the water, while up in the cockpit, four green lights blinked on as though nothing had ever been amiss. There is nothing worse than when a problem mysteriously corrects itself before you have any idea what it is. It feels too much like gremlins.

Our biggest problem now was that we were stuck on this little lake until a big enough wind came up for us to get out. With the load we had, even light on fuel as we were, a takeoff without wind on this lake would be a quick trip into the trees.

Someone eventually came along, and we caught a ride into town to spend the night.

Nature cooperated the next day with the arrival of a strong front and an equally strong wind blowing out of the east. Angus added power for takeoff. He was going to take it over to St. Anthony solo because my extra weight would add to the takeoff distance. I bowed to his greater experience and wondered what the number of the local florist might be in case Angus was overestimating his abilities. The prop was okay as long as fine pitch for take-off was all that was required.

The Cessna made a colossal racket and was soon on the step. It rose up and cleared the trees at the other side, though not by much.

Over at St. Anthony, an Aircraft Maintenance Engineer (AME) looked the aeroplane over. The prop seal was leaking and was replaceable. The gear problem was a complete mystery. He jacked the plane up, started it, cycled the gear—no problem. He thought maybe it was just a faulty microswitch that had failed to send the appropriate "down and locked" signal. After an inspection flight, we were ready to proceed on our way.

Angus was in the left seat this time as we took off to the west, bound for Natashquan, Quebec. We droned on over the Strait to the other shore, then followed it gradually down to the southwest. As we neared the Jacques Cartier Passage, we could see Anticosti Island off to our left in the distance.

We called up the uncontrolled airport on the Unicom frequency and announced our intentions. We were advised of the runway and winds and set up for an approach to land on Runway 14 out of the northwest. The only traffic for us was a company F-27 turboprop that was due in five or ten minutes, but it wasn't in the area yet.

Angus set up for a slow descent. He didn't entirely trust the gear and didn't want to thump the aeroplane on the tarmac if he didn't have to. We landed very gently and began to roll down the runway. As we began to lose speed, and the weight came off the wings and onto the wheels, the left side of the plane started to sink progressively until there was a loud scraping sound and TGN gracefully groundlooped to the left. Angus let loose a torrent of language such as I had never heard him use before. I did what all pilots would do in my circumstances. I gave a silent prayer of thanks that it was him flying the aeroplane instead of me!

We were now stuck fast in the middle of a 4500-foot runway that was supposed to have several tons of turboprop landing on it in minutes. The guys at the ramp had seen what happened and quickly came out in a truck with a jack and some two-by-fours. The plane was quickly raised up and the gear wedged into place with a piece of wood; then Angus started it up and taxied gingerly over to the parking ramp.

We jacked up the aeroplane and tested it again. Again everything worked normally, and we could find nothing to account for the problem. We taxied over to the fuel pumps, filled up and took off again, this time for Baie-Comeau, home of Brian Mulroney. About a third of the way there, we started noticing roughness in the engine and had a not-so-good reading on one of the cylinder-head temperatures. The engine wasn't developing all the power it could, and we couldn't tell if it was something mechanical, like an exhaust valve about to let go, or a fuel problem of some kind. We headed as closely as possible to every potential emergency landing site we could find, just to be on the safe side. The engine wasn't sounding horrible or anything, just not at all like itself.

Finally, we landed at Baie-Comeau without incident. The gear functioned normally, and we would never experience another problem with it. No mechanic ever found the slightest thing wrong either.

We took TGN into a maintenance facility to inspect the engine and quickly found out what its problem had been. The bottom of the fuel tank we'd filled up from in Natashquan must have been full of impurities, because there were black gobs of leaf mulch in the fuel filter and gascolater, and several of the injectors were badly clogged. No wonder the poor old girl had sounded unhealthy. It took all night and much of the next day to take the fuel system apart and clean it before we could be on our way again.

The fall colours were in their full glory as we became airborne again. The fantastic crimsons and russets of the maples and the cheerful yellows of the birch were made more radiant by the brilliant blue of the early autumn sky as we made our way southwest. Everyone should see the Laurentians in early October . . . we were fortunate to be feasting on them at the peak of their beauty.

From Forestville to Quebec City, over to Ottawa, then Peterborough, and finally back to home base at Buttonville Airport. The big adventure was over. There were only three more shooting events to do.

After a four-day rest, we flew TGN up to Lake Muskoka and did a location shoot with Gordon Lightfoot. He was going to sing his song "Knotty Pine" in the show and had contrived to get a couple of his canoes up to the lake to demonstrate his skill as a paddler. He was already taking significant portions of the summer to do long and arduous canoe trips on the Mackenzie and other great rivers. Gord was thin again and fit. He'd forsworn drinking and everything else sometime ago and was much the better for it.

I guess he was nervous that we were going to make him look goofy when it was important to him that his authentic love for canoeing be represented accurately. Something set him off not long after the shoot began, and he went into orbit. He got on a couple of the crew with a torrent of abusive bad language. People stood around not really knowing how to react. Thurling and I took him aside and steered him away from the objects of his fury long enough to quietly point out that, star or no star, he was about to get his ass thrown in Lake Muskoka. Eventually, he calmed down and spent the whole of the next day apologizing at great length to anyone who would stop long enough to listen.

The last trip was back over to Montreal, where we did a shoot with the Acadian star Edith Butler. We staged a sylvan soirée in the woods around Rivière des Mille Îles while Edith, in a sort of Dr. John costume and carrying a staff, led a multitude of people and a cow through her song "Paquetteville."

After that, it was back to Lake St. John for some final point-of-view shots of the aeroplane in action. We spent all day doing takeoffs, landings and low-and-overs while the camera rolled both on and in the aeroplane.

And then it was over.

As a perk for myself, I'd worked it so I had the plane for a few days to use before I'd have to take it back to Collingwood with an expired lease agreement. I just flew it around locally, saying my private goodbyes to the old girl. I took Karin on a flight up to Kempenfelt Bay, where her father's house was, and executed a fairly interesting rough-water landing with a good bounce built in. Then, on October 29, 1984, with a lot of nostalgia in my heart, I flew TGN back to Collingwood all alone.

I dropped the plane off in front of the paint shop, and they lost no time in taking her into the hangar and beginning to strip her down for refinishing. They already had a buyer.

I got a chance to fly John Worts's beautiful de Havilland Beaver CG-DEU back down to Toronto as compensation for the loss I was feeling at being parted from my old friend.

The last time I saw TGN, she was sitting on the ramp at the Barrie Executive Airpark in a proud coat of yellow and black paint, after the manner of Lands and Forests aircraft. She had been bought by a guy who ran a timber company; he was using her to do surveys. I walked over and surreptitiously gave her a little pat on the underside of the cowling. Aeroplanes are like people. If they're around long enough, you get kind of fond of them.

What Else Can You Show Me?

AT THE SAME TIME THAT THE post-production work was starting on *Floating over Canada*, my mother gave us all a bit of a scare. She turned up with a small malignancy in her "plumbing," as she would have said. She underwent treatment at Wellesley Hospital, and I found myself trying to look unconcerned and light-hearted as I picked her up and took her over for the appointments she had at radiology. Once her treatment was over, they said her prognosis was good, so we got on with life. She wasn't nearly as keen to get out on the golf course as she had been, but that wasn't just because of the cancer treatment. She was now seventy-five and had a bad knee and painful arthritis in her neck. Reading mystery novels in her chair was starting to appeal to her more than walking around a golf course.

She had evolved beyond being my mother and had become something more than a friend. She was up to speed on all the events in my life and remarkably nonjudgemental about what was going on. I got over to visit with her as often as possible, and we'd sit around drinking endless cups of tea.

I set up another boat trip on *Tao*. This time my brother Calvin would be coming along with three of his friends. Karin's sister Andrea and her husband were also joining us. We wanted to do something different. I prevailed on Dave

Matthews, the captain, to bring the boat through the Windward Passage between Cuba and Haiti so we could sail the coast of Jamaica.

We all flew down to Montego Bay, then caught a connector flight over to Port Antonio, where the boat was waiting. When we arrived, I was baked and looking forward to just settling in on the boat, putting a drink in my hand and relaxing in preparation for the next day. Right away, I knew I was in trouble because Karin wanted to go into town and see what was what. You could hear the thump of music quite plainly and the whooping of the night revellers. I really wasn't up for fending off admirers while Karin flashed her smile around a bar. She rounded up a couple of the others and went out anyway.

Tourists came to Jamaica in aeroplanes, spent money and went home. That was how it worked. People did not come here in large yachts and anchor in harbours and go back and forth to town as they moved up and down the coastline. The police and customs officials were convinced that we were doing something— running guns, waiting for balefish (floating garbage bags full of marijuana). Perhaps they just wanted us to sweeten their lives in some way.

They hassled us all the time. At first, they wouldn't let us sail out of the harbour for a day excursion and then back in without going through the whole rigmarole of clearing customs both ways. When they finally did relent and let us get on with sailing along the coast, the police tracked us everywhere. Every time a dinghy was put ashore—just a few people wanting to go for a drink or shop— the police would intercept them and make them stand on the beach like prisoners while they went through the charade of okaying it with their superiors. Police and customs constantly came alongside and boarded us for random inspections, during which time they would conspicuously ogle the women and relieve the ship's locker of whatever they felt like taking in the way of booze. I spent a great deal of time accompanying Dave into various customs and police facilities to try to get them to stop harassing us.

There weren't many good harbours along the coast. The waters were fished out, and the reefs that remained were badly damaged by hurricanes, so the fishing was no good. The charm of the place was wearing pretty thin for me after a few days.

To add to my troubles, Karin had developed a friendship with a member of the crew. He was a nice enough guy, but he was everything I was not. He smiled easily, smoked dope when the captain wasn't looking and had no discernible responsibilities—a perfect fling! I didn't think she was flinging, but she sure was spending a lot of time hanging out with the guy. Dave noticed how my face looked, I suppose, and to my embarrassment, spoke to the crewman about the situation. Don't get too friendly with the paying customer's woman, that sort of thing. When Karin got wind of that, it got her back up.

I have a very painful memory of sitting on the boat in the harbour at Montego Bay, watching her disappear around the headland with him in the little Force Five sailboat. She claimed it was to go off and have a smoke because Dave was too stiff to allow any marijuana on board *Tao*. There was plenty on board; he just didn't know about it.

By the time a week had gone by, I was so miserable, insecure and jealous I just felt like leaving Karin her plane ticket and some money, going ashore and walking to the airport. I actually began the journey, but found that at the height of the season, I couldn't get a flight out.

There was a wonderful moment when a miracle of nature cut through my self-absorption. One night, when we were anchored in a place called Mosquito Cove, we noticed that we could see the luminescent trails left by fish in the water as they passed the boat. This was caused by a bloom of little creatures that make light in the water when they are excited by movement of any kind.

Pretty soon someone fired up the outboard motor on the Zodiac and began making rocket trails as they turned. Then a couple of us put on dive masks and fins. We jumped in.

As soon as I hit the water and began to swim, I saw the most wonderful sights. It was surreal. My whole body was outlined in blue-green fire. The outline of every finger as I moved my hand in front of my face was crackling with light. Fish would dart by like showers of meteorites. It was an incredible experience!

But sadly, in spite of the magnificent surroundings, there was little I could do, short of the miraculous, to divert my attention from the fact that *Tao* had seen the beginning and was now witness to the onset of the end of my relationship with Karin.

I never set foot on Dave's boat again.

There was a period of awkwardness as things unwound. We couldn't make love anymore. I would head back from doing pre-production work, and as I drove the last couple of blocks up the street, I'd find I didn't really want to go home.

Finally one night, I just came out with it and said that maybe if she was so unhappy, it was time for her to get her own place. I'd moved out the last time, and now it was her turn.

She found a flat in Cabbagetown, and I helped her move her things in. Once the job was done, I went home and sat brooding for a while. Then I put on a Huey Lewis album and cranked the volume up to "kill the neighbours" level and cleaned the entire house from top to bottom, washed everything that could be washed, vacuumed the fireplace, brushed the dog, stacked the firewood in the garage, bought groceries, bought booze, loaded the fridge, then poured myself a big stiff drink.

I stared out at the Don Valley from the window over the kitchen sink and felt the first roll of hot tears going down my cheek. "Fuck that!" I yelled, and pounded my fist on the counter. I was sick of feeling bad. A couple more drinks and some more loud music and I began to realize that, though I might miss her so my heart would break, I didn't miss the conflict. I felt like I had taken the first step back from the edge of a steep cliff. Now the question I had to answer for myself was, "How do you go about falling out of love with somebody?"

It had become pretty evident to me that Karin had somebody else around, so somewhere in the back of my mind, the switch clicked. The one that had turned me off from looking at anyone else as a romantic partner all the time I was with Karin as a couple.

There was the kicker! This time it was I who had been the faithful one. I had to laugh at myself sometimes. Except for the timing of events, I could have made a convincing case for Karin being hired by my ex-wife to exact revenge on me. I could almost hear Marguerite's voice saying, "Here, asshole, see how it feels!"

I started going out again at night and spending more time with friends. I'd done a good bit of work with Bucky Berger and Terry Wilkins, and I would often go to see bands they were jobbing with or go hang out at an Aces gig. Terry played with a reggae-style band that often worked at the Bamboo on Queen Street, and I started going down there on a regular basis.

There was a lady who worked there named Michèle Williams, a very good-looking almond-eyed smart-aleck who loved to take you down a peg or two if she suspected you had any attitude. I'd keep saying to her, "We should lunch or something. It would be nice to talk to you when you aren't working," and she'd say, "Sure."

I guess I said that a lot, because one afternoon when we happened to be leaving at the same time, I offered her a lift out to a restaurant in the Beaches where she was having dinner with a friend. As she was getting out of the car, I offered the standard, "We should have lunch sometime."

"Fine!" she spat and practically took the door off the hinges as she slammed it. Then she stalked off down the street while I sat there wondering what was wrong with her.

Everybody knew everybody down on Queen Street. A lot of people knew Karin. She'd been hanging around the clubs while I'd been content to remain at home. She was chummy with Cockburn's girlfriend and she knew everybody. In other words, probably within seconds of it happening, the whole world knew that my romantic Titanic had whacked the iceberg and I was going down by the bow.

I still saw Karin, and sometimes that didn't have such a good effect on me. There was still an on-again, off-again character to our relationship that kept me from completely giving up on the possibility of getting back together and making things work. I knew it was insane, but I was susceptible to the drug of hope.

Sometimes when I got too bad, I'd go down into the Don Valley in the dead of night with Corsair and a pint of whiskey and get drunk and scream and kick trees. People who heard the sounds coming up from there in the night must have thought there was a demon loose. I guess there was.

Corsair, the malamute, was my best friend during all of this. Sometimes, after we were back home, he'd come over and put his muzzle quietly on my knee and look up at me with his intelligent golden eyes. I swear I could almost hear his voice in my head saying, "Look, I'm a dog. I have to eat with my face in a bowl. I don't have a quarrel with what I am. She's just a girl, for Christ's sake. What's your problem?"

One night in late spring, I was in a bad post-Karin funk when I walked into the Bamboo for a drink—a drink which I no longer really required. I looked like death warmed over.

Michèle was on duty at the time. She took one look at me and steered me over to a table, sat me down, got me something and made sure I didn't get out of there until it was time for her to get off work.

We went to another place for a while and just talked, then down to the waterfront, to a place I'd told her I liked to walk when I needed to think. As we talked, a lot of the despair I was feeling bubbled up to the surface. I felt like a thoroughly unattractive complete failure. Somehow, the discussion turned around to matters of romantic technique, and I found myself dared into giving her an experimental kiss. "You call that a kiss?" she said. She then showed me how, in her opinion, it should be done.

It is sometimes said that the best cure for somebody is somebody else. It certainly seemed to be true for me. As Michèle and I started dating, I woke right up and got back in the world. She was beautiful, and especially in a certain red dress she was fond of wearing, capable of stopping men dead in their tracks. She could be friendly and vivacious, and was great at dancing. She'd often set fire to the space around the dance floor with a succession of partners, but she always carried about her the message that she was "with someone." I never felt insecure when I was out on the town with Michèle.

She was very social and gregarious, so dating her really got me back into connecting with people again and that had an effect on my work. The only fly in the ointment was that Michèle was making it known that she was "in love." I had been singed so badly that I didn't want to know about falling in love anymore. I liked being with Michèle and cared for her very much. I was happy when I was with her, just doing nothing in particular—reading a book, being together quietly without feeling we had to talk. But I wasn't ready to push off into the land of white picket fences.

Heroes, the special-project album I had released, got a lot of play on CBC radio as well as on some country stations, but it didn't get any major amount of radio. I never expected it to. Right down to its retro-folk cover, it was supposed to be suggestive of the old Vanguard folk albums. It was an art project, not a commercial one.

Unfortunately, though the album was well regarded by everyday people, the music media began to treat me like I was some kind of hockey puck wrapping himself in the flag. The reaction wasn't any more positive from the media hipsters after the TV special aired on Canada Day.

I got to work on a new record in the summer of 1985. For the most part, it was a collection of fairly dark songs, but some were pretty stunning, even though they were hard to listen to. There was a very tough song about a woman who had no option in her mind but to seek an abortion: "Louisa Can't Feed Another Child." "Suppertime in the Milltown" was a hard-driving look at a small town gutted by recession. "Ten People on the Sidewalk" was an autobiographical poem about walking through the streets of downtown Toronto feeling like a ghost in my own life. Several of the songs were about the break-up with Karin and the faint hope of reconciliation.

I made the record down at Manta Studios and used the whole of The Canadian Aces band as the back-up for it, including the Tobin sisters, Marion and Eileen, who did all the background singing.

The album, called *Midnight Break*, was released in the fall. There were two singles from it, each one geared to a different musical genre. "Best at Loving You," which was a really lovely song and one I still sing, got airplay on the country stations. That was the only kind of commercial radio airplay I was getting by this time. Rock stations were full of "New Wave."

We put out a video for the song "Me and Joey," hoping to get a broader exposure for the record, but I didn't really "get" the emerging promotional tool that video was, and the results were mediocre. The album sales were considerably less than underwhelming. I began to feel as though I'd never get it right again. I felt like the world had passed me by. It never occurred to me to think that I might not be doing the best work I could do. It never occurred to me that the business had a lot more people in it now and that a lot of them were pretty good. Most important, it never occurred to me that I was now a generation removed from the one that was making waves on the radio. There were now fifteen-year-old kids who hadn't been born when I'd made my first record!

At least part of the problem, from a commercial standpoint, was that my records were all over the place. As a writer, I moved from rock through blues and country, switching genres as the song dictated. This had worked alright years before, but now the market required an image. Now the category was everything, and there was no crosstalk allowed between radio formats. Generally, rock programmers thought I was country, and country programmers thought I was rock. The result was they all passed. It didn't mean nobody liked me; it just meant I didn't fit anywhere anymore.

Of course, all this stiffing in the record department hadn't gone unnoticed in the touring department. It was harder to get good concert bookings. Guarantees were lower because promoters wanted to minimize their risk. I had to do more work to stay in the same place. There was no longer any discernible interest in me in the U.S., or so I thought.

Apparently Finkelstein thought so too, because one evening in the latter part of 1985, he called me up and said he'd like to come over to my house for a meeting. Once there, he pretty much got right to the point. Bernie had a significant number of problems and was well aware of mine. He was getting burned out himself with the effort of keeping the record company and the management company rolling. He was having trying times in his personal life as well. It was a tired and somewhat disillusioned Finkelstein that sat down opposite me.

"Do you think there's someone else who could be doing a better job for you?" he finally asked. I knew this to be a kind of face-saving code among friends for "I can't carry you along in the business anymore. You're just not happening, and maybe it's time you figured out what you are going to do with the rest of your life." I knew what Bernie was really saying. I'd seen him let talent go before and understood the language.

I gave him my equally face-saving coded reply: "Yes."

We hatched a press release to disguise the truth. All that bullshit about moving on and other opportunities, hoping to stave off the ugly headlines in the trades like "True North Dumps McLauchlan."

That was strike two in the game of life for me. We'd had a long relationship, Bernie and I. We'd been to the wars together, and I was devastated to find that he no longer believed in me. I never thought that maybe he no longer believed in himself!

One afternoon, after Michèle had been staying over at my house for several days running, Karin showed up unannounced at the front door. She was surprised when I was reluctant to invite her in. I explained that I had a ladyfriend with me and it was an inconvenient time to receive guests. She asked me if it was "serious." I said, "It might be, I don't know yet."

That changed the rules of engagement. I still can't believe I fell for it! Shortly after that, a letter arrived—the kind that says things about not losing everything we had. Meetings were held and confessions that there had been someone else were made. Fool that I was, I was still hooked enough that I agreed to break things off with Michèle on the condition that Karin break off her relationship.

I had already reached the point anyway where I felt that if I didn't come clean with Michèle about where things really were with me, I would be doing her a great disservice, and for once, I wanted to face up to the situation and be honest before someone I cared about got really hurt.

I sat Michèle down and told her that I loved her and cared about her very much but I wasn't "in love." I said that at this point, I wasn't over Karin, and I didn't know how long that might take or even if it was possible.

Michèle is such a great woman. That's why she is still one of my best friends after all these years. She went upstairs, hugged a pillow and had a good cry. Then, about a month later, she was perfectly happy being my friend while she dated a new fella. I still laugh with her about how quickly she "got over me."

I didn't lie down and die after life with Finkelstein was over. I called up Bob Burwell, the guy who'd been so taken with "Never Did Like That Train." He'd actually taken the trouble to get in touch. He turned out to have been a fan since my early days when he used to come across the border to see me play at the Riverboat. Bob was working for the Jim Halsey company, the largest and most powerful talent agency in Nashville.

The Halsey company was expanding and branching out into artist management and tour packaging—a wide variety of activities. Bob was an in-house manager who was representing clients on behalf of the company. He was working with Michael Martin Murphey, and this new guy, a sort of retro cowboy singer that no one would take seriously named Dwight Yoakam.

I flew down to Nashville and had a whirlwind of a week. Bob was genuinely interested in working with me as a management client. There was a new phenomenon happening in country music. The old guard was giving way, and artists like Lyle Lovett, Steve Earle and Rosanne Cash were starting to emerge. Bob saw the "Never Did Like That Train" video as the forerunner of what was becoming New Country. In his eyes, it was retro and new at the same time. Bob and Jim Halsey were both well aware of my history. They knew about the Tom Rush recordings, and they knew that there was an undercurrent of respect for what I did in the folk-country music world. I hadn't wasted all those years playing the U.S. club circuit. Kristofferson had performed my song "Honky Red" and so had Waylon Jennings, even though they'd never recorded it. I had a track record.

During that week down in Nashville, I met Garth Fundis, a man I admired a great deal for his brilliant production work with Don Williams. I met Bob Titley, who was managing a new artist named Kathy Mattea, and both of them were looking seriously at my song "Try Walking Away." I met John Prine, my old acquaintance from the Earl of Old Town in Chicago. John had settled into Nashville pretty well and had recently had a writing success with "Love Is on a Roll" for Don Williams. I went to the Bluebird Café with Bob and saw something I hadn't seen in a long time. I saw a packed room full of people who were as quiet as mice and worshipful in their demeanour as they listened to a "songwriters in the round" night with Fred Knobloch, Paul Overstreet and others who among them had written most of last week's hits on the country charts. It felt like a church and the religion was songwriting. I hadn't seen that kind of rapt attention paid to a singer-songwriter in a long time. It was intoxicating. I began to think this was the place for me, and I started moving towards making a deal with Halsey.

Once my week of meetings in Nashville was over, I was faced with turning around the big old Jeep Grand Wagoneer with the 360-cube v8 I was driving at the time and heading it back up north. I read the paper that morning. It was the 19th of October, and the weather in Toronto was just crappy. They were having a premature snowstorm!

I realized I had no pressing reason to go back and only had an empty house to return to. So instead of returning to Canada, I did the sensible thing and drove immediately to Biloxi, Mississippi, most likely because I'd always really liked the Jesse Winchester song by that name. I rented a cheap motel room with a dinky little wire-fenced pool and cheesy awnings on the coast of the Gulf of Mexico. I bought large volumes of cold beer and sat there watching the shrimp boats go by for a couple of days, then headed down to Long Beach. I found a bar there, where the top-selling beer was Moosehead from New Brunswick. They sold it like a premium import because of the Acadian connection between Louisiana and Canada. I got a big kick out of sitting there watching the nets drying and sucking back on a cold one with the mighty moose on it.

I rolled on into New Orleans, rented a little place at an inn located in the French Quarter and spent a couple of days just wandering around listening to music. I remember being amused by the ads on the radio for gris-gris ladies, who would fix you up in marriage or money with the right incantation or read your future and advise you on how to avoid catastrophe. I loved New Orleans. It was the funkiest place I'd ever seen.

Then it was time to go back to Toronto. I drove the whole distance from the Gulf of Mexico in a day. The lady who owned the house I was renting had hit the skids and was going to have to sell it. I had to be there for when the appraisers came. There was also the matter of a final trial date regarding my drunk-driving charge.

Back when I was doing the cbc radio series that became the album *Heroes,* I'd been up at a hotel in Mount Forest, Ontario, trying to get Robert Markle, the painter, back to his farm so I could interview him. Ironically, I had refused a lot of drinks, because everybody in town wanted to buy one for me. When I finally got Bob out of the place, I felt fine. I guess I'd had two bottles of beer in the last hour—not an amount that would make an appreciable dent in me. On the way back to his farm, I hit about a hundred yards of black ice that was covered with freshly drifted snow. I was driving my old red Toyota Land Cruiser, and it was in four-wheel drive at the time.

I wasn't going more than fifty kilometres an hour when the truck broke free on all four wheels at once. It was like being on a skating rink—there was nothing to do but ride the thing wherever it was going. Ever so gently, it slid down towards the roadside, following the camber of the surface. The front wheels and bumper went off into the ditch, which was drifted over with snow. There was just enough momentum for the back end to rise up into the air vertically, and then the four wheeler settled gently over onto its roof.

Some people came by, but they didn't stop. I just heard some really loud woman's voice saying something about calling the cops. Bob and I had already extricated ourselves from the car at this point and were standing there trying to figure out how to get in touch with his wife so we could get to his place and deal with this shit in the morning.

Bob trudged off down the road towards a lit house while I stayed to try and find Corsair, the malamute, who in the confusion, had wandered off to chase girl dogs or something.

Then the Mount Forest police came by. The officer was sympathetic after appraising what had happened and ascertaining that nobody was hurt. He knew Bob and was aware of what an effort was required to get him out of the hotel. Then some shavetail from the OPP showed up. He was all officious and businesslike. A real graduate of police sciences school. He ushered me into the back of the cruiser, after I freely admitted that I had been driving. I never saw this coming. If I'd been thinking, I would have feigned a head injury and said I couldn't remember anything. Whose car is that, Officer? Mine, you say? Amazing, I thought I drove a Ford! He stuck a breathalizer machine in my face, and I was beyond shock when I blew an alert.

Well, it was the crime of the fucking century up there when they caught the famous guy. The prosecutor called the papers himself when I was to appear and made sure they spelled his name right. The judge who convicted me had two convictions himself for the same offence.

To make a long story short, I appealed on various technical grounds and won. My lawyer and I thought that would be the end of it, but Clarence Darrow, the local prosecutor, sensing a great miscarriage of justice, decided on a new trial and overturned the appeal.

By the time I was heading back from New Orleans, I'd decided that the whole process was so expensive and time consuming and inconvenient that I'd just plead and get it over with. Wrong move, Fred!

My licence would be suspended for three months and there would be a fine, but the real long arm of the law reached through the insurance companies. The next time I tried to get car insurance, the premiums would disappear into the stratosphere.

So as I moved into 1986, the Province of Ontario viewed me as a person who had demonstrated sufficient irresponsibility to warrant having his driver's licence taken away. I was grounded! But ever the man with his head screwed on right, I rationalized this setback by thinking, "Who wants to drive anyway? It just cuts down on my drinking."

And I was drinking now—regularly and a lot. I'd given up on cocaine after the experience of making *Storm Warning* with Ezrin. Not only was it something I could no longer afford, but I had begun to realize that I didn't need a drug to help me be an asshole. I'd already proven to be more than capable of accomplishing that on my own.

By the way, I know about all the chest beating with regard to drug addiction. I'd just like to say this. I never stole anybody's money to buy cocaine. When I wanted to stop, I stopped. More accurately, when I ran out of money, I stopped. After a while, I didn't like being around people who were using a lot of it. It made me embarrassed at how I used to be. That shit is about as addictive as Doritos, in my opinion.

I sure did like a drink or two, though. When I rationalized away my driving privileges, I also stopped flying aeroplanes. Life was far too complicated to concentrate on being an aviator.

VII

Goodbye, Mama

ᴊ IN JANUARY OF 1986, I FLED DOWN to Los Angeles just to get away. Shari Ulrich had a house in the canyons above Hollywood that she was renting, and she was kind enough to put me up for a while. I had a good time hanging out with the Canadian Club of expatriates. I dragged Shari over to Malibu to meet Joni and ended up staying up all night at some roadhouse up the coast highway, while they nattered away. I went down to Long Beach with Katherine Moses, the great jazz player who worked in Bruce's band for a while. We saw Howard Hughes' *Spruce Goose*, then had drinks in the bar at the stern of the *Queen Mary*. I even had time to have a brief affair with an actress.

But eventually I had to return to Canada. I had a concert scheduled at the National Arts Centre and preparations to make for a two-week tour of the Maritimes. There was a video shoot scheduled, then a western tour and a concert at Convocation Hall in Toronto that was going to be taped by CBC Radio. Even though the guarantees were lower, I still had a hell of a lot of work to do. I was doing press for the tours, and in between, I had to look for a new house, because the lady I'd been renting from had to sell.

Joanne Perica, my friend Vezi's wife, was driving me around Toronto and helping me look. I still didn't have a licence, although I was due to get it back very soon. When I finally did get it back and went to a car dealership to see about leasing a new car, I found something I liked. I called my insurance agent and just about had a heart attack. Because of the conviction, the bill would be almost four thousand a year. That was more than the lease payments. I crunched some numbers for laughs and found out I could take a limousine everywhere I wanted to go for less money than operating a car. The leasing manager lost a deal because of the car insurance company. I figured if I needed a car, I'd go over to Hertz and rent one.

So I bicycled around town on my old Peugeot ten-speed, or I borrowed a car from a friend. Sometimes I babysat cars for people who were leaving town.

I found a house. It was a charming little bungalow on Wellesley Street in Cabbagetown known locally as Fort Wellesley, no doubt because of the high stockade fence that surrounded it. It had everything I needed. There was a "George Jetson" fireplace and wall-to-wall carpet. The upstairs bedroom had an en suite luxury bathroom with a bidet, no less! The closet ran along one wall and had mirrored doors. It was easy to see what the original owner's hobbies were. It was small and absolutely perfect for the single guy who needed a spare bedroom to stash the occasional friend. On May 1, I moved in and set up my work desk.

I had never really lived in my own place before; I'd always lived with a woman. So I wondered what it would be like to live alone. Here was a spot that could be decorated as I wished—or not adorned, at my discretion. I was answerable to no one for my comings and goings. I could have my friends over and stay up all night yakking and drinking or go out and not be concerned about how late I'd get back. I liked the freedom immediately.

My celebration was dampened when, on the fourth of May, I received a phone call from my brother Calvin. He was calling to say that my mother was back early. She'd been vacationing at his house down in Arizona and there was a problem. (I received this news on the night I'd received an RPM Big Country award.) She'd been experiencing extreme fatigue and had gone to see a local doctor in Scottsdale, who'd been very frank with her about the situation. Basically, he'd said, "Lady, do you want to die at home or die here?" She'd come home on an early flight with an attendant and had been given the wheelchair and supplementary oxygen treatment. She'd gone straight from the airport to Sunnybrook Hospital.

I went to visit her the next day. She was embarrassed by all the fuss being made about her. Typically, she was more worried about the interruptions in our busy lives than she was about herself. She was concerned about becoming a burden. We, her children, had the meeting with the consulting physician, and our worst fears were soon confirmed. Those trips to Wellesley radiation clinic had left some surviving cancer cells, and they had migrated and multiplied. They'd found a particularly fruitful residence in her lungs. The doctor said the concern now was distress and pain management and keeping her comfortable. "How long?" we asked. "Two weeks maybe, a month tops!"

I found a moment to have a little private talk with Mom. I loved her enough that I swore I wasn't going to waste time bullshitting with her. I was also going to try my damnedest not to treat her as though she was already dead when she was still here.

"Do you know what's going on?" I asked her.

"Yes," she replied.

"Are you scared?"

"No! Death holds no terrors for me," she said simply.

I was in the middle of a terribly busy week. I was scheduled to host the CBC program *The Entertainers,* and there were tapings and interviews scheduled with Sean O'Sullivan, the boxer, and Gordon Lightfoot. Between them, I had concerts to do in Montreal and Ottawa over the weekend. I was terribly distracted and upset, and I hated having to be out of town for even two days, but everything was stable and my mom wouldn't have wanted me hanging around the hospital staring at her anyway. She would rather have me get my work done and then come and tell her how it went.

Somehow, I got good interviews, particularly with Lightfoot. Maybe it was the vulnerability I was feeling that affected him, but he opened up in a way he seldom did.

I went for a meeting with the palliative care specialist at Sunnybrook, a very sympathetic and dignified lady named Bonnie Barry. After my mom had spent a few days at Sunnybrook and had a draining procedure done in her chest, they began to give her mild doses of morphine. It was just enough to relax her, but it made her feel good enough and reduced her anxiety enough that she made a firm decision to go home. She wanted to be among her own things, in her own bed!

I had been elected without protest to accomplish the move, and Bonnie was the person whose job it would be to arrange the myriad details—nursing shifts and requirements, special bed, breathing equipment, transport—everything my mother would require at home if I was going to spring her from the hospital. There was nothing I wouldn't have done if my mother had asked me, and I was quite prepared to carry her back home on my shoulders if I had to. Bonnie was like a sympathetic angel.

One afternoon, a day or so before she got out, I noticed her staring intently at the wall.

"What are you looking at, Mom?" I asked.

"You'd just think I was losing my marbles if I told you!" she said.

"Try me."

"Well, there is a door in the middle of the wall and there are people in it. It is surrounded by garlands of flowers. The person closest to me in the middle of the door is a very handsome man who appears to be from India, I think, because he is wearing a turban."

"What are they doing?"

"They're not really doing anything. They're just looking at me and smiling. There isn't anyone there that I recognize. They're all complete strangers."

"Do you think it's the welcoming committee?"

"I don't know, it might be."

On the sixteenth, I went over to her apartment on Yonge Street, where I had so many times sat around having dinner or listening to her talk about family matters. All the medical supplies and the special hospital bed were arriving, and I wanted to at least try to make the place look as normal as possible for when she came home. I didn't want her to feel that she had escaped from a hospital only to find herself in another one.

She came back home the following day. Bonnie and everyone who had helped with her were there to say goodbye and wish us good luck as a family. Mom was loaded into an ambulance and we followed.

For a couple of days, her neighbours and friends dropped by, but she tired easily. They began to realize it was a time to let well enough alone.

We did shifts—Sandy, Calvin and me mostly—but only because we were close by and could be there at a moment's notice. We all did what we could to make her comfortable. We didn't try to distract her with silly conversation, unless she seemed to want to talk. I had to be careful. I sometimes found myself staring at her for long periods of time. I guess I was trying to put her face in my memory against a time when I wouldn't be able to see it anymore.

Once she caught me at this and got a little angry. "Stop staring at me all droopy-eyed! I'm not dead yet!" she barked.

I made custard and applesauce in little glass bowls. She didn't want to eat, but the coolness, the mild sweetness and the texture were soothing. I rubbed her hands and her shoulders and sometimes brushed her hair for a while. Sometimes I just sat quietly and held her hand.

In the last couple of days, it got difficult. She was becoming confused and adrift in time. She would want something, but we couldn't figure out what it was, and she would become agitated. The morphine and lack of oxygen were dissolving a fine intellect. Then, because there was a fear of her choking, I suppose, the nurse on duty wouldn't put her false teeth in and it became almost impossible to understand her. It was extremely distressing to have her taken away by little pieces.

Her breathing became difficult, and she was distressed, anxious and confused until, under the influence of the morphine again, she finally slipped into unconsciousness.

On the evening of May 22, 1986, a very different nurse came to the apartment, one we hadn't seen before. She was very calm and had a religious demeanour about her. I think she was a sister, but I didn't ask. Calvin and I were there as she gave our now sleeping mother a shot and then quietly left. I was sitting by the side of the bed, holding Mom's hand, hoping that in some part of her, she might feel me there with her, when I felt the tips of her fingers grow suddenly cold. Gradually, the line of coldness moved towards her knuckles. My sister Sandy walked in at that moment, and I turned around and looked at her.

"She's going," I said quietly.

Sandy walked around to the other side of the bed and held our mother's other hand, and together we watched and felt the life drain gently from the body of she who had given us life.

When it was over, we let her hands go, and I arranged her a little bit, then we walked out on the balcony with Calvin and stood there quietly for a while. I left them out there and went back to the bedside. I could still feel something of her lingering. I think it was a true feeling, not wishful thinking. I put my head down, and tears poured out of my eyes onto the carpet. I never made a sound.

After a while, the official process took over. The physician came to pronounce, and two sombre young men came, lifted all that remained of my best friend into a plastic bag, zipped it up, put it on a gurney and left.

I was glad to be there when my mother died. I think death is nothing to be feared, and facing it squarely and taking part in the passing makes it easier to accept. That was something I realized later. On the night of May 22, I thought my heart would break under the weight of the grief I felt inside.

True to the Scottish tradition, once she had realized that the game was up, my mother got on quickly with the business of dying. She feared incapacity, senility and dependence more than death, and I couldn't have asked for more than her being independent, lucid and living life to the fullest right up until the last few days of her life.

Picking Up the Pieces

TWO DAYS AFTER MY MOTHER'S funeral, I left Toronto to go back out on tour. I was numb. I suppose I figured that if I kept on doing what I was supposed to do and threw myself at my work, things would gradually feel normal again. It wasn't working.

I had just lost my mother. My career had suffered back-to-back reversals for some years now, with only short periods of relief, finally culminating in the loss of the security I had felt in my management and recording relationship. I had failed to win the heart of the person I loved. Although I was struggling hard to turn things around, I was in a black hole from which there seemed to be no escape. I was finding I couldn't get to sleep at night unless I poured myself several stiff scotches. Then I slept fitfully and woke up feeling rough and depressed. The circle was complete and kept getting harder to escape from. It was a relief to get up on a stage and sing songs, just so I could forget about things for a while.

Joanne Smale, who ran a publicity and promotions company that had done a lot of work for the Finkelstein Fiedler/True North group, had stepped up to the plate in the aftermath of my business separation with Finkelstein. We'd worked out a business relationship. Joanne was a good and loyal friend and ran the kind of company that specialized in taking on strays who needed a leg up in difficult times, putting them to work stuffing envelopes and answering phones. She and her company had taken on all the nuts and bolts duties of a management office for me in exchange for the usual commission on earnings. That meant dealing with agents, advancing tours, handling publicity and coordinating any inquiries. I was clear with her that I was negotiating with Burwell at the Halsey Company and looking to move in that direction. I wanted her to understand that, as much as I thought of her, I wasn't looking for artist management services of a tactical or personal nature. I gave her a limited power of attorney to sign and represent me in certain matters, but I also drafted and signed a private letter with her recognizing that an artist management relationship was not part of our deal. It was quite a satisfactory arrangement, and meant that when I did do a management deal in Nashville, there would be a natural place for her to dovetail into the whole arrangement because Halsey's people were experienced in Canada only from the perspective of being an agency.

In November of '86, Burwell came up for the Juno Awards weekend. I was on the nominations list for Country Male Vocalist of the year (which I won), and Bob came up early to hang out for the celebrations with a final copy of our management contract under his arm. On the eleventh, I signed the deal. I liked it because it all spun around Burwell. I had built a key-man clause into the deal that rendered it null and void if he left the company. I was unnaturally euphoric about this small beginning, and that should have been a warning to me.

One evening a few days later, I had Gary Ledrew over to the house on Wellesley. We were going to have a few drinks and get caught up. Well, I had a few—then a few more!

I knew I had a pile of things to do the next day, including interviews that Joanne had painstakingly scheduled for me—even time that I had put aside to accompany Amy somewhere she needed to go. I drank all night!

By the time the sun came up, I was too drunk, sick, tired and depressed to accomplish anything, even if I could have made it out the door under my own steam. I was now faced with the humiliation of calling Joanne and confessing my helplessness, then asking her to make all the phone calls that would blow away the day—in short, to save my neck! She was angry as hell, but got to work.

After I hung up the phone, I just sat there in the middle of the rug and started to cry. I couldn't stop once it began. During a lull in the outburst of uncontrollable grief and pain that was pouring out of me, I got back on the phone to Joanne. I levelled with her, as best I could, about what was going on. I asked her if there was anyone she could recommend that I could go to, because I knew I needed help. She was more than understanding. She was completely supportive as soon as she found out what the situation was and quickly gave me the number of a professional I could call for counselling. She even made the first call on my behalf, so I wouldn't have to struggle with a cold call.

The first thing I did was to stop drinking completely. I didn't experience any trouble doing this, I just quit. I wanted to get anything that was clouding the issue out of the way. I didn't know if I was depressed because I was drinking way too much, or if I was drinking too much as an anaesthetic because I couldn't take the pain of recent events in my life. Whatever the case, I certainly figured it wasn't helping, so I poured all the booze down the sink and that was that. I never went back to even a social glass of wine for several years after that, and I never drank that way ever again in my life.

Slowly, the pieces began to unravel as I talked my way through things. I began to understand that it had taken a little longer to get to this crossroads than I had thought, and I slowly began to try to do things that would change the outcome of my life.

One of the first things I did was to call up Marguerite and try to extend an olive branch. She had long wanted to stop doing everything through lawyers, and I had come to see that if I ever wanted to be part of Amy's life, I was going to have to learn how to do that. I think she was surprised by the call, but she seemed happy at my apparent softening. By the end of the month, I was back up on the stage, shaky and gossamer, but working!

Karin had put her life on hold briefly. Out of respect for my mother, she had flown into Toronto from out west to be with me at the funeral. During all the emotion of the moment, there was regret for what we had lost. Our families at one time had begun to intertwine as it seemed that a marriage might be in the works. We had done both Italian and Scottish Christmas with the relatives. My mother had been very fond of her, and the feeling was mutual.

Karin had been through a couple of serious affairs by this time, neither of which had worked out. The wind was gone from her sails, and she'd gotten some of the "I might be missing something!" feeling out of her system. I wasn't with anyone at all and was feeling vulnerable. We were actually able to forget all the conflicts and hurts and get along.

I was going down to Arizona in December for two weeks. I needed to get away and rest. I asked Karin to come down and join me at my brother Calvin's place in Scottsdale, and she said yes. I began to think she might be having a change of heart, and I thought we might make a new start if we could just get off by ourselves for a while.

Sometimes, when I simply recount events, I worry about the picture that emerges of Karin. She wasn't a bad person, but rather, a good person trying to learn not to behave destructively. She was just young and struggling to work her way through how confused and conflicted she was about so many things. She never asked me to fall in love with her, but she had to find a way to cope with it anyway at a time in her life when all she wanted to do was to violently push away anything that got too close to her. She was struggling hard in her own way to become a person who could accept love, but she didn't know how yet. She was working as hard as I ever had at growing up, she was just ten years behind! She was tough, resilient and independent as well as beautiful, and I not only loved her, I admired her for not surrendering who she was just because I was hurting. I guess that was why, even though I had my troubles with her, I would speak pretty sharply to anyone else who bad-mouthed her. We had fought a pitched battle for my access to her emotional fortress, and even though I was sure I'd lost, I was prepared to go to Arizona for one last try.

It didn't work out well. First, she delayed her arrival by a week to go hang out in Telluride, Colorado. She was spending time with a guy who'd shown some interest in investing in horses. While I was alone and waiting for her arrival, I played guitar on a beautiful little Mexican gut-string I'd bought down there. It was a wonderful instrument. It was only sixty bucks, it played like a dream and it sounded as sad as a child's tears. I drove around at night in a Chrysler convertible I'd rented and got addicted to listening to the Spanish music coming up across the border. I didn't have to know what it said to know what it was about!

I had plenty of time to think, and what I was thinking about was the nature of love. I had never really thought about what it was before—romantic, spiritual, eros, agape! Was falling in love an experience that was just subjective? Why did so many people seem to fall in love with someone who was completely unsuitable, as I had? Why did people become obsessive and lose sight of who they were in needing someone else? Why were people so vulnerable to being manipulated when they loved someone?

One thing was for certain. I figured out that the only way you could free yourself from being in love with someone was to somehow "kill," figuratively, that part of you that responded to them. If it was an innocent childlike part of you that so completely loved without guile, then you would have to make that child grow up, until innocence was gone. The sadness lay in the fact that, once gone, that child could never be brought back to life.

It was with these thoughts in mind that I sat down at the table and began writing the song "Imaginary Tree." In the lyric, I remember how lovers carve their initials into a heart on the town oak. It is a symbol of their love, for all the world to see. In the song, the image is a metaphor. Love has gone, and now I must cut my name from that heart. It is a way of symbolically "killing" a part of myself.

I wrote several other good songs that week. "Love with a Capital L" compared obsessive romantic love with the spiritual kind. It was a pretty big concept to attack in a short song, but I was pleased with the results.

The crowning achievement, however, was "Swinging on a Star." After I'd finished writing "Imaginary Tree," an incredible lightness had come over me. I realized that I'd been carrying a chain around with me for years. Its links were made of anger, wrongs done to me, failures, disappointments and shortfalls in my estimation of my own worth as a man. It was made of pain, and I had come to think of that pain as me! I had thought that feeling something intensely, even if it was bad, was better than feeling nothing. At least you were alive. But it wasn't me! I made a conscious decision to lay the burden down and stop dragging it along with me anymore. Then I wrote "Swinging on a Star."

When Karin finally did arrive, things didn't go well. We didn't click. I finally sang "Imaginary Tree" for her, and I think for the first time she realized there were no buttons left in me to push.

As 1987 began, I continued my attempts to have a more active part in Amy's life. She was now full of questions about everything, loved music, and even with the difficulties she was experiencing with continuing surgeries and harsh medications for glaucoma, she was flourishing. Under the constant care of her mother, she was doing better than anyone could have expected. I had a grudging respect for how well Marguerite was performing in this difficult role, and that was a long step up for one such as me. I had always arrogantly assumed she'd never accomplish anything! She terrified the medical establishment with her strident activism as a patient advocate. Marguerite and I continued to piss each other off, but at least we were trying.

I made a trip down to Nashville in February to perform on the Ralph Emery show on TNN, and was quite surprised to find people coming up to me in the Chicago airport on the way home and telling me how much they'd enjoyed it. I had wisely sung "Child's Song" to draw an immediate connection between who I was and what Americans might remember of me. A surprising number of fans of the "New Country" music, which had not yet become a dance-fashion craze, were ex-folkies and remembered me well.

In March, I got a call and took a meeting over lunch with a CBC producer named John Dalton. He was planning a special event concert that involved taking a group of performers over to Germany, where a concert would be performed in the town hall in Lahr for the Canadian forces as well as the German people, in honour of Canada Day. He hadn't yet figured out who would be going and was putting out feelers to see if I was interested. It sounded like a good adventure to me, and I'd never been to Germany. I agreed to do it.

Things had calmed down for me a lot. Leaving my abusive habits behind was paying big dividends in extra energy and optimism. I was beginning to find a path through my personal labyrinth of self-delusions.

Michèle had moved into my little house on Wellesley. She'd made plans to go to Singapore with the man she was living with. They'd broken up their apartment when he left to go in advance of her, and I was more than happy to have her come and stay with me. We were great pals now—platonic, of course! It was like having another sister around. She would come home, or I would, and we'd sit up and have a natter. We often cooked each other dinner and caught up with the gossip after I'd been away on a gig. She loved Corsair and referred to him as her "hairy boyfriend." When she was walking down the street at night with him on a leash, absolutely nobody would fuck with her. It was great for me because I could leave for periods of time and not have to worry about the house, the dog or Michèle.

I'd become quite happy with the way life was. It was true that I wasn't romantically involved, but after the last experience, I was more than content to leave it that way. I wasn't lonely. I was occupied by my friends and my work. I was beginning to come to terms with myself and accept me for who I was. I felt it was my time in life to give something to the many instead of everything to the one. There was work to do, and I was making enough to pay the rent. I was beginning to look at the idea of making my own master recording and shopping it independently, which was a big step in taking back the power. It didn't seem impossible to accomplish. I was amassing a great collection of songs.

It was around this time that I started noticing this new person. She would be at music business functions and awards shows. She would be at clubs, interviewing the band. She was full of energy and vitality and quite striking to look at. Whenever I saw her, I would idly find myself watching her, and a little sort of unconscious smile would find its way onto my lips.

Her name was Denise Donlon. She'd been recruited from Vancouver, even though she was a Scarborough girl originally, by John Martin, director of music programming at *MuchMusic*. She'd been running her own promotions company out there after working for some time with Sam Feldman. While she was still in university, she'd set up a college booking company, and now she knew the music game inside out. She was still fondly remembered in some circles as the kind of person who would cook dinner for the band because she thought they might not be eating enough.

I had known John Martin for years and had spent a lot of time hanging around with him. In those days, he had an apartment at Queen and Parliament, just around the corner from where I used to live at Cadillac Johnny's. It was John's creative originality that had defined the emergent music TV style. The fast pace, the guerrilla feel of it—its firm connection to the street. Coupled with Moses' philosophy of bringing the people into the TV studio and the TV studio out to the people—breaking down the boundaries—it was a dynamic creative match.

John was a great guy. He was generous, expansive and occasionally garrulous. He had a tendency to decide what you should be doing and then set the wheels in motion to achieve that goal.

One evening, I was relaxing over at his apartment, and I just happened to mention to him that I thought that person who did *The New Music*, Denise— right?, I thought she was really something special. While I sat there watching TV, John sneaked over to his desk and called her on the phone. He invited her over to hang out and have a drink, mentioning that I happened to be there. I thought it was nothing more than a happy coincidence when, a little while later, she knocked and came on up. We were watching *African Queen,* which has always been one of my favourite movies. I was a bit surprised when a little while later Denise revealed that she didn't care for it that much. How could anyone not like Humphrey Bogart and Katherine Hepburn? While I was explaining to her why it was the greatest of movies, I was rubbing her shoulders. Then, when it was revealed that she'd been on them all day, her feet as well. Now, as any guy worth his salt knows from birth, if a girl lets you rub her feet, you are home free! Especially if you take great care and do it for a long time!

We started going out, and at first, that's all there was to it. I really liked her. She was smarter than any woman I'd ever met and totally unafraid of disagreeing with me on any contentious issue. She also cared a lot about things that were important to me, essentially doing whatever you could in your own way to make the world a better place. She was knowledgeable and enthusiastic about the natural world. She was brave. She was a great swimmer. She was up for any adventure. I really, really liked her!

I brought Denise home for dinner, just before Michèle strategically disappeared for dinner with a friend. I wanted to get an opinion from my surrogate sister. Michèle later confessed that she thought Denise was "terrific." When Miche returned later that night, Denise was seated at the kitchen divider bar, with me pouring her yet another cognac while I read her runes. I didn't know the first thing about runes, but I was doing what I thought was a pretty convincing job of telling Denise what a special woman I thought she was, and hopefully, pouring enough cognac so anything lacking in my delivery wouldn't hurt my case too badly.

It was sort of funny the way things went initially. I still didn't have a car, so on nights where I was going to go to her apartment out in the west end, I would jump on my bicycle and ride over there. It was fun, smelling the smells and hearing the snatches of melody from storefronts as I dodged the opening car doors and homicidal right-turners. I guess it was a good test of Denise's affection, because I was often fairly "manly" by the time I arrived.

She preferred staying at her own place to overnighting at Wellesley. I understood that. If her phone rang, she wanted to be there. Her job was demanding. Hell, she was the first girl I'd ever dated who *had* a job! She couldn't get out of touch. It also might be her father or mother, and she wasn't ready to deal with the inevitable questions just yet.

I didn't mind riding over there. Besides, I did it so often I was beginning to get pretty fit, and that was good for everything, including my love life. When she came over to my place, she'd bring her sports car. She had a white Nissan 300 zx, of which she was justifiably proud. It was her first really good car. It had a T-roof and everything.

I often think of that time with a chuckle. The well-respected Canadian pop performer and folk icon, pedalling around on his bike, not as an ecological ideal, but because he's too cheap or broke to pay for car insurance, while his media-darling girlfriend drives around in the flashy sports car. That wasn't supposed to be how it went, was it?

Somewhere along the line, it dawned on me with delight that I had found love again. I didn't know how, but it had crept up on me when I wasn't looking. Maybe it was precisely because I had love to give, instead of neediness. What was more, there seemed to be very strong indications that it was mutual!

Eventually, I decided to take the plunge again, swallow my resentment and pay off the insurance companies. I leased a car. Girls are always making jokes about guys who drive high-performance cars. The intimation is that they do so because they lack other manly virtues. I decided that if I was going to be driving that particular part of my anatomy, I might as well get the biggest one I could afford. I got a Ford Mustang Cobra convertible with a 5.0 litre v8. I just loved that car. It would do 145 mph right out of the box and was a real licence loser.

Denise looked it over and pronounced it "a burger car." That was Scarborough-ese for the kind of vehicle that guys with not much upstairs drove to the A&W to make a lot of noise and cruise for girls. Yeah, like—you got a problem with that or something?

One of the best things about her in a very long list was that she could take the piss out of me completely and it would never make me mad. I'd gotten pretty good at laughing cruelly at the world, but I'd never cultivated the essential skill of being able to laugh at myself, and I could see right away that she was going to be a valuable teacher.

Our relationship deepened. I began going out to get her at the airport every time she'd come back from a trip, bringing with me little boxes with beads and trinkets. I was in full wooing mode.

In June of '87, I called up Vezi Tayyeb and booked Kensington Sound for a couple of days. I wanted to do a demo-session of all the songs I was considering for a new record. I went into the studio with Bucky Berger on drums, a new guy named Kit Johnson playing bass, Ben Mink, Ron Dann (the funniest man in the universe) and Vezi as engineer. It was only supposed to be a demo-session, but it wound up being the best recording I could make of that particular bunch of songs. It eventually became the record.

We were so relaxed. I was happy. We were working in the middle of Kensington Market, an area of Toronto I've always loved, so every time there was a break, I'd go downstairs, grab a patty from the Jamaican bakery with a Mr. Goudas ginger beer, sit on the bench and watch the world go by.

There was no agenda on this music. It didn't have a goal. I just soaked up the atmosphere of the place it was being made in. The band loped easily through the head arrangements. Everybody contributed ideas, usually good ones. Without knowing it yet, I had gotten to work on that record I'd started in Arizona—the one that tried to look at love from a lot of different perspectives. I really liked the way the tracks were sounding.

I took Denise up to Stony Lake in July for a getaway. My brother had bought an island there some years before with another business associate. Generally, no one was there from Monday through Thursday and the lake was quiet, so I took advantage of Calvin's generosity and often went up there. I loved the place. The huge wood-and-stone house had been built during the 1920s as a retreat for nuns who'd lost the faith or burned out from missionary work. The place was still known locally as Nuns' Island.

We spent our time going for long swims out across the water to a flat rock where the seagulls roosted. We took a canoe into the "Lost Channel" and listened to the screech of the red-winged blackbirds, watched the kingfisher working the water and nosed up silently to listen to the muted vocalizations of the spring crop of young beaver as they chatted amiably with each other inside the safety of their lodge. Denise was like a kid. She got a great excitement from seeing wild things going about their business.

One night we took the canoe out at about two o'clock in the morning. It was a crystal clear night with no wind. It was so still that the loudest noise was the swirl of the water around the paddle. The dark waters of the lake made a perfect mirror of the shapes of the trees, and the brilliance of the millions of stars in the Milky Way shone up from below as well as down from above. The stillness was broken only by the keening of a loon echoing across the night from miles away. There was a perfect illusion of being suspended in space, and throughout that gentle solitude, there was not a word spoken as Denise lay comfortably on pillows in the bow, staring up at a passing meteor. It was then that I stopped being able to see me without her.

After that, we started going to weddings together. We became "announced" socially as a couple. I would sometimes go out to a club where Denise was working at interviewing some band or other and be quite content to watch her work and not get in the way.

She'd been working her way up to buying a house and had made plans for a co-ownership with another young lady. Something went south on the deal, and the other person backed out. I'd just taken advantage of Canada's tax laws regarding capital gains and made a deal with TMP to purchase my publishing back catalogue, resulting in the sudden infusion of a substantial amount of cash, a windfall that needed a safe place to go before my usual habits won the day and I spent it on an aeroplane or something.

I proposed to Denise that maybe she might consider me as co-owner in a house. I didn't want to frighten the life out of her, so I pitched the thing as though it was a straightforward business deal—I cover this, you cover that, here's how we break the deal if it doesn't work out. I didn't want to overemphasize the fact that this meant the big jump of "living together," even though I was already convinced beyond all doubt that things would work out just fine. Why was I so certain?

They always say that if you want to see what the woman you love will become, look no further than her mother. I absolutely adored Denise's mother (still do)! Mavis, as she is known, was the most upbeat person (next to her daughter) that I had ever met. She hadn't had the easiest of lives, but she sailed through her adversities with her head held high. I nicknamed her Mrs. Miniver, after the famous character played by Greer Garson in the movies about England's struggles during the war. Knowing Mavis made me confident about her daughter.

I finally overcame Denise's reservations about living with a musician. Heaven knows she'd met enough of them to merit the opinion she had. With the help of a realtor named Bob Kent, the brother of Darrell, the man who'd been responsible for the renaissance of Cabbagetown, we began looking for a house we could afford.

Bob finally scored for us. After touring like crazy for the whole month of November, I finally put "Fort Wellesley" into boxes, said goodbye to my bachelor days once again, and in December of 1987, Denise and I moved into our first house: a small detached in Riverdale, just around the corner from the park and an easy stroll from all the best Greek restaurants in Toronto.

Swinging on a Star to Swinging on a Star

AS 1988 BEGAN, I WAS STILL UNSURE where my career was going to take me. I didn't have a record deal, and Bob Burwell was having a struggle drumming up enthusiasm in the United States. We were trying to get an American-based signing, figuring that would take care of Canada as well, through whatever branch plant carried the record in our market. We wanted the power to penetrate the U.S. market that a Nashville deal would bring.

I felt that eventually we'd come up with something, but the missing deal was the only major source of uncertainty for me as Denise and I moved into our new house.

No sooner had we established ourselves in the place and had our first festive Christmas together than I all but disappeared. First, I had a tour of the province of Saskatchewan, sponsored by the provincial arts and culture organization. It was twenty-three straight days through the dead of a rural winter playing in community centres and school auditoriums in places with names like Redvers, Moosomin, Watrous and Biggar.

Endless drives without even seeing another vehicle—beating a path through the driving wind and a golden haze of dust and ice crystals. Occasionally, there would be life in the form of a group of shaggy horses, their rumps turned to the wind, their heads low and their tails blowing between their legs. Just the three of us in a van—Danny Greenspoon, Kit Johnson and myself—desperately trying to maintain a level of civility as the endless tour ground on.

I flew back to Toronto for one day for a change of wardrobe, then flew directly to Australia. I was gone for the entire month of February. That must have eased Denise's period of adjustment in the new house. When I got back, everything was changed around and she was happy. I was happy too. It was a lot warmer in Australia in February than it was in Saskatchewan, and I'd pit-stopped in Honolulu on my way home.

In April, I went back into Kensington Sound with Vezi and most of the same musicians to do a bunch of tracks. I had another idea for a record I wanted to try out. I thought that recording, or rather rerecording a bunch of my favourite songs—not necessarily big ones, but the ones I thought were my best work—would be an interesting way to try to reimage some of them and give them a fresh life. Maybe then I might bring out a sort of "classics" collection.

I also recut some of the songs I'd done in the earlier session with the proper care and attention they were due. This was to be the official attempt at making record-quality takes of "Imaginary Tree" and "Love with a Capital L." For some reason, these sessions just didn't gel, and it was perfectly clear to me that they didn't get close to the recordings I already had. It was frustrating to work as hard as I did, paying the bills myself and not get anything I liked.

At the end of April, the time had finally come for the trip to Germany that John Dalton had talked to me about. I drove out to CFB Trenton, where the forces transport wing is based, and met up with John and the group. It was a fun and motley crew: Danny Greenspoon was along for guitar; Nancy White, the humourist-songwriter; Marie-Lynn Hammond, a singer who'd come to prominence in the folk world with Stringband and was currently hosting her own show on CBC radio.

I'd been forewarned that there were certain restrictions on the military 707 that carried personnel back and forth to the bases Canada maintained in Europe as its contribution to NATO. We'd been given a list of don'ts and dos—mostly don'ts.

No jeans. Gentlemen were to wear jackets, although ties were not considered necessary for reasons of comfort—thank heaven for small mercies! At 8:45 in the morning on April 28, we loaded up, red-eyed and dopey, into the bowels of the old-tech jet, along with a bunch of sleepy soldiers.

With all due respect to the Department of National Defence, I guess they figure if they keep their soldiers as uncomfortable as possible, they'll fight that much more ferociously when they get wherever they're going! The comfort level on the plane made Aeroflot look like Cathay Pacific. It was cramped, noisy, stuffy, claustrophobic because of the high-density seating, impossible to sleep in, and just to top it off, there were virtually no refreshments. We arrived at Heathrow after an interminable flight. Then we just sat in the plane on some obscure section of the ramp, unable to walk around or get off, while they refuelled. After the usual English clearance delay, the planeload of now thoroughly exhausted artistes and military personnel blasted off to fly over France to the Rhine.

There was some kind of hooh-hah with France going on at the time about airspace, so the 707 overflew Strasbourg at what looked to be around twenty-five thousand feet, crossed the Rhine, went into a hard sixty-degree bank, chopped power to idle, hung out everything on the aeroplane that would lose lift or produce drag and literally dove it for the base at Lahr. I've done gentler approaches in the Decathlon. I seem to recollect that one of the ladies in our party determined that her life was about to come to an end and volubly expressed this fear.

We landed on the runway at Lahr, hot, high and fast. Then the poor abused jet limped over to a parking area. We got out, picked up our gear and just walked into Germany. I never saw a German official of any kind!

Things got better fast.

Once we'd moved into our hotel, eaten and rested, we went out to look around the town. It was a charming little rural town, with cobblestones and a market area in the old section. We wandered by shops and pastry emporiums, then stopped for tall and delicious glasses of Pils, which took forever to pour. This was my first time in Germany, and I kept wondering as I looked at the squares and old buildings, What transpired there? Who walked there? Dark shades of history could be felt even on this pleasant day. Danny Greenspoon felt this most keenly.

The show in the town hall was packed and a great success, and in the aftermath, we were celebrated with a reception. It was there that I met a fun-loving officer in the forces who would later bring me back to Germany for a different reason.

After things had wound down and there was a quiet moment, John Dalton, the producer, took me aside and sat me down. He said he had an idea and wanted to see how I felt about it. We'd talked about one of my great passions during our previous meeting, and he'd been thinking about it ever since.

It had always rankled me that songwriting, an art form as difficult to master as any other, was never accorded the same respect and appreciation as more visible art forms. Many times, the public confuses the singer with the song and assumes that whoever performed it wrote it. I have often felt disappointed that the "new" art form I'd dedicated myself to, which merged poetic lyrics with folk and pop music, had never been elevated to a legitimate art.

John proposed the idea of doing a brand-new type of show, which would do precisely that. It would celebrate the achievements of songwriters from many different genres by giving them the opportunity to showcase their talent in an informal performance environment. If they weren't good performers, they could even have their favourite artist perform the song for them. That was only half the equation, though. They would also be interviewed about the life situations or the creative necessities from which their work evolved, and about applied technique. It would be slanted creatively, without a word about business.

I told John that I thought the idea was wonderful and that it was precisely the kind of thing CBC Radio did best. But, I suggested, don't make it so typically CBC. Cast the net wide to bring in people who have other styles and views than left-wing folkie or white-bread country. You should see some tough little rockers in there. Bring in people from the black music community. Why not jazz composers?

We had a great rap about the subject, and then John laid on the kicker. He asked me if I'd host the show. He felt that because I was "one of them," I'd have the credibility with the guests that a "normal" CBC host could never hope to achieve. He thought that when approached to appear, with me acting as the host, guests might more readily respond in the affirmative. Most important, he thought I'd have the wit and confidence to carry the show if it was ever losing momentum.

I wasn't at all sure I wanted to become involved. As much as I liked the show concept and believed in what it represented, at least on paper, I was very leery about becoming a "CBC person." By that, I mean I was worried that doing the show might create the perception that I was abandoning my focus on being a musician and writer. I thought my business was making music, not talking to other people about making theirs! I told John I'd think about it.

I was still thinking about it when, after returning to Canada, I went and got my medical renewed and tentatively stepped back into aerobatic flying once again. I'd missed it too much to stay away. I looked on this as a clear indicator that whatever might happen with my career, I was prepared to take it in stride and bounce back. I guess in my mind, flying and living are intertwined.

It was a good thing I was feeling resilient because another disappointment was due in the short term. Bob Burwell was just not having any luck getting me a record deal. Worse than that, the reason he gave me for the resistance coming from the labels was "We like what he does alright, but he's too old!"

I'd never come up so squarely against that one. I was forty years old by now, but I'd never thought of myself as being "old." There was a whole gang of new people coming up in the Nashville music industry, and they were pushing Merle Haggard and Johnny Paycheck off the charts and into obscurity. Not only that, Burwell was becoming unhappy with his relationship to the Halsey Company and was making noises about leaving it. There began to be questions about what he could really do for me. Perhaps I should get a Canadian deal and see what happened. I felt I didn't need him to help me accomplish that, so when he did leave Halsey, I exercised that "key-man" clause and terminated my management agreement with them.

I was back to square one—no record deal, no active management. There was a difference this time, though. I had a master tape full of good songs all ready to mix, and way off on the back burner, I had the offer from John Dalton to consider, so at least there were options.

I started making phone calls to the A&R departments of the record companies and asking for appointments. First, I went over to see John Alexander at MCA. He and Ross Reynolds, the president of the company, both liked what I'd done and could see it in the context of the changing face of country. They felt it was marketable, but they weren't in a position to act.

Next, I went over to see Dean Cameron, who was head of A&R at Capitol EMI at the time. Dean was then and is now a very active champion of Canadian music, and I got a bite right away—not so much on the basis of the record I was offering but more on what I might do next. Dean's assistant, Tim Trombley, thought the way the record was mixed stylistically, plus the soft treatment of the songs on the album, which I was now calling *Swinging on a Star*, were "hokey," to use his own word.

I took an August break to attend the world aerobatic championships in Red Deer, Alberta, where I hung out and helped in any way I could with Canadian champion Gordon Price's effort to compete on behalf of Canada. He was debuting his self-designed three-hundred-horsepower biplane, the Ultimate 10 Dash 300. It was a rocket with an impossibly high roll rate—something around 380 degrees per second, maybe more. It looked splendid in its blue and yellow paint scheme, with the Labatt brewing company advertising that was part of his sponsorship deal not detracting too much from the clean design.

The competition was tough and good. For the first time in North America, there was a full representation from all the Eastern Bloc countries. The aeroplanes said CCCP on the side, but there weren't a lot of KGB people around anymore because of Glasnost.

The Russian pilots, both men and women, were just awesome. They had Sukhoi and Yakovlev monoplanes that employed impossibly strong structures of Kevlar and Carbon fibre. They were big and noisy, with three-hundred-plus-horsepower radial engines barking as they flew—and how they flew.

All you had to do was compare résumés. A typical Russian competitor was totally dedicated to aerobatics and often had very little conventional time. They had the best aircraft, free fuel and all the time in the world to practise. Their logbook breakdown might read: total time twenty-five thousand hours, with twenty thousand hours aerobatic time. By comparison, the average North American or European was usually an airline pilot who flew aerobatics as a sideline for skill enhancement. His summary might read: total time thirty thousand hours, two thousand hours aerobatic. It's amazing the rest of the world did as well as they did. This wasn't a war, though. Everyone got along well and had the utmost respect for each other's skill. I had a ball.

There is a little dance that pilots do before they fly their compulsory sequence in competition. They've just been shown the figures, and in an attempt to memorize them, pilots can be seen doing swooping manoeuvres with their hands as they dance around the tarmac in an imitation of their aeroplane in flight. I felt that Gordon, a biplane pilot, was unfairly penalized in this effort by not having an extra set of hands, so I went to the Red Deer Canadian Tire, bought a bunch of stuff and made him a set of gloves that were appropriate for a biplane aerobat. There was a second set of hands wired to them. The Russians stood around scratching their heads as they watched Gord dance through his sequence with an absolutely straight face. Then the penny dropped, and they all cracked up.

After the events at Red Deer, I went back to Toronto. Kevin Welch, a new friend of mine from Nashville with whom I'd been writing, had arrived to help me record two more tracks—songs we'd written together—for the album. One of them was "Heart upon His Sleeve" and the other was "You Can't Be Fooled." Once that was done, as the end of August rolled around, I went up and signed the record deal with Capitol. They were all pumped, and I was back in business.

I got out on the road by October, working the first radio single like crazy while doing interviews. It was a full-bore campaign, targeted specifically at country radio, and they were proving to be very receptive. There wasn't a song on the advance copies of the record that some country programmer didn't like. We had a good one on our hands. It didn't matter to me that a top-selling Canadian country record then was selling only ten thousand copies and that was nothing to Capitol. I liked the buzz of actually having people be excited to see me walk in their doors again. It had been a long time! The album was officially released at the end of October and very shortly was getting really solid widespread airplay on country stations. That had an immediate effect on concert attendances.

I got back just in time to celebrate Halloween with Amy. It was by far her favourite holiday of the year. She was already demonstrating an off-the-scale intelligence and had reached the point where the kinds of "kid-to-dad" questions she was asking me were, "Dad, how does government work?" She was nine going on forty as we laboured intently over the grotesque face on a pumpkin. She'd started exhibiting a musical precociousness and had developed into a fine singer. Sometimes I'd look at what she was accomplishing, especially given the obstacles she'd had to overcome, and I couldn't help busting my buttons with pride.

I had long ago passed the point where I railed at God and said, "Why are you punishing this child for my sins?" The penny had dropped for me that this was nothing more than a lot of self-indulgent crap. She herself had accepted who she was and gotten on with life. She knew that one day she would probably lose what remained of her sight to glaucoma. That fact had never been withheld from her. Once she was old enough to understand, she was always in the decision loop about what was going to happen. The last thing she needed was some old fart imposing his personal guilt on her struggle to live her life.

I stopped viewing her as a person who was disadvantaged by fate and simply accepted her as who she was. She was developing into a wonderful person—full of questions and with a wicked sense of humour. She was holding down excellent marks in a regular school curriculum with the help of special visual aids. She worked so hard and made it look so effortless that she made it easy to forget just how difficult it was for her to accomplish her tasks.

She had a lot of harsh medications to take for glaucoma and they had nasty side effects: loss of appetite, fatigue and associated difficulty in concentration, an effect on the endocrine system that might result in being a smaller-than-average person in adulthood. Through all that, she was stubborn, single-minded, focused, temperamental and seemingly dedicated from time to time to putting her mother in an early grave. In short, in most respects, she was a normal girl. The most abnormal thing about her was how smart she was. It was hard to get over the feeling that she might be mad at me for the missing years. I hoped one day she'd grow to accept my limitations as a human being.

All through October, I'd been wrestling with another dilemma. I'd become convinced with every fibre of my being that I'd gotten it right this time, and I wanted to propose the idea of marriage to Denise. I felt that if my relationship with her didn't mature to the point where I was willing to stand up and make a commitment in public that I was going to make things work with this person, then maybe not next year, maybe not the year after, but eventually, the relationship would wither.

I think marriage is a bulwark against bailing out when it turns out to be tough sledding. At its best, it is an understanding partnership between two people who love each other, to do better in life together than they could do alone and without each other's support. I think it is a good idea that has been much maligned because of people's embarrassment at and fear of failure. In a world that so often screams, "Me! what about me?" marriage whispers, "You . . . what can I do to make it better for you?"

I got a special table at Fenton's restaurant in Toronto, right by the fireplace. I briefed the *maître d'* on what I was hoping to accomplish. The staff were instructed to make it a memorable evening of effortless elegance—but keep the fuck away from the table unless they make a sign they want you!

I had lunch with Michèle, who was back from Singapore. I asked her if she thought I was crazy to go through with this. She bought me several drinks and shored up my courage by assuring me that I was the most marriageable bachelor in all of greater Toronto. Vezi Tayyeb's opinion was that it was an act of utmost irresponsibility on my part to have inflicted myself upon such a high-quality person as Denise in the first place! No help there.

I went to Birks and got the biggest rock I could afford. The salesman looked upon my effort with pity and condescension, but he put the ring in a blue velvet box for me anyway. And then there was nothing left but to do it!

On the evening of November 1, 1988, Denise and I arrived at Fenton's for what she thought was going to be a nice dinner date. She was happy as a lark all through the evening. The wines were perfect, the food was to die for, the fireplace cheered her on the cool November evening. Dessert came and went, and finally, as we were having coffee and liqueur, I said, "There's something I'd like to ask you."

As soon as I slipped the box out of my jacket pocket, the game was up. Denise was hit with an attack of emotional claustrophobia. Just as I was getting down on my knee by her side to present her with the Birks box and say the magic words, she slammed her hand down on the table rather loudly and hissed, "Don't you dare!"

This wasn't the reaction I'd been hoping for. I didn't realize that what she was reacting to was her desire not to have me make a public spectacle of us by getting down on my knee at Fenton's. As the tables around us went ominously silent, I thought instead that I'd blown the whole thing completely! I thought I'd gone that one step too far, too fast and frightened her off. I was miserable with grief!

I didn't know what to do. I moped around miserably for two whole days, wondering if I should move out or something, before she finally let me off the hook and said yes!

I was overjoyed, and the wheels began to move slowly towards a wedding from that moment on. The biggest problem was finding a hole in our schedules big enough and long enough to accomplish getting married, and then putting to rest all the millions of details about the wheres and whys and whens for relatives and friends.

I finished out '88 by doing a great "Big Ticket" show for John Martin and *MuchMusic* at the Diamond Club. I did all the stuff from the *Swinging on a Star* album, plus Warren Zevon's classic "Carmelita" with Barney Bentall and Lori Yates. Things were moving along well again!

The last bit of business from 1988 stretched over into '89. John Dalton had sold the idea for the radio show to CBC management, and with a solid and important show presented to me on a plate, any resistance I had evaporated in the face of having too much fun. On January 14, 1989, I flew out to Halifax to tape the pilot for the radio series *Swinging on a Star,* with my first-ever guests, Colleen Petersen and Lenny Gallant. It was the start of five years of a top-rated show which succeeded beyond all our wildest imaginings.

And Then Came Duncan

THE AMERICAN EFFORT FOR *Swinging on a Star,* the album, was a mixed success. With help from Dean Cameron, a release through Capitol Nashville was secured. Also with Dean's help, I hired a company called Chart Attack to work the record on U.S. radio. Meanwhile, I joined forces with Evelyn Schriver, the lady who'd made Randy Travis, to do publicity. All this was to no avail, even though we got a lot of visibility on TNN and CMT for the video of "Love with a Capital L."

The first indications that there was something wrong revealed themselves when I got a call from the folks at Chart Attack saying, "We're getting a lot of maybe's from program directors who feel they'd like to add the record, but they don't feel that Capitol is serious about it from a promotions perspective because they're not getting any excitement or sense of commitment from the field reps."

It turned out that Lynn Schultz, head of A&R Nashville, was doing lip service to us Canadian yokels. He had other fish to fry. It turned out he was working this new act named Garth Brooks. I did have the satisfaction of tearing a big strip off Lynn's hide in Dean Cameron's office before his job disappeared in a corporate restructuring at Capitol.

The situation was okay. I was content with the performance of the record in Canada. It fed into the radio show and vice versa. It had reestablished me after a long uphill struggle, and I felt vindicated by its modest success.

I worked the record hard through a long string of good concert dates that I did with my Wall of Folk trio. Actually, it was just two other guys, Danny Greenspoon and Kit Johnson, plus yours truly. We made a lot of noise, though, for three guys banging away on strings.

In May 1989, I began my first tapings for the radio series, and then we were off in earnest. There was a fairly high work load attached to doing them, and I found that I took fewer concert bookings once we got going. When the show travelled to other cities, I would sometimes use the opportunity to schedule in dates around the production, as the band was already there. (I had strongly suggested in the deal I cut with Dalton that it would be really nice if my guys got the gig as the house band for the show. It was good for them and it was extra good for me!)

By the spring of 1990, I was contemplating the making of a new record when I got a communication out of the blue from the officer I'd met when I was in Germany with the radio troupe. His name was Rick Froh, and he was a lieutenant-colonel in the Engineers for the army branch of the Canadian Forces. It turned out he was now some kind of wheel with the Canadian Clubs over in Lahr and Baden Solingen. He'd mentioned that he knew me, and the idea occurred to them that they should invite me over to speak at the clubs in both locations. Rick was calling to see if I'd like to come back to Germany, all expenses paid, guaranteed fun, and I was welcome to bring Denise if I thought I'd like to. I told him I'd see what her response was and get back to him.

The idea of going to Germany was very exciting at the time. There was a lot of energy and celebration because the Berlin Wall had just come down, the collapse of the Eastern Bloc had occurred and everybody was wondering what was going to happen to the balance of power while the people danced in the streets. It took Denise as much as a second to make up her mind. She'd go even if I didn't.

I got back in touch with Rick and told him I'd be happy to speak on one condition. He had to finesse me a ride in the CF-18. I could almost hear him wince over the phone. "The prime minister can't get a ride in a CF-18, Murray," he replied, taking me seriously. I was actually only kidding, really-really! I let him off the hook, and we made the arrangements to get over to Germany. It would be on Lufthansa this time. No more knees-to-your-chin transports.

It was April when we finally flew over. We landed in Frankfurt, and this felt a bit more like the entrance to Germany I'd expected the last time 'round. Polite but firm, with a lot of earnest young men standing around the airport in uniforms carrying light machine guns.

We were picked up by a taciturn German man in a dark suit, who proceeded to whisk us from Frankfurt to Lahr at a zillion miles an hour down the Autobahn in a vw Jetta that was doing everything it could. We were met by Rick, and taken into town to have dinner with his family.

We stayed on the base that night in a suite reserved for married officers. It was like being in a motel when a drunken bike gang is in town. I've seldom heard the kind of language and carrying on, male and female (outside of a jail cell), the likes of which I heard that night.

Bleary-eyed, we got out the next day at the crack of dawn and were whisked off again for a tour of the base. This turned out to be a lot of fun. Among other activities, we got to drive a tank. Denise especially enjoyed this. The thing weighed forty tons, I guess, and went forty-five miles an hour. She was mad with power.

After that, we were taken over to a pistol range and got to blast away with nine-millimetre pistols at a group of targets. I couldn't hit the side of a barn, but Denise, being a cop's daughter, was a crack shot and did a good job of upholding the family honour.

It was a long day, and by the time we'd changed and gone to the mess where the dinner and speech were to be, we were very hungry. We were more than a little slap-happy from jet lag as well.

Denise had been worried about my speech, but then Denise always worries about my speeches. She's got tendonitis from wringing her hands! She's got good reason. I tend to shoot from the hip once I get up a good head of steam, and let the chips fall where they may. This night was no exception.

I had planned my address to touch a wide range of topics, and as long as I stuck to the general and the cultural, things went fairly smoothly. When I got to the part about the controversy that was raging in the country regarding the wearing of traditional Sikh religious clothing, namely the turban and the kirpan, in the RCMP, I hit a nerve.

I made the case that it exposed the undercurrent of vicious racism that exists in Canada that we all love so much to ignore. It was a solid case I made. I pointed out that the RCMP uniform had evolved many times for different reasons, not the least of which was the most recent—to accommodate the presence of women on the force. I pointed out the historic and valiant service the Sikh regiments had done in the Second World War. I pointed out that the question of the turban had easily been dealt with when it was found that a mini-turban, for want of a better word, would fit nicely under a standard battle helmet. In other words, there had been many instances where these issues had been worked out successfully, and there was no demonstrable need for a controversy at all. I suggested that the real resistance was at its root an attempt to exclude Sikhs from the RCMP because many people could not come to terms with taking orders from someone who wasn't white. They were comfortable with Sikhs when they were pushing baggage carts at the airport, but not when they were in a position of authority with a gun on their hip.

I stirred up a bit of a hornets' nest, and things got quite lively. At least one person suggested that they weren't about to take any shit from some "Raghead." There were some unpleasant comments. I stood my ground and argued them down as reasonably as I could.

The next trouble spot was a section where I discussed the potential role for the military in a post-NATO world—responding to ecological disasters, for instance. At this point, a loud male voice boomed, "I didn't sign on to be no goddamned bird-washer!"

After it was over, Rick met me good-humouredly and said in his most understated manner, "Well, that was certainly a thought-provoking evening!" Denise was just relieved that I'd got out alive.

The next morning, we were wakened up before sunrise and whisked off by car to a waiting helicopter. We were in the air, streaking up the Rhine Valley, as the sun was coming up. Denise and I had no sooner landed at the air base at Baden than I was whisked off on my own. I was taken to see an Air Force doctor. He asked me a bunch of routine questions, did a blood-pressure test, listened to my heart and generally poked around for a while. Something was up!

I was taken from the doctor's into another building, where a nice young lady assisted me into a G-suit, fitted me for a helmet, boots and gloves, issued me a set of undergarments and a flight suit, fitted me with an oxygen mask and then instructed me in the arming and use of an ejection seat. Something was really up!

From the equipment dispersal, I was then taken over to the squadron ready room for 439 Squadron and introduced to its commanding officer, Don Matthews. Don filled me in on the details of my good fortune. I was going to go for the ride of my young life in Canada's front-line fighter—two-seat version! The squadron guys made sure I had an egg-salad sandwich with lots of celery and onions, so if I aspirated in my mask, it would be nice and funky. Actually, there was good sense in eating. I know this from flying aerobatics myself. The lower your blood sugar, the less tolerance you have to G loads and the more likely you are to have a problem or even lose consciousness.

I was introduced to the young man I'd be flying with, a Flight Lieutenant named Freidt, squadron name "Frito." Without any delay, we grabbed the helmet bags and trudged out to a jeep in all our flight gear. Denise was back with me now, and getting that uncomfortable look that says, "Do you really know what you're getting yourself into?"

The driver took us to a revetment, the kind built to withstand a small tactical nuke, and we were ushered inside. I'd seen F-18s before, so I wasn't surprised by the appearance, but I couldn't help but notice how hunchbacked and purposeful it looked. There's nothing lyrical about that aeroplane. It's designed for what it does and it ain't called the "Hornet" for nothing.

Frito and I were strapped into the plane by the ground crew, and with his pre-starts done, he fired up the engines. For us, it was a distant gentle whistle. For Denise, standing out on the ramp, it must have been an ear-splitting shriek as the fighter went by and I waved to her from the cockpit.

We taxied down to the holding bay at the end of the active to wait for an IFR clearance up to the north. The weather at Lahr was shitty. Drizzling rain, reduced visibility, but where this aeroplane was going, that was not a problem. We waited for a long time for the clearance, and like any self-respecting fighter pilot faced with a delay, Frito's temperature went up with the amount of fuel he was burning on the ramp. Some pretty colourful language crackled over the intercom. Then he remembered it was a two-seater and he had an audience. I said, "I understand. I'm a pilot, too, and I've been through it myself."

Finally, we blasted off on full afterburner and climbed out into the clag. Not long after getting through the tops, the voice on the intercom came back again, "So you're a pilot, eh?"

"That's right."

"Great! Take me to Frankfurt," he said, throwing a chart over the cockpit divider into the back. I realized he was giving me the stick, and I took it!

That started some serious fun for me. We flew up to the north and did a GCA approach for practice. That's the kind where you're talked in by a ground radar operator who tells you heading, airspeed and rate of descent until you're at the runway. After the approach, we were overflying the runway and the intercom came to life again.

"Okay, give me full burner and your best angle of climb to maintain five hundred knots." I advanced the throttle to afterburner and pulled the nose up to about eighty degrees to see what would happen. It didn't take too long to overshoot the speed, and then I heard the chuckle from the front. I had to pull it vertical, and it still wanted to break Mach 1 unless the power was reduced. We did a vertical climb straight up to the mid-twenty thousands, and then we went off to a practice area that was protected for fighter exercises.

I had a ball, yanking the plane around the sky. The only misstep I made was turning it upside down; a whole bunch of crap came up into the canopy. I mostly rolled it ninety degrees first one way, then the other, and pulled through a turn, delighting in the feeling of the flesh trying to pull itself off the bones of my face.

Finally, Frito took over and demonstrated one or two extreme manoeuvres. As is often the case, what you do yourself doesn't bug you, but when someone else does it, you go all awry. After Frito had done what they call a "Yank and Puke" for a short while, I had enough and told him so. It wasn't a big deal because it was time to return to base according to the remaining fuel, unless we wanted to be sitting on the Autobahn in our ejection seats.

It was a pinnacle experience for an avid civilian pilot, and I owe it to the astute planning of Lieutenant Colonel Froh and to General Jean Boyle. He is now retired, so I don't feel I'm compromising him by telling this story. He and Rick had gone to Royal Military College together and were friends. General Boyle was the commander, 1 Canadian Air Division in Lahr, responsible for Canada's air forces in NATO. I guess he checked up on me, and I came up clean. Between that and Rick speaking up for me, the good general sought the proper approvals and put me through. Thank you, General Boyle! It was the chance of a lifetime for me.

Denise and I got married that summer, in a beautiful ceremony at St. Peter's-on-the-Rock church, where Hell's Gate divides Stony Lake from Clear Lake. We moved the crowd over by barge and boat from the church to Nuns' Island for the reception. It was the social event of the season. I knew that, because for several years after, you could hear the big tourist boat from Viamedes Resort passing by with the loudspeaker going, "And there is St. Peter's church, where Murray McLauchlan was recently married. The McLauchlan family summer at the cottage directly over there, and if you look carefully through your binoculars or the long lens on your video camera, you may catch a glimpse of one of them on the swim dock!"

The wedding was a glorious day for me. All our friends attended. Denise was radiant, and I knew I'd been blessed with the good fortune of marrying a woman whose influence encouraged me to be far better than I am.

We had an idyllic honeymoon on the island of Kauai in a little lanai on the shore, with no telephone and no TV. We could lie in our bed and watch the entire Pacific Ocean through the window. We had a red jeep and used it to go to all the remote beaches to swim. We hiked the Na Pali Trail. We snorkelled every day and marvelled at the skill of the wave-jumping windsurfers. We went horseback riding up over the high ridges. We counted egrets in the taro plantation and blue-footed boobies along the coast. We forgot about the world completely. The U.S. was officially on the eve of the Gulf War, but you would never have known it. The little chunk of Hawaii that we'd found was just like it must have been in the late forties, before the tourists got there. It was paradise, and as our time to leave drew nigh, Denise began to think of business schemes that would allow us to stay. She almost cried when it was time to get on the plane.

There wasn't a conscious decision to have a child, although we talked about it. It was more of a joyful throwing of caution to the wind. I had thought very carefully about whether having another child was a good idea for me. After all, I was already a father. I'd done my biological duty. I didn't know if I wanted to be faced with the prospect of having teenaged children around, with all the angst they go through, when I was in my late fifties and early sixties. I'd looked on that as the time of life when I would breathe a sigh of relief and maybe finally find a place in the sun. And then I began to take a look at what I was saying to myself. I was painting a picture of an ossified old fart who didn't want his well-planned course through the waning years of his life to be interrupted by anything as frightening as further obligation, unpredictability, dirt and unquenchable love.

There was a gentle shifting of the prevailing winds over to, "Well, if it happens it happens, and it won't be at all unwelcome!" So it wasn't so much a decision on my part as it was a sea change about what values I would bring to bear on life. Denise? She had her own reasons entirely, and you'll have to read her book if she ever writes one.

Denise went on a trip to Australia in the spring of 1991. When she was leaving, she asked me if I'd like to have her bring anything special back for me. I said, "Bring me a didgeridoo!" I'd brought back assorted boomerangs the last time I was there, but she was going to hang out with the band Midnight Oil, and they were expert in the lore of the mighty didge. She shopped with the help of the expert player from the band, and at one point, she asked why women never played the thing. They are made by men and played by men in aboriginal culture. Each one that is made has a pattern of decorations inspired by a unique dream that the craftsman has. "Well, women don't play the didge because if they do, legend has it, shortly thereafter, they fall down pregnant." That was the explanation that was offered.

We have a piece of videotape taken on that trip of Denise sitting on a rocky headland overlooking the Pacific and playing notes on the didge she brought home for me.

I was very happy to see her when she got home, and we had the luxury of a few days to relax together and be people for a while. A couple of months later, confirmation arrived that they were right about the didge!

On Friday the seventh of February 1992, Denise, who was now very large with child, was conducting an I-and-I (intimate and interactive) broadcast with the band Cowboy Junkies. She was interviewing Margo Timmins when the water broke. The makeup lady kept coming over and saying, "My goodness, you're sweating a lot!" Denise replied, "I'm in labour!"

The makeup lady just laughed and thought she was kidding. Denise thought there was no immediate cause for concern and finished the broadcast, using the song durations to time her contractions.

I was at the broadcast. We were one week away from the due date, and I wasn't letting Denise out of my sight. The minute the broadcast was finished, we were escorted out to the car by a couple of beefy security guys, and we headed home to get all the stuff we'd packed for the hospital.

A few blocks from home, Denise said, "I think we should go straight to the hospital!"

I said, "Come on now, there's nothing to worry about. You've probably got several hours. Remember what they said in the classes. How much time between the contractions?"

"I'm not sure. Maybe a couple of minutes."

We got home and called the OB. She asked the same question, and by this time, we were just finishing up an actual stopwatch timing. It was three minutes.

"Go to the hospital right now!" said the OB.

When we arrived at Women's College, Denise was already well on the way. It was the fastest possible check-in, and soon we were in the birthing room. Denise was just getting settled when she began getting a series of intense contractions. The nurse and I thought it wasn't time for delivery yet and started going, "Don't push! Try not to push!" and Denise was going, "I'm tryyyyiiiiinnnnngggg!"

The higher-ranking nurse came in to see how much things had progressed and did a "Holy shit!" The baby was already crowning!

"Okay, puuuusshhhh," we all encouraged.

"Jeeeeeez, I'm fucking pushing!" yelled Denise.

I was bracing one of her legs, and the nurse was bracing the other. I looked straight into Denise's face and saw this pure animal concentration take hold of her. She wasn't there anymore. It was as though her eyes were looking back inside her head, even though they were staring at the room. She was magnificent!

Then there was a whole head, then a torso and then our young child was thrust into the world with such force that I had to catch him. After a moment's pause, I took the scissors and cut the cord that bound our new son to his mother. Remarkably calm for what he'd been through, he looked around.

Ten minutes later, Denise was sitting up in bed with the swaddled baby. She still had full makeup on from doing the broadcast, her hair was barely mussed and she was dressed like a Madonna in a lace bedjacket. In a short time, she was legendary on the floor. Jamaican orderlies would make special trips to peer into the room and look at her. Then you could hear them saying as they walked away down the hall, "Now dat's de way to 'ave a baby!"

I had this fantasy in my head. I kept seeing myself and this new person watching *Star Trek* on the couch together. When Duncan Charles Alexander McLauchlan came home with his mother a day or so later, I wasted no time. I checked the listings, opened a beer, sat the little guy on my lap and listened to the voice of Patrick Stewart intone, "Space—the final frontier . . ." At that moment, I knew I was the luckiest man in the world. I was now convinced that there was redemption, even for the slow learner.

One thing is sure: life is unpredictable, random, messy and dangerous. You either shrink away from that because you're afraid to be hurt, or you embrace it because the rewards that it offers are so rich. On the one side lies a slow withering away to death. On the other, the stubborn act of defiance that is being alive. I know I'll have to get out of here one day—not too soon, I hope. *I absolutely insist* on getting out of here *alive.*

Epilogue

❧ AMY EVENTUALLY CHANGED HER name to Sarah, after a singing star named Sarah Brightman. She's now known as Sarah Sackville-McLauchlan. That's good. It's a healthy sign of an independent mind. She phones me now sometimes, and I haven't forgotten how pleased I was the first time that she did. She's in a theatre arts program and singing beautifully (she's been doing quite well in various competitions over the years). I'm as pleased for her and as proud of her as I could be.

Karin got married and had two beautiful children. She's still hot tempered, but motherhood has mellowed her and I think she's finally learned from her kids how to be loved. I still see her from time to time for a lunch or a drink, talk over old times and get caught up on who's been doing what to who. I find that I hope with all my heart that things work out well for her. There's none of that old hurt left in me.

Denise is proving time and time again that she's a far better mate than I had any right to expect. When things have got tough, as they inevitably do, she's always drawn the line against my collapsing into feeling sorry for myself. We've passed the ten-year mark now, and for me it really does seem like only ten weeks. One of the nicer things I find is that occasionally my whirring brain is of some service to her when she's running out of psychological and tactical options. We both go through periods when life gets pretty crazy, what with parallel careers and raising a little boy at the same time (albeit with the assistance of a most valuable grandma). It helps a lot to know that there's someone you love right beside

381

you and they're going to pull their weight. I value Denise a great deal—her advice, her sense of humour and occasionally her criticism, and I think that washes both ways. Sometimes I feel like we're a good farm couple!

The odd thing is, I keep getting these wake-up calls from the gods!

In the summer of 1997, I was up at my brother Calvin's new cottage near Honey Harbour on Georgian Bay. Denise's mother Mavis was up with me to do the occasional bit of child amusing, but otherwise just lolling about in the pleasant summer weather.

Duncan, who was five years old by now, had become quite keen about all things to do with boats and fishing. He'd seen me catch a couple of Northern Pike and was pretty impressed. On a sun-dappled Sunday morning under an acid-blue sky, we set off in a small aluminum open fishing boat. The waters were only mildly rippled by a slight breeze as I opened up the old nine-horse Johnson motor and headed to the first of the spots we'd drop our hooks. The old boat was only planing along at ten miles an hour or so, but it was noisy enough and windy enough that Duncan found it exciting, and he was perched up in the point of the bow with his face to the horizon, happy as a lark in his little yellow lifejacket (he was forbidden to even go near the shore unless he was wearing his lifejacket because he didn't know how to swim yet).

We pulled up and dropped the anchor at a litle bay, but there were too many yachts parked there. The people on them were already coming to life and thundering about, shattering the stillness of the morning. I decided to move on and try another spot that I had seen previously, but never gone into. It was a weedy bay about two miles from where we were.

I picked up the anchor and started the motor. Off we roared with Duncan in his favourite position. We headed out across the open water until I spotted the familiar green of the shore I was seeking, then I turned the boat toward it. We were still quite some distance out from the bay, so I had the motor up to full throttle as my eyes squinted hard into the brightness of the slanting sun. We were heading right into it and the reflections of sunlight from the wavelets were dazzling me. Then Duncan turned his head around sharply and yelled, "Dad!"

No sooner had the word escaped his lips than there was a loud metallic "Bang!" I watched in horror as the front of the boat bucked up into the air and half rolled to the left, launching my little son up into the air and over the side of the boat. He disappeared from view as the boat passed him, and I must have screamed out loud as I thought the boat, or worse, the propeller must have hit him. Just before I was thrown forward onto the metal bench seats and the fishing gear by the impact, I had hit the kill button on the motor with my thumb. The boat kept going on momentum for a short distance, then swooshed to a halt. I picked myself up from the bottom of the metal craft and looked frantically around for Duncan. What was going through my mind? I knew deep in my heart that if I had killed him, I would walk off the side of the boat and take a deep breath.

I spotted him bobbing in the water about fifty feet away. He was looking right at me and he was very quiet. He wasn't carrying on or crying or making a fuss. His eyes were as wide as saucers as he said very clearly and with perfect pronunciation "Save me, Daddy!"

Think? I didn't think about anything! I was cut and bleeding in several places and had a sharp bang in the ribs, but at that moment I never felt a thing. I dove straight over the motor from the back seat and swam for him. I was half crazy. I didn't know if he was cut up from the propeller and bleeding badly or not. His unnatural calm had frightened me.

When I got to him, he did the natural thing and tried to climb out of the water onto the top of my head, so I grabbed him by the shoulders and said, "Honey, here's what you've gotta do so I can swim with you. Now you have to do exactly what I say, alright? Now roll over on to your back and put your arms down by your sides and your legs out straight, so I can grab the ring on your collar and tow you back to the boat, alright?"

He did precisely as he was asked. He was a perfect little trusting soldier as he went limp in the water on his back and I began side-stroking with him in tow— laboriously clawing through the water, for the wounded boat. I stroked hard, and as I inched through the water, I concentrated on the need to get Duncan out where I could examine him. But I wasn't getting much closer to the boat for all the work I was putting into it. I realized that I was tired and I hurt in several places, and dumb shit that I was, I wasn't wearing a lifejacket. I had visions of them finding the boat drifting, Duncan bobbing in his lifejacket, traumatized for life, and me playing poker with the crew of the Edmund Fitzgerald!

The trouble was that the wind had freshened just enough to start the boat drifting, and naturally it was going in the wrong direction. Almost as fast as I was gaining on it, it was moving away. I'm a strong swimmer, but I knew I was cold, shocked and tired. I thought about leaving Duncan and swimming for the boat with the idea of hauling myself in and getting it back over to him, but I just couldn't bring myself to let him go. He trusted me to get him out of the water and I couldn't leave him!

I put everything I had into making it to the boat with Duncan, and I finally put one hand up on the gunwale at about the same time as I got too exhausted to swim anymore. I was too spent to pull myself or him up, so I just hung onto the side with my hand clutching Duncan's lifejacket in a death grip, gasping for breath.

I heard an outboard motor coming, and as I looked up, I saw a Boston Whaler pull up with a couple in it. They knew about the submerged rock that we'd hit, and when they'd seen the boat with nobody in it, they'd come out to investigate.

I begged them to get Duncan out of the water and see if he was broken or cut up, so they took him from me and lifted him gently up. I almost wept with relief when I saw that the worst of his worries was a nasty bump on his forehead and a couple of abrasions. It took me almost ten minutes to get enough strength back in my arms to pull myself into the boat. Our rescuers wrapped Duncan in a towel while I pulled up the motor and examined it. I'd stopped the motor in time, so the drive train and prop were okay, and even though there was a whacking great dent in the bow, the boat itself wasn't leaking. I started the engine, and it fired up first time, as though there'd never been a problem. I thanked our friends from shore with all my heart, and then Duncan and I headed back up the long reach of open water back to the cottage. He was tightly wrapped but shivering, even in the warm sun. As soon as I opened up the throttle to get the boat going, he started crying and carrying on. He did not want to go fast—period. So we putt-putted all the way back home, and it took a couple of hours to get there as Duncan, his eyes tight shut, held onto my leg with his cheek against my thigh, clinging for dear life!

When I finally got the boat back and tied it up at the dock, Duncan had been warmed up a bit by the sun. I got him out of his lifejacket and briskly towelled him off. He hadn't said anything for a very long time, and I was a bit worried about him. Suddenly his head came up and he looked me square in the kisser with two of the most penetrating eyes I've ever seen and said angrily, "YOU SHOULD WATCH WHERE YOU ARE GOING!" I knew he was going to be alright then.

Duncan was nervous around little boats for a while, but the longer-term effects were on me. In some subtle way, I'm no longer as confident as I was since that day when something bigger than me reached down and slapped me upside my head and said, "Look, you arrogant man, I can take your child anytime I want and there's nothing you can do about it. You just remember that!"

I finished this book in the wee small hours of the morning which was the dawn of my fiftieth birthday. I had wanted it to skid in under that self-imposed deadline, and I was in a celebratory mood and flushed with the warm glow of accomplishment as I poured a large single-malt scotch in a tumbler and knocked it down before wandering off upstairs to go to sleep. I finally dozed off at about four-thirty, I suppose, but was wakened up again an hour later by a distant rumbling—rather a lot of rumbling, in fact. I remembered that there was a big cold front coming through and I'd forgotten to button up the house. It was a hot night, and not only were all the soft cushions and vulnerable stuff still out in the screened-in porch; all the windows were open as well. I hauled my tired corpse out of the sack and went down to prepare for the storm.

I had just finished when the squalls hit. The violence was remarkable, and I watched the trees in our backyard bending over at impossible angles as they were hit with lashing rain and gust after gust of fierce wind. I went back up to the bedroom, where Denise was awake by now and gazing out the window at the tempest. Duncan was sound asleep.

I was just having one of those moments of contentment, looking at Denise, knowing that I'd finished a long and arduous project, when there was the most God-awful noise I have ever heard in my life. It was as loud as the atomic bomb but sharp and short-lived. We were deafened by it.

There's an eighty-foot poplar tree not fifteen feet from the head of our bed, and a bolt of lightning had picked that exact moment to strike it, blowing shrapnel from its massive trunk from our backyard all the way out to the street in front. Coincidence? I don't know. But please—enough with the wake-up calls already! I'm awake for Christ's sake!

Discography

TRUE NORTH RECORDS
Songs from the Street
Murray McLauchlan
Day to Day Dust
Sweeping the Spotlight Away
Only the Silence Remains
On the Boulevard
Hard Rock Town
Greatest Hits
Whispering Rain
Live at the Orpheum
Into a Mystery
Storm Warning
Windows
Timberline
Heroes
Midnight Break
Gulliver's Taxi

CAPITOL EMI
Swinging on a Star
The Modern Age

Index

Abrams, Shelley, 93
Ace Bristol (car), 59
Adilman, Sid, 134
aerobatics, 311–12, 366, 367–68
aeroplanes, 29–30, 262; first ride in, 134; and gear problems, 328–31; learning to fly, 245–46, 252–54, 257–59; used for filming, 308–24; weather and flying, 265–66, 275–78, 284–86. *See also* individual types
After the Gold Rush (album), 187
Ahearn, Brian, 204
alcohol, 184, 325–26, 343–44, 353–54
Alexander, John, 366
Alexenburg, Ron, 196
A&M (record label), 153–54
Andersen, Eric, 148, 209
Andersen, Jørn, 240, 241
Arrow (plane), 38–39, 309
Ash, Niema, 143, 144
Ashley, Elizabeth, 260, 261
Austin Healy Sprite (car), 59
Austin Princess (car), 16
awards: Hallmark cards, 68; Juno, 353; RPM Big Country, 348; RPM Gold Leaf, 206
Aztec (plane), 262, 264–66, 268, 272; from Nassau to Toronto, 283–86; for tour, 273–78

Bahamas, 231–36, 282–83
Bain, Michael, 86
ballet, 216–17
Ballon, Paula, 206
Band, The, 160, 168, 186
Banks, Sid, 134
Barry, Bonnie, 349, 350
Bateman, Robert, 42, 43, 76
Bates, Charlene, 44
Batten, Jack, 190
bear, grizzly, 118–19
Beaver (plane), 333
Beckwith, Skip, 204
Bellanca Decathalon (plane), 311–12
benefit concerts: for Crees, 201, 203; flood relief, 280; Olympic team, 241, 242–44
Bentall, Barney, 371
Berger, Bucky, 336, 360
Berry, Frank, 30
Bikel, Theodore, 177
Black Swan (Stratford club), 143
Blackwell, Chris, 239, 255
Blajer, Matt, 309
Blood, Sweat and Tears (band), 153
BMW (car), 10
Bohemian Embassy, 85, 86
Boris's (club), 149
Boulderwood (summer camp), 39–40
Boyd, Liona, 241, 243

Boyle, Jean, 376
Brand, Oscar, 134, 136, 177
Brazilian George, 150, 156–57, 184, 192–93
Briggs, David, 189, 213
Bromberg, David, 177
Brown, Doug, 93, 130, 131
Buckley, Tim, 148
Buffalo Springfield (band), 152, 187
Burwell, Bob, 308, 341, 362, 366
Butler, Edith, 332
Butterfield, Paul, 204

Cad-Allard (car), 59
Cadillac Johnny, 194–95, 358
Café Le Hibou (Ottawa club), 143
Cameron, Dean, 366–67, 371
Campbell, Doug, 271, 272
Canadian Aces (band), 339
Canadian recordings, 153, 190–91
Canso (plane), 257
Capitol Records, 366, 368
career, 137, 140, 143, 147; crucial breaks in,
    147, 191–92, 206, 239–41; early gigs, 87,
    89, 93, 95, 133–34; finances, 218, 255–56,
    289, 295, 303–304; first engagement, 87;
    first gig at Riverboat, 187; invitations to
    Mariposa, 142, 146; in New York,
    173–80, 196–97, 200–201; hardships in,
    167, 172, 255–56, 299, 306; managers. See
    Finkelstein, Bernie; Garber, Hope;
    Grossman, Albert. See also television
    broadcasts; tours; travelling; songs,
    writing
Caribbean, 333–35
Cash, Johnny, 57
cat, infected, 293–94
Catcher in the Rye (book), 71
Cavendish, Mike, 93
Central Technical School, 58–59, 65, 67–72,
    82–84, 95
Cessna (plane), 210, 245, 253, 257, 270, 310,
    311
CF-100 (plane), 29
Charles, Bobby, 204
Charles, Ray, 57
Chart Attack (company), 371
Chevrolet Belaire (car), 44

Clark, Bobby, 242
Clark, Jim, 60
Clayton-Thomas, David, 152–53
Cockburn, Bruce, 148, 151, 165, 166, 169, 170,
    183; recording with MM, 219, 298
Cockburn, Kitty, 166, 167, 169
Cohen, Leonard, 88, 95
Commander Cody (band), 198, 199
Cooper, Myron, 93, 133, 138, 155
Corvair (car), 87
Costa, Ed, 72
Cowley, David, 45
Craig, Gordon, 268
Crandall, Brad, 139
Croce, Jim, 207
Crosby, David, 136
Crowley, Bob and Ellen, 45
Crowley, David, 47, 48
Cunningham, Jack, 221, 226–28

Daigle, Ted, 206
Dalton, John, 356–57, 363, 365, 371
Danesbury Public School, 26, 34, 50, 51
Dann, Ron, 220, 263, 360
Daroux, Alex, 150, 156, 157, 163, 164–65
Dash 300 (plane), 367
Davis, Paul, 206
Day, George and Marjorie, 66
Day of the Triffids, The (book), 28
Day to Day Dust (album), 211
Debolt, Daisy, 135
Detroit Renegades (motorcycle club), 162
diabolism, 169, 170–72
Dickie, Karla, 155, 162, 185
Dixon, Maxine, 297, 299
Docherty, Anna, 5–8
Don Baby, 157, 172
Donlon, Denise, 361–62, 372–76, 378–79,
    381–82; affair with MM begins, 357–60;
    engagement to MM, 369–70; and MM's
    wedding, 376–77
Donlon, Mavis, 362, 382
Downchild (band), 184
drawing, 31, 41, 43, 51, 57–59, 67–68
Driftwood, Jimmy, 134, 136
drugs, 151–52, 157, 162, 167, 188; cocaine,
    202, 211, 226, 214, 299, 344; heroin,

192–93; LSD, 151; marijuana, 91, 153, 275; MDA, 150, 168, 198
Dylan, Bob, 88, 143; influence of, 75, 91–92, 94

Eagles (band), 152
Ebony Knight (club), 131, 143
Eisencraft, Gary, 146, 155
El Patio (club), 149
Elder, Jim, 304
Elliot, Ramblin' Jack, 185, 188
Ellis, Don, 196
Empire of the Sun (book), 38–39
Everly Brothers, 198–200
Ezrin, Bob, 295–300

F-18 (plane), 374–76
F-86 (plane), 29
Faulkner, Dennis, 143
features about MM: *Toronto Star*, 146; Canadian Aviation, 310
Fecan, Ivan, 310, 313–14
Federation of Ontario Naturalists, 41
Fiedler, Bernie, 137, 140, 187, 192, 256; apartment, 218; and Joni Mitchell, 202
Finkelstein, Bernie, 156, 157, 164, 169–70, 172–73; as deal-maker, 149, 150; and True North Records, 183–84; as MM's manager, 186, 192, 208, 220, 239, 255, 262, 273, 294–95; ends business with MM, 339–40
Finkelstein Fiedler Management, 193–94, 196–97, 241, 242
fire, 158–59, 188
Fisken, Grandma, 23, 27
Flast, Barry, 176–77, 189
Flohil, Richard, 207
Florida, 264–60
Flye, Tom, 201
folk festivals, 131, 206, 207–8. *See also* Mariposa
folk/pop music, 57, 74, 75
Ford Mustang (car), 360
Ford Prefect (car), 4
Free Wheelin' Bob Dylan (album), 75
Freeman, Ed, 197–98
Friesen, Kenny, 241, 249, 262, 263

"Frito" (F-18 pilot), 375–76
Froh, Rick, 372, 376
Fulghum, Barbie, 130
Fulghum, Billy, 93, 129, 130, 133–34, 146, 151
Fuller, Jesse, 92
Fundis, Garth, 341

Gallant, Lenny, 371
Gann, Ernie, 313
Garber, Hope, 92, 153; as manager, 146, 153, 157
Garber, Lisa, 92
Garber, Nick, 92, 93, 98, 130, 146, 153
Garber, Victor, 92
Garrett, Amos, 85, 86, 204, 205–6, 211
Gart, Herb, 129
Geffen, David, 193, 197
Germany, 356–57, 363–65, 372–76
Gerrard, Denny, 149
Gibson, Bob, 84
Gibson, Luke, 150, 151, 163, 164, 169, 184
Glatt, Harvey, 166
Glotzer, Bennett, 168, 174
Godovitz, Greg, 298
Goffin, Gerry, 187
Goldhammer, Charles, 59
Goldstein, Al, 175
Goodman, Steve, 207
Gordon, Alison, 211
Gordon, Angus, 311, 312–13, 315–33
Graham, Bill, 150, 215
Greatest Hits (album), 262
Green, Lloyd, 263
Greenspoon, Danny, 363, 365, 371
Grin (band), 212, 213
Grossman, Albert, 149, 168, ; as manager, 174–75
Grossman's Tavern, 184
guitar, 57; developing repertoire for, 74–75; Echo, 106; Fender Jazzmaster, 165; first, 69; Kay, 69, 89; learning to play, 69, 86; playing for food, 106, 108; Travis, 75
Gzowski, Peter, 230

Haliburton, 76–81
Haller, Leslie, 3
Halsey, Jim, 341

Hamilton, Joyce and Ian, 156, 167, 171
Hammond, Marie-Lynn, 363–64
Hammond Chord Organ, 31–32
Hapanovitch, Nick, 72, 85, 94, 96, 98, 99–125
Hard Rock Town (album), 249, 254
Hardin, Tim, 187–88
harmonica, 31, 75
Harvard (plane), 29
Hatfield, Richard, 274–75
Havens, Richie, 148
Hawkins, Bill, 148, 166, 210
Hawkins, Ronnie, 44, 186–87
Hayden, Michael, 250–51, 264, 268, 269, 270
Helm, Levon, 326
Hendrix, Nona, 210
Here Come the Seventies (TV series), 151
Heroes (album), 314, 338
Hershoran, Anne, 129
Higgins, Dee, 217
Hill, Dan, 217, 280
Hill, Graham, 60
hockey, 22, 25–26
Hodgkins, Diane, 231, 232
Hodgkins, Gary, 230–35
Hollingshead, Jeanine, 98
homes of MM: Albert Hotel (New York), 175–76; Alexander Street (Toronto), 216; Augusta Avenue (Toronto), 184, 188; Brunswick Avenue (Toronto), 133; Don Valley (Toronto), 308, 324; Hayden Street (Toronto), 138, 158–59; Hazelton Avenue commune (Toronto), 159–62; at Michael Hayden's, 250; Moore Park (Toronto), 303; Paisley (Scotland), 4–8; Pape and Danforth (Toronto), 290–91; Riverdale (Toronto), 362; Queen and Parliament (Toronto), 194–95; Queen near McCaul (Toronto), 166–67, 169, 170–71, 172; Stayner Avenue (North York), 20–24, 56–57, 66; Sunderland (Ontario), 306–7; Wellesley Street (Toronto), 348, 357; Withrow Avenue (Toronto), 251–52
Hooker, John Lee, 148
Hootenanny (TV series), 134
horses, 290, 304, 323

Hunter, Alistair, 23, 44
Hurricane Hazel, 20–21
Hurricane (plane), 272
hydroplanes, 47–49

Into a Mystery (album), 282, 294
Inuit, 320–21
Isla (yacht), 231–35

James, Rick, 152
Jason, Neil, 297
"Jeanie the Tailor," 154
Jeep Grand Wagoneer, 342
Johnson, Kit, 360, 363, 371
Jordanaires (back-up group), 263
Joyous Lake Bar, 188, 205

Kadonaga, Jimmy and Gus, 194–95
Keane, Barry, 189
Keith, Ben, 204, 212
Kensington Market (band), 149–50, 156, 163
Kensitt, William, 223–24, 272–73
King, Carole, 187
Klein, Estelle, 208

LaBelle, Patti, 210
Lawrence Heights Junior High School, 52–54
Ledrew, Gary, 185, 230–35, 306, 353
LeFevre, Mylon, 206
Lennon, John, 160, 186, 305
Levon and the Hawks (band), 186
Lightfoot, Gordon, 186, 193–94, 217, 220; benefit for Olympic team, 241; location shoot with MM, 332
Lincoln (car), 221, 226, 227, 228
Lofgren, Nils, 212, 213
Lograsso, Joe, 72
Lola Ford GT (car), 60
Lovin' Spoonful (band), 176
Luke and the Apostles (band), 150
Lumley–Smith, Elizabeth, 88, 95
Luz, Virginia, 72

MacLellan, Gene, 204, 205
Macon Special (car), 59
managers. *See* Finkelstein, Bernie; Garber,

Hope; Grossman, Albert; Smale, Joanne

Manuel, Richard, 168
Mariposa Folk Festival, 137, 146–48, 207–8
Markle, Robert, 310, 342–43
Martin, John, 357, 358, 370
Martin, Mary, 261
Martynec, Gene, 150–51, 163, 164, 189, 240, 241
Massey Hall, 91, 221–22, 239, 294
Matthews, Don, 374
McAdam, Gerry, 184
McCarthy, Doris, 72, 82–83
McCarthy, Jim, 85, 86, 260, 261
McCracken, Melinda, 146, 155
McDonnell, Tom, 156
McGhee, Brownie, 57, 84, 137
McHugh, John, 85
McKenna, Mike, 219–20
McKie, Keith, 150, 163, 164
McLauchlan, Amy. *See* Sackville-McLauchlan, Sarah
McLauchlan, Bill, 14, 22, 23, 29, 44, 45, 59–62
McLauchlan, Calvin, 14, 17, 23, 56–57, 87, 140, 264–65, 333
McLauchlan, Duncan, 10–11, 382–85; birth of, 378–79
McLauchlan, Ian, 14, 23, 45, 220
McLauchlan, Margaret, 9, 16, 66, 214–15; employment, 24, 37; as friend to MM, 224–26, 333; and terminal illness, 348–52
McLauchlan, Murray: birth of, 11–12; early chilhood of, 5–43; emigration to Canada, 15–20; early musical education, 31–32, 33, 39–40, 50, 52–53, 57; and Patty Sockwell. *See* Sockwell, Patty; and Karin Ucci. *See* Ucci, Karin; and Denise Donlon. *See* Donlon, Denise; career. *See* career
McLauchlan, Rosemary, 10–11, 14, 17, 23, 44, 56
McLauchlan, Sandra (Sandy), 14, 23, 24, 32, 39
McLauchlan, William, 14, 19, 35–37, 49, 94, 96–98, 145; employment, 23–24, 56;

love of music, 31–32; illness, 216, 219, 221–24
Meeker, Howie, 242
Mellotron, the, 209
Mendez, Raphael, 33
Meraska, Ron, 242
Mercedes (car), 192–93
Midnight Break (album), 339
Midnight Cowboy (movie), 179
Mills-Cockell, John, 150–51, 163, 184
Milne, Alec, 46
Mink, Ben, 219, 240, 262, 360
Mitchell, Adam, 149
Mitchell, Joni, 135, 136, 148, 153, 197, 201–4, 208
Molina, Ralph, 212
Monroe, Bill, 147
Moog, Professor, 151
Morris Oxford (car), 139–40
Moses, Katherine, 347
Moses (of the Vagabonds), 146, 151, 155, 160–62, 184
Mothers of Invention (band), 162
motorcycles, 140–41, 147, 151, 158, 159
Mountain (band), 150
Mousehole coffeehouse, 85, 142
Mustang (car), 129
Mynah Birds, (band), 85, 152

Neiman, Tannis, 98
Nelhams, Austin (and family), 27
"New Country" music, 307, 356
Newmark, Andy, 189, 297
Nissan 300 zx (car), 359

Ochs, Phil, 137, 140
O'Keefe, David, 315, 319, 326, 327
On the Boulevard (album), 240, 246
Only the Silence Remains (album), 239
Ono, Yoko, 160–61
Otter (plane), 317
owls, Artic, 30–31

Paisley (Scotland), 3–15
Pappalardi, Felix, 149–50, 163
Parker, Chris, 204, 211, 219
Paupers (band), 149

Pendrith, Dennis, 189, 198, 223, 226, 240, 241, 274
Penny Farthing (club), 85
Perica, Joanne, 347
Perold, Frank, 155, 162
Petersen, Colleen, 98, 165, 371
Petlock, Guy, 53–54
Piper Navajo (plane), 269
Pitts s-2b (plane), 268
Pontiac Parisienne, 218–19
Pope, Carole, 291, 296
Powell, Bill, 131, 132
Presley, Elvis, 32, 263
Price, Gordon, 367, 368
Prine, John, 207, 341
Provenzano, Carlo, 72
Purple Onion (club), 84

Queen's Own Rifles, 70–71

radio, 25, 57, 69, 74–75, 190–91; first performance on, 19; hosting cbc show, 365–66
Raitblatt, Noni, 93, 133, 138, 158, 159, 180
recording sessions, 189–90, 296–99
reviews, 190, 243, 254, 306; in Rolling Stone, 239
Reynolds, Ross, 366
riding the rails, 100–104, 107, 108–9
Rigby, Heather, 86
rights to songs, selling of, 147, 174
Rive Gauche (club), 87
Riverboat coffeehouse, 85, 137, 140, 148, 187
Rizzo, Ratso, 204
Roberts, Elliott, 148, 153, 157, 193
Robertson, Eric, 189, 262
Robertson, Scottie-Belle, 139–40, 145, 154–55
Robinson, Carol, 85, 204, 205
Ross, Bob, 82, 83
Rough Trade (band), 291
Royal Ontario Museum, 41–42
Rush, Tom, 137, 146–47, 148, 165, 168, 173, 187; buys rights to mm's songs, 174; recording mm's songs, 147, 186

Sackville-Hunt, Marguerite de. See Sockwell, Patty
Sackville-McLauchlan, Sarah, 324, 356, 368–69; birth of, 286–87; changes name, 381; and rubella virus, 291–92, 295–96
Saint-Marie, Buffy, 310, 322, 323
Sakimoto, Ron, 310
Saskowski, Henry, 189
sawmill, working in, 113–18
Scace, Dave, 274, 306
Schaeffer, Penelope and Ted, 210
Schoales, Bart, 190, 194–95, 211, 246
Schriver, Evelyn, 371
Schultz, Lynn, 371
Schwartz, Joey, 27, 40–41
Screw (magazine), 175
Sebastian, John, 176
Sergeant Pepper (album), 136
sex education, early, 55, 73–74, 88–89
Shack, Eddie, 242
Shafer, Joan, 308–9, 310, 313
Sharpe, Neil, 73
Sheas (band), 152
Shepard, Sam, 175
Shimmin, Ian, 244, 245, 253, 264, 268–71, 280, 314; on Bahamas trip, 282–86
Siffert, Jo, 60
Silver Tractors (band), 151, 241, 243, 246, 249, 254
Simone, Sally, 74
Sirynx (band), 151
Skein, Chris, 189
Skipper, Buddy, 263
Smale, Joanne, 352–53
Smith, Cathy, 217, 220
Snider, Bob, 84, 88, 95
Snikkar, Allan, 73
Sockwell, Herman Maurice, 139
Sockwell, Michael, 139
Sockwell, Patty, 93, 130, 131, 216, 232, 235–36; living with mm, 132–33, 158–60, 166, 169, 178–80, 249–50; marriage to mm, 144–45; and mm's wedding, 154–55; changes name, 249; and marriage troubles, 278–79, 278–79, 281–82; and pregnancy, 280–81, 282,

286; and birth of daughter, 287; divorce, 295, 304, 324–25

Solomon, Bernie, 194

Song from the Street (album), 190

songs, writing, 95, 129, 142, 176, 274, 303, 307; "As Lonely as You," 90; "Child's Song," 98, 142; "Don't Put Your Faith in Men," 291; "Hiroshima," 305; "I Hate Your Gun," 305; "If the Wind Could Blow My Troubles Away," 296; "Imaginary Tree," 355; "Into a Mystery," 282; "La Guerre, C'est Fini Pour Moi," 240; "Louisa Can't Feed Another Child," 338; "Love with a Capital L," 356; "Never Did Like That Train," 307; "On the Boulevard," 240, 243; "Out Past the Timberline," 307; "Red River Flood," 307; "Rockin' on the Sea," 291; "Suppertime in the Milltown," 338; "Swinging on a Star," 356; "Tell Your Mother She Wants You," 297; "Ten People on the Sidewalk," 338; "Ten Thousand Miles from Shore," 327; "Train Song," 239; "Try Walkin' Away," 291; "Trying to Stop the Sun from Going Down," 307; "Wouldn't Take Another Chance on Love," 297

songs by MM: "Back on the Street," 186; "Child's Song," 186, 222, 223; "Coat of Colours" ("More Than a While"), 142; "Do You Dream of Being Somebody," 220; "Down by the Henry Moore," 219, 220; "Farmer's Song," 174, 200–201, 206, 248; "Hard Rock Town," 254; "Honky Red," 186; "Immigrant," 249; "Linda, Won't You Take Me In," 211–12; "Maybe Tonight," 220; "Old Man's Song," 186; "Poor Boys," 249; "Shoeshine Workin' Song," 219, 220; "Sixteen Lanes of Highway," 186; "Well, Well, Well," 249; "Whispering Rain," 261, 262, 263. *See also* songs, writing

Sonny and Peter (duo), 93

sound systems, 163, 185–86, 243

squirrel, Arctic ground, 319

ss *Samaria* (ship), 16–18

Stamfel, Peter and Antonia, 175

Stanford, Lester, 139

Storm Warning (album), 303; recording sessions, 296–300

Stuart, Mary, 30–31

Sukhoi (plane), 367

Sweeping the Spotlight Away (album), 219, 220, 262

Swinging on a Star (album), 220

Swinging on a Star (radio series), 371

Syrinx (band), 184

Talbot, Billy, 212

Tao (ship), 268, 269, 271, 333, 335

Tate, Howard, 244, 245

Taylor, Elizabeth, 90

Taylor, James, 187

Taylor, Vicky, 142–43

Tayyeb, Vezi, 296, 360, 370

television broadcasts about or by MM: *Adrienne Clarkson Presents*, 5; "Big Ticket," 370; CBC special, 242; *Entertainer, The*, 349; "Floating over Canada," 308–33; *Let's Sing Out*, 134–35; simulcast (CityTV/CHUM), 254

Telfer, Jay, 184, 189, 217

Tenzen, Mike, 310, 311

Terry, Sonny, 57, 84, 137

Three's a Crowd (band), 142, 148, 165

Thurling, Peter, 310, 313–14

Timberline (album), 307

Timmins, Margo, 378

Titcomb, Brent, 142, 165

tobacco, priming, 141–42

Tobin, Marion and Eileen, 339

Toronto Junior Field Naturalists' Club, 41–42

Toronto Maple Leafs, 25–26

tours: Australia, 363; Canada, 226–29, 246–48, 280; Germany, 372–76; "Hard Rock Town," 254–56; with Neil Young, 212–15; price of, 249; Saskatchewan, 363; "Swinging on a Star," 368; U.S. club, 206–7; west coast, 198–200; "Whispering Rain," Eastern Canada, 273–78; "Windows," 306

Toyota Land Cruiser, 343

travelling; for "Floating over Canada,"

308–33; to Los Angeles, 259–62; west, 99–125

Tremblay, Sylvie, 325

Tressy (girlfriend), 131–32

Trillium (Toronto Islands ferry), 73

Troiano, Dom, 298

Trombley, Tim, 367

Trudeau, Margaret, 310

True North Records, 183–84, 189, 197

Tyson, Ian, 84, 230, 323

Tyson, Sylvia, 84, 241

Ucci, Andrea, 282, 286, 290; wedding of, 305

Ucci, Karin, 265, 266, 267, 268, 269, 381; affair with MM, 271, 278–79, 280, 288–90; living with MM, 290–91, 303–7, 324–25; end of affair with MM, 305–6, 334–38, 354–56

Ucci, Peter, 290, 324

Ulrich, Shari, 347

Upper Crust Café, 150, 156

Vagabonds (motorcycle club), 146, 151, 162

Vanguard (toy car), 18

Vauxhall (car), 53–54

Veitch, Trevor, 142, 165, 168, 173

videos: "Me and Joey," 339; "Never Did Like That Train," 307–8

Village Corner Club, 84, 92, 95, 98–99, 129–30

Viscount, Vickers (plane), 135

Vosse, Michael, 153

Wachtel, Waddy, 198

Wainwright, Loudon, III, 207

Waldhauser, Karl, 52–53

Walker, Jerry Jeff, 161–62

Wall of Folk (trio), 371

Walsh, Rick, 184–85

Wanakita (summer camp), 76–81

Ward, Max, 310, 316–17

Warner, Donna, 142, 165

watercolours, 82, 83

Waterman, Dick, 207

Watkins Glen, 59–60

Watson, Doc, 148

Watson, Jimmy, 163, 164

Webster's (restaurant), 151

Weitzman, Steve, 239

Welch, Kevin, 368

West, Leslie, 150

Westcott, Lorna, 48

Whispering Rain (album), 250, 273; recording, 262–64

White, Bukka, 148

White, Nancy, 363

Wiffen, David, 142, 165

Wilcox, David, 262

Wilkins, Terry, 336

Williams, Michèle, 336–38, 340–41, 357, 370

Wolf, Howlin', 147–48

Woodstock Royals (band), 168

Wyndham, John, 28, 29

Yakovlev (plane), 367

Yanofsky, Zal, 176

Yates, Lori, 371

Yetnikoff, Walter, 196

Yorkville, 84–87, 140, 146–56

Young, Neil, 85, 152, 187, 208; MM opening for, 212–15

Young, Rusty, 198

Young, Scott, 215

Zappa, Frank, 162

Zevon, Warren, 198

Znaimer, Moses, 220

Zurakowski, Jan, 39, 309